China Adams

Trevor Hernandez

About the Authors

FRANCIS D. ADAMS is an independent scholar. BARRY
SANDERS teaches at Pitzer College, The Claremont
Colleges, in California. Both authors live in southern
California.

ALSO BY BARRY SANDERS

*A Is for Ox: The Collapse of Literacy
and the Rise of Violence in an Electronic Age*

Sudden Glory: Laughter as Subversive History

The Private Death of Public Discourse

ALSO BY FRANCIS D. ADAMS
AND BARRY SANDERS

Three Black Writers in Eighteenth-Century England

ALIENABLE
RIGHTS

THE EXCLUSION OF AFRICAN AMERICANS IN A WHITE MAN'S LAND, 1619–2000

Francis D. Adams
and
Barry Sanders

Perennial

An Imprint of HarperCollins*Publishers*

To Teresa, China, and Joseph for their
unfailing love and support.
—FDA

To Grace, Kali, Pebber, and Trevor:
For listening, enduring, responding. All my love.
—BRS

A hardcover edition of this book was published in 2003 by HarperCollins Publishers.

HarperCollins books may be purchased for educational, business, or sales pro-
motional use. For information please write: Special Markets Department,
HarperCollins Publishers Inc., 10 East 53rd Street, New York, NY 10022.

First Perennial edition published 2004.

Designed by Phil Mazzone

The Library of Congress has catalogued the hardcover edition as follows:

Adams, Francis D.
    Alienable rights : the exclusion of African Americans in a white man's land /
Francis D. Adams and Barry Sanders—1st ed.
        p. cm.
    Includes bibliographical references and index.
    ISBN 0-06-019975-X
    1. African Americans—Civil rights—History. 2. Slavery—United States—
History. 3. African Americans—Segregration—History. 4. Racism—United
States—History. 5. United States—Race relations. I. Sanders, Barry. II. Title.

E185.A233 2003
305.896'073'00904—dc21

                                                        2003040686

ISBN 0-06-095911-8 (pbk.)

04 05 06 07 08 ❖/RRD 10 9 8 7 6 5 4 3 2 1

ACKNOWLEDGMENTS

Our thanks to Miriam Altshuler, Terry Karten, Sara Lippincott, and Andrew Proctor for their care and concern in turning *Alienable Rights* into a book.

Special thanks to Dave Schwartz; also to Jose Aguilar, Manuel Hernandez, and Brian Hopkins for making it possible for me to find time to complete this project. Thanks also to Dick Willis and Gail Borden for their insightful comments after reading an early draft of the initial chapters. Finally, I owe a debt of gratitude to Mickey and George Canillas and Bankole Paris, childhood companions who were often in my thoughts while writing.

—FDA

I am grateful to Adam Rosenkranz, head of research at the Honnold Library, for his wisdom, and to all the librarians for their help and direction and, most important, their patience. I held a good many of their books hostage over a long stretch of time.

—BRS

CONTENTS

CONTENTS

INTRODUCTION

The bus driver didn't change his mind, Rosa Parks changed hers.

—REVEREND AL SHARPTON, *THE NEW YORKER*, 2002

Whatever his faults may be, no one has ever accused Al Sharpton of gullibility—at least not in relation to white folks. In that regard, Sharpton resembles most African Americans, who remain convinced that racism still lives in the dark recesses of the nation's heart, despite the millions of dollars that black athletes and black entertainers earn and the high-end luxury that many black executives and professionals routinely attain.

On the other side of the racial divide, however, night passes for day. Where blacks see only darkness, a majority of whites find sunshine—and they are exasperated when they hear African Americans blame white people for whatever is wrong in their lives. In 1995 a national survey jointly sponsored by the *Washington Post*, the Kaiser Family Foundation, and Harvard University found that most of the 1,057 white respondents believed that American blacks fare "as well as or better than the average white in such specific areas as jobs, education, and health care," and "the overwhelming majority" believed that blacks were to blame for their own economic and social ills. Nor does proximity to blacks seem to make white Americans like them any better. A 1994 study by the Urban Institute found that blacks and whites live together on reasonable terms as long as the number of blacks in the neighborhood stays around 3 percent. When the black population starts to rise, whites begin to leave. The Kaiser Foundation completed the survey by asking respondents for their estimate of the size of the nation's black population. While African Americans constitute some 12 percent of the population, the survey found that "white respondents gave estimates that averaged 23.8 percent." So much did blacks concern or frighten those white respondents that they saw, on average, nearly two for every one that exists.

In 1700, Samuel Sewall, one of the judges who presided over the Salem witch trials, wrote *The Selling of Joseph*, often called America's first antislavery tract. Sewall condemned "Man Stealing" as an atrocious capital crime, but also expressed something unsettling—white desire to have nothing to do with blacks. "There is such a disparity in their Conditions, Colour & Hair, that they can never embody with us, and grow up into orderly Families, to the Peopling of the Land," Sewall wrote, "but still remain in our Body Politick as a kind of extravasat Blood." Rather than availing themselves of African slaves, Sewall suggested, the citizens of Massachusetts ought to revert to the old system of white indentured servants. Blacks would always be outsiders—"extravasat Blood" running separate from and never mixing with the white blood of the Massachusetts Body Politick.

There are striking parallels between Samuel Sewall and Al Sharpton. Though readers may find it hard to imagine two people more removed from each other—the one a Puritan jurist in the Massachusetts Bay Colony, the other a contemporary Harlem preacher turned activist—both recognize, from opposite ends of our national history, the same enduring attitudes that white Americans have always had in relation to blacks. Though time may have taught the country's white citizens to be more circumspect, their deepest feelings remain essentially unchanged. Sharpton also understands—just as Sewall predicted—that white attitudes toward blacks seem unlikely ever to change. The agreement between the two is startling—not only because of their obvious differences but because it raises questions about the received historical view of America and the progress of race relations in this country over the last three hundred years. Was Sewall's observation that blacks would never successfully integrate with whites incorrect? Is Sharpton's pessimism mistaken? Have white feelings about African Americans changed? Or is there a river of truth, as we argue in this book, connecting the two men, both of whom recognized a continuing reality? Is

America's racial history far bleaker than many Americans would like to believe?

History usually gets written by the victors. For example: The founding fathers believed that all men were created equal and endowed with the same natural rights; those ideals are embodied in our Constitution; the North fought the Civil War to end slavery; the 1960s civil rights movement eliminated discrimination. Such noble ideas are easy to absorb but may have driven truth from the marketplace. An alternative way of viewing the past broadens our understanding instead of narrowing it. Critical history examines not only a nation's triumphs but its failures. In the preface to his history of the Middle Ages, the French social historian Pierre Chaunu suggests that we should "look squarely at what people have done their best to forget or ignore" in order to recognize "the price that was paid, the sacrifice required" at any historic moment.[1] In that spirit, we have sought to understand more clearly the price paid and the sacrifice required by the nation's black citizens to preserve white privilege.

Though most Americans learn about the nation's past as a series of clearly delineated periods, each of which achieves a reassuring resolution as it comes to a close, a more realistic view describes the relationship between blacks and whites as a continous arc of white animosity, reaching from the early seventeenth century, when slaves first came to the mainland colonies, to the present day. Animosity toward blacks has over the centuries shaped a good deal of American polity, the Constitution itself being perhaps the outstanding example. Contrary to what most of us would like to believe, the story of its birth is not an uplifting tale of American genius and accomplishment of which we can all be proud. Its final form belies its difficult birth: the Constitution came into being through a series of nasty battles and uneasy compromises between the northern and southern states, primarily over a single festering issue—the status of black Americans. Early in the proceedings, James Madison, the guiding intellect of the Constitutional Convention, identified the crucial problem: "The States were divided ... partly from climate (that is, from the varying economies possible in the North and South), but principally from the effects of their having or not having slaves."[2] That signal division also informed the mechanics of later admissions to the Union: the Northwest Ordinance, the Missouri Compromise, the war over Texas, and the subsequent enlargement of the country all the way to the Pacific.

For a variety of reasons—some entirely innocent—most Americans have only the foggiest notion of the enduring nature of black exclusion. Slavery, of course, constituted its most brutal form, with whites casting blacks as creatures more akin to draft animals than to their masters. In the first half of the nineteenth century, as the debate intensified between North and South over the growing number of freed blacks, by far the most popular solution was the so-called colonization movement, a scheme to transport blacks to the Caribbean or back to Africa. In 1896, long after the Civil War and the extension of citizenship to black people, the Supreme Court sanctioned another variety of exclusion—*separate but equal*, which legitimized southern Jim Crow laws for the entire nation. And when civil rights leaders forced the overthrow of segregation in the 1950s and 1960s, whites fled to private schools and the suburbs, hoping to contain blacks in the inner city.

The average white citizen has little patience with the claim of perpetual prejudice and abuse—which is understandable. No one wants to view the United States as a villain without a heart. More than that, it's hard to imagine that a nation with such a vibrant and dynamic history has not managed to solve a problem that arose nearly four hundred years ago. In an essay entitled "A Testament of Hope," published after his death, Martin Luther King Jr. asked why "the issue of equality" remained "still so far from solution . . . in a nation that professes itself to be democratic, inventive, hospitable to new ideas, rich, productive, and awesomely powerful?" The only possible answer, he concluded, was that whites were "deeply racist," and few had ever been willing to address racism seriously.[3] More than thirty years later, King's question still hangs in the air and his answer is still largely ignored by the white majority. Most blacks understand that though they live *in* the same nation as whites, they do not live *within* the same system. Sooner or later, for every black child, the time arrives when he or she discovers that America's most sacrosanct rules are not the same for blacks and whites, and that color determines that one must go through life as an exception, without many of the guarantees and opportunities that whites enjoy. It is hoped that the following history will encourage readers to confront America's painful racial legacy and recognize that every one of us bears a degree of responsibility for the nation's treatment of African Americans. Just as stockholders in a corporation that in the past created an ecological disaster cannot walk away from their obligation to make good the damage, so white citizens cannot deny their involvement in America's moral failure by maintaining that it all happened before they were born, and, consequently, it has nothing to do with them. In our willingness to dismiss the manifold social disadvantages that most blacks endure as simply the result of their own personal failings, we all share in the responsibility for America's continuing exclusion of its black citizens.

CHAPTER 1

"TWENTY NEGARS": SLAVERY IS PLANTED IN THE COLONIES

All Negroes or other slaves shall serve durante vita.
—MARYLAND LEGISLATURE, 1663

In 1772, Lord Mansfield, the chief justice of the King's Bench, adjudicated the case of James Somersett, an African slave who had been brought by his master from Virginia to England. Somersett had run away but had been recaptured, taken aboard ship, and held there against his will. Demanding his client's freedom, Somersett's lawyer petitioned Mansfield for a writ of habeas corpus, which the chief justice reluctantly issued, affirming that Somersett could not be held, because "as soon as any slave sets foot upon English territory, he becomes free." Mansfield's decision, which resulted in the uncompensated emancipation of as many as fourteen thousand blacks residing in Britain, not only made it clear that slaves automatically gained their freedom the instant they arrived on English soil, it also asserted an even more fundamental principle: that slavery could have no legal standing in a society unless "positive law" existed that provided it with an unequivocal legislative mandate. Slavery was so odious, Mansfield maintained, that its legality could not be based on mere custom or usage. Anything short of statutory action, which had the power to preserve slavery's mandate long after the "reasons, occasion, and time . . . from which it was created . . . were erased from memory," was insufficient to give it legitimacy.[1]

Somersett v. Stewart represents a judicial landmark because it effectively ended slavery in Britain, where black servants had grown increasingly fashionable throughout the eighteenth century. It also raises important questions about the development of slavery in America. The basis for the *Somersett* decision—that no statutory law existed in Britain pertaining to slavery—meant that no English precedent had been established to justify slavery in Britain's colonies. Nevertheless, over the preceding 150 years, each of the colonies had built its own independent system of bondage and evolved an elaborate legal code that had come to represent the positive law sanctioning the institution. By the 1770s, the thirteen colonies had created a unique form of American slavery, unlike any the world had ever seen.

How did slavery become so firmly entrenched in the colonies, when it appears never to have received the approval of English law? The answer lies in a century and a half of organic development that allowed the colonists to formulate their own brand of bondage, responding as they went along to the constant changes that accompanied the introduction of slavery into new and relatively unstable societies.

From the beginning, the English Crown had granted the colonists an unusual degree of freedom to govern themselves. Unlike the Castilian monarchy, which maintained tight controls throughout Latin America, the English Crown wanted to avoid the expense of colonial development. Thus it granted substantial independence to private merchant-adventurers, who were willing to raise money and risk their lives for speculative enterprises on the American continent. Virginia's 1611 charter, for example, granted to that colony's leaders "full power to ordain and make such laws and ordinances . . . as to them, from time to time, shall be thought requisite and meet."[2] Though the king retained control over international relations and commerce, the colonies exercised the broadest powers in relation to their internal affairs.

In the New World, the English stand as relative latecomers both as colonists and as exploiters of blacks. In 1501, Spain officially sanctioned the introduction of slaves into its Caribbean and South American colonies, and by the end of the sixteenth century the Spanish had brought nearly a million Africans to Latin America. The English colonists arrived in the West Indies and Virginia only at the start of the seventeenth century and began importing blacks a few years later. The first recorded instance of blacks arriving on the American mainland came in 1619, when the planter John Rolfe noted that "a dutch man of warre" had called at Jamestown and sold the colonists "twenty Negars."[3] In all likelihood, these first blacks were slaves who had been kidnapped from the Spanish West Indies by English or Dutch privateers, secretly financed by gentlemen from Virginia and Bermuda.

Whatever their background and status, this original group of blacks landed in a country that knew servitude quite well but in which slavery barely existed, if at all. The English Puritan theologian Paul Baynes delineated two types of servants: "either [the] more slavish," created "forcibly, as in captivity," or the "more free and liberall," who became servants voluntarily. But the terms of both sorts of servitude were temporary, and included apprentices and indentured laborers along with bound convicts and Irish and Scottish prisoners of war. They made up the colonies' primary source of labor throughout the seventeenth century.[4] Before 1700, roughly two-thirds of all the immigrants south of New England arrived as bond servants. A steady stream of Britain's poor and dispossessed contracted for a period of voluntary servitude in order to escape their blighted prospects as subsistence laborers at home. These bondsmen agreed to serve their colonial masters for a period of four or five years and in return received passage, maintenance, and "freedom dues"—which might include a sum of money and a piece of land—when their term of service expired.[5] Generally, they bound themselves to farmers, who cultivated a small area carved out of the wilderness with no more than four or five indentured laborers. Conditions were harsh, and often master and servants lived in close quarters in an environment that, at least in the early years, was exclusively male, with everyone crammed into the single habitable structure that typified the earliest colonial farm.

Alien in appearance, language, and culture, the first blacks fell into this system of servitude as if from the sky. In the English concept of indentured service, master and servant were both white; there was no provision for people as strange and forbidding as Africans. The colonists surely understood that slavery was thriving throughout Latin America—and also in the East Indies, Greece, and the Middle East—but anything resembling Baynes's "slavish" servitude, with the exception of convicts and prisoners of war, had ended in Britain during the Middle Ages. Thus the colonies' first blacks, welcomed for the potential man-hours of labor they represented, found themselves slotted into the prevailing system merely as another group of servants, akin to indentured English laborers but employed for the general good. Acquired by trading provisions from the government's common store, they had been purchased as public rather than private servants, for use throughout the colony in a variety of public works projects.

From the beginning, a degree of ambiguity existed in their situation that set them apart from British bondsmen. Although, unlike whites, they had never contracted voluntarily to surrender their freedom—and thus, in Bayness terms, were being held as slaves, "forcibly, as in captivity"—they could look forward to eventual freedom after seven or eight years of service (a considerably longer term than that of white servants), which made them seem more like the indentured British. Nevertheless, their presence undoubtedly aroused a fair amount of apprehension among the colonists, who housed them in small groups with farmers linked in various ways to the colonial government. In other respects the colonists treated them more or less like their other servants—and perhaps accorded them as much equality as blacks in America would ever see again. But certainly there was not much enthusiasm for increasing their numbers: four years after the arrival of the "twenty Negars," the 1623 census in the *Lists of Living and Dead in Virginia* includes only twenty-three blacks in the entire colony.

Given America's future accomplishments, it is easy to forget that in the early years there was little to suggest that its success was guaranteed. The first colonists endured appalling physical hardships, as well as the psychological burden of living in a wilderness, far away from family and the comforts of the civilized English landscape. No doubt the early generations of colonists often felt themselves teetering on the edge of failure. They desperately needed a way to prosper, in order to transform their rough colonial outposts into European-style communities. For those colonies staking their future on agriculture, the problem appeared essentially the same: how to produce crops of substantial value that they could trade for money or goods in England and the British West Indies. Until about midcentury, however, the small farm—the traditional model that the colonists had brought from Britain—remained the basic unit of colonial agriculture. Though tobacco already represented their most valuable export crop, particularly on the eastern shore of Chesapeake Bay, individual planters, who cultivated it with just a few indentured servants, managed to make only a modest profit.

This small-scale agriculture, coupled with a reliable supply of British bondsmen, meant that there was little economic pressure on colonists either to increase the number of blacks or to expand white control over them. Black servants remained few in number, and many enjoyed essentially the same rights as their white counterparts. After their term of service, they normally went their own way, often acquired land, and established themselves as independent farmers with indentured servants of their own. They also appear to have exercised a broad range of civil rights, particularly in the courts, where they regularly became involved in litigation with both blacks and whites. In 1624, for example, John Phillips, "a negro, Christened in *England* 12 years since," testified against a white defendant in a Jamestown court proceeding. Nevertheless, at least for some blacks, their status both as free men and as indentured servants began to erode. In 1639, a Maryland statute introduced the term *slave* to distinguish certain blacks (and some Indians) as subsidiary members of society, who could not expect the same treatment as whites: "[A]ll the Inhabitants of this Province being Christians (Slaves excepted) shall have and enjoy all such rights liberties immunities priviledges and free customs . . . as any naturall born subject of England."[6] A year later, in the case of John Punch, the General Court of Virginia recorded the first unambiguous example of the enslavement of an individual Negro, as punishment for having run away. Punch and two other indentured servants had escaped to Maryland, where authorities eventually apprehended them. After they were returned to their master, the courts tried and convicted all three of the crime of absconding, but Punch received a far harsher penalty than his companions, a Scot and a Dutchman. While the two whites received sentences of four additional years of service, three of which would be spent working for the colony as public servants, the judge ordered that John Punch should "serve his said master or his assigns for the time of his natural life here or elsewhere."[7]

Virginia's treatment of John Punch is a watershed in the development of American slavery. As judicial punishment, it fell short of legalizing slavery, which would have required statutory action by the colonial government, but the sentence suggests that an official body of Virginia's leaders viewed not only Punch but the growing number of blacks as peculiarly suited for enslavement—either as inferior creatures who lacked the basic rights routinely accorded to whites and who thus could be dealt with as less than human beings, or as individuals particularly prone to criminal behavior who were too irresponsible ever to be allowed to go free. How widely Virginians accepted these beliefs no one knows, but both would become important elements in the white stereotype of American blacks.

Punch's punishment also suggests that the division between blacks and whites would require two separate justice systems. His sentence differentiated him not just from his two fellow defendants but from every white servant in Virginia's history, none of whom the courts had ever dealt with so severely. Punch's lifetime of servitude was a draconian penalty that reduced him from a man to a slave and, even for far more serious offenses, would have been unthinkable in relation to a freeborn Englishman. Unlike an indentured servant, who could expect to recover his freedom at some future date, Punch would exist at the will of his master for his entire life, as a piece of property that could be sold or disposed of in whatever manner his owner wished.

With the enslavement of John Punch, the judicial system crossed the line between indentured service and slavery. From that moment forward, cases of perpetual servitude begin to show up fairly frequently in Virginia court records. In 1646, for example, Francis Pott sold a black woman and child to be used by their new owner "forever." The growth of service in perpetuity also became evident in the values assigned to blacks in estate inventories and bills of sale. Previously, when owners bought and sold servants, indentured whites tended to be worth more than blacks if their future obligations were roughly the same. But the prospect of lifetime service raised the value of black bondsmen. In 1648, when James Stone of York County inventoried his six white workers, all with a few years left to serve, he placed an average value of about 1,300 pounds of tobacco on each one. Stone set the value of his two blacks at 2,000 pounds each.[8]

By the middle of the seventeenth century, perpetual servitude among blacks was common, but the actual number of cases remained small because relatively few blacks had reached North America. In 1648, Virginia, which had the largest black population of any of the colonies, counted only about three hundred of its fifteen thousand inhabitants as Africans.[9] The situation would soon change, as colonial agriculture shifted into high gear, spurred by events in the British West Indies and a drop in the number of white servants coming from England.

Though the first English had arrived on Barbados, Saint Kitts, and the other Leeward Islands about the same time that the colonists came to Virginia, by midcentury the islands had become overpopulated and offered few opportunities to those indentured whites who had completed their terms of service. With little chance for advancement, thousands emigrated—either to North America or, after 1655, to Jamaica, which the British had taken from the Spanish. Though many Caribbean emigrants arrived in the mainland colonies with only limited capital, they also brought extensive knowledge of the plantation system, particularly about the growing of tobacco, the crop of choice in the islands until cotton and sugar supplanted it in the 1640s.[10] At the same time, the flow of white servants coming from England slackened. After 150 years of continual growth, in which the English population exploded from 3 million to over 5 million, the increase in numbers fell to almost nothing. No one knows for certain what caused the change, but by the fourth quarter of the seventeenth century English complaints of overpopulation had stopped and pressure on the poor to leave England began to recede. The ravages of plague and the great London fire of 1666 may have played a part by reducing the labor pool and raising wages for workers at home; whatever the reasons, the colonies received fewer indentured whites.[11]

A decline in English servants and a growing number of immigrants with plantation experience led to the expansion of slavery. Farmers who had come from the Caribbean recognized almost immediately that the colonists could increase their tobacco output dramatically and make far greater profits by shifting to large-scale production. Two of the three elements necessary for success they already had in place—managerial expertise and inexpensive land. They needed a steady supply of cheap labor, which the Virginia legislature encouraged in 1660 by exempting Dutch slavers from local duties. The adoption of slavery slowed temporarily when the British government demanded a share of the potentially lucrative enterprise and blocked the entry of Dutch ships, but it quickly resumed after the Crown chartered its own slaving company, the Royal Adventurers—which in 1672 changed its name to the Royal African Company.[12]

In the quest for African slaves, the colonists appeared to be at a disadvantage in competing with the Caribbean sugar growers, primarily in Barbados. Though it cost more to raise than tobacco, sugar also generated significantly larger profits. Thus, island planters attracted more investment capital than tobacco growers on the mainland and could afford more slaves. In the earliest years that yield reliable figures for comparison, Barbados acquired 150,000 slaves between 1712 and 1762, while Virginia imported only 45,000 from 1700 to 1750.[13] Though these figures indicate that American colonists lagged behind in the acquisition of slave labor, they fail to tell the whole story. At the end of the same fifty-year period, the black population on Barbados had increased by only 28,000, while the number of slaves in Virginia had grown from about 10,000 to more than 100,000. Cultivating sugar demanded backbreaking labor that quickly used up workers, and as much as 6 percent of the island's labor force had to be replaced annually. In Virginia the mortality rate was much lower; the cultivation of tobacco was easier work, which preserved the slaves' health and enabled them to multiply.

As one might expect, the slave populations of the Caribbean and North American colonies developed substantial differences. The sugar plantations needed rugged, durable workers, preferably robust males between fourteen and twenty-five years of age. With less wealth, the colonists had to take the slave traders' leftovers: older men, those who had become sick in passage, women who were considered too frail, and seasoned island rejects who had done their time in the cane fields but no longer had the stamina for such strenuous work or had become rebellious and represented disciplinary problems. No hard evidence exists to fix the ratio between the sexes, but it seems likely that the number of women in relation to men, though always a minority, stood significantly higher in the colonies than on the islands. The mainland birthrate, substantially greater than that on any of the islands, created over time a new type of slave society. By 1740, most colonial slaves could no longer be called Africans. They had become *Creoles*, the contemporary term for American-born blacks.

As the labor forces of the tobacco planters grew, importation expanded in the other colonies. In New England, a handful of blacks had arrived in the 1630s, but with no interest in large-scale agriculture the Puritans lacked a compelling economic incentive to acquire slaves and only slowly increased their numbers. Despite an occasional complaint that the northern colonies would never thrive until they had taken in a sufficient number of slaves to do all their work, most austere New Englanders took no comfort in being relieved of the burden of labor; moreover, they tended to view slavery as morally justifiable only as a form of imprisonment for captives taken in war or as punishment fairly imposed by some authority. "There shall never be any bond-slavery . . . amongst us," the Massachusetts Body of Liberties recorded in 1641, except for prisoners of war and "strangers" whose status as slaves had been established before they were purchased.[14]

The Massachusetts pronouncement implied, of course, that only outsiders—people of different nationality, religion, or race—could properly be held as slaves. Massachusetts had acquired its first shipment of blacks in an exchange on Isla de Providencia, off the coast of Central America, where sailors received them in trade for Indians they had captured and enslaved in the colony's Pequot War of 1637. The Puritans felt uncomfortable enslaving members of their own race who professed the same religion, and though they briefly experimented with the penal enslavement of whites, they discontinued the practice in 1642, freeing a number of men in less than a year who had initially been sentenced to perpetual servitude.

Though New England usually tolerated slavery under rather narrow circumstances, Rhode Island resisted altogether, going as far as to outlaw bondage in 1652. Acknowledging that it had become "a common course . . . amongst English men to buy negers" and keep them as "slaves forever," the colony's fathers ordered that for "the preventigge of such practices, no black mankind or white" could be forced to serve more than ten years. Any master attempting to hold an individual longer would forfeit £40 to the colony.[15] In 1680, there were only a few hundred blacks in New England, and even as late as 1700 their numbers remained at less than a thousand.

In 1698, however, the British government ended the Royal African Company's monopoly, allowing private individuals to enter the slave trade. Northern merchant-sailors rushed in to carry human cargo to the islands of the Caribbean and the North American mainland. Ships from Boston and Rhode Island—which raised no objection to its citizens embarking on a lucrative economic opportunity—led the way. From 1700 on, slavers from New York, Philadelphia, and Baltimore joined the hunt. Over time, this traffic increased the North's black population, as a ship's captain would often reserve a few likely members of his cargo to carry home, where they might fetch high prices as apprentices to tradesmen or as house servants. Perhaps one in five of these northern blacks eventually gained emancipation, either through the generosity of a sympathetic master or by buying their freedom with money earned in their spare time. Given a chance for education and a strong community of their own, particularly in the Boston area, many of these freedmen became powerful advocates for the liberation of southern blacks and would later work with white abolitionists throughout the nineteenth century.

Though slavery developed separately in each of the colonies, regional similarities tended to produce two systems: one in the North, which included Massachusetts, Rhode Island, New Hampshire, Connecticut, New York, New Jersey, Pennsylvania, and later Delaware; and another in the South, made up of Virginia, Maryland, North Carolina, South Carolina, and after 1733, Georgia. With a growing reliance on large-scale plantation agriculture, the South demanded a vast slave population in order to cultivate tobacco, rice, and eventually cotton. The North, in contrast, built a manufacturing economy, which required skill rather than numbers, and thus its demand for blacks remained relatively small. By 1715, blacks numbered about fifty-nine thousand throughout the colonies, nearly forty-seven thousand of them concentrated in the South. Of the remaining twelve thousand, fully a third resided in New York, which had far more slaves than any other northern colony, having already acquired a substantial number of blacks before the English took it from the Dutch in 1664.[16]

In spite of the differences in their slave populations, northern and southern colonies alike moved to exert greater control over blacks as the pace of importation increased. In 1667, the English Parliament's Act to Regulate the Negroes on the British Plantations had asserted that blacks possessed a "wild, barbarous, and savage" nature and had to be treated with "strict severity." The regulations—against reading and writing, free movement, intermarriage, and so on—reflected the fears of the West Indian planters for whom they were written, but the American colonists would later come to share those fears. The rapid expansion of slavery in the eighteenth century poisoned whatever goodwill had existed between blacks and whites on the North American mainland, fostering not only anger and resentment among the enslaved but fear and a need to demonize blacks in their masters.

Though the colonies never undertook an organized effort to create a single, unified system of slavery, they all tended to move in a similar direction; at bottom, they had the same intentions. In the Punch case, Virginia had sentenced a recalcitrant servant whose skin color marked him as an outsider to a lifetime of servitude, transforming him with the bang of a gavel from a man to a piece of property. More than just a punishment, this transformation enabled Punch's master to see him as an object, a tool to be employed for his owner's benefit, instead of as a human being. The dehumanization of black servants assuaged white consciences by making enslavement morally acceptable. To this end, colonial legislatures took steps to codify exactly what it meant to be a slave. The Punch case—the first recorded instance of perpetual servitude—became an accepted principle of customary, as opposed to statutory, law throughout the colonies; however, after 1660 the elaboration of slavery shifted to statutory enactment. Though Massachusetts and Connecticut (in 1641 and 1650, respectively) took the lead in recognizing slavery, the Virginia Assembly of 1661 set off a flood of legislation sanctioning slavery throughout America. Blacks who had run away were "incapable of making satisfaction by the addition of time," Virginia noted, because their earthly days already belonged to their masters. "All negroes or other slaves shall serve *durante vita*," Maryland agreed in 1663.[17]

The growing number of slaves raised new and confusing questions that colonial leaders urgently needed to address. Was the offspring of a union between master and slave bound or free? In English common law, the status of a child always derived from its father. But to grant automatic freedom to children of a mixed union threatened to blur the color line. Treating mulattoes as an intermediate category between the races—dark in color but white in entitlement—would have obliterated class and social distinctions that whites had no intention of surrendering. In 1662 Virginia responded to this problem by enacting a statute to resolve "doubts [that] have arrisen whether children got by any Englishman upon a negro woman should be slave or ffree. . . . All children borne in this country," the colonial government affirmed, contradicting the practice of the mother country, derived their status from "the condition of the mother." As the eminent English jurist William Blackstone explained, the colonies departed from English law and followed the Roman principle of *partus sequitur ventrem*, which held that among "tame and domestic animals, the brood belongs to the owner of the dam or mother."[18] Thus a master gained an absolute paternal power over his black offspring, while the child was denied any rights it might possess under normal circumstances.

The application to human beings of a principle intended for animals was yet another way to dehumanize blacks, but its true significance lay in extending the term of slavery past a mere lifetime. The statute made slavery heritable. Not only would an individual remain a slave forever, but one could be born a slave. Slavery became a condition that each generation of the slave's family passed on to the succeeding one. The practice quickly became customary usage throughout America, and most of the colonies eventually worked out similar laws: Maryland in 1663, Massachusetts in 1698, Connecticut and New Jersey in 1704, Pennsylvania and New York in 1706, South Carolina in 1712, Rhode Island in 1728, and North Carolina in 1741.

Heritability represented an important step in extending the concept of slavery, by applying it not only to individuals but to a whole class of people defined by an absence of any hope for social mobility and, thus, unable to escape their servile destiny. Legislation clarified the meaning of slavery by limiting the criteria for the type of person who could be enslaved—criteria based primarily on race or creed. Historically in slave societies, both those issues had been traditional justifications for enslaving outsiders, but the colonists reinterpreted them to fit their own needs. Early Portuguese slave traders, who often carried out mass baptisms on entire boatloads of blacks, had argued that slavery represented a benefit to the enslaved because it saved Africans from paganism. But did baptism also mean that blacks should be emancipated as fellow Christians, deserving to be embraced as brothers and sisters rather than dehumanized as slaves?

The question had enormous significance for the American colonists, for two reasons: First, they wanted to clarify the status of slaves who had become Christians before importation began in earnest or who had arrived in the colonies already baptized. Second, they needed to determine whether to encourage or discourage religion among American-born blacks— whether "the propagation of christianity" should be permitted, as the Virginia Assembly asked in 1667, and whether "those of greater growth ought to be admitted to that sacrament." The gospel message of forbearance in the face of suffering and the promise of a heavenly reward in the afterlife inclined slaves toward patience and docility, but if Christianity also represented a pathway to freedom for blacks, its disruptive revolutionary potential outweighed its advantages.

Not surprisingly, the colonists settled the issue with a practical rather than a theological answer, enabling them to preach obedience and stoicism without ever acknowledging that the acceptance of Christ might also lead to a slave's emancipation. "Baptisme doth not alter the condition of the person as to his bondage or freedom," the Virginia statute of 1667 asserted, defying not only traditional Christian belief in the universal church but severing the connection between body and spirit. Though Christ possessed the power to free the soul, in America the slave's corporeal being still belonged to his master. The principle was affirmed repeatedly and spread throughout the colonies, denying blacks the normal blessings that accompanied baptism.[19] Historically, heathenism had represented one of the primary criteria of slavery, but the assertion that becoming a Christian made no difference rendered religious orientation meaningless, leaving race to stand alone as the defining characteristic of a slave.

Throughout the colonies, men had experimented with the use of indigenous slaves—Indian captives who had been taken in war or purchased from other Indians—but the practice seldom produced satisfactory results. Indians proved less adaptable to agricultural work than blacks, and colonists never held a sufficient number of captives to meet the rising labor needs of the southern plantations. Moreover, Indians inspired a different reaction among whites than blacks did. Confronting an unfamiliar wilderness, the colonists could not help but admire Indians as masters of the forest—primitive and frightening but peerless in their independent spirit and their knowledge of nature. The mere fact that they were dealt with as nations indicates the respect they commanded among the colonists, and as more and more blacks arrived from Africa, Indians gradually became exempt from slavery. In 1670, Virginia outlawed their enslavement, reinstating it in 1682 after a period of hostilities, and then prohibiting it finally in 1691 by implication, when a statute was enacted that legalized free trade with all Indians.

By the last quarter of the seventeenth century, blacks and slaves had become essentially the same thing to the colonists. The "two words, Negro and Slave," the Reverend Morgan Godwyn wrote in 1680, had "grown Homogeneous and Convertible, even as Negro and Christian, Englishman and Heathen represented Opposites."[20] Colonists isolated blacks racially—not as a separate class exactly, which would have implied that they still belonged to the human community—but as a kind of property, lacking human and legal rights. Slaves could be transferred from one owner to another or seized by creditors to satisfy a debt, and an owner could separate a husband and wife or mother and child as he saw fit.

Inevitably, the relationship between blacks and whites took on a schizophrenic quality. As property, slaves received none of the consideration and respect routinely accorded to human beings. At the same time, because of their proximity and daily interactions, whites could not avoid the reality of blacks as men and women who constantly chafed at their inferior status and needed to be restrained by a series of restrictive laws. Over time the colonies formulated elaborate codes aimed at the enforcement of three essential principles: First, the conduct of blacks had to be carefully regulated by colonial legislatures in order to avoid economic disruption and ensure the safety of whites. Second, masters themselves needed broad and incontestable power to keep slaves in their place. And finally, the color line between black and white had to be vigorously defended in order to maintain the separation of the races.

By its very nature, slavery created an unending battle between repression and resistance. A "new *Negro* required more hard Discipline than a young Spaniel to be broke [from] Obstinacy," the English traveler Edward Kimber wrote after touring America in the 1740s.[21] Driven by a powerful urge for control, the planters responded with obstinacy of their own, determined to tighten the screws on their truculent workforce. As Virginia's governor Alexander Spotswood warned the state assembly in 1710, blacks longed to "Shake off the fetters of Slavery"; consequently, the colonists needed to strengthen the militia and make laws "to prevent The Consultations of . . . Negroes, which might lead to an Insurrection [that] would surely be attended with Most Dreadful Consequences."[22]

Colonial legislatures designed the contours of enslavement to isolate and weaken blacks by wiping out their individual identities and encouraging a sense of powerlessness in relation to whites. In the waterfront slave auctions, both seller and buyer recognized the wisdom of separating Africans who had a common background or had formed a desperate friendship during their crossing. Similarly, owners promptly stripped their new purchases of their African names, the last vestige of their personal identity, and taught them to respond to odd sounds in a meaningless tongue, which the Africans were forced to adopt in order to survive. Except for religious meetings or gatherings that involved plantation business, both of which required white supervision, blacks were not allowed to congregate and needed a written pass from their masters to go from one plantation to another.

Blacks bold enough to run away received particularly brutal treatment. Their flight openly challenged their masters' dominion; if allowed to succeed, they might encourage others to follow in their footsteps. Plantation slaves in colonial times, rather than making their way north, usually went no farther than the nearby wilderness, hoping to join other escapees, known as *maroons*. These bands of runaways formed small, armed outlaw communities, daring enough to raid local plantations and determined to fight for their freedom. To colonial authorities the escaped slaves represented a constant anarchic threat, and they waged regular campaigns to suppress them, either by force or by granting them autonomy in exchange for their help in capturing other escaped slaves. When the runaways were apprehended by vigilante groups, the awful power of colonial law awaited them. Though masters often dealt with minor offenses privately, local authorities punished runaways whenever possible in public, in an attempt to send a message of graphic horror throughout the slave community. For a first offense, slaves might be whipped and branded on the cheek with the letter R, so that they could be easily identified as runaways, or rogues, if they tried to escape in the future. Repeated offenses likely would result in dismemberment—the loss of an ear or, for a slave who appeared unrepentant or bent on fleeing again, castration. In special circumstances, local authorities executed runaway slaves and put their mutilated bodies on public display, to intimidate others who might follow their example.

In general, offenses fell into two categories: minor infractions, which resulted in a slave's being whipped, pilloried, or mutilated; and felonious crimes, punishable by loss of life or dismemberment.[23] In the Virginia code of 1748, felonious crimes included insurrection or the plotting of insurrection, murder, manslaughter, burglary, and hog stealing. Less serious infractions included the killing of deer out of season, going off the plantation without a pass, attending an illegal meeting, or raising a hand against a white person. Under constant scrutiny, blacks were always aware that anyone in the white community could impeach them for some crime they could never satisfactorily deny. A formal system of patrols empowered to enter the slave quarters on every plantation reminded blacks that they were constantly being watched. Often arbitrary and unruly, these local patrols represented the precursors of the Ku Klux Klan, night riders whose mission extended beyond simply policing to terrorizing and intimidating blacks.

Though colonial law sharply restricted their freedom, slaves found themselves subject to a second, more immediate source of control. The master's property right to his slaves gave him broad discretion to regulate their conduct, and colonial authorities only reluctantly interfered between a master and his bondsmen. In Virginia, in 1669, if a slave died while resisting punishment, no crime had occurred. At least theoretically, self-interest dictated a sane limit to the degree of force a master would employ against his own property; a deceased or disabled slave, after all, represented lost man-hours, a loss ultimately borne by the planter. The list of offenses for which a slave might be disciplined and the accompanying punishments were arbitrary and inconsistent from one plantation to the next. Without a fixed code, each plantation owner felt empowered to formulate his own set of rules and alter them as he pleased. The code of conduct on any plantation became a reflection of the owner's personality, liable to be marked by individual idiosyncrasies which might amount to nothing, but given the wrong master could represent a terrible burden for those living under it.

By most measures, William Byrd II, the son of Virginia's largest landholder, was a man of admirable intellect and refinement. He had studied law at the Inns of Court, and before inheriting his father's estate in 1705 had lived in Europe for fifteen years, acquired a Continental education, and hobnobbed with London's literary elite. A compulsive diarist, he kept a minute record of his daily life, portraying both good and bad with the supreme indifference of one who never intended his journal to be read by others. At home on his plantation in Westover, Virginia, Byrd described a placid, privileged existence regularly upset by one jarring distraction—the constant need to discipline unruly servants. Byrd recorded thrashing, beating, and soundly whipping a sixteen-year-old slave girl named Jenny for such minor offenses as being unmannerly, spilling water on the sofa, or concealing the bed-wetting of a servant boy, Eugene. On one occasion, Byrd's wife went as far as to brand the unfortunate girl with a hot pressing iron on the cheek. When Eugene tried to run away Byrd had him soundly whipped and forced him to wear an iron boot. When his bed-wetting became chronic and the branding iron failed to teach him self-control, Eugene found himself at the receiving end of an even more diabolical punishment. The gentlemanly Byrd notes in one matter-of-fact entry: "I made him drink a pint of piss."[24]

Sadly, we cannot dismiss Byrd's treatment of Jenny and Eugene as exceptional cruelty. In South Carolina, the missionary Dr. Francis Le Jau observed far greater atrocities. Carolinians could not be "persuaded that Indians and Negroes are otherwise than beasts, and use them like such," he wrote. A slave was "burnt alive without any positive proof of the Crime" because someone suspected her of arson. Masters were accustomed to "hamstring, maim, & unlimb slaves for small faults." Punished for losing a parcel of rice, a man had been put into "a hellish Machine contrived . . . into the shape of a Coffin and kept there Several Dayes & Nights" by an overseer who had already murdered five slaves.[25] Almost certainly, the misery that Byrd inflicted on Jenny and Eugene remained within normal bounds and typified the penalties meted out on many plantations, designed to humiliate and frighten blacks into submission but not to seriously injure property that belonged to the master. Casual cruelty represented the linchpin of the plantation system. As George Mason, one of Virginia's delegates to the Constitutional Convention, later observed, every slaveholder became "a petty tyrant." Masters preferred fear as a method of maintaining order, and while most owners harbored no particular personal animosity toward their slaves, they believed that in order to control them they needed an absolutely free hand. Colonial planters were determined to profit from the rough resources available to them, and they developed a strict and brutal form of discipline as a way of managing a workforce they regarded as lazy, dishonest, and potentially dangerous. The outrages that Le Jau saw in South Carolina, a colony notorious for the cruelty of its planters, surely would have been condemned in Virginia or Maryland, but throughout the South owners used controlled violence as the chief weapon to maintain their dominance over a burgeoning slave population.

Of the three principal ways that colonial law shaped slavery, the third, a strict separation between the races, filled a deep emotional and psychological need, as the colonists—living in a wilderness only recently and tenuously claimed from savages and increasingly populated by slaves—struggled to maintain their identity as civilized Englishmen. In the early years in Virginia, far more men than women had arrived from England. The first three ships that came to Jamestown had carried only men; in the 1630s, the ratio of male to female immigrants ran about six to one. Not surprisingly, the scarcity of white women led the colonists to seek out Indians and blacks for female companionship. While colonial authorities sometimes tolerated liaisons and even marriages with Native Americans—particularly when they had positive political implications, as in the case of John Rolfe and Pocahontas—intimacy with blacks inspired violent reactions. As early as 1630, Virginia's governor ordered that a white man, Hugh Davis, "be soundly whipped ... for abusing himself ... in lying with a negro." In a similar case ten years later, the court convicted a second indentured servant, Robert Sweet, of fornicating with a black woman, but in Sweet's case the court ordered his unfortunate partner to receive the whipping.[26] Surely the Davis and Sweet liaisons did not represent isolated incidents, and the choice of public punishment in both cases—aimed at discouraging other fornicators—suggests that soon after the first blacks arrived in Virginia, sexual congress between blacks and whites became a serious issue that grated on colonial leaders. The Virginia act of 1662 that defined an infant as slave or free based on the condition of its mother came as a direct result of white fears about miscegenation, and a series of statutes intended to prevent the "spurious and mixt issue" resulting from biracial parentage quickly followed. In 1691, the Virginia legislature enacted a statute permanently banishing any white who married a black, mulatto, or Indian, and bound children resulting from such a union to service for thirty years, even if both parents were free.

As a class, free mulattoes represented a particularly confusing problem for colonial legislators. In everyday practice, individuals were black as long as one could see a trace of African heritage in their features—skin, hair, facial structure, and so on. If they could pass for white, in effect they had transmogrified into whites. Under ordinary circumstances, the distinction seemed clear enough, but legally the colonists needed a more exact definition of blackness to establish a bright line in the gray area where the blood of the two races ran together. As with blacks and Indians, laws denied free mulattoes most of the rights accorded to whites: to vote, to bear witness, to hold office, to join the militia, and so forth. Legally, however, their status demanded clarification. When, if ever, should free biracial children be regarded as essentially white and thus eligible for the same rights as normal citizens? At precisely what point would the stain of inferior blood be sufficiently diluted so as to become meaningless? In 1705 Virginia offered a startling answer to the question—one that appeared to single out blacks as the lowest, least trusted element in colonial society.[27] As part of a disabling act that lumped blacks, Indians, and free mulattoes with criminals, the Virginia Assembly denied each group permanently the fundamental rights of citizenship, with one exception. Children of mixed heritage could gain their rights, but only after a prescribed period of time: two generations for individuals with Indian blood, four for free mulattoes. Thus the assembly deprived only the first generation of mixed Native American children of its rights, while it excluded from citizenship all the children, grandchildren, and great-grandchildren of free blacks. Black blood required two extra generations of dilution before its bearers could be included in white society.

By the 1720s, laws against racial mixing prevailed throughout the southern colonies and had become common in the North, where blacks remained relatively few in number. In Pennsylvania, in 1700, the Chester County Court instructed a black man "never more to meddle with any white woman

. . . uppon paine of his life."[28] Massachusetts enacted strict prohibitions against intermarriage five years later, ordering offending blacks and mulattoes sold out of the colony and fining whites £50. In South Carolina, where whites more openly pursued interracial relationships than anywhere else in America, a grand jury in 1743 condemned "THE TOO COMMON PRACTICE of CRIMINAL CONVERSATION with NEGRO and other SLAVE WENCHES as an Enormity and Evil of general Ill-Consequence."[29] Marked by their skin color not only as outsiders but as subhuman creatures destined for enslavement, blacks were forced to spend their lives laboring for whites but not allowed to intermingle with them. Even before it had become a nation, America had clearly and indelibly drawn its color line.

By the time Lord Mansfield declared that England had no "positive law" sanctioning slavery, the American colonies had developed their own full-blown system of bondage, based not only on custom and usage but on an extensive body of statutory law formulated in bits and pieces by all thirteen colonies. Developed essentially without legal precedents, American slavery became a reflection of the conflicting forces at work on the colonists: the need for an ever-expanding pool of servile labor coupled with an insistence by whites that blacks, brutish and duplicitous creatures, needed to be kept under strict control and at arm's length. Blacks responded by feigning ignorance, subtly malingering, running away, and even violently rebelling. With no possibility of real accommodation, masters and slaves were locked in a tense battle that promised endless cycles of increasing repression and resistance.

In 1711, only a year after Governor Spotswood had called on the Virginia Assembly to strengthen the militia and legislate tighter controls over blacks, the colonists' greatest fears were realized in South Carolina, where a group of maroons led by a runaway named Sebastian carried out a series of raids on local plantations. The South Carolina militia eventually suppressed Sebastian's band of rebels, but their boldness incited some two dozen blacks in New York City, who revolted in 1712, setting fires and killing nine whites before being captured. White fear rose to panic levels, and city authorities publicly hanged twelve blacks, burned two at the stake, and slowly roasted another over an open fire for an entire day. In 1739, the pattern repeated itself, starting again in South Carolina. The trouble began in Charleston, where a group of slaves, urged on by Spanish missionaries, set out for Florida, determined to kill anyone who stood in their way. Eventually, they were surrounded and massacred, but not before twenty-one whites and forty-four blacks had died. Colonial authorities conducted another public horror show, displaying the decapitated heads of the rebel leaders on mileposts along the road. Two years later, again in New York, blacks conspired to terrorize the city by setting a series of incendiary fires, which came to be known as The Great Negro Plot. In retaliation, eighteen blacks were hung and thirteen more burned at the stake. The cycle of resistance and repression had taken another turn in an established pattern that would last until the Civil War.

CHAPTER 2

ATTITUDES HARDEN IN THE PROMISED LAND

Comparing them by their faculties of memory, reason, and imagination, it appears to me that in memory they are equal to the whites; in reason much inferior . . . and that in imagination they are dull, tasteless, and anomalous.
—THOMAS JEFFERSON, 1784

Though northerners and southerners felt a similar contempt for blacks, they held fundamentally different attitudes toward them. The prevailing southern view grew out of the region's economics. The labor-intensive plantation system depended on cheap manpower, and slaves annually produced millions of dollars in wealth at a relatively low cost. By ignoring the slave's humanity, owners were free to use whatever methods they pleased to generate maximum amounts of labor. For a southern master to think of slaves as his equals—to have to base their treatment on that assumption and also consider the moral issue of enslaving other human beings—would have been in direct conflict with the economic interest that led him to acquire slaves in the first place. Southerners sustained the system on which their lives depended by believing that the gulf between the two races could not be bridged. This radical racism, which not only insisted on white superiority but locked blacks into a permanent position of inferiority, arose out of necessity. In practical terms, it provided the rationale that allowed masters unbridled freedom in the treatment of their bondsmen and, even more important, assured southerners that even if they had no way out of their moral dilemma they could at least leave things unchanged and prosper indefinitely. Southern whites had built a society that planted the seeds of its own destruction. Since the arrival of the plantation system at the end of the seventeenth century, the South had gradually become, at least numerically, a land that blacks and whites shared. From 1787 until the Civil War, blacks represented about 35 percent of the southern population. With every third person a black, whites could imagine no other arrangement but as masters and slaves. The idea of sharing the South with blacks in any way that implied equality between the races—socially, politically, or economically—was unthinkable.

Given the imposing number of blacks in the South, almost any imaginable future that admitted the possibility of change pointed to a mixed society. The contrast between what whites could bring themselves to accept and what seemed likely to happen was stark and unyielding. The slaveholders' only hope of preserving what they had was denial—an insistence that, in defiance of human experience, life on the plantation would never change. Against all reason, Southern whites were betting that time could be stopped in its tracks. When Alexis de Tocqueville toured the United States in the 1830s, he quickly came to understand that slavery was "the most formidable of all the ills that threatened America." Southerners "chose their slaves from an inferior race," he wrote, and any notion of intimate union with blacks horrified them. "*They must have believed that slavery would last forever* [italics ours]," he continued, "since there is no intermediate state . . . between the excessive inequality produced by servitude and the complete equality that originates in independence."[1] To hold that the inferior status of blacks resulted from their inherent, fixed nature meant that blacks could never rise to a higher level of civility or understanding; thus, blacks would always have to be kept in their place in a society dominated by whites.

In the North, though nearly everyone agreed on black inferiority, the idea meant something different from the extreme southern view. By the mid-1780s, a revolutionary wave of egalitarian enthusiasm had produced laws abolishing involuntary servitude, either immediately or by gradual emancipation, in all the northern states except New York and New Jersey. Whites in the North, free of the plantation owners' desperate need for control over an imposing servile population, could allow themselves far more latitude than southerners in their thinking about blacks. Northerners even sympathized with blacks, as long as they considered them in abstract political terms, as victims of injustice and mistreatment who had been forced into servitude and deprived of perhaps the most important universal human value, the inalienable right to freedom. Northern attitudes turned sharply critical, however, when whites ceased viewing blacks abstractly and had to deal with them personally. As free agents, able to determine what they might freely do or not do, blacks made northerners wary and uncomfortable: a bedraggled, alien race that represented an affront to the good order and finer sensibilities that whites recognized in themselves.

Soon after the first blacks arrived in the North, this heartfelt ambivalence became nearly universal. Not just their enemies but even, quite remarkably, whites who proved themselves outspoken friends of blacks, took black inferiority for granted. The Puritan judge Samuel Sewall wrote one of the earliest antislavery tracts, *The Selling of Joseph*, in 1700.[2] Disturbed by the "Numerousness of Slaves" in Massachusetts—then surely no more than five hundred—he turned to Scripture to prove that "Man Stealing" ranked among the most atrocious of crimes. "All Men, as they are the Sons of *Adam* are Coheirs and share One Blood," Sewall wrote, his prose boiling with indignation. "In taking Negros out of *Africa*, and Selling of them here, men do boldly rend asunder that which GOD has joyned together: . . . Men from their Country, Husbands from their Wives, [and] Parents from their Children. . . . How horrible . . . the Uncleanliness, Mortality, if not Murder, that the Ships are guilty of that bring great Crouds of these miserable Men, and Women." Nevertheless, he also harbored powerful reservations about blacks. Favoring the use of white indentured servants instead of slaves for life, Sewall voiced his personal suspicions of blacks, which he assumed most members of the Massachusetts Colony shared. "Few can endure to hear of a Negro's being made free," he wrote. Blacks could do nothing but cause trouble, either as unwilling servants or as creatures who, when given their freedom, were unable to cope. The root of the problem lay in blacks themselves, as God had made them. "There is such a disparity in their Conditions, Colour & Hair," Sewall observed, "that they can never embody with us, and grow into orderly Families, to the Peopling of the Land." Biblical examples of human kinship aside, in his heart of hearts the evidence convinced Sewall that God had constituted blacks as creatures wholly unlike whites. Ignoring his own earlier assertion that all people shared "One Blood," he concluded that blacks would always remain outcasts—"a kind of extravasat Blood in the Body Politick" of Massachusetts.

Sewall's lifelong friend, the Puritan divine Cotton Mather, held similarly conflicted views about blacks. Mather owned slaves himself and had no trouble reconciling his religion and slaveholding. When his congregation gave him a young house servant, he exulted over the gift as a "mighty smile of Heaven upon my family" and would doubtless have maintained that fortune had likewise shone on his new bondsman, Onesimus. A Christian master, according to Mather, represented a great blessing for a slave, because religion "wonderfully Dulcifies, and Mollifies, and Moderates the Circumstances of bondage." Mather took seriously his Christian responsibilities, governing his manservant only through what he called principles of reason: teaching him daily to read and write, instructing him in religion, encouraging him to lead an exemplary life. Not only privately but publicly, Mather insisted that a conscientious Christian had an obligation to uplift the benighted souls of blacks. In *The Negro Christianized* (1706), he encouraged slaveholders to view their charges not as beasts but as human beings who deserved education and baptism. "Their *Souls* . . . are as white and good as those of other Nations . . . but are *Destroyed for lack* of *Knowledge*," he wrote. He prided himself on the many good offices he had done for slaves; contrary to the white-only policy of most New England ministers, he not only included "a Number of black Sheep" in his own congregation but in 1693 formed a Religious Society of Negroes, which still held regular meetings twenty-five years later, "to pray with them, and preach to them, and enquire into their Conduct, and encourage them, in the ways of Piety."[3]

Mather recognized a Christian obligation to blacks, but he also never doubted their inferiority. Intent on bringing them religion, he prepared a simplified catechism, insisting that he needed a shortened version to instruct "poor Stupid Abject Negro's." "Indeed their *Stupidity*" represented such "a *Discouragement*," he admitted, that "it may seem, unto as little purpose, to *Teach* as to *wash an Aethiopian*." At home, Mather's ambivalence clouded his household routine. He not only devoted hours to instruction and counseling for Onesimus but also felt compelled to keep a strict eye on the young man, whom he constantly suspected of sinfulness, particularly of thievery. Mather maintained his belief in a single humanity—that all men and women originated with Adam—but his feelings about blacks obviously tested his faith. Ultimately, everyone would gather in Heaven at the Table of Abraham, he wrote, "even, the *Indians*, and the *Negro's*," which should "wondrously encourage the *dark-hued Ones*, with their Despised Complexion, to become *seekers of GOD*." Mather's invitation to the feast seems less encouraging than he imagined, with its implicit suggestion that at least temporally blacks wore their skin color as a permanent badge of inferiority.[4]

One figure among the nation's earliest leaders from whom we would expect understanding and humanity surely would be Benjamin Franklin, America's great exemplar of philanthropy and public idealism. Though we associate his name with Philadelphia, his adopted home and the city that bears the imprint of his public interests, Franklin originally came from New England and had grown up in the Puritan tradition that spawned Mather. In his *Autobiography*, Franklin credits Mather's writing with influencing his thinking and his life. Though the practical-minded Franklin had little time for Mather's theology, the older man's commitment to virtuous action attracted him, and his assertion in *Poor Richard's Almanac* that "the noblest question in the world is What Good may I do in it?" was taken almost verbatim from an essay by Mather.[5]

In the second half of his life, Franklin belatedly added the well-being of blacks, both slave and free, to his already lengthy list of civic concerns, but as a young man his thinking reflected the typical prejudice of most whites. Starting out as a printer in Philadelphia, he regularly carried ads for slaves and runaways in his newspaper, though at least one of his competitors refused to publish them. The casual cruelty of the slave traders' vending notices apparently failed to move him: "A very likely Negro Woman aged about thirty Years . . . She has a Boy of about Two Years old, which is to go with her . . . And also another Boy aged about Six Years. . . . He will be sold with his Mother, or by Himself, as the Buyer pleases."[6] Franklin also kept slaves as servants for more than thirty years, as did his son and daughter. In contrast to family members who frequently mention their household slaves in letters to him, Franklin seems to have taken almost no personal interest in his servants. In his letters he had little to say about the blacks who waited on him, except for an occasional generalized complaint. In 1750, for example, he wrote to his mother that he intended to sell his two slaves—a plan he never carried out—because, he said, he did not like Negro servants. Later, when he was in England and one of his male bondsmen, King, ran off, Franklin complained that Peter, the remaining slave, behaved "as well as I can expect in a Country where there are many Occasions of spoiling Servants." With only Peter to care for him, he could manage pretty comfortably, he assured his wife, as long as he contented himself with low expectations, "seeing with only one Eye and hearing only with one Ear."[7]

In 1751, at age forty-five, Franklin wrote his "Observations Concerning the Increase of Mankind," which included the principal statement of his views on blacks during the first half of his life. Intending to reassure the British that "the Danger of [the] Colonies interfering with their Mother Country in Trades that depend on Labour, Manufacture, &c." remained slight, Franklin considered the part that blacks should play in America's future. Arguing against the economics of slavery, Franklin insisted that it was "an ill-grounded opinion that by the Labour of Slaves, *America* might vie in cheapness of Manufactures with *Britain*." Fascinated as always with lists, he enumerated the separate costs that made slave labor uneconomical: the initial expense of slaves; lost interest on the purchase money; insurance, maintenance, and support; sickness and loss of time; the price of an overseer; and, of course, "Pilfering from Time to Time, almost every Slave being by *Nature* a Thief."[8] In Franklin's view, not only did slave labor prove expensive but its presence seemed certain to diminish a nation. The white population of the Caribbean, he suggested, had been ruined by the introduction of blacks. The possibility of a harmonious, cooperative society in which everyone lived modest, upright lives—Franklin's ideal community—had been destroyed by the plantation system, which allowed a few to profit lavishly but left most people with little or nothing. The use of slaves also had disastrous individual consequences, according to Franklin. In terms of masculine power and raw muscle, hard physical work represented a form of self-improvement, and whites who relied on slave labor would no doubt experience a decline in male virility accompanied by a falling birthrate. Such a situation would also likely ruin white children, because a slave society failed to inculcate the virtues of modesty and hard work: "Slaves . . . pejorate the Families that use them," he explained. "The white Children become proud, disgusted with Labour, and being educated in Idleness, are rendered unfit to get a Living by Industry."[9]

Franklin's "Observations" are quite remarkable for the selective, one-sided humanity with which he viewed the master-slave relationship. Franklin believed slavery to be an evil institution, but he seemed indifferent to the fate of the slaves themselves—in fact, he barely acknowledged their misery. Slaves were "work'd too hard, and ill fed," their constitutions so broken that their mortality rate exceeded their birthrate, but this, to Franklin, was merely additional proof of the prohibitive expense of using slaves, for "a continual supply was needed from *Africa*." The cruel and inhumane treatment of black slaves appeared less important to him than slavery's harmful effect on whites. Franklin feared the hordes of darker-skinned people who inhabited most of the earth and represented a threat to white racial purity, and at least in part he intended the "Observations" to sound an alarm—to alert his fellow whites to the danger of corruption by inferior races. "Why should Pennsylvania, founded by the English, become a Colony of Aliens, who . . . will never adopt our Language or Customs, any more than they can acquire our Complexion?" he asked. He divided the world into two neat groups: the "purely white People," which included only the English and some Germans and was "proportionably very small," and the rest of humankind, who threatened to undermine white purity. "All *Africa* is black or tawny," he noted, "*Asia* chiefly tawny. *America* (exclusive of the new Comers) wholly so. And in *Europe*, the *Spaniards, Italians, French, Russians* and *Swedes* are generally of what we call a swarthy Complexion; as are the *Germans* also, the *Saxons* only excepted." Franklin wanted to make sure that America protected its purity. The colonists had brought white civilization to "this side of our Globe" so it "reflect[ed] a brighter Light," he explained, and it would be tragic to cloud America's prospects by "darken[ing] its people." Blacks represented the ultimate threat. "Why increase the Sons of *Africa*, by planting them in *America*," he asked, "when we have so fair an opportunity, by excluding all Blacks and Tawneys, of increasing the lovely White and Red?"[10] Franklin made no apologies for his desire to keep America white, believing as he did that being "partial to the Complexion" of one's own race was a normal, wholesome instinct. Such partiality helps to explain his frequent callousness toward blacks, who lived in this country not just as men and women of a different color but as an exotic, troublesome people that threatened white society, a potentially corrupting influence that could be allowed no permanent home in a land destined for whites.

The "Observations," originally circulated privately and not published until 1755, mark the low point in Benjamin Franklin's opinion of black people. From that time forward, his attitude gradually softened, in part perhaps because of his experience with an English philanthropic group in establishing a separate school for blacks in Philadelphia. Noting the formidable obstacles to African education—widespread "Prejudice that Reading and Knowledge in a Slave are both useless and dangerous and the Unwillingness . . . of common Schools to take black Scholars because Parents of the white Children should be disgusted and take them away"—Franklin voiced his pleasant surprise at the progress of the school's black pupils, announcing that he had "conceived a higher Opinion of the natural Capacities of the black Race than I had ever before entertained. Their Apprehension seems as quick, their Memory as strong, and their Docility in every Respect equal to that of white Children."[11] Still, Franklin's new attitude toward blacks took time to develop. Beginning in 1764, he lived primarily in Europe for almost twenty years—in England as the representative of several of the individual colonies, and after the war began, as the United States' ambassador to France. In the 1770s, seeking the Crown's approval of Georgia's draconian slave code, he remained deeply suspicious of blacks as a group. "Perhaps you imagine the Negroes to be a mild tempered, tractable Kind of People," he wrote in the 1770 *Conversation on Slavery*. "But the Majority [are] of a plotting Disposition, dark, sullen, malicious, revengeful, and cruel in the highest Degree."[12] When he returned to America in 1785 at nearly eighty years of age, Franklin had gained enormous respect as a humanitarian, philosopher, patriot, and politician; and in 1787, when he became a delegate to the Constitutional Convention in Philadelphia, he also assumed the presidency of the Pennsylvania Society for the Abolition of Slavery. In an address to that society he acknowledged that his youthful preconceptions had led him astray, noting that "you will wonder perhaps that I should ever doubt [their abilities], and I will not undertake to justify all my Prejudices, nor to account for them." At the Convention, he prepared a petition calling on the coastal states to close American ports to the slave trade, which he ultimately withheld, fearing that it would disrupt negotiations between the North and South.[13]

"Life," Franklin once wrote, should be "conducted with Regularity, but methinks it should finish handsomely. I am very desirous of concluding with a bright Point."[14] In 1790, with his life coming to a close, he presented a memorial to Congress, fulfilling his wish for a final shining moment, one that aroused a bitter debate in the House of Representatives and that George Washington himself privately declared "very mal-apropos." Franklin noted that the Constitution intended to promote the welfare and liberty of all the nation's inhabitants, and pleaded for an end to slavery.[15] Not only the "political creed of Americans" but Christian religion demanded the removal of this "inconsistency from the land of liberty." The same God had created everyone, he argued, and embraced both whites and blacks as "objects of his care and equally designed for the enjoyment of happiness. . . . Step to the very verge of the power vested in you," Franklin urged Congress, to discourage "every species of traffic in the persons of our fellow men." His humanity toward black Americans had obviously expanded as he grew older, but whether he ever fully overcame his conflicted feelings about them remains an open question. Even as he asked Congress to abolish slavery, he conceded that blacks too frequently sank beneath "the common standard of the human species."[16] Throughout his life, Franklin rarely passed up an opportunity to promote upbeat American values: openness, optimism, a sunny disposition, and good intentions; and blacks represented the very antithesis of these ideals: a "dark, sullen, malicious" race that violated Franklin's fundamental conception of what men should be and threatened to undermine the nation's future.

Raised in the strict moral atmosphere of Puritan New England, Franklin, Mather, and Sewall all felt a sincere humanitarian responsibility toward the blacks in their midst, while at the same time remaining wary of them and unwilling to view them as equals. Most antislavery whites shared these ambivalent feelings. The shortcomings of Franklin, Mather, and Sewall do not alter in any way the reality that they sincerely and conscientiously strove to better the condition of black Americans. The important point lies not in the personal failures of essentially good men but in what their contradictory statements and behavior reveal about the attitudes of their white contemporaries. If people who unquestionably counted themselves as friends of the Negro and had an authentic humanitarian commitment to blacks could not overcome their private feelings of distaste, what does it say about the great majority of their fellow Americans, who felt no particular moral obligation to blacks but certainly experienced the same profound personal confusion in relation to them?

When he sought to justify the exclusion of "all Blacks and Tawneys," Franklin had asserted that to prefer one's own race was "natural to Mankind," but this was not the case universally. In Latin America, for example, the Spanish intermixed with blacks relatively easily. Anglo-Americans had a much harder time accepting blacks, and led by Thomas Jefferson's *Notes on the State of Virginia*, a substantial body of speculative and pseudoscientific literature developed, aimed at fathoming the growing alien presence that whites in both the North and the South desperately wanted to reject.

In 1781, at the request of the Duc de Barbé-Marbois, a French diplomat stationed in Philadelphia, Jefferson began writing a guide to his native state, which ultimately contained an overview of its fauna and flora, geography, economy, government, and social order. Though it would eventually be published in America, Jefferson intended the *Notes on the State of Virginia* to be circulated in Paris only among a select group of close friends; thus, Jefferson felt free to express his unguarded views on the question of blacks and slavery. However, along with men like Franklin, Thomas Paine, and the chemist Joseph Priestley, Jefferson played a leading role in the American Philosophical Society, and he also had an apparently less controversial, scientific goal in mind. Ideally he wanted to assume the guise of dispassionate observer and describe Negroes with scientific detachment. In "a century and a half," he wrote, they had "never yet been viewed by us as subjects of natural history," and he hoped that his observations would be the first of many that, in true Aristotelian fashion, would lead to a precise, scientific understanding of one of the distinct varieties of the human species, *Homo sapiens Afer*.[17]

No doubt Jefferson sincerely wanted to be objective, but the *Notes* provides an instructive example of the influence that personal feelings can exert on an individual's perceptions. By 1781, Jefferson had already won international fame as the author of the Declaration of Independence. Nevertheless he remained a Virginia aristocrat, with an estate of ten thousand acres and two hundred slaves, and in terms of direct experience nearly all his personal contacts with blacks came as a member of the slaveholding class. Jefferson had been waited on and cared for by African Americans, had bought and sold them, rewarded their industry and punished their indolence, dealt with them daily as a master on every conceivable matter, and no doubt believed that he understood them intimately. He reported that his earliest recollection was of a mounted Negro bondsman carrying him from place to place on a pillow. And in fact, he surely must have understood them, though from the terribly restricted perspective of a Virginia slave owner whose privileged life depended on the continued subservience of his bondsmen.

Jefferson presented his description of blacks to explain why they could never be incorporated into white society. He offered not only political reasons—"deep rooted prejudice entertained by the whites and ten thousand recollections, by the blacks, of the injuries they have sustained"—but physical and moral barriers as well, enumerating a number of ways in which the two races differed. Blacks required "less sleep, were at least as brave, and more adventure-some [and] more ardent after their female," he observed. None of these traits, however, indicated black advantages; on the contrary, even when blacks seemed in some way superior to whites, closer consideration revealed their inferiority. Negroes appeared to need less sleep only because they exhibited more irresponsibility. "A black after hard Labour through the day, will be induced by the slightest amusements to sit up till midnight or later, though knowing he must be out with the first dawn of the morning." Black bravery turned out to be nothing more than foolhardiness, proceeding "from a want of forethought, which prevents their seeing a danger till it be present." The fervor of black love also revealed a deficiency: their lack of tender feelings. Love among Negroes was "more an eager desire, than a tender delicate mixture of sentiment and sensation." And just as they demonstrated a lack of feeling in love, Jefferson added, blacks showed an insensitivity to pain. "Their griefs are transient," he wrote, "less felt, and sooner forgotten." All in all, he decided, black "existence appears to participate more of sensation than reflection," a conclusion that led to a final, demeaning observation: "To this must be ascribed their disposition to sleep when abstracted from their diversions, and unemployed in labour. An animal whose body is at rest, and who does not reflect, must be disposed to sleep, of course."

Jefferson also judged black mental powers as inferior. "Comparing them by their faculties of memory, reason, and imagination," he wrote, "it appears to me that in memory they are equal to the whites; in reason much inferior . . . and that in imagination they are dull, tasteless, and anomalous." As evidence, he pointed out that he could find scarcely one black "capable of tracing and comprehending the investigations of Euclid," and none who had ever uttered "a thought above the level of plain narration." Poetry, painting, and sculpture all remained beyond their reach, he insisted. Though misery often gave birth to "the most affecting touches in poetry"—and certainly, blacks had misery enough—still they had no poetry. Only in music did Negroes display a greater gift than whites. "Whether they will be equal to the composition of an . . . extensive run of melody, or of complicated harmony, is yet to be proved," Jefferson observed, but they did have an accurate ear for simple tunes, which they played on "the instrument proper to them," the banjo.

Though his flimsy science was little more than a recapitulation of black inferiority that most whites already accepted as established fact, Jefferson believed that he had gone out of his way to be scrupulously fair. To describe blacks as morally inferior based on faculties like imagination and reason, which defied calculation, could only be "hazarded with great diffidence," he warned. For himself, he could go no further than cautiously theorizing—"as a suspicion only"—that the races were unequal. Nevertheless, their physical differences, particularly their color, convinced Jefferson that they should never be allowed to intermix. Not only did blacks lack the beautiful flowing hair and elegant symmetry of form that characterized whites but their "unfortunate difference of colour" defined their whole being. Though many whites sincerely wanted "to vindicate the liberty of human nature" by freeing their slaves, they were immobilized because they also wanted "to preserve [human] dignity and beauty." The aesthetics of race evidently weighed heavily on the author of the Declaration—even against an individual's right to freedom. "What further is to be done," he asked, when the Negroes' blackness represented such "a powerful obstacle" to their emancipation?

Skin color, for Jefferson, provided "the foundation of a greater or less share of beauty in the two races." Surely one must prefer the "fine mixture of red and white," he maintained, to the "eternal monotony that reigns in the countenances" of Negroes. The difference between the races literally appeared as day and night. A white complexion shone like the midday sun, revealing "the expressions of every passion by the greater or less suffusions of colour," while the Negro face seemed as forbidding as midnight, with its "immovable veil of black" muting any sign of expression and "covering all the emotions" in darkness. For Jefferson, differences in skin color symbolized the differences in character between the two races. Whites dealt with people in an open, straightforward, and trustworthy manner; blacks interacted in the most secretive, morose, and devious of ways.

The idea of blackness as a permanent, defining characteristic can be traced back to the Old Testament. "Can the Ethiopian change his skin / or the leopard his spots?" Jeremiah asked, implying that just as evil could not be removed from the soul of the sinner, blackness served as an indelible mark that defined the Negro. The Bible also provided a historical explanation for the origin of African skin color. Since every human being ultimately derived from Adam and Eve, how did they produce both black and white offspring? The explanation lay in the transgression of Noah's son Ham. After the flood, when his father had fallen into a drunken stupor, Ham immodestly gazed upon Noah's nakedness, while his brothers, Shem and Japheth, averted their eyes and covered their father. When Noah awoke, he punished

Ham by cursing his son, Canaan, dooming him to act for all time as a servant of servants unto his brothers. Ham's progeny, condemned to slavery, had been marked by God with black skin to separate them from Noah's more deserving descendants. Blackness thus became a manifest sign not only of inferior status but of the Almighty's permanent displeasure with Negroes.[18]

A biblical explanation of black skin color failed to satisfy everyone, of course. Southerners, committed to the proposition that blacks had to remain slaves because their essential nature could never change, embraced the idea that God had blackened them as punishment because it affirmed their conviction that slavery would have to last forever. But for those who believed that environmental factors—the rigors of life in Africa and slavery in America—had degraded blacks and that by changing their circumstances they could be made essentially the same as whites, skin color became a subject of intense debate. Most northerners, even those sympathetic to Negroes, saw black skin color as a sign of inferiority, but many of them questioned its permanence. Was it possible that blacks could be made white—that eventually the two races would become indistinguishable?

The Reverend Samuel Stanhope Smith, a member of the American Philosophical Society and later president of Princeton, believed that environment determined skin color. In *An Essay on the Variety of Complexion and Figure in the Human Species*, first published in 1787 and revised in 1810, Smith maintained that all humankind represented a single race, and that "climate," "state of society," and "habits of living" had caused the variations in human appearance. According to Smith, human beings originated in Asia, and God—in keeping with his own perfection—had created them not as savages but as civilized whites. As men spread out around the globe, those who settled in more primitive regions gradually were altered in appearance and degenerated into savagery. Writing more than a century before rudimentary genetics was understood, Smith believed that the key to human difference lay in heat, or climate. The white progenitors of blacks had concentrated in the tropics, and even the most casual observer could see that both heat and human color increased as one moved from the Poles down to the equator. Over time, the inhabitants of the tropics had slowly acquired their blackness from the scorching sun. Heat thickened the skin and released bile from

Smith's views on skin color

within the body, which congregated in the skin's middle layer and appeared as color, Smith explained. Blackness, in effect, represented a skin blemish that covered the entire body—in Smith's words, "a universal freckle."[19]

Smith believed in "the unity of the human species"—that all men belonged to a single human family; thus he remained more sanguine than many of his contemporaries about the future of black Americans. Along with climate, the "state of society and habits of living" powerfully affected human development, particularly in relation to complexion. A wild, untamed landscape and savage life exacerbated blackness, because "the vapours of stagnant water with which uncultivated regions abound; all great fatigues and hardships; poverty and nastiness tended to augment the bile." America not only occupied temperate "latitudes that have ever been most favorable to the beauty of the human form," Smith wrote, but also led the world as a model of civilization, a benign setting in which man could attain "the greatest perfection . . . of his whole nature."[20] Smith anticipated that as time passed, the American environment would gradually lighten the skin of blacks. By 1810, in the revised edition of his *Essay*, he had discerned evidence suggesting that the process was already under way. Apparently oblivious to the libertine nature of many slave owners, Smith considered the great difference in color and features that had developed between domestic and field slaves a hopeful sign. While the field hands remained as dark and primitive as blacks in Africa, he observed, the uplifting influence of a civilized household had begun to alter many African American domestics, who now appeared "as handsomely formed as those of the inferior and laboring classes, either of Europeans, or Anglo-Americans." For blacks, this represented an important development, because it indicated that if they were "perfectly free, enjoyed property, and were admitted to a liberal participation of the society, rank and privileges of their masters, they would change their African peculiarities much faster." Allowed to mingle on an equal footing with whites, blacks eventually might recover their original whiteness.[21]

Others besides Smith formulated ostensibly scientific theories to explain black skin color and suggest the possibility that it might be changed. The physician Benjamin Rush, one of the truly fascinating figures of the Revolutionary period, was a signer of the Declaration of Independence and a member of the Continental Congress, and for a time served as surgeon general of the Continental Army. He performed heroically during Philadelphia's yellow-fever epidemic of 1793, did pioneer work in the fields of psychiatry and dream interpretation, and helped found the nation's first antislavery society. A staunch abolitionist who declared slavery a national crime, Rush published in the *Transactions of the American Philosophical Society* of 1799 his "Observations Intended to Favour a Supposition That the Black Color (As It Is Called) of the Negroes is Derived from the Leprosy."[22]

Many of the personal characteristics that whites cited to demonstrate black inferiority Rush categorized as symptoms of a disease. Not only a blackening of the skin but a fetid body odor accompanied leprosy, Rush noted. Thick lips and a flat nose indicated the spread of the disease, as did woolly hair, a sure sign that the infection had traveled to the scalp. Leprosy also accounted for many of the unsavory behavioral traits that had been noted in blacks: their lethargy, their insensitivity to pain, their notorious sexuality—all constituted traits common to other victims of the disease. "Lepers are remarkable for having strong venereal desires," Rush noted, and blacks, even after working all day in the hot sun, were willing to "walk five or six miles to comply with a venereal assignation."

Contemporary accounts of blacks who apparently transmogrified into whites fascinated Rush. At its 1784 meeting, the Philosophical Society presented as curiosities two individuals with mottled skin, and the Charles Peale Museum showed a third in Philadelphia in 1790. For Rush, the opportunity to examine a black man undergoing a color change came in 1795, when Henry Moss, who had straight white hair and extensive white blotches over much of his body, arrived in Philadelphia. One of Rush's students, Charles Caldwell, paid for Moss's upkeep and exhibited him for money at various museums, schools, and fairs throughout New England. Moss attracted wide attention—so much that Caldwell remarked that his name "was almost as familiar to readers of newspapers and other periodicals . . . as that of John Adams, Thomas Jefferson, or James Madison." Apparently, eighteenth-century medical practitioners did not understand vitiligo, and Moss appeared to Rush as a fascinating example of leprosy in spontaneous retreat. "The change from black to a natural white flesh color began about five years ago . . . and has extended gradually over the greatest part of his body," Rush noted in the *Transactions of the American Philosophical Society*. Moss's "wool also had changed into hair." Rush was confident that "the cure was nearly complete" and that Moss would soon regain all his normal, healthy whiteness.[23] He offered no documented evidence for this novel theory, but he clearly longed for a rapprochement between blacks and whites.

Though linking blacks with leprosy would seem to accentuate their status as outcasts, in fact Rush aimed at inspiring just the opposite reaction among his fellow whites. Claims of superiority "on account of color," he insisted, "were founded alike in ignorance and inhumanity. . . . If the color of the Negroes be the effect of disease," he wrote, "instead of inviting us to tyrannize over them, it should entitle them to a double portion of our humanity, for disease . . . has always been the signal for immediate and universal compassion."[24]

Instead of treating blacks as pariahs, Rush suggested, whites ought to combine science and humanity to discover a cure for leprosy, for several reasons. In the first place, it would destroy one of the chief arguments in support of slavery: that God made black skin as a mark of divine judgment. Also, it would add greatly to the Negroes' own happiness, because although "they appear to be satisfied with their color, there are many proofs of their preferring that of the white people." Finally, a cure that restored the Negroes' true skin tone would prove that blacks and whites had both descended from the same original parents, which would "not only add weight to the Christian revelation" but unite the races by removing "a material obstacle to the exercise of universal benevolence."[25]

Though their theories may now seem absurd, Smith and Rush both approached the controversial subject of black skin color with lofty humanitarian intentions. Realizing the formidable power that skin color had to separate the races, both hoped to prove that beneath their skin blacks and whites remained essentially the same—that blackness was not permanent but temporary, and that underneath the Negro's mantle of darkness one would find skin as white and pure as anyone's. But they were victims of the same corrosive prejudice that infected nearly all whites. The possibility that blacks *as they existed* could be the equal of whites simply never occurred to either man. For both, a black skin marked Negroes as degenerates, either from the tropical sun or from disease; if they ever hoped to be thought of as equals, blacks would have to be restored to the white standard of perfection. Nor did Rush or Smith provide an answer to the question of how the races should live together until they had eventually attained the same white skin tone. They could do no more than counsel a great deal of patience based on a common humanity. For Rush, in fact, the immediate problem of color presented a public health issue. As a physician, he had read reports of white women whose skin had begun to darken from living with black husbands; for the time being, he recommended that blacks, in effect, be quarantined.

Whites needed to keep up "that prejudice against such connections with them, as would tend to infect posterity with any portion of their disorder."[26] Ironically, Rush—whose abolitionist sympathies cannot be doubted—called for the isolation of blacks to protect the purity of the white race; in his mind, of course, the measure would be only temporary. Having seen with his own eyes Moss's miraculous cure, Rush felt confident that a remedy for leprosy would soon materialize, but for the moment he suggested that the races should scrupulously avoid intimate contact until blacks became white—an open-ended prescription that would please the most adamant racist.

Black skin color—or said another way, the visible sign that one was a Negro—represented the defining barrier between the races, one that could not be overcome no matter how a black American acted or thought. As one commentator put it in the 1820s, a "broad and impassable line of demarcation existed between every man who has one drop of African blood in his veins" and every other class of American inhabitants. In reality, of course, men and women of African ancestry frequently crossed over and assumed white identities, and the true racial test became a person's appearance—most obviously, color.

White Americans did not invent racism. The prejudice of light-skinned people against black Africans existed more than a thousand years before the first Europeans came to the New World, and white Americans surely drew on the longstanding European perception of blacks as little more than savages, somewhere between the great apes and the whites in their development. Whites had also absorbed the traditional connotations that allied whiteness and light with the desirable and blackness with the undesirable—the night, the cold, "the outer darkness." A thousand such analogies dwelled in the white imagination, inevitably linking the African's color with the negative connotations surrounding blackness. Historical antipathy and linguistic usage produced a brand of prejudice that racists everywhere shared, but something peculiar to the American attitude—namely, the image of superiority that white Americans had of themselves—made them unrelenting in their insistence on black inferiority. Black skin color repelled whites, but it was not the only cause of their prejudice. The assumption that color indicated inferiority was a judgment by whites that reflected their own deeply held beliefs about themselves. White Americans believed in black inferiority because they saw themselves as a superior variety of the human species.

How did whites become convinced of their own superiority? The answer requires a good deal of historical background, but it goes a long way toward explaining the peculiarly consistent hostility of white Americans toward the country's black inhabitants. Tocqueville observed that an overweening pride based on their English origin and their belief in democratic liberty had kept the European inhabitants of the United States from "mixing with the Negroes."[27] Surely the remarkable experience of many of the early settlers in New England, from the days of their religious persecution in Europe through the Revolution, contributed to the American people's special sense of themselves. Early in their collective history, whites developed a belief in their election as a chosen people, setting them apart from the rest of the world.

To understand the belief in the nation's special destiny, one must look back to the Protestant Reformation. In a little over a hundred years, in a series of disputes over doctrine and policy, the monolithic Catholic Church and its two great offshoots, the Lutheran, or Evangelical, movement and the Church of England, successively splintered into a variety of Christian faiths, and in the process a body of ideas came together that fed the belief of white Americans that God had elected them as a chosen people. If one theme can be said to dominate the division and redivision of Christianity, it is the repeated desire of sincere and earnest believers to forge a more direct, intimate relationship between themselves and God. Just as Martin Luther challenged the accretion of clerical dogma and authority that had taken place in Catholicism, each successive defection in the chain reaction of the Reformation arose from one group or another accusing an established church of interfering with the practice of true religion by interposing itself between themselves and the Almighty. Succeeding denominations each tried to create their own purer form of Christianity. Calvinists disagreed with Lutherans over the interpretation of the Lord's Supper, giving birth to the Reform Movement. Puritans believed that the Church of England had retained too many trappings of Catholicism and chose a more rigorous path. And in a move that perhaps can be called the logical culmination of the Reformation, the Quakers broke with the whole notion of a formally structured church and set out entirely on their own, maintaining that the individual's inward light was enough, and that there was no need for either theologically trained priests or church ritual to achieve communion with God.

Along with the hope for a purified, more vital Christianity, each of these dissenting groups also believed in its own specialness. This was not, as one might imagine, a form of sanctimonious vanity but something that flowed naturally from what they saw as their divinely directed mission. Though we may now think of the Lutherans, the Calvinists, the Puritans, and so on as having established a series of new churches, that was never their intention. Rather than creating new institutions, each group in its turn aimed at returning Christianity to its uncorrupted roots by restoring the original, primitive church of Christ and the apostles. The dissenters believed not that they were breaking away but that they were taking the path back to true religion. According to biblical prophecy, the children of Israel, God's chosen people, would carry out that mission; thus, as each dissenting group left the corrupted church, its members departed with the sense that God had selected them as special messengers to cleanse the tabernacle and restore the world to its original purity.

Among the numerous sects that made their way to North America, none felt more confident that it had been specially chosen, nor would prove more influential, than the Puritans who formed the Massachusetts Bay Colony. The Puritans believed, literally and absolutely, that they represented the fulfillment of divine prophecy—that as the modern-day embodiment of the children of Israel they had been sent into the wilderness to build not just a church but a commonwealth, intended to herald the return of Christ and the New Jerusalem. They divided history into two types: providential and redemptive. The first, essentially secular, concerned itself with ordinary people and everyday issues, like politics, economics, and culture, and held little interest for the Puritans; but the second, the study and explanation of events in relation to Christian salvation—and applied only to the spiritual elect—seemed to provide the key to understanding their own experience. In the Puritan mind, the development of the Bay Colony was the last act in the great unfolding drama of human redemption. The Puritan preacher John Higginson wrote in the preface to Cotton Mather's ecclesiastical history of New England that just as "the *Holy Scriptures* showed the wonderful works of God towards his church and his people," the Puritan experience in Massachusetts revealed "the wonderful works of God in . . . America."[28]

All temporal events, whether in the Old Testament or in the future,

Puritans interpreted in terms of Christ as the incarnation of the Almighty. The biblical past could be understood properly only as foreshadowings of Christ, and the future was revealed on the basis of the Incarnation itself or in Old Testament events as one interpreted them through Christ. "*Prophecie is Historie antedated* and *Historie is Postdated Prophecie,*" Nicholas Noyes explained in 1698; "the same thing is told in both." The Puritans' Great Migration reenacted an exodus that the Bible had prefigured repeatedly— the Israelites fleeing their oppressors in Babylon, Moses leading his people out of Egypt—and more recently the true church turning its back on Rome. Similarly, the very discovery of America had been accompanied by events rich in portent. Could it be mere coincidence that monumental accomplishments like the Reformation and the invention of the printing press, which put the Bible in the hands of everyone, had come at the very moment that God had provided a new continent that fulfilled his promise?[29] The vast continuum of time, from the creation to the Second Coming, when time would cease to exist—what Cotton Mather called the "long line of *Inter-Sabbatical Time*"—had but one meaning: Humankind would be redeemed through Jesus.

An abundance of prophetic signs pointed to the Puritans as a people destined to play an important role in redemptive history. As they set out for the New World, John Winthrop, the first governor of the Bay Colony, understood that "the other Churches of Europe had been brought to desolation," and that God had chosen New England as a haven for those he meant "*to save out of this generall callamitie.*" Over the next hundred years, as the Puritans tamed the Massachusetts landscape and made America their home, various religious leaders expanded that vision of their future. By the early years of the eighteenth century, in the words of Cotton Mather, all of America had become "*pulcherrima inter mulieres,*" Christ's most beautiful bride, in which a "*Holy City*" would arise with streets of "*Pure Gold.*" The Puritans and the continent had, in effect, merged, so that the land itself shared the Puritans' redemptive role. The holy city of the future one could find inscribed in Scripture, Mather maintained, where "AMERICA was Legible in these Promises." The Puritans' focus widened from their own backyard to a broader view of the entire continent, and at midcentury, as New England struggled through a dark season of dissension and spiritual turmoil, the evangelical divine Jonathan Edwards remained confident that in the ultimate, coming spring "the Sun of Righteousness" would "rise in the west, contrary to the course of . . . things" and reveal to "America a brighter type of heaven."[30]

In the spacious setting of a new continent, with a new world of opportunities unlike anything Europeans had ever known before, the single-minded preoccupation with their spiritual destiny grew into a broader conception of the part America and its people would play in the future. Like earlier Puritans, Jonathan Edwards surely continued to view the world as a Christian millennialist, but by the second half of the eighteenth century America's role as a redeemer nation had become more secular. In the approaching millennium, Edwards affirmed, America would not only serve as a spiritual model but would also provide the world with material wonders, such as "inventions to facilitate . . . secular business and better contrivances to expedite . . . communication between distant regions." In the meantime, American prosperity was a foreshadowing of the spiritual riches that awaited the new pilgrims. "The changing of the course of trade, and the supplying of the world with its treasures," Edwards insisted, "is a . . . forerunner of what is approaching in spiritual things, when the world shall be supplied with spiritual treasures from America."[31]

Just as secular concerns made their way into the Puritans' essentially religious vision, their belief in a special role for which they had been selected became part of America's national and political mythology. The idea blossomed to include Americans in general as God's chosen people. Instead of creating the New Jerusalem, Americans would spread the secular ideals of freedom and enlightenment throughout the world. God still sanctioned America's new role, but it would be played out in the political institutions of men. "The settlement of America [is] the opening of a grand scene and design in Providence for the illumination of the ignorant, and the emancipation of the slavish part of mankind," John Adams wrote in 1765.[32]

America could accomplish relatively easily the change from religious to worldly redeemer because a common history linked the two ideas: the Reformation also represented the beginning of a political revival, intended to wipe out hundreds of years of civil corruption that paralleled the religious corruption of the Catholic Church. Writing ten years before the Declaration of Independence, John Adams explored the links between political despotism and Catholicism in "A Dissertation on the Canon and Feudal Law." Throughout the Middle Ages, an evil conspiracy between the "Romish clergy and the temporal grandees" had kept the people in a state of "cruel, shameful, and deplorable servitude."[33] At the same time, and for reasons Adams admitted he did not fully understand, human beings continued to grow more intelligent, and "wherever a general knowledge and sensibility have prevailed among the people, arbitrary government and every kind of oppression have . . . disappeared in proportion." The Reformation, a direct result of humanity's growing awareness, brought an end not only to "ecclesiastical, but to civil tyranny," and with the colonization of America the torch of liberty passed to the New World. More than other men, the colonists, who had fought so hard to preserve their religious freedom and resist political oppression, had recognized that "popular powers must be placed as a guard . . . to the powers of the monarch and the priest" or government would soon become a "great and detestable system of fraud, violence, and usurpation."[34]

For Adams, the Reformation had ended oppression by both church and state and welcomed in a new age of human liberty, but he warned of a fundamental class conflict that keeps humankind in a state of perpetual struggle: the love of power accounted for "the soaring ambitions of princes" and likewise led "the common people to aspire at independency" as a way of confining "the power of the great within the limits of equity and reason."[35] Common people must limit their rulers, Adams maintained, because all human beings had inalienable rights, "*Rights* that cannot be repealed or restrained by human laws—*Rights*, derived from the great Legislator of the universe." We should remember that Adams wrote these passages a decade before the Revolutionary War, but he appears already prepared for the coming conflict, because in his mind ruler and subjects engage in a never-ending battle of opposing wills in which the one strives for domination while the others seek to limit that striving in order to protect their natural rights.

In this context, America's secular mission takes on added meaning. Throughout the world, ordinary people battled against oppression that by its very nature seemed endless; fortunately, however, the settlement of America had put in motion a providential design to protect individual freedoms. God, the "Legislator of the universe," had chosen the American colonists to lead the struggle to preserve the rights He had granted to everyone. Though still only a loose collection of thirteen colonies, America seemed—to Adams, at least—prepared to play a prominent part in the future of human civilization. For Adams, the colonists were blessed with a passion for liberty that was racial in origin and, thus, would be passed on to succeeding generations.

*   *   *

Rather than an embodiment of the children of Israel, however, Adams' freedom-loving Americans were one and the same as Franklin's "purely white People," direct descendants of the ancient Anglo-Saxons, celebrated by Adams for their spirit rather than their skin color. As we have already seen, in his "Observations Concerning the Increase of Mankind," Benjamin Franklin spelled out an American future in which the continent would become a shining example for the rest of the world. But to fulfill its destiny, its population had to be limited to "purely white People" and exclude "all Blacks and Tawneys." From a modern perspective, Franklin seems to have had a surprisingly narrow view of exactly who constitutes "purely white People." All Europeans, including the French, Swedish, and Germans, with the exception of the Saxons, appear swarthy to Franklin; only purebred descendants of the Anglo-Saxon tribes that originated in Europe meet his standard for true whiteness. Behind Franklin's apparently extreme vision of racial purity lies a complex set of questionable beliefs, the *Anglo-Saxon myth*, lost to most of us now, but which had a powerful grip on the imagination of many eighteenth-century Americans.[36]

Reverence for Anglo-Saxons had come into fashion among the English in the middle of the seventeenth century, in what has been called the Whig view of history. Like the interpretation of ecclesiastical history that derived from the Reformation, the Whig version of the English past told a story of initial purity perverted and then blessedly restored by the recovery of original values. In the Whig view, the inherently fair and democratic government of ancient England consisted of Anglo-Saxon tribes that had come to Britain more than a thousand years earlier. In 1066, the Norman Conquest destroyed or perverted the nation's original governmental institutions, and only after a series of dramatic victories, like the signing of the Magna Carta and the execution of Charles I, had English liberties been restored.

The Whigs found an idealized description of their Anglo-Saxon ancestors in the Roman historian Tacitus. In the *Germania*, Tacitus used the primitive Germanic tribes of the first century A.D. as foils to attack the corruption and immorality of his Roman contemporaries, and he portrayed the Anglo-Saxons as paragons of nobility, endowed with both a love of freedom and a remarkable purity. "In the peoples of Germany," Tacitus wrote, "there has been given to the world a race untainted by intermarriage . . . a peculiar people and pure, like no one but themselves."[37] This virtuous people, he observed, had a profound respect for individual rights and a cohesive sense of community which enabled its members to live together in nearly perfect harmony. As much imagining as fact, the Anglo-Saxons of Tacitus were ideals that he used to castigate his fellow Romans, and 1,500 years later the English fastened onto them in much the same way, making their own use of the Germanic tribes by celebrating their courage and purity in order to endow modern English political institutions with an ancient lineage.[38]

After 1750 the Anglo-Saxon myth took hold quickly in America because the colonists could adapt the Whig view of history so easily to their own troubles with the English Crown. Seeking to justify their resistance to British authority, Americans portrayed themselves as trying to recover their ancient rights, which the king, under the sway of institutions still corrupted by Norman influences, continually abused. Standing up to the king became part of the providential design for world freedom that John Adams had detected in the settlement of America, and as the conflict with the British intensified, comparisons to the Anglo-Saxons became a staple of colonial protest literature. A variety of writers, including Josiah Quincy Jr., Samuel Adams, James Otis, and Benjamin Franklin, invoked the memory of the Anglo-Saxon past to argue the growing list of American grievances. No one clung more strongly to the idea of Anglo-Saxonism than Thomas Jefferson, who in his *Summary View of the Rights of British America* (1774) addressed the Virginia delegation to the first Continental Congress, which had convened to formulate a uniform list of complaints to submit to George III.[39] Hoping to embolden the Virginia representatives, Jefferson enumerated a long series of "unjust encroachments and arbitrary acts" that violated American rights, and he insisted that the king had no power over them as free people of the colonies unless they voluntarily surrendered it to him. Jefferson's *Summary*, a justification of the colonists' rights, rested on ancient English principles that, he maintained, had originated with the Anglo-Saxons. According to Jefferson, when the Germanic tribes left Europe and settled in Britain, they established their own system of government "without any claim of superiority or dependence asserted over them by that mother country from which they had migrated." Surely the American colonists possessed the same right "which nature has given to all men," Jefferson argued, free to depart "from the country in which chance, not choice, has placed them, [to go] in quest of new habitations, and [to establish] new societies, under such laws . . . as shall seem most likely to promote public happiness."[40]

Jefferson also rejected the British claim that the colonists owed allegiance to the king if only because he had granted them their American landholdings. Before the Norman invasion, Jefferson wrote, "our Saxon ancestors held their lands, as they did their personal property, in absolute dominion, disencumbered with any superior." In 1066, William the Conqueror had changed all that, by parceling out the estates of his enemies who had fallen at the Battle of Hastings "subject to feudal duties," which he imposed on a newly created class of vassals. Thus began the history of feudalism in England, and throughout the Norman period England recognized two forms of real property: that which was held feudally by serfs and villeins and encumbered with obligations to the Crown, and that which "was left in the hands of [the king's] Saxon subjects," held outright and not tied to feudal conditions.[41] In the colonies, Jefferson insisted, this distinction made a crucial difference, because most Americans labored as farmers, not as lawyers, and they had been led to believe the mistaken Norman notion that all lands belonged to the king. Jefferson turned to "the Saxons' laws of possession, under which all lands were held in absolute right" for the true principle that should apply to their descendants in America. The king had "no right to grant lands of himself," Jefferson asserted, because "all the lands within the limits which any particular society has circumscribed around itself are assumed by that society, and subject to their allotment only."[42] For Jefferson, with his penetrating legal brilliance, the Anglo-Saxons represented a foundation of early English precedents on which to build the case for American independence.

Perhaps more than anyone in America, Jefferson had a passion for the Anglo-Saxons that continued throughout his life. In his reading of Whig history, although Anglo-Saxon England had an elected king, it had been a land of small, independent farmers who voluntarily formed their own political units and settled most issues locally. The system left the people essentially free to rule themselves, and though they had been defeated by the Normans "their will to recover the Saxon constitution continued unabated." To Jefferson, the Saxons represented a nearly exact model of the utopian future he dreamed of for America, and he constantly looked for opportunities to incorporate Anglo-Saxonism into American culture. As the founder of the University of Virginia, he insisted that the curriculum include the Anglo-Saxon language because "the histories and laws left us in that . . . dialect must be the text-books . . . of the learners, [and] they will imbibe with the language their free principles of government." Similarly, in 1784, when he proposed names for new states in the western territories, Jefferson suggested calling the northern region between Lake Huron and Lake Michigan Chersonesus, the name of the original Saxon homeland in northern Europe. Even at the end of his life and well over eighty years old, Jefferson still carried on about the wonders of the Anglo-Saxon language and culture, sheepishly admitting that the study of the language was "a hobby which too often runs away with me."[43]

For our purposes, the most intriguing instance of Jefferson's love affair with Anglo-Saxon mythology comes from a letter that John Adams wrote to his wife, Abigail, in August 1776, after the signing of the Declaration of Independence. At the time, both Adams and Jefferson sat on a committee to consider designs for the Great Seal of the United States, and—as Adams wrote to his wife—Jefferson proposed a seal divided down the middle, which on one side would show "Hengist and Horsa, the Saxon chiefs from whom we claim the honor of being descended and whose political principles and form of government we have assumed." The two Saxon heroes were a logical choice for Jefferson, but what makes the design fascinating is the image he proposed for the other half. Next to the Saxon leaders, Jefferson wanted a rendering of "the children of Israel in the wilderness, led by a cloud by day and pillar of fire by night."[44] Attuned to the temper of the times, Jefferson brought together the two historic symbols that had been conflated to confirm white America's belief in its own greatness and its special mission.

Just as it changed everything else in America, the Revolution would alter the image that Americans had of themselves as a chosen people. Most of all, it strengthened the nation's sense that God had truly selected America to lead the struggle for human liberty and provide an example for oppressed people everywhere. How else to explain the fantastic odds the colonists had overcome to defeat one of the great nations of the world with a ragtag army of poorly trained citizen-soldiers? Surely events had demonstrated that God chose America's side and had great things in store for the American people. The Revolution also altered the definition of who made up the "purely white People." The narrow conception that included only descendants of the Anglo-Saxons and left out not only darker races but most other Europeans as well simply would no longer work. Cynically, one might conclude that necessity forced white Americans to begin thinking more broadly once the country extended halfway across the continent and an ample supply of pure Anglo-Saxons could not be found—anywhere in the world—to fill the nation's population needs. But it was also true that the Revolutionary experience changed American attitudes, and if it did not succeed in convincing whites to embrace blacks, it did open the door to an enlarged understanding of whom the nation's leaders deemed white enough to be counted an American.

In 1818, John Adams looked back at the Revolution and tried to explain exactly what had happened during that glorious time. The *"real American Revolution"* one could not find in the war itself, according to Adams, but in what had taken place before the conflict began. "The revolution was in the hearts and minds of the people," he wrote, and represented a *"radical change in [their] principles, opinions, sentiments, and affections."* The miracle of the Revolution threw together people "of so many different nations, with different customs, manners, and habits," who had only an imperfect knowledge of one another, to form almost immediately a cohesive nation. "The complete accomplishment of it, in so short a time . . . ," Adams observed, "was perhaps a singular example in the history of mankind. Thirteen clocks were made to strike together—a perfection of mechanism, which no artist had ever before effected."[45] Whether he intended it or not, Adams accomplished more than merely recounting history; he also created mythology. At the heart of the Revolutionary story lay the belief in the emergence of a new, unified American people—not a race exactly but a single, tightly knit nation of individuals who had renounced their Old World ties, with their cultural heritage still admittedly European but determined to lead the world into a new age of divinely ordained political bliss. The Revolution made all white Americans into a bona fide chosen people.

In *Federalist II*, John Jay celebrated the nation's wondrous coming together. We can call Americans, he wrote, "one united people—a people descended from the same ancestors, speaking the same language, professing the same religion, attached to the same principles of government, [and] very similar in their manners and customs." All this commonality had been achieved, Jay continued, as Americans shared their "counsels, arms and efforts, fighting side by side, throughout a long and bloody war." Jay's description of his countrymen is remarkable in two ways. First, though Jay himself was descended from Dutch and French Huguenot stock without a drop of English blood, he willingly and completely subsumed that heritage in his post-Revolutionary identity as a new American man, "descended from the same ancestors" as every other American. Second, and perhaps even more important, just as Jay willingly ignored his historical ancestors, he also shed

America's spiritual forebears. With the Revolutionary experience behind them, Americans finally could stand on their own as a "band of brethren, united to each other by the strongest ties," still meaning to play a leading role in the grand design of providence but no longer needing to insist on themselves as either the modern embodiment of the children of Israel or the inheritors of ancient Anglo-Saxon traditions.[46]

By the 1780s, Americans stood defiantly convinced of their divine selection, their moral righteousness, and God's intention to provide them with special blessings. In the words of George Washington, the nation's people had been chosen "as the Actors on a most conspicuous theater, which seemed to be peculiarly designated by Providence for the display of human greatness and felicity." The nation's citizens had been placed "in the most enviable condition as the sole Lords and Proprietors of a vast tract of Continent, . . . abounding with all the necessaries and conveniences of life."[47] White Americans, those specially chosen people, had also been given a rich, unspoiled landscape in which to work out their national destiny. Like Washington, Jay felt certain that America's "connected, fertile, wide-spreading country" was a special blessing that Providence had granted to the "western sons of liberty." Its "variety of soils and productions and its innumerable streams" God meant "for the delight and accommodation of its inhabitants," Jay wrote. Its "navigable waters formed a kind of chain round its borders," and its noble rivers, "running at convenient distances, represented highways for the easy communication of friendly aids, and the mutual transportation and exchange of . . . various commodities."[48] God had made such felicitous arrangements for one reason only: to gratify America's chosen people.

Given this view of themselves, one can more easily understand why white Americans were unwilling to embrace blacks. More than just specially chosen by God, Americans had been given a new, untouched continent—a second Paradise—in which to carry out the grand and mysterious scheme of Providence. Though only later would America be called the land of opportunity, surely the possibilities that seemed to exist for the nation's founders were not just the chance of a lifetime but an opportunity for all time. Had ever a nation of men been so blessed by the Almighty? Not only had the Lord signaled his intention to provide for them bountifully, but the onrushing tide of history already had put them on the way to creating human institutions in which American citizens would recapture the natural rights God intended for them.

Where did blacks fit into this picture? America's leaders, despite their optimism about the country's future, recognized that they faced horrific problems. "The cup of blessing has been reached out to us," Washington observed, but the American people had to "seize the occasion and make it our own or become contemptible and miserable as a Nation."[49] Washington referred specifically to the crisis created by the Articles of Confederation, but he might as easily have been writing about blacks. The nation's cup overflowed with prospects, but its spiritual strength—the homogeneity in *principles, opinions, sentiments, and affections*" that had made the thirteen colonies miraculously act as one—was endangered by an alien, unsavory fraction of the population that not only divided Americans on the basis of black against white but also threatened to turn white against white over the question of what could be done. And to make matters worse, whites had only themselves to blame for introducing blacks into America in the first place. The Anglo-Saxon myth and the quest for national identity left no place for an American Negro. In 1790, the first federal naturalization act restricted citizenship to "free white persons" only. The Negro was not an American.

CHAPTER 3

THE DARK SIDE OF THE CONSTITUTION

When you assemble a number of men to have the advantage of their joint wisdom, you inevitably assemble . . . all their prejudices, their passions, their errors of opinion, their local interests, and their selfish views.
—BENJAMIN FRANKLIN, 1787

A covenant with Death and an Agreement with Hell.
—WILLIAM LLOYD GARRISON, 1845

The fifty-five delegates who convened in May 1787 at the State House in Philadelphia would have no need of a naturalization act to recognize their countrymen. Having assembled to revise and strengthen the federal government, they would be representing only the nation's white population. While the South's slaves clearly would be on the delegates' minds throughout the convention, the document they finally approved gave blacks absolutely nothing—certainly none of the universal natural rights the Declaration of Independence asserted everyone had at birth, and not even the narrow protections slaves were given by the French in Louisiana under the Code Noir.

Exactly what transpired in the Constitutional Convention's deliberations remained secret for over fifty years, not because the delegates felt a need to hide the way in which they dealt with the nation's blacks—few white Americans would have objected—but because they wanted to minimize any appearance of conflict, which they feared would jeopardize ratification. In

1840, however, the precise details of what had gone on behind closed doors in Philadelphia became public, ending the voluntary silence the members had voted unanimously to impose in 1787. At the Convention, the delegates had appointed an official secretary who took careful notes, but James Madison also kept his own even more detailed record. Friends repeatedly urged him to publish his account, but he insisted that it remain private until all the framers had died. In 1836, Madison, the last surviving member of the Convention, passed away, and his *Notes of Debates in the Federal Convention of 1787* was released four years later.[1] Its publication shocked many of his countrymen, not because Madison's account showed that slavery had been an issue at the Convention, but because it revealed that slavery had been the delegates' overriding preoccupation. Slavery prompted almost every serious disagreement—disagreements that the delegates managed to resolve only because northerners and southerners alike were willing to trample on the human rights of the nation's black population.

Once the Convention's deliberations became public, the abolitionists angrily condemned the proceedings. In 1845, William Lloyd Garrison described the Constitution as "a covenant with Death and an Agreement with Hell." "Inhuman, unjust, and affronting to God and man," Frederick Douglass echoed. One may choose to dismiss Garrison and his followers as extremists—after all, they argued not just for emancipation but for immediate abolition and rejected anything less than an all-out attack on slaveholders. But even a moderate like the Reverend Samuel J. May, who continued to defend the Constitution, declared that the publication of Madison's *Notes* had disconcerted him: "I could not so easily maintain my ground in the discussions which afterwards agitated so seriously the Abolitionists themselves—some maintaining that the Constitution was, and was intended to be, pro-slavery." Another of Garrison's colleagues, Wendell Phillips, scrutinized the *Notes* and concluded that a "compromise . . . was made between slavery and freedom . . . granting to the slaveholder distinct privileges and protection for his slave property, in return for certain commercial concessions upon his part toward the North." Phillips believed that the North and South had entered into a malicious bargain, "willingly and with open eyes," and thus the "free and slave States were partners in the guilt, and responsible for the sin of slavery."[2]

Though Madison's *Notes* reveals that members of the Convention spoke freely about "slaves," "blacks," and "Negroes," the final form of the

Constitution avoided these words, cryptically referring to African Americans as "Persons," or "Persons held to Service or Labour." As Abraham Lincoln later observed, the delegates hid away slavery in the Constitution "just as an afflicted man hides away a wen or cancer which he dares not cut out." Reticence over slavery had appeared initially in Congress under the Articles of Confederation, the nation's first attempt at a constitution, because—as William Paterson of New Jersey, who later became a Supreme Court justice, noted—the members "had been ashamed to use the term 'Slaves.'" Many delegates to the Philadelphia Convention had similar qualms. When one of them included the phrase "importation of slaves" in a proposal on the African trade, Roger Sherman of Connecticut asked that it be changed, indicating that he preferred "a description better than the terms proposed, which had been declined by the old Congs. & were not pleasing to some people."[3] Nearly forty years later, Luther Martin of Maryland remained mortified by the Convention's hypocrisy. Though the delegates had "anxiously sought to avoid the admission of expressions which might be odious to the ears of Americans," he wrote, ". . . they were willing to admit into their system those things which the expressions signified."[4]

How did southern proslavery leaders exert such inordinate influence? As individuals, many delegates expressed antislavery sentiments. Luther Martin surely spoke for many of his colleagues when he said that he viewed slavery as "inconsistent with the principles of the revolution and dishonorable to the American character."[5] Did northerners make a bargain, as Wendell Phillips maintained, merely to gain commercial concessions? True, the South granted certain advantages to the North, but larger historical events made the need for agreement imperative. By the mid-1780s it was clear that the Articles of Confederation had produced a weak, inefficient government, and many American leaders believed the Union was ready to collapse. Though slavery would become a defining issue at the Convention, the delegates did not arrive in Philadelphia with that expectation. Nearly all the northern states had outlawed slavery by 1787 and thought of it as primarily a southern problem, at least for the foreseeable future. To understand why the representatives of the separate states had come to Philadelphia, we must go back to the Revolution and recall the colonies' initial, hesitant efforts to form a national government and the period of ineptitude that followed when the war ended.

*   *   *

In 1774, the colonists banded together to protest their treatment by George III, and an assembly of representatives from the separate colonies, the First Continental Congress, prepared a series of grievances for presentation to the Crown.[6] In subsequent meetings, the Congress created the Continental Army, appointed George Washington its commander, and adopted the Declaration of Independence. A year later, it approved the Articles of Confederation, seeking to give the makeshift government that had evolved in the previous meetings a formal structure. Defining the relationship between the separate states as a permanent "league of friendship," the Articles envisioned a loosely constructed confederation of independent states that retained their individual sovereignty except in certain areas expressly delegated to the central government.

To go into effect, the Articles required acceptance by all thirteen states, and discussions dragged on until 1781, when Maryland, the last holdout, finally agreed to ratification. Though the Articles gave the federal government a fairly wide range of powers—over defense, foreign affairs, treaties, Indian matters, land disputes among the states, the postal service, a national currency, and military forces—they made it nearly impossible for the new government to meet its responsibilities. The states retained the power to levy taxes, muster troops, and regulate commerce, and even when they agreed with the national authorities, the federal government had no power—that is, no money or men at its command—to act. Instead, it had to petition the states for troops or dollars, or both. More often than not, the states refused to answer these requests, or responded to them tardily—particularly when they saw little or no direct benefit for themselves. Even more disabling was the fact that amending the Articles required approval from all thirteen states; thus each individual state held an effective veto over any effort to increase the strength of the national government.

Geography also worked against establishing national loyalties. New England and Georgia lay a thousand miles apart. Overland routes could barely qualify as roads or did not exist at all; people could more easily cover distances by sea than by land. During the Revolutionary War, northerners and southerners alike had been much more inclined to aid their neighbors than distant states, which seemed as far off as the West Indies or Europe, and the coming of peace did not help matters. Independence created increasingly complex national problems, but it also compounded local concerns, and the states felt, if anything, less willing to supply the federal treasury than they had during the war. Of the six federal budget requisitions between 1781 and 1786, the states complied with only four.

The Treaty of Paris in 1783, which ended the war with the British, more than doubled the size of the United States. Its 890,000 square miles extended from the Great Lakes to Spanish Florida, from the Atlantic to the Mississippi. Throughout Europe, politicians questioned whether a loosely linked confederation of disparate states—the largest territorial entity since the Roman Empire—could possibly survive. The Comte de Virgennes, France's foreign minister, certainly doubted it, observing in 1784 that "the American Federation has a great tendency toward dissolution." Others were even less kind. "Little by little, colony by colony," Frederick the Great, the king of Prussia, scoffed, "Americans will rejoin England and their former footing."

To become internationally respectable, America needed to adopt a resolute and responsible policy in its dealings with other nations, but the government's structural weakness made it hesitant and unreliable. Without troops, it could not respond to provocations by the British along the Canadian border or by the Spanish, who controlled the mouth of the Mississippi. Without money, the government behaved more like a common bankrupt than a great nation. Not only unable to meet its obligations to European creditors, from whom it had borrowed over $10 million during the war, by 1786 America could no longer pay its current accounts. With the national treasury nearly empty, the federal government paid its employees and troops sporadically or not at all. Even when American lives were at stake, the government had no money to save them. In 1783 and again in 1785, when Barbary pirates kidnapped American sailors for ransom, Congress lacked the funds to meet their demands. The pirates never released their hostages, and the government had no alternative but to warn American ships to avoid the Mediterranean.[7]

The federal authority also lacked the power to tame the nation's commercial chaos. After the war, the British had shut American traders out of the West Indies, their most lucrative market. American merchants wanted desperately to reestablish the Caribbean trade and expand to European ports that previously had been closed to them as British subjects, but the unwillingness of the states to cooperate with one another made it impossible to formulate a coherent national trade policy. The English economist Lord Sheffield, whose hawkish tract, *Observations on the Commerce of the*

American States, argued against the easing of Britain's trade restrictions, recognized the problem from across the Atlantic: "No treaty can be made with the American states that can be binding on all of them. . . . When treaties are necessary, they must be made with the states separately."[8]

In 1782, only a year after the Articles had been ratified, Alexander Hamilton warned that America's prospects would remain "diminutive and contemptible" as long as the nation remained "a number of petty states, with the appearance only of union, jarring, jealous, and perverse, without any determined direction, fluctuating and unhappy at home, weak and insignificant by their dissension in the eyes of other nations."[9] By 1786, the accelerating collapse of the American government had shown that Hamilton was correct, and a growing number of the nation's political leaders echoed his sentiments, including George Washington, who warned in a letter to Madison that only extraordinary measures could "avert the humiliating and contemptible figure we are about to make in the annals of mankind."[10]

The gathering that became the Constitutional Convention evolved from a series of meetings that began at Mount Vernon in 1785. Representatives from Virginia and Maryland came together to discuss questions that had arisen between the two states: fishing rights, tolls, plans for a canal to link the Potomac to the system of rivers west of the Allegheny Mountains. The participants, who made headway on many of their problems, judged the meeting a success; consequently, when the Virginia representatives made their report to a state commission chaired by Madison they suggested an annual conference to which all the states would be invited. Madison presented the idea to Washington, and their discussions led to a proposal by the Virginia Assembly calling on the thirteen states to assemble to make recommendations on the nation's patchwork commercial policy.

Madison led the Virginia delegation to that gathering, which took place in Annapolis on September 11, 1786.[11] He hoped the meeting would set in motion a larger process of constitutional reform, but he doubted whether that could happen. "Though my wishes are in favor of such an event," he wrote in his diary, "yet I despair so much of its accomplishment at the present crisis that I do not extend my views beyond a commercial reform." He read the situation correctly. As might be expected, several states wanted no part of a conference they suspected had been called to undercut their individual powers. Though nine states agreed to send representatives, only twelve delegates—from New York, New Jersey, Delaware, Pennsylvania, and

Virginia—appeared for the convention's opening. The poor turnout made it impossible to conduct business, but it also meant that nearly everyone who attended felt reform-minded and inclined toward the federalist view. Seizing the opportunity, the delegates, led by Madison and Hamilton, expanded their subject from trade to the larger question of constitutional reform and issued a call for another convention the following year to discuss not only commercial matters but "further provisions as shall appear . . . necessary to render the constitution of the Federal Government adequate to the exigencies of the Union."

This second meeting, which later became known as the Constitutional Convention, opened in Philadelphia on May 14, 1787. Tensions ran high. By calling for constitutional reform, the Annapolis gathering had caught nearly everyone's attention and forced them to the table. Rhode Island and New Hampshire resisted the call, but the other states that had declined the earlier invitation to discuss trade issues felt they could not ignore a conference intended either to reform the old federal government or to frame an entirely new one. In general, the states feared, as Caleb Strong of Massachusetts pointed out, that without sufficient compromise the Union would soon dissolve. But there was also widespread fear of surrendering the protection in the Articles of Confederation of each state's right to chart its own course, and many of the delegates arrived in Philadelphia anxious and uncertain. Throughout the colonial period and under the Articles, Americans had grown to think of themselves as citizens of their separate states; in fact, long after the states had ratified the Constitution, Thomas Jefferson would insist on referring to Virginia as his "country." Now it appeared that they might be asked to shift their primary loyalty to a national government, a difficult adjustment for many in both the North and the South.

Four days into the Convention, Edmund Randolph introduced a series of resolutions formulated by Madison which came to be known as the Virginia Plan.[12] These proposals represented a radical new outline for a stronger national government, made up of an executive, a judicial, and a bicameral legislative branch in which population would form the basis for representation in both houses. By accepting the Virginia Plan for discussion, the delegates took the first tentative step in constructing an entirely new government. The assembly then resolved itself into a committee of the whole to consider each of the plan's proposals.

The first serious disagreement arose over congressional representation.

In 1781, the Articles had established a single legislative body in which each state had one vote. Despite their considerable difference in size and population, all states had the same power in the national congress. The Virginia Plan aimed to correct that inequity by establishing proportional representation in both legislative houses. As a representative of Massachusetts when the Articles were originally formulated, Elbridge Gerry had approved the equal vote. Now he insisted that it had always been recognized as an "injustice" and maintained that with the Revolutionary War in progress, the equal-vote provision had passed "under the pressure of public danger, and the obstinacy of the lesser states."[13] Naturally, smaller states like Delaware, Connecticut, and New Jersey resisted the Virginia Plan, fearing, as Delaware's John Dickinson wrote in his private notes, that they would be "delivered into the absolute power of the larger [states] who may injure them in a Variety of Ways."[14] The delegates from the smaller states pressed for one-vote-per-state representation in at least one of the two houses of the new Congress, but when their motions failed they responded by offering their own plan, which repeated the formula of the Articles, calling for the states to share equal power in a single legislative body. This New Jersey Plan, as the delegates named it, proved more of a tactical maneuver than a serious proposal. As Dickinson explained privately to Madison, the smaller states did not necessarily oppose "two branches in the General Legislature, [but they] would sooner submit to a foreign power, than . . . be deprived of an equality of suffrage, in both branches."[15]

Just as it had earlier in formulating the Articles of Confederation, the obstinacy of the smaller states prevailed. Digging in their heels and insisting that they would accept nothing less, the smaller states got the larger ones to agree to precisely what they had been after from the start—equality in one of the two houses of the new Congress. Connecticut's aristocratic William Samuel Johnson, who had been appointed president of Columbia College on his way to the Convention, supplied the common sense needed to head off a potentially endless controversy. The larger states wanted to consider states strictly as "districts of people composing one political Society," he noted, but the truth was that the states also existed as political societies, and a government needed "to be formed for them in their political capacity, as well as for the individuals composing them." Instead of these two ideas being opposed to each other, Johnson argued, they should be combined— "in one branch the *people* ought to be represented; in the *other* the States."[16]

The Great Compromise, as historians have called it, resolved the conflict between the large and small states, but Madison, whose mind invariably raced ahead of the daily proceedings, stood firm as one of several delegates who continued to object to any concessions to the smaller states. Unlike his colleagues, who thought primarily of the interests of their own constituents, Madison held a broader, national view. In his mind the Convention continued to overlook a far more serious problem, one explosive enough to shatter the whole idea of union. The states stood divided not by size but by geography. "The great danger to our general government," Madison insisted, lay in the differences between the North and the South. One of the main functions of a national authority was to provide protection, and like "every peculiar interest of any class of citizens," the interests of the small states ought to be guarded as far as possible. But Madison opposed casting the Congress in a bicameral form that did not reflect the authentic fundamental division within the nation. If the government offered any special protection in the formula for representation, it ought to be accorded equally to North and South vis-à-vis one another. Madison made a stunning suggestion: "[I]nstead of proportioning the votes of the States in both branches, . . . they should be represented in one branch according to the number of free inhabitants only; and in the other according to the whole number counting the slaves as if free."[17]

Madison's proposal surely must have surprised many of his colleagues, but no one responded to it. Even though they passed it by without comment, it represented the single most significant development of the Convention. Madison had brought the unspoken issue of slavery out into the open by identifying it as the nation's deepest and most troublesome division. More than that, he had raised the question of how the delegates should consider slaves in relation to the free population, a highly charged issue that would become the Convention's next great point of disagreement.

The question had first arisen in 1777, during the drafting of the Articles.[18] The decision to reject proportional representation for the Continental Congress in favor of a single vote for each state eliminated the problem of how to count slaves in relation to representation, but it left unresolved the knotty economic question of how they would be dealt with in apportioning taxes. The original draft of the Articles provided that the colonies would pay into the national treasury in proportion to the number of their inhabitants, except that Indians would not pay taxes. Southerners rejected the proposal, complaining that it unfairly saddled slaveholders with punitive tax levels by including slaves in the population count. They suggested instead that taxes be apportioned according to the number of white inhabitants only. A critical point in the southern argument turned on the status of slaves. Would they be treated as human beings or property? If the states had to debate whether or not slaves were property, Thomas Lynch of South Carolina asserted, the confederation could not survive. Why should one's property be counted as citizens, he asked, any more than the sheep, cattle, and horses of the North?[19]

This was a disagreement about money—specifically, how much each region would be required to pay to support the national government. Unlike our current system, in which the Internal Revenue Service collects an unspecified amount of total revenue accruing from individual tax payments, taxation under the Articles began with an annual request, or requisition, by the federal government for a specific amount of money, with states expected to pay their proportional share. This meant that the amount northern states would remit in relation to the southern states would depend, finally, on how slaves figured in the population count.

With both northerners and southerners looking for a way to end the standoff, a new strategy entered the slavery debate: to count slaves as fractional percentages of whites. Searching for an answer that would satisfy the North's belief that slaves should be included in the population tally and the South's contention that they should be treated the way the North treated its livestock, Benjamin Harrison of Virginia suggested that the delegates accept a numerical compromise, valuing two slaves as one white—though he did not feel confident, he confessed, that a slave could perform half the work of a white man.[20] Harrison's suggestion failed to break the deadlock, and the delegates finally dropped population entirely as the basis for taxation and agreed instead that the expense of government would be apportioned according to the value of all the land within each state. As many expected, a tax system based on real property proved unworkable because no one could ever agree on the relative value of land in places as different as South Carolina and Massachusetts. By 1783 the system had failed, and the question of taxation remained a continual source of contention among the states. The nation sorely needed a more efficient way of assessing taxes. The Continental Congress formed a committee, appointing Nathaniel Gorham of Massachusetts as chairman, to address the problem of how to fund the federal government, and included among its suggested reforms a proposal to reconsider making population rather than land values the basis for taxation.[21]

Once again the divisive question arose: how to count slaves in calculating the southern states' tax obligations. Northerners had rejected Harrison's earlier suggestion that two slaves count as one white because they felt that reducing the number of slaves in the population count by half handed the South too great a concession. The Gorham committee first considered setting the ratio at three slaves to two whites, but southern members balked at the prospect of paying direct taxes for two-thirds of their slaves as if they were white. Splitting the difference between one-half and two-thirds, the committee finally compromised on the so-called *federal ratio* of five slaves to three whites—which set the value of a slave, in relation to taxation, at three-fifths of a white person.

The ratio passed out of the Gorham committee as part of a measure that would replace real property with population as the basis for apportioning taxation, and the measure went to the states for ratification. In keeping with the government's practice of avoiding any reference to slaves, the explanation accompanying the proposal indicated that the ratio had been arrived at through mutual concessions in order to find a fair and acceptable way to balance the difference in value "between the labour and industry of free inhabitants and of all other inhabitants."[22] As an amendment to the Articles, the measure required unanimous approval by the states, which it never received.

In 1787, as the Constitutional Convention opened, the proposal remained in limbo, still unapproved by two northern and two southern states: New Hampshire, Rhode Island, South Carolina, and Georgia. By the time the delegates in Philadelphia addressed the question of counting slaves, the issue had taken on both greater complexity and new significance. All the earlier discussions of population-based apportionment had occurred in relation to taxation. At bottom, the argument about counting slaves had always been about a rather limited amount of money: the difference between what the North and South would have to pay as their shares of the national government's costs. Based on $3 million, the amount sought by the national government in the requisition of 1785, the difference for states like Massachusetts and South Carolina amounted to only about $30,000 each—or nine cents for every individual in the population count—depending on whether states included slaves on a one-to-one basis with whites or counted them in accordance with the three-fifths ratio.

At the Convention, the stakes rose dramatically. Now when the delegates took up the question of how to count slaves, they did it with the understanding that they had already agreed on a population-based apportionment in one house of Congress; thus the relative strength of the two regions in the legislative branch would depend on the value given to slaves. For the delegates, comparatively minor questions of taxation and money had been superseded by weightier issues of representation and political power. The formula for counting slaves had taken on a new and crucial significance. The North and South both generally favored proportional representation in at least one house of Congress. Philosophically, it accorded with the egalitarian belief that equal numbers of people ought to have an equal number of representatives. Practically, it appeared to offer both regions immediate political benefits—the North because no one doubted that it would have control of the apportioned legislative house in the new government, and the South because it stood to gain a larger share of votes than the 38 percent it had in the old equal-vote Congress. Still, the delegates needed to work out the precise ratio of voting power between the two regions. If they included whites alone in the population count, the South would have only 41 percent of the votes in the lower house of Congress. If they counted slaves on a one-to-one basis with whites, it would give the South 49.9 percent—virtual equality with the North. And in a compromise based on the three-fifths federal ratio, the South would have 46.5 percent of the voting power.[23]

In the past, when the issue had been taxation, the South had hoped to minimize its obligation by excluding slaves from the population count. The North, seeking to reduce its own tax burden, had argued to include them. Now, with the South attempting to maximize its representation in Congress, the two regions reversed themselves, each taking up the position it had argued against in the earlier debates. When they were trying to minimize their tax obligations, southerners had contended that slaves were mere property and should not be counted as human beings. Now, when the South wanted to increase its population count, northerners turned that argument against them. Why should blacks "be in the rule of representation more than the Cattle and horses of the North?" Elbridge Gerry asked, with more than a hint of irony. William Paterson of New Jersey, pointing out that "Negro slaves are no free agents, have no personal liberty . . . but on the contrary are . . . entirely at the will of the Master," asked, "If Negroes are not represented in the States to which they belong, why should they be represented in the Genl. Govt?"[24]

The southerners made no effort to argue that slaves had somehow been transformed and now should be regarded as human beings. The Southern position was never that slaves should be included in the population tally on the basis of a human equivalency with whites. Such an idea would have led to the preposterous conclusion that there should be members in the new Congress sitting there to actually *represent* slaves—a situation that no one, from either North or South, would have tolerated. Instead, the South wanted credit for the wealth that slaves represented by including them in the population count, so that slaveholders would receive a greater share of representation for themselves. Government "was instituted principally for the protection of property," Pierce Butler of South Carolina asserted. "The states ought to have weight in the government in proportion to their wealth."[25] Many northerners felt great sympathy with the claim that slaves, who undeniably constituted a measure of southern wealth, should be included in the formula for determining representation. "Property," rather than "Life & Liberty," was "the main object of Society," Gouverneur Morris of Pennsylvania affirmed, and it "ought to be one measure of the influence due to those . . . affected by the Government."[26] The next logical step, of course, was to ask why northern manifestations of wealth, such as ships and factories, should not be considered in determining representation, but no one seriously raised the question.

From early in the Convention, one reality stood out clearly. The majority of the members understood that no matter where the debate went, eventually it had to lead to a compromise. The major disagreement in the deliberations—the special consideration the South demanded for slavery—could blow apart the marriage between the North and South. Southerners would support the creation of a powerful federal government only as long as they received assurance that it would not threaten the existence of the South's servile labor force.

Compromise offered the only way to simultaneously save the Union and create a strong national government. Members on both sides at times took extreme regional positions. Pierce Butler and Charles Cotesworth Pinckney argued that blacks, the peasants of the South, should be counted as whole beings—one for one with whites.[27] On the other side, Gouverneur Morris at one point rejected even the three-fifths rule, insisting that Pennsylvania would never agree to any sort of representation for Negroes. Such moments of posturing increased as the Convention moved inexorably closer to accepting the three-fifths ratio. No amount of talk would enable the two regions to see eye-to-eye on slavery, but both recognized the necessity of reaching a political agreement. James Wilson of Pennsylvania, who had won wide notice as a pamphleteer during the Revolution, puzzled over the dilemma of his northern colleagues. He could see no wisdom in the three-fifths principle: "Are they admitted as Citizens? then why are they not admitted on an equality with White Citizens? Are they admitted as property, then why is not other property admitted into the computation?" Wilson heard nothing from the Convention floor to put his doubts at rest, but those difficulties, he finally conceded, must be solved by compromise.[28]

In "Federalist 54," Madison added a fascinating footnote to the debate over the three-fifths rule. The Convention delegates had by now approved the federal ratio as part of the new Constitution, and Madison was writing to America at large to encourage ratification by the states. In Philadelphia, the North and South had managed to reach a wholly political agreement that left their fundamental differences intact, but Madison wanted to avoid any suggestion that the delegates had adjourned in anything less than perfect harmony; consequently, he portrayed the compromise on representation not as a political solution but as the result of a rigorously reasoned determination of the status of slaves. As Madison described events in Philadelphia, the North had acted somewhat unreasonably. Northerners had insisted that slaves had always been regarded only as property and thus should be included in estimates of taxation but not in representation, which should be regulated by census. Could it be reasonably expected that the southern states would agree with such an analysis? Madison asked. The answer, of course, was no, since it did not reflect reality in the South. "The true state of the case is, that [slaves] partake of both these qualities," Madison pointed out, "being considered by our laws, in some respects, as persons, and in other respects, as property."

Slaves could be "compelled to labor," they were "vendable from one master to another," and could be "restrained" from liberty and "chastised in . . . body"; and thus, they were "degraded from the human rank, and classed with those irrational animals, which fall under the legal denomination of property." On the other hand, Madison noted, the slave also was "protected in his life & his limbs" and was "punishable himself for all violence committed against others," which showed "no less evidently" that the law regarded him "as a member of the society; not as a part of the irrational creation; as a moral

person, not as a mere article of property." Madison laid bare the dark reality
of slaveholding: it destroyed the slaves' humanity, reducing them to creatures
that appeared half irrational animal and half moral person. Later in life he
would draw a very different conclusion from the same text, but for now he
pronounced himself quite satisfied with his odd, lawyerish argument. "It
may appear to be a little strained in some points," he admitted, but "I must
confess, that it fully reconciles me to the scale of representation, which the
Convention [has] established."[29]

Agreement on the three-fifths ratio solved the immediate problem of
how the North and South would share power in the new Congress, but it
fell short of settling the representation issue for either section. Both the
North and South recognized the inevitability of demographic changes; consequently, each wanted additional constitutional guarantees that it hoped
would protect or increase its share of representation in the future. Along
with the rest of the country, the delegates realized that the nation was undergoing a population shift south and southwest that could alter the balance of
power between the North and South. "People are constantly swarming from
the more to the less populous places," Madison observed, "from Europe to
America, from the Northern & Middle parts of the U.S. to the Southern &
Western. They go where land is cheaper, because their labour is dearer."[30]

Contemplating the future, northerners feared that the South would soon
surpass them in population and gain control of Congress. "It has been said
that North Carolina, South Carolina, and Georgia . . . will in a little time
have a majority of the people in America," Gouverneur Morris warned. The
result, he argued, was sure to be "an oppression . . . of [northern] commerce."[31]
According to the three-fifths ratio, a difference of only about 250,000 people separated the two regions; thus, a shift in power in the not so distant
future seemed to northerners a real and frightening possibility. They worried
that by agreeing to the three-fifths rule they had put in place a mechanism
that the South could exploit to hasten its domination of the North. With
slaves being counted along with whites, the South could increase its population simply by importing a greater number of slaves; adoption of the three-
fifths rule had thus unwittingly given encouragement to the slave trade. A
few years later, John Quincy Adams, determined to amend the rules of representation, would complain that the Constitution offered an "alluring bounty
to the slave-holding states." The Constitution promised that for every five
thousand new Africans, the South would add three thousand individuals to

increase its proportional representation in Congress and in the electoral college. The previous presidential election had been a heartbreaking experience for Adams. Jefferson had defeated the reelection bid of his father only because of the fifteen electoral votes added by black slaves to the southern total, and many embittered northerners who had opposed Jefferson's election (including John Quincy Adams) had excoriated him as the "Negro president" who rode into "the Temple of Liberty upon the shoulders of slaves."[32]

At the Constitutional Convention, Gouverneur Morris tried to protect the North by insisting that the delegates write a balancing disincentive into the Constitution to discourage the South from padding its population count by importing extra slaves. He proposed that the national government be given power to impose a direct tax, or capitation, levied in proportion to representation. Separate from other, indirect taxes on exports and imports, this simple head tax would empower the federal government to assess the states based on their population counts. Morris understood that most Americans had little actual currency and could not pay direct taxes, but he never meant the head tax as a regular annual assessment. Instead, Congress would levy it only "in case of absolute necessity"—if, for example, the South began adding slaves simply to increase its population count. Morris intended the tax to deter slaveholders by forcing them to weigh their desire for more representation against their wish to avoid increased taxation.

Morris's proposal met with almost no opposition. Southern delegates knew they had to cooperate. Like their northern counterparts, they also wanted additional constitutional protection, and they planned to give the North what it wanted in order to win passage of their own measure. With America's population moving in its direction, the South had every reason to be optimistic about the future, but it remained suspicious of northern intentions. The South feared that even if it managed to gain a majority of the nation's population, the North would still retain control of the government and could deny the South its right to majority power. The South wanted a constitutional guarantee that the number of representatives allotted to each state would be adjusted periodically, based on a national census conducted at regular intervals. Northerners, of course, preferred to leave all questions regarding a census to the discretion of the new Congress. The representatives would be bound by "their duty, their honor & their oaths" to represent the entire country fairly, Morris argued, which prompted Madison to reply that he was "not a little surprised to hear this implicit confidence urged by a member who on all occasions, [has] inculcated so strongly, the political depravity of man."[33] Madison's levity lasted for only a moment, however. Southerners refused to budge and continued to insist that the revision of the census could not be left to the good judgment and honesty of the legislature. Once again, the delegates had reached a point where they would have to resolve their regional differences by mutual concession. To calm its fears that southern slaveholders might be tempted to expand the population count by importing slaves, the North engineered a constitutionally protected head tax which, though it was never collected, at least theoretically meant that any suspicious increase in the number of slaves could invite punitive taxation. In return, southern fears that the North might misuse its legislative dominance to hold on to power found relief in a guarantee that the government would count the population every ten years, and that it would adjust the apportionment of Congress to conform to the new numbers. Together, the measures eased the anxieties of both regions that political chicanery might pervert the balance of power. The Convention bundled the two measures and the three-fifths rule into a single proposal, which gained approval six states to two, with the members from Massachusetts and Georgia divided among themselves and unable to cast votes.[34]

The delegates in Philadelphia worked hard to provide for both the present and the future in dealing with representation, but an additional, related issue needed to be considered outside the Convention. Once again the delegates found themselves forced to address the future of slavery. The old Congress, still sitting in New York, had jurisdiction over most of the nation's western territories, and it needed to clarify their future. Both the North and the South understood that while the western lands would gradually be broken up into states, how that would affect the balance of power between the regions remained in doubt. Delegates had to determine how many states the West would produce and, more important, whether they would be slave or free.

From the very first days of the Revolution, the United States had laid claim to the vast expanse of land stretching from the western extremities of the thirteen states to the Mississippi, but within that wilderness no one agreed on who owned what. Based on prewar charters or military action, seven states—New York, Massachusetts, Connecticut, Virginia, North Carolina,

South Carolina, and Georgia—all claimed portions of the territory, often with conflicting boundaries. The remaining six states insisted that the national government should have jurisdiction over the West, and in 1780 some of the northern states had begun relinquishing their western claims. Gradually, Congress gained control of all the land north of the Ohio River. The southern states continued to maintain their separate claims, but the national government now possessed millions of northern acres and needed to formulate a plan for their development.

In 1784 Virginia surrendered its western claims and Jefferson submitted a development scheme to Congress not only for the land north of the Ohio but for the southern territory as well. Jefferson's plan included a provision that after 1800 the West—in both the north and the south—would practice neither slavery nor involuntary servitude, except for the punishment of certain crimes. Though six states voted in favor of the proposal, the South unanimously rejected it—even the Virginia delegation, which overruled Jefferson. The rest of Jefferson's scheme received congressional approval, but Congress never put it into effect—in part because northerners continued to press for the inclusion of a statement outlawing slavery in future states of the West.[35]

The establishment of a definitive plan for the western territories—one that dovetailed neatly with the agreement on representation at the Constitutional Convention—coincided with the deal-making in Philadelphia. Both the North and the South worried that the eventual disposition of the territories might work against them in the contest for congressional power. Northerners feared that western farmers, "calling out for slaves," would naturally align themselves with the slaveholding, agrarian interests of the South. At one point in the Convention, northerners suggested limiting the admission of western states, to make sure that the Northeast would continue to dominate the single-vote upper house in the new Congress. Speaking for his northern colleagues, Elbridge Gerry advocated admitting new states on "liberal grounds, but not . . . putting ourselves in their hands. . . . Like all men," Gerry argued, "if they acquire power, Westerners would abuse it," and he suggested adding a provision to the Constitution guaranteeing that the representatives from the new states would never outnumber those from the established states on the Atlantic seaboard.[36]

The South also had good reason to feel threatened without an agreement on the future of the territories; southerners feared that the North would exercise its majority power in the new Congress to put Jefferson's earlier proposal to ban slavery in the West into effect. Though no records of specific communications exist, the delegates in Philadelphia kept in close contact with members of the Congress in New York; the fact that congressional approval of a plan for western development came just one day after the three-fifths rule passed in Philadelphia suggests that the two bodies had reached an agreement.

The plan for western development, known as the Northwest Ordinance, represented another compromise easing tension between the North and the South. It applied to all lands above the Ohio River and effectively halved Jefferson's earlier proposal for all of the western lands, guaranteeing that it would not permit slavery in the area covered by its provisions. Of the lower half of the West, much of which individual southern states still controlled, the Ordinance said nothing, but the omission spoke volumes. It signified that although the region would lie under federal control, the compromise had cut off all further opposition to the spread of slavery throughout the southwest. The North and South had split the western lands down the middle, extending the Mason-Dixon line along the Ohio River to the Mississippi. The North also gained under a provision that put a firm limit on the number of states the northwestern lands would produce, accomplishing essentially what Elbridge Gerry had tried to do at the Convention. Earlier committees of Congress had suggested that the region might produce as many as fourteen states; the Ordinance reduced that number to not less than three or more than five states, thus ensuring the continuation of northeastern dominance for the foreseeable future.

The South won a further concession by insisting on the inclusion of a fugitive-slave clause in the Ordinance. Edward Coles, Madison's secretary during his presidency, later noted that that clause, an important element in the compromise, resulted from conferences and communications between members of Congress and the Convention delegates.[37] A few weeks later in Philadelphia, members would also insert a similar measure in the Constitution without debate, suggesting that it, too, had been previously agreed upon, perhaps when the delegates discussed the idea in relation to the territories: "If any person bound to service or labour in any of the United States shall escape into another state, he or she shall not be discharged from such service or labour, in consequence of any regulations subsisting in the state to which they escape, but shall be delivered up to the person justly claiming their services or labour."[38]

Whatever the intricacies of its birth, the fugitive-slave clause—intended to invalidate northern state laws protecting runaways and force northerners to turn them over to their masters on demand—ultimately created a multitude of problems not only for escaped slaves but for free blacks, who became targets of unscrupulous slave catchers, and for anyone who tried to aid them. In 1772, Lord Mansfield's finding in the *Somersett* case had suggested that slaves became free the moment they entered a free jurisdiction. The fugitive-slave clause enabled the South to tighten its grip on the slave population by using the federal government to extend the power of southern law beyond the region's borders into the free areas of the North and West. As Madison explained at the Virginia ratifying convention, laws in the North had been uncharitable to slaveholders, but the fugitive-slave clause promised to protect owners by closing the loophole that allowed a runaway to escape to "any of those States where slaves are free and be emancipated by their laws."

The Northwest Ordinance was the last piece in the representation puzzle, settling the question, at least temporarily. The Convention next considered the manifold issue of federal powers. A committee of five of the most active and influential framers—John Rutledge of South Carolina, Randolph of Virginia, Wilson of Pennsylvania, Gorham of Massachusetts, and Oliver Ellsworth of Connecticut—undertook to prepare a draft of the entire Constitution, including a list of the government's enumerated powers.[39] Once again, slavery drove the discussion. When the committee returned after two weeks with a series of proposals, the North immediately accused the two southern delegates of having dominated the committee's deliberations. The North and South had potentially serious disagreements on three crucial issues, and in every case the committee had recommended adoption of resolutions that seemed to favor the South. First, southerners, holding to slavery as a local matter, argued that the federal government should have no power to regulate slavery or the slave trade. They also insisted that Congress should not be allowed to levy taxes on exports—specifically, on the rich crops of tobacco, sugar, rice, and cotton that provided the foundations of southern wealth. Finally, southerners demanded that navigation acts— which would regulate shipping in and out of the nation's ports—should require special two-thirds majorities for passage. To the consternation of northerners, the committee's enumeration of governmental powers incorporated all three of these proposals. It prohibited any federal limitation on the slave trade, denied the levy of any duty or tax on exports, and vetoed all navigation acts unless they received the approval of two-thirds of the members of both branches of Congress.

Speaking for his northern colleagues, Rufus King of Massachusetts, a late convert to the federalist view after having initially opposed the idea of a constitutional convention, expressed bitter disappointment over the report. He had approved including slaves in the rule of representation because he had hoped it would lead to a greater trust between the regions that ultimately would strengthen the general government, but the committee report dashed his hopes. Slaves made both foreign invasion and internal sedition more likely, King argued, and the committee's recommendations asked northerners to increase their exposure to danger without any compensation for their burden. If the South wanted to continue importing slaves, King believed, then "the exports produced by their labour ought to supply a revenue . . . to enable [the government] to defend their masters." Instead, the committee had recommended that the South be allowed to import slaves without limitation, for which it would be rewarded with increased representation. The report contained so much inequality and unreasonableness, King concluded, that the northern states could never be reconciled to it.[40]

Obviously angry, King also made clear what he expected from the South. The North had allowed slaves to be included in the population count, and now the time had come for the South to make some accommodation to northern feelings. King felt less sure about precisely what he wanted—a time limit on the importation of slaves, perhaps, or the power to tax exports—but it was certain that he and many other northern delegates had grown weary of the steady stream of southern demands and would resist the committee's one-sided proposals unless they were adjusted to gain northern support.

As it turned out, the North and South finally agreed on no export taxes. The southern, or staple, states, and the carrier states of the North, whose ships transported the products of southern agriculture, had a shared commercial interest that at least temporarily aligned them against the nonexporting middle states. Two other issues remained for which no one had easy answers: Would navigation acts require a two-thirds majority? And, more troubling, what role if any would the federal government play in relation to the slave trade?

Before the Revolution, the British had imposed on the colonies a rigid monopoly that closed shipping in and out of North America to foreign vessels, restricting trade to ships owned and manned by English subjects; having thrown off the yoke of British oppression, southerners had no desire to give similar power to the North, wanting instead to gain an economic advantage by opening their ports to competitive shipping. Only a year before, the New Yorker John Jay had attempted to negotiate a treaty for trading privileges with the Spanish Empire by partially giving up American rights to navigate the Mississippi.[41] The treaty would have benefited New England merchants at the expense of settlers in the Ohio River valley, but negative votes by five states succeeded in blocking it, because the old constitution required nine favorable votes—essentially two-thirds—for the acceptance of treaties and alliances. The incident demonstrated two things to southerners: the increased protection that a supermajority requirement gave to the minority and the untrustworthiness of northerners, particularly when they saw an opportunity to advance their own interests.

The question of who would have the upper hand in relation to navigation acts was fundamentally an economic one, but when the delegates turned to the slave trade they finally confronted an issue that the North, at least, regarded as a dispute over principles. Slaves were a constant presence in the South, and southerners viewed them as a sometimes difficult but indispensable part of their everyday lives. They accepted the slave trade in the same complacent manner; some of the more aggressively pious southerners were even ready to argue that enslavement did Africans a favor, that their lives improved after being brought to America, as their masters treated them in accord with Christian principles. When pressed, the majority of southerners would admit the shame of man-stealing and all its attendant horrors, but whenever possible they chose to overlook the evils of the trade. The less said, the better, became the slaveholders' unofficial motto. Southerners simply avoided thinking about the African trade, or they justified it as an unfortunate but necessary element in the region's economic and social system, to which they felt intense loyalty.

Northerners, however, made a clear distinction between the slave trade and the domestic institution of slavery. Though they would have preferred that slavery had never come to North America, they could not wish away its formidable existence. No one could doubt that slavery had put down deep roots in the South and become a critical element in the nation's economic system, and northerners reluctantly accepted its continuation as their only realistic political choice. The slave trade was another matter. Though it worried northerners in practical terms—more Africans would no doubt accelerate the expansion of the slave system—their deepest objections remained philosophical and moral. The kidnapping and commitment to bondage of free Africans, who at least theoretically were endowed with the same natural rights that whites enjoyed, presented a troubling contradiction that weighed heavily on northerners, who had ostensibly gathered in Philadelphia to write a Constitution giving concrete form to the idealistic principles of the Declaration of Independence.

Breaking with the rest of the South, Virginia also spoke out against the slave trade. Though committed to slavery, Virginia opposed importation. The Revolutionary War had been hard on large southern planters, and recovery had been particularly difficult for the Virginia plantations. Slaveholders had far too many bondsmen and not enough work, and some resentful southerners suggested that the Virginians' opposition to the slave trade was hypocritical, having more to do with economics than morality. Virginia "will gain by stopping the importations," South Carolina's Charles Pinckney observed. "Her slaves will rise in value, & she has more than she wants."⁴² Virginia's economic circumstances likely influenced its opposition; only a few years later, it was derisively being called the "Guinea of the Union" because of the large number of slaves it sold to the Deep South and the Southwest. At the same time, many illustrious Virginians, including Washington, Jefferson, and Patrick Henry, were deeply troubled by the African trade—which they tried to blame on the British—and wanted to distinguish between it and domestic slavery.

In one of the Convention's most memorable speeches, George Mason, who had written both the Virginia constitution and its bill of rights, passionately argued for an end to the slave trade. The "infernal traffic" had been forced on the colonies by "the avarice of British Merchants," he maintained, but already many of the individual states had acted to prohibit it. "All this would be in vain" if the Deep South remained "at liberty to import." Mason feared for the country's future because slavery discouraged "arts & manufactures," prevented "the immigration of Whites, who really enrich & strengthen a Country," and produced "the most pernicious effect on manners. Every master of slaves is born a petty tyrant." A continuation of the slave trade, he predicted, would bring the judgment of heaven on the country. "By an inevitable chain of cause & effects providence punishes national sins, by national calamities."[43] Delegates from Georgia and the Carolinas responded that they had no intention of surrendering their individual rights, guaranteed under the Articles, to decide whether or not they would import slaves, and they threatened to dissolve the Convention. Charles Pinckney declared that even if he and his colleagues "were to sign the Constitution & use their personal influence, it would be of no avail towards obtaining the assent of their Constituents. S. Carolina & Georgia cannot do without slaves." John Rutledge agreed: "If the Convention thinks [the southern states] will ever [accept] the plan, unless their right to import slaves be untouched, the expectation is vain. The people of those States will never be such fools as to give up so important an interest."[44]

With the two sides once again apparently deadlocked, members of the Connecticut delegation stepped in—just as they had in the conflict between the large and small states—and tried to steer the Convention toward a compromise. Better to let the southern states import slaves than to have them splinter off on their own, Roger Sherman suggested. Raising the specter of dissolution, his colleague Oliver Ellsworth concurred: "If we do not agree on . . . middle & moderate ground . . . [states] may be disposed to stand aloof . . . and fly into a variety of shapes & directions, and most probably into several confederations and not without bloodshed."[45]

The Convention finally turned the whole thorny matter—the slave trade and the navigation acts—over to a committee of eleven delegates, who were instructed once more to seek a compromise. Two days later, the committee returned with a proposal that satisfied the North in three ways: by eliminating the two-thirds majority on navigation acts, by giving power to the federal government to eventually end the slave trade (if Congress decided to), and by establishing a nominal head tax on all imported blacks. As Charles Cotesworth Pinckney later explained at the South Carolina ratification convention, southerners relented on navigation acts because they recognized the North's need for consideration on the issue. The war had badly damaged the North's shipping industry—"some ports . . . which used to fit out one hundred and fifty sails of vessels, do not now fit out thirty"—and "justice, friendship, and humanity" required that the South help relieve the northerners' distress. Southerners conceded control over American shipping to the North, and in exchange, they got what they wanted most, the uninterrupted continuation of the slave trade. The compromise guaranteed that the federal government could not prohibit the importation of slaves before 1800.

The measure passed a day later, with two added northern concessions. At the insistence of Charles Pinckney, the Convention extended the life of the slave trade to 1808 and perhaps indefinitely, if the South could gain control of Congress within twenty years. In addition, the delegates passed by acclamation the previously agreed upon fugitive-slave clause. Once again, the Convention had found a way to preserve the Union, but it had required a constitutional guarantee that the South would be free to import slaves for many years into the future. As Madison ruefully noted, "Twenty years will produce all the mischief that can be apprehended from the liberty to import slaves."[46] And indeed, during that time hundreds of thousands of additional captive Africans would be brought to the shores of America.

Throughout the Convention, the need for compromise had undermined the North's willingness to aggressively address the nefarious institution fashioned by southern slaveholders, resulting in a blueprint for government that doomed black Americans to a miserable future. With a clear majority, northerners repeatedly conceded elements of power in order to satisfy the South's desire to protect slavery. The North also allowed slaves to be included in the rules of representation, a concession that radically distorted the selection processes of the new government and gave the South undue influence throughout the nation's political system. Not only had the Convention handed extra votes in the Congress to southerners but it also gave them additional power in the electoral college, in candidate selection within political parties, and in the appointment processes to the Supreme Court, the federal judiciary, and federal bureaucracies. Similarly, when the North agreed to a fugitive-slave clause in both the Constitution and the Northwest Ordinance, it granted southern agents the right to enforce on free soil laws which many northerners bitterly resented and ultimately resisted.

The northern delegates agreed to all these concessions and compromises with a reasonably clear understanding of what they had negotiated away, but they faced another, entirely separate question at the Convention, which at the time no one thought of primarily as a slavery issue. No one ever openly linked the question of how much power the states would retain to the slavery debate, but the Convention's decision to adopt the principle of states' rights—allowing the states the lion's share of local control—would eventually become the South's main defense against federal action to curb racial injustice. After the Civil War, individual states would regularly use the argument that the national government had no right to meddle in local affairs as a shield to deprive blacks of constitutionally guaranteed liberties.

Like the regional conflict over slavery and the division of large and small states, the split between federalists and antifederalists represented an important difference of opinion that had the power to temporarily realign the delegates in Philadelphia. The antifederalists thought of themselves as representing individual states in a voluntary confederation from which they could withdraw at any time, and they intended to protect their independence. The federalists believed that the confederation had revealed America's weakness as thirteen separate, squabbling mini-nations and that the best hope for the future lay in a single great country, in which the states would play a subsidiary role to a unified national authority.

In the original Virginia Plan, Madison had proposed two houses of Congress, both of which would have some form of proportional representation. Madison recognized that the concentration of power in the hands of so many locally focused states had been a source of endless contention under the old constitution, and he hoped to promote national unity by creating an encompassing federal authority in which the citizenry would be directly represented as individuals rather than as members of thirteen separate interest groups. A number of delegates pushed Madison's views even further. "The idea of distinct states . . . would be a perpetual source of discord," George Read of Delaware warned. "There can be no cure for this evil but in doing away [with] states altogether and uniting them . . . into one great society."[47] But the most outspoken of all the federalists was Gouverneur Morris. It had been one of America's greatest misfortunes that the interests of the nation had been sacrificed over and over again to local interests, he observed, but with a new constitution the time had come for the states to unite and support the dignity and splendor of a great American Empire. The country could not enjoy an efficient national government while at the same time allowing the separate states to freely follow policies that were, in his view, "evidently unjust, and pursue them in a manner detrimental to the whole body." If "their conduct should deserve it," Morris bluntly asserted, "*particular*

States ought to be injured for the sake of a majority of the people" (italics ours). For his own part, Morris pronounced himself ready to take "all the Charters & Constitutions of the States" and throw them "into the fire, and all their demagogues into the ocean."[48]

Even when the small states had succeeded in thwarting Madison and preserving an equality of votes in the upper house of the new Congress— which to Morris made the new body like the old one, "a mere wisp of straw"—this did not end the fight to diminish the states' individual powers. Having lost the battle for proportional representation in both houses, Madison introduced another measure, arguing this time that the federal government should have the power to overturn state laws before they ever went into effect. The proposed measure would have given the legislative branch an opportunity to review state law much the way the Supreme Court does, but its power would have been preemptive rather than exercised after states put their statutes into practice. As Morris had, Madison maintained that the states had a propensity to push their own local interests in disregard of the general interest, and that the federal government needed a way to control these constant disturbances in the national system. He suggested that as a means of preserving harmony, the government should have the power of "negativing" state laws it found improper. The federal government would become the guardian of national equality, charged with balancing the scales of justice throughout the country. "Nothing short of a negative on [state] law," Madison insisted, would protect the efficacy and security of the new federal government.[49]

The delegates quickly defeated Madison's proposal, with just one northern and two southern states voting in its favor. Though no one ever mentioned slavery in the discussions that led to the retention of significant power by the states, it surely lurked in the background, influencing the thinking of southern delegates about states' rights. Above all else, they battled to keep slavery under local control, and this naturally led them to maintain that with the exception of certain specific powers expressly ceded to the national government, the states should be in charge of their own separate destinies.

Northerners saw the issue in a more convoluted way. Certain states, like diminutive New Hampshire, concentrated mainly on retaining their independence, fearing that they would utterly lose their minuscule voice in an expansive national union. But slavery also influenced northern thinking about states' rights. At least theoretically, eliminating the autonomy of the individual states would have removed the main obstacle to the federal government's ending both slavery and the slave trade. Though that was what northerners generally believed they wanted, they also recognized that it was politically impossible, and they were most comfortable regretfully accepting slavery while distancing themselves from it as a problem of the southern states. The end of state power would have forced northerners into a much more difficult position, both intellectually and morally. If the federal government, which represented the entire citizenry, had the power to control slavery, it meant that the North could no longer think of slavery as purely a southern problem. Northerners would have to bear a share of the responsibility for it. At the Massachusetts ratifying convention in 1788, William Heath ruminated on the North's dilemma. Did the people of Massachusetts become "partakers of other men's sins" by entering into a compact with the slaveholding South? Heath answered in the negative, but this "No" held true only as long as the states could call themselves "sovereign and independent to a degree" and had the right to control their own affairs.[50] If the states lost sovereignty, then everyone would share the responsibility for slavery. Looking at slavery from a distance, as outsiders, northerners were able to recognize it as a moral quagmire, and their reluctance to be drawn closer to it made them hesitant to curb states' rights.

With its work completed, the Constitutional Convention adjourned, after four long months of haggling, on September 17, 1787. The framers left Philadelphia with a sense of optimism—tempered, at least for many northern delegates, by a recognition of what they had failed to accomplish. They had achieved their overriding goal: to bring the thirteen states closer together and create a constitution that would save the Union. They had also fostered a spirit of compromise that made the future appear brighter than it had seemed at the meeting's beginning. "When you assemble a number of men to have the advantage of their joint wisdom," Benjamin Franklin noted on the final day, "you inevitably assemble . . . all their prejudices, their passions, their errors of opinion, their local interests, and their selfish views." Franklin had to admit that the Constitution had several parts of which he did not approve, but still he declared himself more than satisfied. He found it astonishing, he said, that the Convention had managed to create a "system approaching so near to perfection as it does."[51]

Where the delegates had failed, and failed badly, was in dealing with slavery. While subsequent changes partly mollified Gouverneur Morris and he finally signed the Constitution in order to avoid "general anarchy," his speech midway through the Convention had spelled out the cruel ironies preserved in the document's final form. Though the nation was founded on principles of equality and justice, the delegates had made domestic slavery "the most prominent feature in the aristocratic countenance of the proposed Constitution." Even worse, the delegates had put their stamp of approval on the slave trade. "When fairly explained," Morris had told the Convention, "it comes to this: [an American] who goes to the coast of Africa, and in defiance of the most sacred laws of humanity tears away his fellow creatures from their dearest connections & damns them to the most cruel bondages" will have more power "in a Government instituted for the protection of the rights of mankind, than the Citizen . . . who views with laudable horror, so nefarious a practice." Posterity, Morris concluded, should not be saddled "with such a Constitution."[52]

CHAPTER 4

THE FOUNDING FATHERS AT HOME

No man will labour for himself who can make another labour for him.
—THOMAS JEFFERSON

When the framers forwarded their final document to Congress, George Washington, as chairman of the Convention, added a cover letter praising the delegates' spirit of cooperation. Without exception, the members had in their hearts "the greatest interest of every true American, the consolidation of our Union," Washington wrote, which fostered "a spirit of amity, . . . mutual deference and concession."[1] The reality, of course, had been quite different. As Benjamin Franklin had suggested, discord was the rule, and the verbal sparring continued even after the Convention closed. Men who objected to the Constitution on a variety of grounds moved swiftly to block its approval, while its advocates—led by Madison, Hamilton, and Jay, the authors of the *Federalist Papers*—worked overtime defending the Constitution against a variety of charges: that it would foster an aristocratic government in which the rich few would lord it over the many, that it would destroy harmony among the independent states by making universally binding laws, and that it would create a system of dramatically unequal representation.

Critics even attacked the revered Washington and Franklin for their part in the Convention. It was all very well that Washington had "wielded the sword in defence of American liberty," a letter from the yeomanry of Massachusetts exclaimed, "but it did not alter the fact [that] to this day, [the general is] living upon the labours of several hundreds of miserable Africans, as free born as himself." A New Yorker from Dutchess County, who wished "for the Sake of Humanity [that] the Convention never had existed," excoriated Franklin in a similar fashion: "The Doctor is at the Head of a humane Institution for . . . abolishing Slavery; yet lends his Assistance to frame a Constitution which . . . not only enslave[s] those whom it ought to protect; but . . . encourages the enslaving of those over whom . . . it has [not] the least shadow of Authority."[2] Anger and recrimination dominated the discussions of slavery—to such a degree that one wonders how the North and South managed to reach any kind of agreement, much less write a new constitution that at least theoretically brought two regions of a vast country closer together than they had ever been before. Surely the constitutional crisis represented a grave incentive, encouraging both sections to reach agreement. The commercial advantages that the North received, particularly the power over navigation acts, also may have led to concessions—but even those inducements hardly explain the North's readiness to accommodate southerners on the issue of slavery.

To understand how slavery's opponents could argue so vociferously against it and at the same time concede so much, one must first recognize that slavery involved three distinctly separate issues: domestic slavery, which most northerners reluctantly accepted, believing they had no choice but to let it continue; the slave trade, which southerners—particularly in the Deep South—insisted on as necessary to maintain domestic slavery; and finally, the broader question of white acceptance of blacks as human beings. On this last point, the entire nation—North and South—essentially agreed. In the discussions at the Constitutional Convention, no one had considered blacks as anything but slaves; similarly, in all the state ratifying conventions—with the exception of Rhode Island's, which in 1790 suggested a constitutional amendment condemning the slave trade—not a single proposal designed to relieve the suffering of black Americans was entertained, though hundreds of amendments were offered on scores of other topics.[3] Like southerners, nearly all northerners believed in black inferiority. This shared contempt, amounting to a national creed, is the key to the bargain struck between the North and the South in Philadelphia. The comprehensive distaste for blacks represented the bedrock of agreement on which the framers constructed a shaky constitutional edifice held together by a series of unstable compromises.

The ratification of the Constitution solved crises that had come perilously close to ending the very existence of the United States, but as long as the issue of race remained unresolved, there could be no lasting peace. The struggle between whites and blacks, and between the North and South, doomed American society to endless rancor and conflict, casting a shadow of bitter frustration over individual lives on both sides of the color line. While blacks suffered under the obvious burden of bondage, whites had no answer to what could be done with them. The dilemma of slavery turned the dedication to liberty and equality of even the nation's greatest heroes— Washington, father of his country; Jefferson, author of the Declaration of Independence; and Madison, the guiding force behind the Constitution— to ashes.

All three owned a substantial number of slaves, of course, and each lived a privileged life supported by the fruits of slave labor. Between them, they occupied the office of chief executive for twenty-four of the first twenty-eight years of the nation's existence. All claimed Virginia as their birthplace, and their roots among the state's planter aristocracy powerfully affected their attitudes toward slavery. "We all look up to Virginia for examples," John Adams wrote in 1776, and just as it figured centrally in the intellectual ferment that created the Revolution, Virginia was the crucible in which the conflict over race boiled most intensely. The large-scale importation of slaves into the state, begun in the 1680s, continued well into the eighteenth century, but gradually a combination of increasing competition, exhausted fields, and the dilatory inefficiency of a resistant workforce slowed its momentum. The impact of the Revolution dealt a final blow to Virginia slaveholders, and by the 1780s the state's plantation system was in disarray. In a hundred years, Virginia had gone through a boom-and-bust economic cycle, and the time had come to tote up the costs. When the importation of slaves began in earnest, Virginians had simply asked how much money could be made; now, with slavery no longer able to deliver the same lucrative rewards, the question became, What is slavery's price in terms of the happiness and good order of white society? With a dangerously Africanized population that included nearly three hundred thousand blacks, many of Virginia's leading citizens seemed ready to concede that slavery—more exactly, the continued presence of African Americans—had become a mistake they longed to eliminate.

* * *

Of the three men, Washington was the eldest. A generation ahead of Jefferson and Madison and lacking their formal education, he was an authentic frontier prodigy who had worked as a surveyor on the western side of the Blue Ridge Mountains while still in his teens and by twenty-five had risen to commander in chief of the Virginia militia, a leader of the colonial forces in the French and Indian Wars. Washington had just turned eleven when his father died, and he inherited his first slaves, a company of ten that eventually would grow to over three hundred. Nine years later, tragedy struck again, when his older brother succumbed to tuberculosis; Washington became master of Mount Vernon and inherited an additional eighteen slaves. For the next six years, he spent most of his time as a soldier, but in 1758 he surrendered his Virginia commission, married the wealthy widow Martha Dandridge Custis the following year, and embarked on a new life as a gentleman farmer.

Washington's training as a soldier had taught him the value of discipline, and he brought a powerful sense of order to Mount Vernon. A tireless worker, he demanded that everyone be busy from first light until darkness and insisted that slaves needed strict supervision. "There is no other sure way of getting work well done and quietly by negroes," he explained, "for when an Overlooker's back is turned the most of them will slight their work and be idle altogether."[4] Washington preferred a preemptive watchful eye to harsher forms of discipline, but he remained military to the core and refused to tolerate servile insubordination. "If the Negroes will not do their duty by fair means," he wrote, "they must be compelled to do it."[5] Intensely practical, he demanded that his overseers treat blacks with proper care, but he was also willing to deal out harsh punishment to anyone whose actions threatened to upset Mount Vernon's precarious calm. In 1766, when authorities returned a runaway identified only as Negro Tom, Washington sent him to the West Indies to be traded for molasses, rum, and spirits, warning the ship's captain to "keep him handcuffed till you get to sea."[6]

When Washington became commander in chief of the Continental Army in 1775, he initially opposed the idea of including blacks among his troops. The colonies, fearful of providing blacks with weapons or training that might encourage them to revolt, had legally excluded them from militias throughout the colonial period; still, military units allowed them to serve during wartime when manpower shortages became acute. By 1775 a number of these battle-tested black veterans had joined the Massachusetts

Minutemen, acquitting themselves with honor at Lexington and Concord and later at Bunker Hill, but despite their exemplary service the Revolutionary leaders wanted to exclude blacks from the Continental Army. Whether discomfited by the obvious contradiction in asking blacks to fight for the freedom of their oppressors or concerned that slaves who went to war might one day return to lead their fellow bondsmen in revolt, both Washington and Congress agreed not only that no "stroller, negro, or vagabond" should be allowed to enlist but that blacks already in uniform should be discharged at the end of their current terms of service. In November 1775, Washington's headquarters issued orders that "neither Negroes, Boys unable to bear Arms, nor old men unfit to endure the fatigue of the campaign" would be allowed to serve.[7]

Washington's plan for an all-white army ended abruptly when Lord Dunmore, the royal governor of Virginia, offered freedom to any slaves who consented to join His Majesty's troops and take up arms against the colonies.[8] Dunmore's proclamation, an arrow aimed at the Achilles' heel of the South, produced an Ethiopian Regiment, whose members wore the slogan "Liberty to Slaves." It also spurred many previously undecided slave-holders to commit to the cause of independence. Wild rumors circulated of black insolence: plans to massacre women and children when the soldiers had gone to fight, the refusal of blacks to step aside for whites on the street, black mothers naming their newborns after the British governor. Angered and terrified by what they perceived as a growing rebelliousness among their bondsmen, Virginia planters excoriated Dunmore for plotting against his own race, "carrying on a piratical and savage war against us, tempting our slaves by every artifice to resort to him, and training and employing them against their masters."[9] John Adams wrote in his diary that southerners had warned that in South Carolina and Georgia alone, twenty thousand Negroes anxiously awaited the arrival of British troops, ready to join them at a moment's notice. If Dunmore, an "arch-traitor to the rights of humanity, was not instantly crushed," Washington wrote in December 1775, he could become the nation's most formidable enemy.[10] Washington feared a massive servile defection that would force the rebels to fight not only the British but a vast army of former slaves who, even more than his own troops, would be engaged in a life-and-death struggle for freedom. The outcome of the war might ultimately depend on which side succeeded in arming blacks, the general concluded, and he quickly retreated from his earlier insistence against allowing blacks into the Continental Army.

In January 1776, acting on Washington's recommendation, Congress sanctioned the reenlistment of free blacks who had served faithfully in the war's early skirmishes around Boston—an opening in the color line that gradually widened to allow the enlistment of all able-bodied blacks, slave or free, in order to fill Washington's chronic need for troops.[11] Even if Dunmore had not forced his hand, Washington would have needed black recruits. When the war began, the period of voluntary enlistment lasted a scant three months, and most whites, who still thought of themselves as citizens of the separate colonies, resisted fighting at any distance from home. Though Congress ordered the formation of eighty-eight voluntary troop battalions in September 1776, the response was less than enthusiastic, and in December Washington's army included only about three thousand men, half of them unfit for combat.

While we know little of Washington's personal experiences with blacks during the war, we do know that he never singled out any of the five thousand or so who served under his command in either the Continental Army or state militias for heroism or distinction of any kind. Though Washington appears never to have been entirely comfortable with the blacks in his command, he granted them the same rights and privileges given to white troops, and his wartime experience may have altered his attitude toward them. Whatever the cause, during the war he first began to question the ownership of slaves and consider how he could manage to do without them. "Every day," he noted in a letter to his estate manager, "I long more and more to get clear of bondsmen."

At the war's end, when Washington returned home, he brought with him a sense of personal confusion about American blacks that continued for the rest of his life. Over the next fifteen years, he repeatedly expressed his opposition to slavery. "I can only say that there is not a man living, who wishes more sincerely than I do, to see a plan adopted for the gradual abolition of it," he wrote in 1786 to Robert Morris, who had served as secretary of finance during the war.[12] Still, though he had decided never to buy or sell another slave, he occasionally allowed practical matters to overcome his resolve. He never placed another slave on the auction block, but he did acquire them when it represented a sound business decision. As an expression of that business acumen, he offered to accept six blacks as payment for a debt owed to him by a certain John Mercer, an old family friend who apparently had no money.[13] Expedience and self-interest seem to have guided him in this context, as is evidenced in another letter, written around the same time to Henry Lee, a fellow Virginian and Revolutionary War hero. Animated by plans for projects at Mount Vernon, Washington wrote, "It is not my wish to be your competitor in the purchase of any of Hunter's tradesmen; especially as I am in a great degree principled against increasing my number of slaves by purchase. Yet, if you are not disposed to buy the bricklayer, which is advertised for sale, . . . I shall be glad if you shall buy him for me. I have much work in this way to do this summer."[14]

With northerners, Washington grew cautious. Like most plantation owners, he believed that outsiders could never understand the peculiar southern system, and eager to protect his national reputation, he hid his involvement with slavery when his business spilled over into the North. Seeking to recover a runaway, he advertised for the slave's return but allowed his name to be used in newspapers only in the South. Above the Mason-Dixon line, the ads appeared anonymously. In another incident, in 1791, when Washington was president and the national government had moved from New York to Philadelphia, he suspected that Quakers might try to entice his house servants to run away, based on a Pennsylvania statute that freed any slave residing there for six months, and he instructed his secretary to send them back to Virginia in a way that would deceive both the slaves and the public.[15]

As chief executive, Washington signed into law the Fugitive Slave Act of 1793, the only official action he took in relation to slavery during his presidency. Washington never commented on the legislation, consistent with the low profile he kept on the issue of slavery. He took the position that slavery's demise appeared inevitable but that it should be given every legal protection until it withered away. In 1792, when South Carolina failed to extend its ban on the importation of slaves, Washington quickly recorded his disappointment, noting that he had hoped "the direful effects of Slavery . . . would have operated to produce a total prohibition." At the same time, however, he continued to defend the legal rights of slaveholders as he had in 1791 when he ordered the border with Spanish Florida closed to block the escape of runaways from Georgia.[16]

In 1797 Washington returned to private life for the last time. Mount Vernon had been in a state of neglect for many years, and he immediately

began setting things in order. The estate's slave population had nearly doubled, though it was only marginally more productive. Hard times had
arrived, and though Washington still described himself as "principled against
this . . . traffic in the human species," he was consumed by daily responsibilities and frustrated by providing for a workforce that had grown out of all
proportion. The problem with slavery, as he now saw it, was its cost. In the
summer of 1799, he prepared what would be a final inventory of the Mount
Vernon slaves; of the 317 he owned, he could count only about half as available to work, and even with this reduced labor force he still had too many
able-bodied slaves. Soon he was complaining of his increasingly unmanage-
able situation: "On this estate I have more working Negroes . . . than can be
employed to any advantage in the farming system. . . .What then is to be
done? Something must, or I shall be ruined."[17]

A few months later he was dead. Ten years earlier, David Humphreys, his
longtime military aide, had begun a biographical sketch of his former commander, and the unfinished manuscript includes Washington's own marginal
note revealing his most intimate feelings about slavery. "The unfortunate condition of the persons, whose labor . . . I employed had been the only unavoidable subject of regret throughout my life," he wrote, and he hoped to ease his
mind and begin to satisfy "the justice of the Creator by laying a foundation to
prepare the rising generation [of blacks] for a destiny different from that in
which they were born." In a move widely applauded in the North and frowned
upon by southerners, he took the momentous step, in his last will and testament, of freeing his slaves.[18] Unfortunately, his executors and heirs could not
easily untangle the web of confusion that slavery had cast over his life, and
Washington's final gesture left them with a series of problems.

Hoping to provide for the future of his slaves, Washington had stipulated
that they should "be taught to read & write; and . . . be brought up to some
useful occupation." Though he set aside funds to support the project,
Washington's wishes could not be carried out, because Virginia law prohibited the education of blacks. Even more problematical was the question of
how to proceed with the manumissions. Of the 300 or so slaves at Mount
Vernon, only 124 belonged to him outright. Washington had kept a close
accounting of the estate's bondsmen, separating them into two categories:
those he had acquired and those that Martha Washington owned as part of
her original dowry or who had descended from dowry members. Freeing the
124 slaves who were his own property upon his death would have been

Washington's first choice, but it would also have created "insuperable difficulties on account of their intermixture" with his wife's Negroes. Forty years of living together had melded Mount Vernon's blacks into a single community, linked to one another by marriage and ties of intimacy; by freeing only a portion of them, Washington feared, he would "excite the most painful sensations, if not disagreeable consequences" among the dowry Negroes.[19] Understanding that Martha's slaves would be dispersed to a number of separate heirs when she died, Washington elected to delay the emancipation of his own bondsmen until his wife's death so that the entire Mount Vernon black population would be dissolved at the same time. The plan seemed prudent in terms of the slaves' relations with one another because it eliminated any immediate grounds for jealousy or division among them, but for Martha Washington it had serious consequences that her husband had not foreseen or mistakenly chose to ignore.

Following a visit to Mount Vernon in December of 1800, Abigail Adams described the distressing circumstances in which Martha found herself only a year after George's death. Martha did not feel that her life was safe in the hands of her Negroes, Abigail wrote, because many of the slaves understood that they would be free when she died, and rumors abounded that her own servants planned to poison her. Depressed by the loss of her husband and weakened by age, Martha struggled not only under the burden of an estate falling into decay and an insufficient fortune to support three hundred slaves but in fear that they understood that it was in their interests to get rid of her. Her situation finally prompted her to manumit any slaves who wanted to leave Mount Vernon. To Abigail Adams, the lesson seemed clear. If people wished to discover "the baneful affects of Slavery," she wrote, "the torpor and indolence and . . . Spirit of domination it created, let them come and take a view of the cultivation of this part of the United States."[20]

Martha may well have been prompted to act by a wave of white fear that had swept Virginia earlier in the year. In August, a slave, "General" Gabriel Prosser, led an armed march on Richmond. Frightened Virginians read the abortive revolt as a conspiracy of vast proportions that had carried the state to the brink of catastrophe, though Gabriel's plan had been leaked to the authorities by two of his men—whom the Virginia Assembly later rewarded with manumission—and a torrential rainstorm had washed out the rebellion just as it was getting started. When word of the outbreak spread beyond Richmond, southerners talked of the apocalypse. Gabriel's revolt appeared to be not just an isolated local event by a few disgruntled blacks but a large, well-planned insurrection. James Monroe, then the state's governor, added to the confusion by announcing, incorrectly, that the plan had "embraced most of the slaves" in the city and the surrounding area and had "pervaded other parts, if not the whole, of the state." Though the authorities had put down the uprising quickly, with no whites or Negroes killed, its subsequent investigation and the court proceedings that followed, which resulted in the hanging of Gabriel and some thirty-five others, created a climate of panic. Southerners persuaded themselves that the scheme represented the arrival in the United States of the violent black resistance that was tearing apart the island of Haiti.[21] In 1791, Haiti—or Sainte-Domingue, to use its contemporary name—had exploded as 480,000 slaves, mostly African-born, turned on the island's French rulers and their mulatto functionaries. Haiti became a prize in a larger international conflict between France and England, and the rebellion raged for years as the ex-slaves fought against successive waves of foreign troops—first French, then English, and then French again. The blacks fought with unbelievable fanaticism—laughing at death, the French commander reported to Napoleon—and in 1804 they would finally expel the last remnants of the French army and establish Haiti as the first black nation in the Western Hemisphere.[22] Reports of the island violence constantly reached the American mainland, trebling the anxiety with which the South already viewed its Negro population.

For Washington, slavery represented a practical matter that he struggled with as a plantation owner, but for Thomas Jefferson it had darker, more troubling implications, arising from contradictions between his public and private life. A self-proclaimed champion of the small, independent farmer, he lived lavishly at Monticello in the manner of a European aristocrat, which eventually brought him to the verge of bankruptcy. Priding himself on his scientific understanding of blacks, he still could not escape thinking of slavery in religious terms and dreaded the divine retribution that awaited America for its sins. Though his countrymen looked to him for leadership on the slavery issue, more often than not he turned them away, insisting that the controversy had passed him by and that he had nothing to offer.

There can be no doubt that Jefferson found slavery repellent when he equated it with the oppression of his countrymen by the British or viewed it theoretically in relation to natural rights. In the case of blacks laboring in the fields of the South, however, his indignation rapidly cooled. Though publicly Jefferson cultivated his reputation as a staunch defender of freedom and revolution, privately he loved the pampered existence of a plantation owner and balked at destroying the system that made it possible. These positions could never be made compatible, and Jefferson settled into a kind of double life, privately offering encouragement to antislavery advocates but making it clear from about 1785 on that he would take no active part in their movement. During the Revolution, he and his contemporaries had served the nation heroically on the great stage of history, but he insisted that a rising generation of younger men would have to undertake the next step in the march of human progress.

In many ways, Jefferson lived as an exceedingly private person. Late in life, he noted that he had become "too desirous of quiet to place myself in the way of contention," but even as a younger man he resisted close scrutiny. No doubt his longing for privacy arose in part from his vulnerability to charges of inconsistency, but it now seems clear that he also had a dark secret to hide. DNA testing strongly suggests that Jefferson fathered a number of children with Sally Hemings, a house slave at Monticello.

Accusations of a sexual relationship between Jefferson and Hemings first surfaced in 1802. James Callender had been Jefferson's attack dog and had written a series of anti-Federalist tracts with his financial assistance, savaging John Adams, Alexander Hamilton, and even Washington. Following Jefferson's election as president in 1800, however, the two men fell out over precisely what patronage had accrued to Callender.[23] After an acrimonious parting, Callender began writing for an anti-Jefferson scandal sheet, and in short order his explosive accusations became public. Callender brazenly described Jefferson's extended vacations at Monticello as a return to the arms of his "black Venus." And he warned that if eighty thousand white Virginians each produced five mulattoes, as Jefferson had, the state would have four hundred thousand additional blacks to deal with and "the country no longer would be habitable, till after a civil war, and a series of massacres."[24]

Naturally, the charges created a political furor. The Federalists gleefully assumed that Callender spoke the truth. Jefferson had his own supporters in the Democratic-Republican Party, as well as Thomas Paine, who branded the story "the blackest calumny that ever escaped the envenomed pen of a villain."[25] The public lost interest in the scandal only when Jefferson returned to Monticello at the end of his second term. With partisanship a fading issue, his relationship with Hemings gradually became a matter of history rather than politics, and for 150 years historians either ignored the accusations or dismissed them as unfounded slander. Only in the last thirty years or so have scholars reopened the question, revealing a much more troubling picture of Jefferson.[26]

The story of the Jefferson-Hemings relationship, which begins with Jefferson's father-in-law, the wealthy planter John Wayles, provides a glimpse into the sordid secrets of the southern plantation. Apparently Wayles fathered a number of light-skinned children with Elizabeth Hemings, one of his slaves who was half white, and Elizabeth and her children came to Monticello as part of Martha Jefferson's inheritance in 1774 after her father died. Sally Hemings was Elizabeth's youngest child, and an infant at the time. As the offspring of John Wayles, she and her siblings, Mrs. Jefferson's half sisters and half brothers, were given preferential treatment and trained as house servants or artisans. Martha Jefferson died in 1782, and three years later Jefferson accepted a post in Paris, where his daughter, Mary, joined him a year later, accompanied by her personal servant, Sally Hemings, then only fourteen. While in France, Jefferson made Sally his mistress and began a relationship that he carried on for essentially the rest of his life and which produced at least five and perhaps as many as seven children. Back at Monticello, Sally became Jefferson's personal chambermaid, and documents show that she and Jefferson were together—at the same location, at least—nine months prior to the birth of each of her children.

Needless to say, the confirmation of both Jefferson's involvement with Sally Hemings and the paternity of his black children has disconcerted many white Americans, who would prefer that their heroes remain untarnished, even at the cost of ignoring the reality of the past. In Jefferson's case, people find his relationship with Hemings especially hard to deal with because it brings up issues that are unpleasant to contemplate. While few people still doubt that Jefferson and Hemings were intimate for many years and produced several children, the confirmation of these facts—rather than giving us a definitive answer—poses disturbing questions about the nature of their relationship. In 1861, in her memoir, *Incidents in the Life of a Slave Girl*, Harriet Jacobs recalled her youthful experience with an abusive master who took advantage of her sexually. "Slavery is terrible for men," she mourned, but "it is far more terrible for women." What W. E. B. Du Bois called "the legal defilement of Negro women" we can today in fact call rape, institutionalized as a prerogative of white males who controlled a system in which blacks remained powerless.[27]

Jefferson's relationship with Sally Hemings raises several other moral issues. When Hemings first arrived in Paris, Jefferson not only was her master but should have been her protector as well. Hemings was somewhere between fourteen and sixteen years old when she became Jefferson's mistress; according to Abigail Adams, she lacked all sophistication and acted particularly childlike for her age. On the way to France, Hemings and Mary Jefferson had stopped in England to visit Abigail, who afterward wrote to Jefferson, alerting him to Hemings's inexperience: "She wanted more care than the child [Mary], and is wholly incapable of looking after her without some superior to direct her."[28] Later in life, Sally Hemings revealed that she had gone to France dreaming that she would learn the language and remain there as a free woman, but she had been overcome by Jefferson's persistence and the promise that any children resulting from their relationship would be given their freedom when they became adults. Whatever their feelings for one another later were, the image of a worldly Jefferson in his mid-forties taking advantage of an inexperienced teenager, whose life he controlled absolutely, is bleak testimony to the hidden sins that the slave master accepted as God-given rights.

Both publicly and privately, Jefferson sought to conceal his guilty secret—a natural though pusillanimous reaction, given the time, the place, and the circumstances of his involvement with Hemings. But what did his desire for secrecy mean for their children? "I deem the composition of my family the most precious of all the kindnesses of fortune," Jefferson wrote in June 1791 to his daughter Maria, but his sense of gratitude extended only so far.[29] Clearly, he was a doting father to his white daughters, but to his black offspring he was master as well, and he possessed not only a powerful need to hide his connection to them but the awful right to determine what their status would be, either by making them free human beings or burying them as creatures enslaved for life. Were his black children to be considered, at least in some sense, as members of his own family who deserved special treatment and parental affection, or could they be dismissed with the same insouciance shown to the rest of Monticello's black population?

At some level, Jefferson must have faced the tumultuous reality that he was dealing with his own flesh and blood; by forsaking his children and leaving them enslaved, he would be imprisoning his best moral self in unbreakable chains of guilt. Still, overwhelming forces most certainly pulled him in that direction. Jefferson had grown accustomed to treating blacks as property, and Virginia legislation made it clear that a child, rather than deriving its status from its father, merited enslavement or freedom based on the condition of its mother. Sally Hemings was a slave, and therefore her children had to live out their lives as slaves.

In addition, Jefferson had feelings about miscegenation and the purity of the white race that even among Virginians appeared unusually strong. Racial mixing troubled him so much that in the late 1770s, in the years between the Declaration of Independence and his departure for France, he had tried to get the state legislature to pass a law banishing any white woman bearing a child by a Negro or a mulatto. Similar statutes had been in existence for almost a hundred years, but the remarkable thing about Jefferson's proposal was that it called for a far harsher punishment than the fines imposed in the past. The Virginia legislature seems to have agreed that Jefferson's views were excessive and defeated the measure, but his attitude apparently never softened. Even after his relationship with Hemings had continued for a period of years, Jefferson publicly called miscegenation a sin not only against the nation but against the white race. "Amalgamation with the other color," he wrote in 1814, when his black firstborn was nineteen years old, "produces a degradation to which no lover of his country, no lover of excellence in the human character, can innocently consent."[30]

What did all this mean for Jefferson and Hemings's children? As long as Jefferson lived, they remained unacknowledged, and in all his voluminous notebooks he never mentioned them in any way that might hint at their familial relationship. According to the one record available from the children themselves—a newspaper interview given by his son Madison in 1873—Jefferson's bearing toward them never revealed their connection, and Madison could not recollect a single instance of fatherly affection.[31] Jefferson accorded them a degree of special consideration, but nothing more than the favors granted to the other light-skinned descendants of Elizabeth Hemings, whose family generally received good treatment because of her relationship with John Wayles. Of Jefferson's four children with Hemings whose names we know, none received a formal education, but all learned a trade. His daughter Harriet became a weaver in the plantation factory, and his three sons, Beverly, Madison, and Eston Hemings, he apprenticed out as carpenters. Without question, Jefferson's children enjoyed many privileges in contrast with most blacks, who were forced to labor in the fields, but can anyone doubt the withering resentment they must have felt in the face of their father's cruel silence and hypocrisy.

Unlike Washington, who elected to emancipate all of his Negroes when he died, Jefferson freed only eight slaves throughout his life. In part, this was undoubtedly because his extravagant living kept him constantly in debt and forced him to think in terms of selling slaves, rather than freeing them at a loss. From 1784 to 1794, he sold at least eighty-five slaves, and when he became president he continued to auction them from Monticello. Even if he had wanted to manumit all his bondsmen when he died, it would have been impossible, because Jefferson's creditors had the legal right to demand that they be sold to contribute to the repayment of his debts. Of the eight slaves Jefferson freed, all belonged to the Hemings family, and three of them were his own children: his daughter Harriet and her two younger brothers, Madison and Eston. Harriet ran off in 1822 and made her way to Philadelphia with her brother Beverly. Jefferson freed Harriet after she had escaped but never emancipated Beverly, leaving him in the precarious legal position of a runaway, perhaps because he blamed Beverly for having instigated his sister's flight. Both Harriet and Beverly found new lives in Philadelphia, where they married whites and quietly passed into the majority community.

When Jefferson died in 1826, his will granted Madison and Eston, still minors at the time of Jefferson's death, their freedom once they became adults. Surprisingly, Jefferson never emancipated Sally Hemings. In fact, Harriet, who had forced Jefferson's hand by running away, was the only woman he ever freed, but perhaps he believed that he was protecting Sally by not granting her freedom. Slaves were "brought up from their infancy without necessity for thought or forecast," Jefferson maintained, which rendered them "as incapable as children of taking care of themselves." The master had a burden, he self-righteously explained, to provide for "those whom fortune has thrown on our hands, to feed and clothe them well, protect them from all ill usage, . . . and be led by no repugnancies to abdicate them and our duties to them."[32] Somehow Jefferson always managed to wind up on the side of the angels, and perhaps he convinced himself that he was doing Sally Hemings a favor by keeping her enslaved.

Jefferson's lifelong involvement with slavery brought both triumph and torment. In his private life, he surely believed in the slavery system and his own entitlement to the luxuries it provided, including his right to use Sally Hemings in whatever way he pleased and to deny their children the paternal support they would have had under normal circumstances. As noted, in all Jefferson's papers nothing suggests the existence of his other family, and thus it is impossible to know how he truly felt about them.

Though it was the Declaration of Independence that established Jefferson's fame as a spokesman for universal liberty, he also addressed the specific question of slavery in America in his *Notes on the State of Virginia*. Along with his tainted examination of black inferiority, the *Notes* also contains his most extensive reflections on the institution of slavery, which scholars often cite as proof of his commitment to antislavery principles.[33] In spite of his poor opinion of blacks, Jefferson held that slavery had to end, because of the terrible threat that it represented to white society. Jefferson recognized that slavery destroyed any hope that blacks had for the future, and he further feared that it made them hate America. But he found another problem much more pressing: slavery's "unhappy influence" on southern whites. Though some of his contemporaries had argued that the presence of slaves enhanced the South's love of freedom, Jefferson would have none of it. In his mind, slavery's existence created a culture with disastrous consequences for all its members. "The whole commerce between master and slave is a perpetual exercise of the most boisterous passions," Jefferson wrote, "the most unremitting despotism on the one part, and degrading submissions on the other.... Our children see this, and learn to imitate it. The parent storms, the child looks on, ... and thus [is] nursed, educated, and daily exercised in tyranny.... The man must be a prodigy who can retain his manners and morals undepraved by such circumstances." Slavery not only destroyed a society's moral fabric, it also discouraged industry. "No man will labour for himself," Jefferson observed, "who can make another labour for him." Even worse was the gnawing realization that whites lived in a perpetual state of sinfulness as long as slavery continued. Slave owners certainly invited divine punishment in the form of violent and prolonged slave rebellion. "I tremble for my country when I reflect that God is just: that his justice cannot sleep forever," Jefferson mournfully wrote. "The Almighty has no attribute which can take side with us in such a contest."

The *Notes'* pessimistic ruminations represent Jefferson's most thoughtful conclusions about slavery—views he affirmed forty years later in his

Autobiography. The races obviously had grown no closer, and America could not avoid its cosmic comeuppance forever. "Nature, habit, and opinion have drawn indelible lines of distinction between blacks and whites," Jefferson wrote, "and nothing is more certainly written in the book of fate than that blacks are to be free; nor is it less certain that the two races, equally free, cannot live in the same government."[34]

These powerful, absolute statements crystallize Jefferson's opposition to slavery, but our faith in his words runs up against our knowledge of the conflicting loyalties that stopped him from living in a manner consistent with his principles. Ironically, even with the *Notes'* honesty and outrage in relation to slavery, Jefferson hoped to prevent his views from reaching Virginia and tried to suppress their publication in English. In 1784, when they first appeared in France, he wrote the Marquis de Chastellux, insisting that he did not want the book's contents known at home. "The strictures on slavery and on the constitution of Virginia," he explained, "might produce an irritation which would indispose ... people," and thus would likely do more harm than good. Obviously, one could not call oneself an ardent foe of slavery in any meaningful way and at the same time remain hypersensitive to the feelings of Virginia's plantation owners. Once again Jefferson attempted to mask his true feelings by making sure that the wrong message never reached home.

Of all the great American leaders, Jefferson stands out as the most complex and most tragic. Hopelessly conflicted in relation to slavery, he dug himself deeper and deeper into a life of subterfuge and denial, constantly at odds with his own innate moral sense that urged him to *"do what is right."*[35] Near the end of his life, Jefferson compared America's problem with slavery to a man holding a wolf by the ears: "We can neither hold him, nor safely let him go," he wrote. "Justice is in one scale, and self-preservation is in the other."[36] The image of the wolf captures the awful dilemma slavery posed for the nation, but the metaphor also illuminates Jefferson's individual predicament. On the one hand, he believed firmly that divine justice cried out for an end to slavery; on the other, he recognized that the preservation of Virginia's planter class and the life he dearly loved depended on its survival. Tragically, Jefferson felt trapped between two alternatives, both of which carried consequences he refused to accept. Instead, he continued astride the wolf, desperately clinging to its ears, unwilling either to commit to antislavery or to acknowledge his tacit approval of bondage in Virginia.

*   *   *

Born eight years after Jefferson, James Madison had been too young to play a leadership role during the Revolution and achieved national prominence only at the Constitutional Convention. Recognizing slavery's critical place in the nation's political dynamics, he hoped to point the delegates toward a practical compromise that balanced the conflicting interests of North and South. When the Constitution in its final form fell short of his desires, Madison nevertheless worked tirelessly for ratification, believing that the need for a strong central government outweighed every other question, including slavery.

Publicly, Madison subordinated his views on slavery to the need for national unity; privately, he remained convinced that the ownership of slaves was a stain on the nation's claim to moral superiority. Unlike most Virginians, Madison appears not to have harbored strong feelings of racial antipathy. As a realist, he recognized prejudice as a powerful social force that had to be reckoned with, but for his own part he seemed willing to accept blacks as human beings with essentially the same aspirations as whites. In 1783, when his term in the Continental Congress ended, Madison realized that his valet, Billey, who had been with him for an extended period in Philadelphia, had become "too thoroughly tainted to be a fit companion for fellow slaves in Virginia," and he arranged for him to become an indentured servant in Pennsylvania, where he would be freed after seven years. As Madison explained in a letter to his father, he could not think of punishing Billey "merely for coveting that liberty for which we have paid the price of so much blood, and have proclaimed so often to be right, and worthy the pursuit of every human being."[37]

Early in the 1790s, Madison recorded his inmost thoughts on slavery in a series of notes for essays he intended to write for the *National Gazette*. In contrast to most whites, he accepted the reality of blacks as members of American society and raised the boldest of questions: What did the violation of their rights mean for the nation at large? What precise influence did domestic slavery have on government? What did slavery reveal about the nation's politics?[38]

Madison began with a broad proposition that exposed the contradiction at the heart of American democracy: Given the institution of slavery, a government, however fervently it pursues democracy in theory, must remain aristocratic in fact. America's problem went well beyond the simple notion that as a republic it failed to protect the human rights of its black minority:

the southern half of the nation did not have a republican form of government at all. The power of "the rich and easy" held sway over the great mass of the region's inhabitants. In Virginia, the aristocracy maintained power through the rule of suffrage, which enabled the wealthy to control the other three-quarters of the state, made up of blacks and nonfreeholding whites, who did not have the right to vote. "Were the slaves freed and the right of suffrage extended to all," Madison calmly observed, "the operation of the Government might be very different."[39]

Madison discerned the larger national picture and comprehended the role that slavery played in shaping American politics. He realized that the constitutional compromise of 1787 really had solved nothing—that the country remained divided between North and South, where two antagonistic forms of government prevailed. Without the burden of slavery, northerners had established a true republic, but in the southern states the old aristocracy remained in charge. In the long run, the nation faced an explosive, fundamental clash of differing societies, but in the meantime Madison resolved to keep his own counsel and direct his energy toward strengthening the federal government to make it powerful enough to withstand whatever internal shocks might come.

For the next twenty-five years, Madison had little to say about slavery. Carving out a name for himself in government, he recognized that his opinions would make him few friends and could damage him politically. Instead, he occupied himself with projects of national importance, deeply involved in the day-to-day operations of the federal government, first as a member of Congress, where he proposed the establishment of the Bill of Rights, then as secretary of state during the Jeffersonian era, and finally as a two-term president, beginning in 1809, when he succeeded Jefferson. At his best dealing with practical problems of governance, Madison allowed slavery to sink to the bottom of his political agenda, and when it became an issue during his presidency, it represented little more than a source of frustration. Though Jefferson had outlawed the importation of blacks in 1808, it was left to Madison to enforce the ban, but his efforts to suppress what he called those "unworthy citizens, who mingle in the slave trade under foreign flags" met with only marginal success, and traders imported more than a quarter of a million blacks illegally between 1809 and 1860.

In 1817, at the end of his presidency, Madison retired to Montpelier, his Virginia estate. Two years later, in a letter to the editor Robert Walsh, who had asked his help in preparing a response to attacks on the United States in British periodicals, Madison reflected on the changes that had taken place in Virginia since the Revolution. The establishment of republican values, he observed, had uplifted the character and morals of the state's people. The unequal distribution of property had been repaired by abolishing entails and primogeniture; the desire for luxury had been quenched; the indolent and irregular members of the clergy had reformed; and all the demoralizing causes of corruption tainting the citizenry under the colonial government had ceased, or were, with one exception, wearing away. Of all the old vices, only slavery remained, but even in relation to slavery Madison insisted that the country had made progress. Slaves were "better fed, better clad, better lodged, and better treated in every respect," he observed, and "what was formerly deemed a moderate treatment, would now be a rigid one; and what formerly a rigid one, would now be denounced by the public feeling."[40] Choosing his words for what ultimately would be a British audience, Madison sounded more like Jefferson than like himself, maintaining that Virginia, moving at its own deliberate pace, would eventually put an end to slavery. The larger reality, however, was that it still flourished, and many of the Virginia plantations had become heavily involved in the domestic slave trade, sending thousands of blacks to the Deep South and the Southwest, where they were not only separated from loved ones but faced harder work and more brutal living conditions. In order to maintain the rigid American color line, legislators in the Louisiana Territory had made conditions considerably worse than they had been under the French. The Gallic Code Noir had granted them a series of humane guarantees, such as the right to be instructed in religion, to cultivate a garden for their own sustenance, to take Sunday as a holiday, to be sold together if they were husband and wife, and for any child under fourteen years of age to remain with its mother.

Just three months later, responding to a letter from the antislavery advocate Robert Evans, Madison offered a more candid and considerably less optimistic view. A thorough incorporation of blacks and whites seemed impossible, he lamented, as long as blacks were "strongly marked by physical . . . peculiarities." Doomed to live "under the degrading privation of equal rights," they would always be "dissatisfied . . . secretly confederated against the ruling and privileged class, and uncontrolled by . . . the most cogent motives to moral and respectable conduct."[41] Madison acknowledged that the principal cause of the division between the races was white prejudice. All the power in American society belonged to whites, after all, and if blacks felt any resentment their anger was reactive, growing out of circumstances that whites controlled. Freed from the demands of daily political activity, Madison's mind dwelled on the continuing problem of slavery, and for one final time he returned to public life to confront the issue. In 1829, at the age of seventy-eight, Madison traveled to Richmond to join the state constitutional convention, hoping his accrued wisdom could aid his fellow Virginians as they attempted to solve their own slavery crisis.

Almost since its inception, the Virginia state constitution of 1776 had been under attack for its conservative leanings. In the *Notes on the State of Virginia*, Jefferson had argued that the document's approach to both suffrage and apportionment flew in the face of republican principles. It not only disenfranchised the majority of adult males by limiting the vote to freeholders but it also gave disproportionate influence to the state's eastern elite through a system of county representation tilted in their favor. Reformers were stymied as long as Virginia's western lands remained sparsely inhabited, but in the early years of the nineteenth century the state underwent a dramatic demographic shift. From 1790 to 1830, the white population in the western part of the state nearly tripled, while the eastern increase registered a modest 17 percent, and the two regions approached parity in white population. At the same time, the vast majority of the state's slaves was concentrated in the east, with the western total never rising much over 10 percent of Virginia's black population.

As the number of whites in the western part of Virginia grew, the east's near monopoly on power rankled them more and more, and finally the Virginia Assembly agreed to a constitutional convention, which everyone anticipated would focus on the issue of representation. The stage was set for a struggle between the state's westerners, who wanted to expand their power by broadening the vote and apportioning representation on a white-only basis, and its easterners, who were looking for a way to retain as much of their advantage as they possibly could. Madison hoped to serve as a peacemaker, seeking a principled compromise between the two parties. Recognizing the aristocratic leanings of the eastern elite, he realized that westerners had a legitimate grievance, but he also understood that the east would never surrender an iota of power unless it gained something in return. Relying on his national experience, he suggested that the key to a settlement could be the status of slaves. Like the federal government, the Virginia legislature had two separate houses, and

Madison proposed that one be apportioned on a white-only basis and the other be formed by using the federal ratio, counting five slaves as the equivalent of three whites. For both sides, the plan promised to reduce tension and restore stability by ensuring that each region would have dominant voting strength in one of the two houses; thus, each had a way to assert its own interest and check the ambition of the other.

Presenting his views to the convention, Madison returned to the under-lying principle of "Federalist 54"—that blacks were not merely property but also human beings and therefore ought to be included in the population count for at least one of the two legislative houses. This time Madison shifted the grounds of his argument, however, making the status of slaves a moral rather than a practical issue. Whether or not Virginia law assumed the traditional dual nature of blacks was no longer the primary question. Instead, Madison argued that on the basis of moral and ethical considera-tions alone, slaves ought to be viewed, at least in part, as human beings.

If blacks had the same pale color as whites, much of the difficulty they created would be removed, Madison insisted; slaves naturally would be included in population counts without a second thought. Obviously, the cir-cumstance of complexion alone should not be enough to deprive blacks of "the character of men," and they deserved to be treated as human beings. It was "due to justice; due to humanity, due to truth," Madison said, "to the sympathies of our nature; in fine to our character as a people, both abroad and at home, that they should be considered, as much as possible, in the light of human beings, and not as mere property." He called on the delegates not only to adopt the legalistic and practical measure of including blacks in the population count but to undertake the moral—and far more radical—step of embracing them not on the basis of equality but something very close to it. Consider them "as making a part, though a degraded part, of the families to which they belong," he pleaded.[42]

Unfortunately, Madison's proposal ran counter to the mood of the dele-gates. Neither western reformers nor eastern conservatives had much interest in either reaching a Madisonian-style political compromise or being lectured by an elder statesman who urged them to acknowledge their common humanity with blacks. Instead, westerners continued to argue that both houses of Virginia's legislature should be apportioned on a white-only basis, while easterners remained just as adamant that property as well as popula-tion had to be taken into account, a semantic subterfuge that allowed them to include slaves in calculating apportionment without accepting blacks as human beings. Ultimately the delegates in Richmond narrowly approved a pair of proposals giving westerners a somewhat broader franchise and white-based apportionment in both houses, but eastern slaveholders more than held their own by insisting on the permanent use of the 1820 census for population figures and blocking any provision for future change based on a new count. Westerners got far less than they had hoped for, while easterners managed to maintain power indefinitely by neutralizing the demographic tide that clearly seemed to be moving in the west's favor.

In Madison's view, the Richmond convention had produced mixed results. As usual, he was inclined to find the good in things and consequently more willing to accept many of the new state constitution's flaws as compromises necessary for the delegates to reach agreement. The document—a "pudding," Madison called it—also contained a number of plums after all, and he was particularly gratified that the representatives finally had found a way out of the apparent deadlock that developed midway through the proceedings.[43] As he wrote to Lafayette, the convention had proved once again that America's form of government, destined to endure, was able to survive through perilous times. "The *peculiar* difficulties which will have been overcome," he observed, "ought to render . . . new evidence of the capacity of men for self-government, instead of an argument in the hands of those who deny and calumniate it."[44] Still, Madison surely felt a considerable degree of personal disappointment. One can imagine his frustration when many of his colleagues scornfully dismissed his call for a moral consideration of slaves, sneering at his principles as "fatuity" and "vacillating conduct." In his letter to Lafayette, who was a strong opponent of slavery, Madison attempted to explain the mood among the convention's slave owners, which had stopped him from going further than he had and proposing eventual emancipation. Their morbid and violent disposition against any such discussion had made it impossible, Madison wrote, "And I scarcely express myself too strongly in saying that any allusion . . . to the subject you have so much at heart would have been a spark to a mass of gunpowder."[45]

For Madison, the convention was a bitter experience on two counts. First, he had always insisted that important decisions about government should be left in the hands of the elite, who would make rational and principled judgments balancing the contending ambitions of the mass of people. The Virginia convention put the lie to his theory of government. As Madison acknowledged to Lafayette, the elite of the community had taken

part, but they had behaved like ordinary self-centered citizens, squabbling
mightily among themselves to advance their own ambitions at the expense
of one another. Madison's other great disappointment arose from his colleagues' refusal to budge on the question of slavery, a direct result of the
Virginia aristocracy's intellectual and moral selfishness. When the delegates
had gathered, Madison still clung to the mistaken notion that in their hearts
many Virginia leaders wanted to end slavery. Thus, when he pleaded with
them to treat blacks in accordance with the highest principles and to accept
their slaves as something akin to junior members of their own families, he
was urging the assembly not only to affirm the moral strength of the
American character but to carry out its own deepest convictions. Instead,
eastern slaveholders continued to treat blacks as mere property and would
take them into account only as a measure of wealth, for which the owners
should be given an added share of representation. This intransigence, which
blocked even a token gesture toward more humane treatment for blacks, was
a crushing blow to Madison's hope that slavery might disappear through the
good offices of the slaveholders themselves.

When the convention ended, Madison returned to Montpelier with a
heavy heart. Recognizing that he had failed "to promote a compromise of
ideas between parties fixed in their hot opinion by . . . local interests," he no
doubt felt, as he once quipped, that he had managed to outlive his own influence. His adversaries were much younger men, who for partisan reasons
ridiculed rather than respected him and dismissed his opinions, ignoring his
illustrious history and the wisdom of his youth. Temporarily they had won
the battle, and the convention's questionable settlement brought outward
calm to Virginia, but within eighteen months, in August of 1831, the peace
was shattered by the fulfillment of every Virginian's worst fears: an organized slave rebellion, which came in the form of the Nat Turner insurrection,
taking the lives of nearly sixty whites and, in its aftermath, resulting in the
death of over one hundred blacks.[46]

Many Virginians had been looking over their shoulders for years nervously
anticipating the arrival of someone like Turner, a fearless, self-possessed black
leader charismatic enough to inspire open defiance among the slaves. After
the Turner uprising, the question for many Virginians became how many
potential rebels were hiding in their midst—not necessarily bold warriors
like Nat Turner but enigmatic kitchen workers or brooding house servants
who might poison their food or steal upon them and catch them unawares.

If Turner had managed to accomplish nothing else, he had cranked up the blood pressure of white Virginians and robbed them of the ability to get a sound night's sleep. A sense of panic spread through the white community, affecting even the legislature, which began formally debating the significance of Turner's rebellion and questioning slavery's future in Virginia.

To some it seemed that the time had come for the state to rid itself of an institution that had grown increasingly dangerous, and in fact the Virginia House of Delegates passed a compromise resolution calling for emancipation, though only at some unspecified, distant time. The majority of representatives were not ready to surrender so easily, however, and they answered their troubled colleagues in two ways: by maintaining that slavery functioned as a positive good—one that southerners should never let go, because their well-being depended on it—and by insisting that northern radicals were responsible for Turner's reckless violence and that the South's slaves, contented and happy when left on their own, needed to be sealed off from outside agitators.

Virginians had already been shocked by the distribution in Richmond of the radical David Walker's *Appeal . . . to the Coloured Citizens of the World* to blacks to take up arms, and only a few months after Turner's insurrection William Lloyd Garrison's abolitionist newspaper, *The Liberator*, began publication. Many became convinced that an army of wild-eyed northern radicals hell-bent on the destruction of southern society had them under siege, and they embarked on an aggressive campaign to defend slavery and solidify southern resistance to the revolutionary madness emanating from up North. On the heels of the legislative session that took up the Turner insurrection, Thomas Roderick Dew, an economics professor at William and Mary College, published his *Review of the Debate in the Virginia Legislature of 1831–1832*, the first of a flood of assertive proslavery arguments that appeared over the next thirty years.[47] Dew dismissed Virginia's emancipationists as "chimerical philanthropists deluded by splendid but unworkable visions." Slaves represented property, he insisted, and the rights of slaveholders needed to be guarded at all costs because property was the keystone of civilization. Governments had been formed to provide the possibility of happiness by securing the ownership of each individual's belongings. Dew urged Virginians not to panic over the Turner uprising and embrace ill-considered antislavery sentiments. The revolt was certainly unfortunate, he agreed, but he also urged people to keep in mind that Turner had led the only massacre in Virginia history. For the South, slavery represented a valuable asset, and Virginians needed to focus on ways to constructively maintain it, rather than indulge in wishful thinking about how to end it. Emancipated blacks would never be incorporated into American society, Dew prophesied, because they carried an indelible mark that no amount of time could erase. Without whites to govern them, "the animal part of [their nature] gains victory over the moral"; thus, rather than freeing their slaves, whites had to strengthen their control or face the staggering reality of many more Turners bloodying the pages of southern history.

Only a month before the Turner rebellion, Madison had expressed his fears that men on both sides of the Mason-Dixon line had lost any realistic sense of how dreadful the consequences would be if they failed to sustain a compromise on slavery: "If the states cannot live together in harmony under the auspices of such a government as exists, and in the midst of blessings such as have been the fruits of it, what is the prospect threatened by the abolition of a common Government, with all the rivalships, collisions, and animosities inseparable from such an event?" Madison now was in his eighties, but his intellect remained acute, and a young English writer, Harriet Martineau, who visited Montpelier, found him to be a charming "little person wrapped in a black silk gown, a warm gray and white cap upon his head, blessed with an uncommonly pleasant countenance and a particularly lively manner of speaking." For all the pleasure that seeing Madison gave her, however, Martineau was most impressed by his inexhaustible faith, his belief that "a well-founded commonwealth may . . . be immortal . . . because the principles of justice in which such a commonwealth originates never die out of the people's heart and mind. This faith shone brightly through the whole of Mr. Madison's conversation except on one subject." Only on the question of slavery had his faith wavered, and on that subject Madison admitted that he was "almost . . . in despair."[48]

Throughout his life, Madison had devoted himself to establishing and protecting the great American experiment of self-government, working tirelessly to bring the nation together through patient reasoning and compromise, but he also understood the threat that slavery represented to America's stability. Madison never doubted that the South's insistence on keeping slaves had the potential to destroy the Union, and he had vainly hoped that at some point southerners would choose the moral high road and end slavery themselves. The Virginia constitutional convention, the growing stridency of northern abolitionists, Nat Turner's rebellion and the reaction it provoked: all these suggested that the slavery question was beginning to spin out of control and the chance for a rational solution to the problem based on mutual concessions by the North and South was growing more and more remote. And as if things were not bad enough before the Turner insurrection, the growing proslavery resolve it engendered seemed sure to make the situation worse. Northerners and southerners were moving in opposite directions, and Madison feared that the combination of pride and resentment would overwhelm the dictates of prudence.

Although he believed that the South had to solve the slavery problem, Madison felt inclined to blame the North for the growing rift between the regions, because Garrison and his sympathizers had been allowed free rein to incite the nation against slavery. Unfortunately, the South's response to the excitement over abolition had produced deplorable effects, as southerners met one form of extremism with another. Abolitionism encouraged southerners to imagine slavery as not only a constitutional right but a useful endeavor and was responsible for the arrest of the emancipation movement and the rise of men like Dew, who not long after the publication of his response to the Turner rebellion had become president of William and Mary. Before the advent of the abolitionists, Madison complained, no Virginia professor would ever have defended the moral advantages of slavery.[49]

In his last years, Madison had to face the melancholy prospect that his dream of a stable Union was fading and might never be realized. Personally, he still held about a hundred slaves, and like Washington and Jefferson before him, he saw them as an economic burden draining his slender resources; their needs forced him to sell parcels of his best land. To Harriet Martineau, Madison observed that "the whole Bible is against negro slavery; but . . . the clergy do not preach this, and the people do not see it."[50] Coming from Madison, who for so long had been the nation's apostle of reason, this seems an odd observation, perhaps reflecting the depth of his despair. Was Madison reaching out for a higher moral authority because he had lost faith that reason would ever be strong enough to deliver men from themselves? Surely in the last days of his life the younger generation of American leaders badly disappointed him, for they seemed to have repudiated the idealism of the Revolution and appeared ready to risk the union of North and South rather than sacrifice their own interests for the common good.

*   *   *

Clearly there were powerful social forces at work on Washington, Jefferson, and Madison making it difficult for them to oppose slavery. As members of the Virginia elite, tremendous pressures existed for all three men to support, or at least not to attack, the southern labor system. As one plantation owner explained, for a man to consider freeing his slaves was like setting fire to his own building knowing that his neighbors' houses would also be destroyed. Besieged by outsiders, slave owners had taken on an "us against them" mentality, and though it remained marginally acceptable, as an expression of one's humanity, to bemoan slavery and favor some vague form of emancipation in the distant future, any concrete proposal calling for action represented a breach in planter solidarity that the community viewed as treasonous. Additionally, all three men lived well, enjoying a degree of luxury that would have been impossible without the labor of slaves; thus on a purely personal level they no doubt felt reluctant to act decisively against slavery. As Madison himself admitted, his desire as a young man to obtain a decent and independent livelihood had led him to accept his position as a slave owner rather than to repudiate slavery on moral grounds.

"There is not a man living, who wishes more sincerely than I do, to see a plan adopted for the gradual abolition" of slavery, Washington claimed, a sentiment echoed almost exactly by Jefferson: "Nobody wishes more ardently to see an abolition, not only of the trade, but of the condition of slavery." Still, even when opportunity handed solutions to them, all three refused to step forward and align themselves with even relatively mild anti-slavery activities. At the conclusion of the Revolutionary War, Lafayette wrote to Washington proposing that they "unite in purchasing a small estate where we may try the experiment to free the Negroes, and use them only as tenants," in hopes that Washington's influence would turn their example into a general practice. In his reply, Washington seemed to favor the scheme but suggested that they put off going into the details until they met face-to-face. Sixteen months later, Lafayette visited Mount Vernon, and though we have no record of his conversations with Washington, the usual assumption is that the two men discussed Lafayette's idea but Washington balked at going forward. Within two years, Lafayette had acted on his own and carried out his plan in South America, establishing a model plantation in the French colony of Cayenne, which ultimately failed; but he remained an active spokesman for abolition throughout his life, though the subject virtually disappeared from his correspondence with Washington.[51]

Both Jefferson and Madison had experiences similar to Washington's, in which each was asked to lend his name to a private experiment in emancipation. For Madison, the opportunity to ally himself with one of these utopian ventures came in the 1820s, when Lafayette introduced him to a young Scottish heiress, Frances Wright, who had toured the United States and written a book praising the nation's commitment to equality, justice, and freedom. Wright proposed creating a community in which slaves would be taught vocational skills and paid a regular wage that would enable them to buy their freedom after a period of five years. Acquiring property in Tennessee, she set out to establish a model farm, Nashoba, and wrote to Madison, soliciting his support. Madison responded with polite skepticism, praising Wright's dedication but offering no more than passive interest, while reminding her that prejudice against the physical appearance of blacks precluded their ever gaining entrance to white society. As he wrote to Lafayette a year later, he admired Wright's genius and spirit of benevolence but believed that her plan to give blacks economic independence was misdirected. Emancipation had never been just an economic problem, Madison said. If it were, he pointed out, it could be solved easily by the government's purchasing all female slave infants at their birth and immediately manumitting them, which after a period of a little more than forty years would make every black newborn free, based on the condition of its mother.[52]

A few years earlier, in 1814, Jefferson had been approached in much the same fashion by Edward Coles, Madison's personal secretary. As a student at William and Mary, Coles had been inspired by Jefferson's antislavery rhetoric and had developed a passionate hatred for the southern institution of bondage, privately vowing never to own slaves. When his father died and left him ten blacks, he resolved to leave Virginia and take them to Illinois, where he wanted to establish them as freedmen with farms of their own. Addressing Jefferson as the "revered father of all our political and social blessings," Coles exchanged letters with him, suggesting that it was Jefferson's duty, given his philosophy and outlook, to exert his influence in arousing public sentiment to end slavery. Though Coles represented just the sort of younger leader Jefferson had hoped would appear, when asked for his support he quickly declined. Coles was a welcome voice, Jefferson replied, but he himself was too old and tired to get involved.[53] Instead of support, Jefferson offered Coles a place in his prayers and a healthy dose of advice reflecting the pessimism of his old age. Like most Virginians, Jefferson routinely opposed the freeing of adult slaves, and he warned the younger man about their inability to take care of themselves, adding that free blacks quickly became pests in society because of their idleness. He offered Coles a better alternative: to stay at home and reconcile himself to Virginia and its unfortunate state of affairs. Over time, Coles might succeed in enlisting other Virginians in the war against slavery, if he would "become the missionary of this doctrine [and] insinuate and inculcate it softly but steadily." Promoting emancipation while making sure not to offend anyone was similar, of course, to the ambivalent path Jefferson himself had traveled over the preceding thirty years.

Though none of the three would willingly declare himself an active enemy of slavery, it would be a mistake to think that slavery did not deeply trouble Washington, Jefferson, and Madison, and that at least part of them would not have applauded its demise. The three men struggled with frustration and contradiction, recognizing the moral depravity of slavery but effectively prevented from taking any decisive action against it. Washington's eleventh-hour attempt to put himself on the side of emancipation represented a desperate personal solution to the dilemma of slavery; for Jefferson and Madison, the problem loomed larger than that. Rather than on their individual souls, both men focused their attention on the fate of the nation. The suffocating paradox in which white Americans had placed themselves has been noted: With the exception of only the most rabid slave-owning southerners, they could not help but recognize that slavery represented a moral abomination, but they also believed with equal conviction that emancipation provided no answer because America was meant to be a racially pure society reserved strictly for whites. By 1790, the black population had surpassed 700,000, however, and within ten years it would exceed the 1 million mark.

What possible alternatives were available to whites? Either they could surrender their view of themselves as specially chosen moral exemplars, try to keep an exploding Negro population under their thumb, and remain a nation that sanctioned the sin of slaveholding; or they could give up their dream of a homogeneous, purely white society, end slavery, and become a multiracial nation. White people needed, at nearly any cost, a third alternative that would enable them to escape from the dead-end paradox that slavery had left them with—a radically different plan of action that would not only abolish the practice of keeping slaves but guarantee America's racial purity.

CHAPTER 5

FREED BLACKS: THE HEART OF THE DILEMMA

Be their industry ever so great and their conduct ever so correct, whatever property they may acquire or whatever respect we may feel for their character, we could never consent, and they could never hope to see . . . free blacks or their descendants visit our houses, form part of our circle of acquaintances, marry into our families, or participate in public honours or employment.

—FEDERALIST ROBERT G. HARPER, 1818

In 1792, Jonathan Edwards the younger, in a rare attempt to face the issue of slavery head on, addressed the Connecticut Abolition Society on the subject of America's future and questioned whether blacks and whites would ever be able to live in harmony with one another. With a moral intensity that typified the Puritans of a hundred years earlier, Edwards insisted that in any shared future between the races, whites had to face the fact that "their posterity will infallibly be a mungrel breed."[1] Rejecting the continuation of slavery as morally unthinkable, Edwards argued that whites were left with only two choices: "To balance their accounts for the injury which they have done" to blacks, whites either had to take them "into affinity with themselves, giving them their own sons and daughters in marriage, and making them and their posterity [their] heirs," or desert America entirely and leave "all their houses, lands, and improvements to [the blacks'] quiet possession and dominion." To Edwards, the radical injustice of slavery demanded a radical recompense, but he also made clear which option whites must choose. Intermarriage might raise the Negro's color "to a partial whiteness, whereby a part at least of that mark which brings on them so much contempt will be wiped off," but for whites, "the mixture of their blood with that of the Negroes" would be a solution "inconceivably more mortifying than the loss of all their real estates." As outlandish as the idea seems, Edwards maintained that whites had to accept responsibility for their sins and indemnify blacks "at the cheapest possible rate" by surrendering the continent to them.[2]

Perhaps more than any of his contemporaries, Edwards managed to look beneath the surface and recognize the bitter struggle raging in the hearts of his countrymen. The future teemed with possibilities. Americans had not only been singled out by God to accomplish great things but they had been given an earthly paradise in which to prosper and multiply. But by 1790, white Americans held seven hundred thousand black souls in bondage, casting a dark shadow over all their good fortune; worst of all, they could see no conceivable way out of their predicament. What could be done? Intermarriage and the transformation of the white race into a "mungrel breed" of mulattoes was unthinkable—but so was Edwards's conclusion that whites should simply walk away and abandon not only the land that God had given them as a manifest sign of his approval but their identity as an independent people with a special destiny.

The removal of blacks, however, and the establishment of colonies for them in Africa, the Caribbean, or some other distant location represented a way out of their dilemma—a far-fetched idea requiring more willing suspension of disbelief than common sense normally allowed, but one that perfectly fitted the nation's needs. Slavery would end and blacks would be free, but rather than remain in the United States they would be removed to a distant land, where they could establish their own independent communities and toil for themselves.

The dream of removal and colonization was nothing new. The impulse to deal with blacks by simply making them disappear seems to have occurred to people soon after the first Negroes arrived in the colonies, perhaps while their status as heritable property remained unclear and a number of them managed to gain their freedom after a period of indenture. If some whites found slaves in chains morally upsetting, nearly everyone had trouble with blacks exercising a newfound freedom and roaming the countryside, and by 1691 the desire to get rid of them had been incorporated into Virginia law in a statute requiring masters who freed slaves to pay for their transportation out of the colony within six months.

A generation later, the idea surfaced again, this time in New England, a region with few blacks but enough resentment for people to begin questioning how to eliminate them. In 1701, in reply to Samuel Sewall's *The Selling of Joseph*, John Saffin, another member of the Massachusetts provincial court and also a slaveholder, defended the practice of keeping slaves, though he admitted they represented a great inconvenience. Saffin expressed his readiness to give them up, but only under certain conditions: First, masters would have to be reimbursed out of the public treasury; and second, all blacks needed to be sent out of Massachusetts or the remedy would end up worse than the disease. Saffin's ideas suggest that soon after whites encountered blacks, idle talk about sending them away became common.

Jefferson was a relatively early convert to a formal scheme of colonization, which he discussed in the *Notes on the State of Virginia* as part of his plan to revise the state's legal code. Jefferson proposed that all slaves born after the new code went into effect be emancipated, educated at public expense, and sent to colonize some unnamed but appropriate location. The loss of their labor could be minimized, he wrote, by sending "vessels at the same time to other parts of the world for an equal number of white inhabitants; to induce whom to migrate hither, proper encouragements will be proposed."[3] Like Jefferson, Madison first endorsed colonization in the 1780s, when he voiced his approval of a scheme put forth by William Thornton, a Quaker physician who wanted to establish a community on the west coast of Africa for freed slaves. Such an asylum might encourage southerners to manumit blacks, Madison wrote, and thus it seemed "the best hope yet presented of putting an end to the slavery in which not less than 600,000 unhappy negroes are now involved."[4] As time passed, Madison clarified his views on colonization and came to believe that if it were to succeed, several conditions would have to be met. First, colonization would need to proceed gradually, in order to minimize the disruption of the southern labor force. It would also have to be agreed to not only by planters but by slaves, many of whom regarded America as their home and would only reluctantly leave for an uncertain future in Africa. And finally, if it were to be expanded to include the great majority of blacks, it would need to be conducted by the federal government, which would be able to bear the substantial expense through the sale of the nation's rich inventory of uninhabited western lands.[5]

In 1816, Robert Finley, a wealthy Presbyterian minister from Basking Ridge, New Jersey, saw additional advantages in sending free blacks and freed slaves to Africa: Christianized Negroes might turn other Africans toward God, and they would also achieve a degree of equality in Africa that they could never enjoy in America. Like Madison, Finley believed that to succeed, the plan would have to be carried out under the auspices of Congress, which could exert jurisdiction over the entire nation. Finley went to Washington to plead his case and managed to convince Henry Clay, the Speaker of the House, to convene a meeting of government officials interested in the idea. After hearing Finley out, Clay told the assembly that there could be no nobler cause "than to rid our country of a useless and pernicious, if not dangerous part of its population, [while at the same time] spreading the arts of civilized life, and . . . [redeeming] from ignorance and barbarism . . . a benighted quarter of the globe." With Clay as champion of the idea, the American Society for Colonizing the Free People of Color in the United States came into being, attracting many distinguished political and civic leaders, including the secretary of the treasury and future president, Andrew Jackson.

By 1822, the American Colonization Society, as it came to be known, had raised enough money to buy land at Cape Mesurado on the west coast of Africa and send a white Congregationalist minister, Jehudi Ashmun, to organize a colony. He lasted only months and was succeeded by a black minister, Ralph R. Gurley, who named the settlement Liberia. The same year, small bands of freed slaves began crossing the ocean to their new African home. In the meantime, the colonization society located its chapters in slave states, aiming its program squarely at attracting the support of slave owners. Clothed in humanitarian rhetoric, colonization—at least as the southern founders of the society conceived it—was an oblique attempt to eliminate the troublesome influence of free blacks. Northerners ridiculed the southern plan almost immediately. Questioning its narrow focus, the *New York Courier* mocked the society's unexpected tenderness and humanity toward free blacks and freedmen. "Why was not something proposed for enslaved blacks?" the paper's editor wondered, observing that the scheme's true intent was to minimize the dangerous mixture of slaves and free blacks, who represented a bad influence likely to lead them astray. The possibility of getting rid of black Americans certainly appealed to many northerners, but why consider only those who had been emancipated? Why not carry it further and cleanse the nation of every black face, slave or free?

As the American Colonization Society spread North, its message

changed, winning it approval from many of the national church organizations and state legislatures. Though its representatives in the South still confined their meetings to the problem of free blacks, northern spokesmen
shifted their attention to a general removal of all blacks, including southern
slaves, and in 1824 the Ohio legislature passed a resolution calling for a
national plan of gradual emancipation. Under the state's scheme, all children
of slaves would be freed at the age of twenty-one, as long as they agreed to
leave for Africa. Acknowledging that "the evil of slavery is a national one," the
resolution maintained that "the people and the States of this Union ought
mutually to participate in the duties and burthens of removing it." The legislature promised a generous offer of compensation to slaveholders, which
some northerners found troubling, insisting that sinners ought not to receive
compensation for their iniquities. The Ohio legislature sent the measure to
the other state governments and to the national Congress, and while most
northern states quickly approved the plan, the Deep South—Georgia,
Alabama, Mississippi, Louisiana, and South Carolina—voted as a solid bloc
to reject it. As Georgia governor George Troup complained, once again the
South had been subjected to enormous outrages caused by outsiders med-
dling with its domestic concerns. Southerners needed to be on their guard,
he cautioned, because the national government appeared willing to "lend
itself to a combination of fanatics for the destruction of every thing valuable
in Southern life."[6] Convinced that northerners would go to any lengths to
destroy slavery, southerners suspected that the colonization idea had been a
northern plot all along, purposely misrepresented to lower the South's guard
and strip it of its slaves.

Madison's analysis of colonization revealed many of the scheme's sticki-
est problems. As one might expect, there was little enthusiasm, particularly
in the North, for the national government to assume the project's cost, and
Madison himself knew how difficult it could be to convince blacks to cooperate in their own removal; he told Harriet Martineau that he had finally
given up and sold a particular group of slaves because they had recoiled in
horror when he raised the possibility of emigration to Liberia. But colonization faced an even greater difficulty because no one seemed to be able to
make the numbers work. Calculating the cost and counting the available
ships and the number of crossings they could make annually, the sum of all
the blacks that could be removed never approached the number of Negroes
born each year. As Harriet Martineau noted, in the first eighteen years of its

existence the colonization society had managed to remove "only between two and three thousand persons, while the annual increase of the slave population in the United States was upward of sixty thousand."[7] Rather than making progress, it seemed that every year colonization was taking another giant step backward in the effort to remove blacks from the United States.

In 1832, Thomas Dew sent Madison a copy of his defense of slavery, asking for his reaction, particularly in relation to colonization, which Dew dismissed as a stupendous folly. Madison responded in two ways: He wrote to Gurley, now secretary of the colonization society, accepting his offer to become the group's president, which publicly linked his name to the society, something he had previously refused to do; and he answered Dew with a long letter explaining his continuing support for the removal of blacks. Madison thanked Dew for his thoughts and acknowledged that his pamphlet contained numerous obstacles to ridding the country of slavery; nevertheless, he asserted, he could never agree with Dew's conclusions. Though he concurred that slaves almost universally preferred their present condition to the uncertainty of an unknown land, this resulted from the slaves' distrust of white reports, which had presented a favorable picture of Africa. Once blacks had firsthand information from members of their own race, their suspicions would vanish, Madison maintained, and their aversion to removal would disappear.

Madison went on to to concede the existence of nearly every problem Dew had raised; but still, he argued, wasn't it better to search for solutions to the difficulties accompanying colonization than to accept the continuing existence of slavery or an "extinguishment of it by convulsions more disastrous in their character and consequences than slavery itself"? For Madison, supporting colonization, no matter how slim its chances of success, represented the only alternative available. Even if the scheme collapsed completely, he added, America would still be better off for having attempted it. "An entire failure," he wrote, would "leave behind a consciousness of the laudable intentions with which relief from the greatest of our calamities was attempted in the only mode presenting a chance of effecting it."

As often happened, Madison recognized more clearly than his contemporaries what was at stake for the nation. Americans really had no choice but to support colonization, even though the impossibility of the idea appeared crystal clear. In 1862, in the dark days of the Civil War, Harriet Martineau recalled her visit nearly thirty years earlier and Madison's desperate battle to keep despair at bay. "Rather than admit to himself that the South must be laid waste by a servile war, or the whole country by a civil war," she wrote, "he strove to believe that millions of negroes could be carried to Africa, and so got rid of."[8] There was no need, she added, to comment on the weakness of such a hope.

Unfortunately, most of the Liberian pioneers did not fare well, many falling ill with fever or dying in violent clashes with the indigenous population. Even so, in 1827 the American Colonization Society sought a congressional appropriation to underwrite the transportation of blacks to Africa. The Maryland, Ohio, and Virginia delegations voted for it, but Georgia and South Carolina argued so strongly against using public funds for colonization that the bill failed. By 1831, after nearly ten years in business, the ACS had managed to send only a few shiploads of emigrants to Liberia, in part because of continuing opposition from northern blacks, who adamantly resisted the call for the removal of the entire black population, which at that point had reached about 2 million, 320,000 of whom were free. Still, whites continued to support colonization, and only a year later every state except Rhode Island and South Carolina had an ACS chapter. In some southern states, like Virginia, where the focus remained on freedmen, state governments still favored the plan, taxing free Negro males between the ages of twenty-one and fifty-five to help pay for removal.

Colonization provides a key to understanding the confused reaction that white Americans had to slavery in the years between the Revolution and the Civil War. While the Revolution had affirmed the special destiny of the American people, the Constitution melded America into a single political state, suggesting northerners and southerners had an equal share of the responsibility for slavery. Americans could never again view slavery in quite the same way, and their new attitudes heightened the differences between the regions and destroyed the frail consensus that had existed before 1787. The immediate question, of course, was what could be done? Colonization stood out as the lone proposal to end slavery which had a wide following throughout the first half of the nineteenth century, and even beyond the Civil War. Though the scheme now appears bizarre, and we may wonder how anyone could have believed it could succeed, there is no denying its attraction.

In 1851–52, when Harriet Beecher Stowe first published *Uncle Tom's Cabin* in serial form, it became an immediate sensation, and the book version that followed sold over three hundred thousand copies in its first year of publication, an unheard-of figure at the time. No one could rightly call Stowe, who believed she had written in partnership with God, a radical abolitionist, but her description of the cruelty and inhumanity of the southern plantation became a clarion call that aroused antislavery sentiment throughout the North. Though today's readers often overlook her advocacy of colonization as a permanent solution to slavery, the novel's conclusion urges Christians to "receive" slaves as their brothers, educate them "until they have attained to somewhat of a moral and intellectual maturity, and then assist them in their passage" to Africa. *Uncle Tom's Cabin* enjoyed enormous success because Stowe captured the latent feelings of her vast audience. The widespread support for the draconian alternative of colonization revealed the nation's discomfort and disaffection with itself as it struggled to find a way to escape the dilemma posed by the blacks in its midst, more and more of whom were becoming free.

Whites could easily look down upon Negroes categorized as slaves. Slaves were inferior beings, plain and simple. But increasingly America's white citizenry had to confront a new and troubling presence—emancipated Negroes—and deal with them for what they were, independent beings with black skin. And if slaves were difficult for nonslaveholders to accept, growing numbers of black men and women over whom no one had direct control were nearly impossible for every class of whites to abide, whether they held slaves or not. Alien in their habits, their features, their desires—their lives—free blacks represented a threat to the good order of American society on two counts. Not only were they likely to inspire discontent and rebellion among blacks still in chains, but as free members of the communities where they lived, many believed they had a right to claim a share of the economic and social rewards that previously were available only to whites. Segregation begins here, with emancipated Negroes.

Before the Revolution, barely two thousand free blacks lived in Virginia, Jefferson's friend St. George Tucker estimated. By 1790, however, the national figure had risen to sixty thousand, and seventy years later, on the eve of the Civil War, nearly a half million free blacks lived in various small towns and cities across the nation, about 55 percent of them in the South.[9] The rapid increase in the number of free blacks had been set in motion by the

Revolutionary War. The most noteworthy effect of Lord Dunmore's inflammatory proclamation was the unprecedented opportunity it presented for blacks. Dunmore's offer struck at the heart of the master-slave relationship by opening a number of avenues of escape, giving blacks a greater sense of hope than at any time since their arrival in America. Dunmore not only promised freedom for those who would fight for the British, he also forced the Americans to respond by accepting black troops on essentially the same terms. Taken together, these actions, which separated slaves from the immediate control of their masters and put them on the move throughout America, encouraged others simply to run away, flee to a new locale, and claim they were members of the expanding population of free blacks.

Though the statistical evidence is meager, somewhere between eighty thousand and one hundred thousand slaves left their masters during the Revolutionary War.[10] Virginia was said to have lost thirty thousand slaves, perhaps 65 percent of them men between the ages of fifteen and forty, who represented about half of the South's best agricultural workers and artisans. Throughout the war, blacks continued to flock to the English. When the British surrendered at Yorktown, they stipulated that any American property in their possession would be returned to its rightful owners. To the Americans, of course, this meant the recovery of all runaway slaves, but when it came time for the British to depart—from Savannah and Charleston in 1782 and New York in 1783—they refused to hand over many of the blacks who had joined them during the war, saying that they had promised the runaways freedom and returning them to their former masters would be a violation of public faith. Though Washington personally tried to intercede, the British carried off about fifteen thousand American blacks in the final stages of their evacuation, including a substantial contingent of slaves forced to depart with their Tory masters. Earlier, the British had sent away thousands, and some American officers and their French allies also refused to surrender blacks who had run away and joined them during the war. Black escapees spread not only throughout the nation but around the world. The majority ended up in the Caribbean, particularly in Jamaica and the Bahamas; the British took others to Europe, the Atlantic coast of Florida, South America, Canada, and Nova Scotia, and even resettled a few in Liberia.

For many whites in the North, blacks had represented an ideal solution to the shortage of troops in the Continental Army. With the promise of unconditional freedom, slaves were induced to enlist for the duration of the war, and even more important to individual slaveholders, army service could be avoided altogether by sending a slave as a substitute in exchange for freedom.[11] "No regiment is to be seen in which there are not negroes in abundance," because a slave could "take the field instead of his master," a Hessian officer noted in 1777.[12] By the war's end, a significant number of blacks had spent six or seven years under arms and had become the professional core of the Continental Army's foot soldiers, leading the charge in many of its major battles. When the war ended, so did the most pressing logic for setting blacks free, but at least for a few years a residue of Revolutionary enthusiasm survived, enabling the surge in black freedom to continue. Though some masters tried to renege on their earlier agreements and reenslave bondsmen who had been promised emancipation, several states passed legislation guaranteeing the freedom of blacks who had served as substitutes for white conscripts, going as far as to accept their testimony as evidence against their masters. Moreover, after independence many states adopted new constitutions with relatively liberal attitudes toward freed blacks. Even in several of the southern states, legislatures briefly granted them the right to own property, to testify against whites, to travel freely wherever they chose, and to vote—despite the fact that the federal government still had not conferred the status of citizenship on them. That discrepancy became moot, however, as whites quickly tired of blacks roaming the countryside free from supervision. Soon the rights they had been granted during the Revolutionary period vanished in a cloud of second thoughts and legislative remorse. As the war ended, Maryland lawmakers set the tone for their southern colleagues, resolving that any slaves manumitted in the future would not be entitled to the rights of free men and thus creating two classes of emancipated blacks within the state: those who had been freed before 1783 and, at least theoretically, could vote, hold office, and testify against whites; and those who gained their freedom later and were denied these rights.

In the North, the goodwill that blacks had earned, coupled with a continuing faith in the Revolutionary creed of natural rights, spurred a movement to outlaw bondage altogether, and over the next twenty years, this so-called First Emancipation brought an end to slavery throughout the northern states.[13] In New England, the abolition of slavery began soon after the start of the Revolution and by 1784 had won approval in every state. In 1777, Vermont, a territory with few slaves and no national connection with the

South, drew up an independent constitution explicitly prohibiting bondage of any kind. Among the already established states, the process leading to emancipation was less forthright. In Massachusetts, though strong sentiments existed to end slavery, leaders like John Adams also felt considerable apprehension that such a move might jeopardize relations with the South. In a remarkably straightforward speech at the state's constitutional convention, the Reverend William Gordon, chaplain of both houses, blasted his colleagues for their refusal to emancipate blacks and allow them to vote. Their stance proved that whites cared about "their own rights only, and not those of mankind" when they called for freedom from oppression. Is it honest, he questioned, "to exclude *freemen* from voting . . . because their skins are black, tawny or reddish? Why not disqualified for being long-nosed, short-faced, or higher or lower than five feet nine?" As for the claim that blacks were not Americans, he continued, most of them had been born in this country, and those who were not "were forced here by us, contrary, not only to their own wills, but to every principle of justice and humanity." Massachusetts should write its new constitution to show the South that blacks stood solidly side by side with whites as citizens, he insisted, or frankly admit that color, and color alone, set them apart as foreigners.[14] Gordon's speech fell on deaf ears, and the convention delegates chose instead the familiar ambiguity of the Declaration of Independence, granting freedom and equality to all men but avoiding any specific statement on slavery.

With no clear direction coming from the convention, the responsibility to decide the status of Massachusetts's slaves devolved to the courts. The constitution of 1780 fostered a series of freedom suits, including the case of Quok Walker, who claimed that he had been promised emancipation by a previous owner and thus could not be held in bondage by his current master. When the lower courts agreed with Walker, his owner carried the matter to the state's chief justice, William Cushing, who also decided in Walker's favor. Though slavery had been tolerated in the past, Cushing conceded, the new constitution effectively abolished it by granting to blacks rights and privileges totally antithetical to the institution of slavery.[15] Cushing, in effect, had taken on the cruel contradiction undermining the argument of the Declaration and—at least, at the state level—resolved it on the basis of principled consistency.

Similar hesitation preceded abolition in the other New England states. Like the Massachusetts document, the New Hampshire constitution of

1783 included a broad guarantee of the universal right to freedom, but in practice the status of blacks remained unsettled until 1789, when the legislature removed slaves as taxable property from the state's revenue rolls. Leaders in Rhode Island and Connecticut also proceeded cautiously, finally agreeing in 1784 to gradual schemes that allowed owners to keep their adult slaves but freed children at the end of their minority. Though abolition had begun hesitantly in New England, it gathered strength rapidly. More than 13,000 slaves resided there at the beginning of the war; by the first national census, in 1790, the number had been reduced to 3,763, and twenty years later it had fallen to 418, all of them elderly blacks living in Rhode Island and Connecticut.[16]

In the lower northern states—Pennsylvania, New Jersey, and New York—efforts to end slavery met with greater resistance. New York had the largest slave population in the North, and taken together the bondsmen in the three states represented a substantial accumulation of wealth that slaveholders had no intention of surrendering. In addition, the war had thrown the middle states' antislavery leaders, the Quakers, into disarray. As pacifists, the Friends had refused military service and been widely criticized as Tory sympathizers, forcing them to retire from public life. Nevertheless, Pennsylvania managed to pass a gradual abolition bill in 1780. Though the measure had to withstand several court challenges, it survived, guaranteeing that all blacks born in Pennsylvania in the future would be given their freedom at the age of twenty-eight.

Abolitionists in New Jersey and New York had a more difficult time. With the exception of a New York law that emancipated slaves who had enlisted with their masters' blessing, neither of the two states made any effort to abolish slavery until after the war's end, and well into the 1790s the issue remained unresolved but hotly debated. For every person who believed that slavery represented a national sin, another pinned the problem on the abolitionists themselves and accused them of engaging in nothing more than criminal attacks on personal property. Like Pennsylvania, both states eventually passed gradual abolition laws, New York in 1799 and New Jersey in 1804, freeing the children of slaves after a period of service—up to twenty-eight years for males and twenty-five for females. In both states, the key to passage turned on indirect compensation meant to insure that owners would suffer no loss for slaves who would be emancipated. Under the system of abandonment, owners surrendered enslaved one-year-olds to local authorities as paupers, and the overseers of the poor would return them to their owners as bound servants, with a monthly stipend paid by the state for their maintenance.[17] The system was an attractive inducement to win the support of slave owners, who could look forward to some twenty years of labor in addition to more than $1,000 in regular payments before granting a slave freedom. After a period of only a few years, however, both states repealed the plan, which had proved to be prohibitively expensive, consuming as much as 30 percent of New Jersey's state budget in 1808, the last year of its existence.

Though many whites conceived of emancipation as a long-term process that compensated owners and ignored adult slaves, blacks made remarkable progress from 1776 well into the 1800s. Indeed, they experienced their own revolution, which began in the shadows of the larger national conflict. Before the war, Virginia had very few free Negroes, petitioners to the Virginia legislature affirmed in 1805. These free Negroes were normally either the mulatto children of white mothers, whose color determined their offspring's status, or men and women too crippled or too elderly to work. They barely survived, with no community of their own and little or no provision made for them by whites. The disruption of the war, military service, and the subsequent emancipation of slaves in the North radically altered the free black population. War veterans, runaways, and a flood of vigorous young people, the beneficiaries of gradual emancipation—combined with a healthy birthrate—made free blacks one of the fastest-growing and most troubling segments of American society. Clearly, if blacks set freedom as the prize, they had taken a great step forward.

Still, they could not surmount a major barrier. While many blacks had won their freedom, acceptance in white society remained as elusive as ever. Writing in 1818, the Maryland Federalist Robert G. Harper spoke for most whites: "Be their industry ever so great and their conduct ever so correct, whatever property they may acquire or whatever respect we may feel for their character, we could never consent, and they could never hope to see . . . free blacks or their descendants visit our houses, form part of our circle of acquaintances, marry into our families, or participate in public honours or employment."[18] By 1810, Maryland had more emancipated blacks than any state in the Union: free blacks made up nearly 10 percent of its population. "Beggarly blacks have been vomited on us" from the Deep South, whites complained to the state legislature; but even in the North, black freemen quickly became unwelcome.[19] "The popular feeling is against them—the interests of our citizens are against them," a Philadelphia Quaker noted in 1831. "The small degree of compassion once cherished toward them . . . appears to be exhausted. Their prospects either as free, or bond men, are dreary, and comfortless." To Fanny Kemble, the English actress who married Georgia planter Pierce Butler but grew to be a bitter foe of slavery, free blacks were "marked as the Hebrew lepers of old . . . not slaves indeed, but they are pariahs; debarred from all fellowship save with their own despised race."[20]

Initially attracted to the egalitarian doctrine of white churches, particularly the Baptists and Methodists, free blacks soon discovered that whites had no intention of allowing them to worship as equals. Some churches used benches painted black and white to designate the separation of the races. Even the Quakers, among the nation's most active and best-organized supporters of blacks, were reluctant to accept them as partners in faith. In the first half of the eighteenth century, a rift had opened among the Friends between the diligent and the pious—Quaker merchants who saw the African trade as an economic opportunity and those who viewed the importation of human beings as a moral outrage. But by 1774 the Quakers had completed a conscientious and thorough self-cleansing, threatening to disown members who continued to trade slaves and requiring masters who still held blacks to treat them with the same humanity afforded white servants and to free them at the earliest opportunity. The Quakers not only attacked slavery among their own members but also dedicated themselves to aiding and protecting runaway slaves and campaigning for universal emancipation. When Benjamin Franklin became president of the Pennsylvania Society for the Abolition of Slavery, it counted fully 75 percent of its members as Quakers. In the South, their efforts naturally were more circumscribed; nevertheless, they deserve credit for bravely carrying the banner of antislavery into hostile territory. Often, they limited themselves to lobbying for better treatment for bondsmen, but individual Quakers, like the wealthy Virginia planter Robert Pleasants, pledged themselves to the moral reconstruction of southern slave owners. Pleasants delivered the Friends' message not only in words but through his actions, experimenting with privately freeing slaves in defiance of state law and treating his bondsmen as tenant farmers, allowing them the freedom to roam at large, for which he was attacked by his neighbors and heavily fined.[21] All in all, the pacifist Quakers proved to be ubiquitous and remarkably persistent in the early antislavery movement.

But despite their place in the movement's vanguard, most Quakers had little stomach for mingling with blacks, even those who had been freed by their own members. Above all else, the Society of Friends ran an exclusive brotherhood, intent on guarding the purity of their own lives, and they gently but firmly persuaded blacks to seek religious communion elsewhere. Not surprisingly, a number of the unswervingly righteous members of the society objected, pointing out, as Joseph Drinker did in 1795, that Christ had not said "there should be one fold of Black sheep and another of white."[22] Internal pressure gradually forced a degree of change, and Quakers slowly admitted blacks to their meetings, but kept their numbers small and often made them feel unwelcome, even as full-fledged church members. In the 1830s, Sarah Douglass, a black schoolteacher and lapsed Quaker, recounted the experiences she underwent in Philadelphia's Arch Street meeting hall as a child. She remembered having regularly been seated on a separate bench, with a church member at each end to stop other whites from inadvertently sitting next to her. At one meeting in particular, she recalled, she heard "five or six times . . . this language of remonstrance addressed to those who were willing to sit by us, 'This bench is for the black people. This bench is for the people of color.' And oftentimes I wept, at other times I felt indignant and queried in my own mind are these people Christians." Sarah Douglass gave up on Quaker fellowship, but her mother still attended meetings and—just as in the past, Miss Douglass noted—she often had "a whole long bench to herself." There were no indications that misgivings about blacks had declined among the Friends; on the contrary, it appeared to Miss Douglass that the more "intellectual and respectable" blacks became, "so in proportion do the disgust and prejudice of the Quakers increase."[23]

Undaunted by the near-universal rejection, a Delaware black named Richard Allen, who had been born a slave and converted by Methodists at the age of seventeen, taught himself to read and write and purchased his own freedom with money earned on the plantation. In the 1780s, Allen began preaching locally, to both blacks and whites, and earned for himself a fairly wide audience. He then moved to Philadelphia to attract larger black crowds. There Allen founded, around 1787, the Free African Society, an association to provide aid and spiritual comfort to blacks. After being tossed out of one white church after another, he established the Bethel Church for Negro Methodists in 1793 and that year was ordained a Methodist deacon. In 1814, he and a group of other blacks succeeded in establishing their own denomination, the African Methodist Episcopal (AME) Church. Though whites ridiculed and sabotaged their efforts at religious independence, destroying several of their earliest churches, Allen and his followers managed over the years to control the AME Church themselves. The congregation appointed Allen the church's first deacon in 1816, and he led the church against sometimes violent interruptions until his death in 1831.

Similarly, when African Americans found themselves unwanted in white schools, black leaders established their own. In 1811, Christopher McPherson, a successful black businessman who liked to refer to himself as "the first son of Christ," hired a white teacher, Herbert Hughes, and set up a night school in Richmond, Virginia, for freemen and slaves whose masters approved their attendance.[24] Students spent three hours each night studying grammar, arithmetic, geography, astronomy, and other subjects, and McPherson suggested that blacks ought to establish similar institutions throughout the United States. White leaders took a different view, insisting that it was impolitic and improper for such an institution to exist, and they outlawed the school, driving Hughes out of town and locking up McPherson in the Williamsburg Lunatic Asylum.

Black education fared no better in the North. In the 1830s, in Connecticut, a relatively liberal state, two incidents occurred that demonstrated northern resistance to African American book learning. In the city of New Haven, antislavery leaders wanted to establish a black college, where students could gain a mechanical or agricultural education while also pursuing classical studies. A raucous town meeting scotched the idea as destructive to the best interests of the city, a decision supported by several northern newspapers, which noted that an enlarged "unwholesome colored population" would only undermine the city's morals and scare away prospective students for Yale and the local girls' school.[25] Around the same time, in Canterbury, a short distance from New Haven, a second, more vicious reaction followed when a young Quaker schoolmistress, Prudence Crandall, agreed to accept a black girl at the boarding school she had established. Parents protested and withdrew most of the white children. Not to be deterred, Crandall enlisted the support of abolitionist leaders throughout the North and reopened the school exclusively for "young colored Ladies and Misses." A town meeting voiced its unqualified disapproval, and when the school opened, local residents poisoned its well with manure, merchants refused to sell their goods to Crandall, and the citizenry insulted and humiliated her students whenever they went out in public. The state legislature passed a law prohibiting institutions "for the instruction or education of colored persons who are not inhabitants of this state," and a Connecticut court eventually tried and convicted Crandall, concluding that blacks were not citizens and thus not protected by the federal or state constitutions. Shortly afterward, the school closed and the gallant Miss Crandall left Connecticut and moved to Illinois.[26]

It may seem surprising that whites, who constantly decried the idleness, drunkenness, and dishonesty of free blacks, would have taken such a dim view of black efforts at self-improvement, but in fact prosperous and respectable blacks, intent on bettering not only their own lives but the condition of their race, troubled whites far more than aimless, dissipated exslaves, who confirmed the prevailing belief in black inferiority. Though some whites warned that emancipation would set free a "vast Multitude of unprincipled, unpropertied, vindictive, and remorseless Banditti," who would terrorize the nation with "Rapes, Murders, and Outrages," calmer minds recognized that the steady advancement of righteous, upright African Americans represented a far greater threat.[27] St. George Tucker noted in 1805 that when Dunmore had issued his proclamation at the start of the Revolution, blacks "sought freedom merely as a good; now they . . . claim it as a right."[28] Black advancement, even in the form of laudable self-help, needed to be resisted because it was the first step toward the destruction of white America. Give slaves freedom, they ask for equality. Allow them to enter business and public life, they will demand social and personal contact with whites. Accept them on a level of intimacy, and you set the stage for racial amalgamation.

Such fears may seem hysterical today, but in the nineteenth century they were the commonly held views of most of the white population. A father would rather consign "his daughter to a silent tomb," a Maryland legislator observed, "than see her led to the hymenial altar by the hand of a colored man."[29] At its deepest level, the white response to "freenegroism," as the emancipation of blacks came to be called, was a graphic reassertion of what whites had known all along: that blacks could never be accepted in American society. Whites focused on a number of specific, practical problems created by the presence of free blacks. In the North, working people quickly grew to resent the appearance of blacks in a labor pool they had reserved for themselves. As a group of petitioners told the Connecticut legislature in 1834, competition with "the most debased race that the civilised world has ever seen" had deprived the white man of employment and "forced [him] to work for less than he requires."[30] The usual southern complaint, on the other hand, arose from the planters' fear that blacks beyond their control might disrupt the slavery system, a class paranoia that by the 1830s infected even Madison, who confided to Harriet Martineau that the plantations of Virginia were "surrounded by vicious free blacks, who induce thievery among the negroes, and keep the minds of the owners in a state of perpetual suspicion, fear, and anger."[31]

More than anything, however, southern whites complained most bitterly about their loss of immediate control over emancipated blacks. Though owners liked to portray slaves as members of their families, they could scarcely overlook the built-in tension in the relationship—particularly after so many blacks had demonstrated their questionable loyalty by disappearing during the Revolutionary War. White confidence in the faithfulness of their bondsmen had been badly shaken, and slave owners grew deeply suspicious of free blacks, worried not only that they harbored ill feelings toward their former masters but that they represented a fifth column, with freedom to travel from one place to another and spread discontent wherever they visited. Anxious about their security, southern whites acted to control the movement of free blacks so that they could keep track of where they were and precisely what they were up to.

In 1793, Virginia prohibited the immigration of emancipated blacks from other states, and Georgia and North Carolina soon followed with laws of similar intent, the one insisting that blacks show proof of their good character or face deportation, and the other demanding a bond of £200 before a black was allowed to enter the state. In 1806, Virginia ordered newly manumitted slaves to leave the state within six months, which caused Kentucky, Maryland, and Delaware to enact legislation banning their entry. Throughout the South, restrictions on interstate migration severely limited the ability of emancipated blacks to travel freely, but the states still needed to deal with the problem of movement within their borders.[32]

Generally, manumission laws required emancipated blacks to carry freedom papers, which could easily be forged, rendering them almost meaningless. In 1785, North Carolina embarked on a more serious scheme to control free blacks in towns and cities where they congregated, requiring new arrivals to register with local authorities and wear shoulder patches inscribed with the word "FREE." In 1793, Virginia installed a similar plan—minus the badges—that forced blacks to list themselves in the local "Register of Free Negroes" along with a description that included name, age, sex, identifying marks, and a record of the individual's manumission.[33] By 1810, most southern states had enacted not only registration laws but a whole series of statutes restricting black freedom, including prohibitions against vagrancy, which gave local authorities the power to sell indigent blacks back into slavery.

The North enacted less onerous legal restrictions, but only because it had far fewer emancipated blacks, so whites could control them in less formal ways. After touring both regions, Tocqueville noted with some surprise that racial prejudice appeared "stronger in the states that have abolished slavery than in those where it still exists."[34] The South, with its draconian laws, no doubt feared blacks more than the North, which was content to control its black population through custom and community pressure. In most places in the North, no laws prevented miscegenation or barred blacks from the polls. Instead, public opinion exerted powerful pressure on them not to intermarry or to vote. At one time or another, almost every northern state debated the question of free movement for emancipated blacks. Northerners wanted desperately to protect themselves from a flood of former slaves, whom they regarded as the South's responsibility. A committee of Massachusetts legislators warned in 1821 that growing restrictions in the South were bound to drive free blacks to places like New England, which would increase the ranks of the dependent poor, take jobs from whites, and upset the order and tranquility of northern communities.[35]

Newer western states like Ohio (1803), Indiana (1816), and Illinois (1818) explicitly barred blacks or insisted that they post a prohibitive bond, from $500 to $1,000, before being allowed to enter. Both Illinois and Indiana included provisions against black immigration in their constitutions, which, as one Indiana citizen explained, showed the "strong and irresistible tendency of the American mind to accomplish a separation of the two races."[36] Ohio required blacks to post a $500 entry bond but seldom enforced the ordinance until 1829, when the civic leaders of Cincinnati decided that its black population had grown alarmingly and gave blacks thirty days to pay up or leave the state. A delegation of Cincinnati blacks departed for Canada seeking asylum, after requesting an extension of the deadline to allow them time to prepare for resettlement. Canada agreed to accept the immigrants, but

white mobs in Cincinnati grew impatient and attacked the black sections of
the city, destroying property and terrorizing the inhabitants. As the local
Gazette later reported, about two thousand blacks ultimately left for Canada,
including the most "sober, honest, industrious, and useful portion of the colored population."[37]

The problems presented by free blacks stemmed from their ambiguous status in American society. The 1790 Naturalization Act had made it clear that
America would welcome only whites as new citizens: no others need apply.
Constitutional and statutory law, at both the federal and the state level,
embodied the same principle; but having gained their freedom, the burgeoning population of emancipated blacks appeared perilously close to pos-
sessing citizenship, which threatened to confound the definitive categories of
slave and free and scramble the national distinction—that is, the color
line—between black and white.

Confused and more than a little defensive, white leaders sought to carve
out a third, necessarily contradictory designation—one in which blacks
would be free, no longer slaves, while at the same time denied the liberties
that whites routinely expected and enjoyed. Black codes, updated specifically
for emancipated blacks and depriving them of the right to vote, to hold
office, and so forth, represented one of the measures used to shunt free
blacks into a racially defined limbo, formulated specifically to insure that the
nation remained white and that any Negroes, even though born free, would
never become citizens.

Most of the states continued to search for ways to legally separate free
blacks from whites well past midcentury, even going so far as to consider
whether free Negroes could be restored to servitude, as Maryland slave owners did in 1858, when they assembled to debate the future of the state's siz-
able population of what they deemed nonproductive blacks.[38] Today we
assume that the federal government has responsibility for establishing criteria for national citizenship, and that its power could have been invoked to
protect blacks in the individual states, but prior to the Civil War this was
never the case. Though it outlines specific qualifications for the presidency,
the Senate, and the House, the Constitution is mute on the issue of citizenship, suggesting instead—in Article IV, Section 2, which guarantees recip-
rocal "Privileges and Immunities to the Citizens of the several States"—that

each state had the power to set its own standards to decide which of its inhabitants were eligible to be United States citizens.

Even if the federal government had possessed the right to determine national citizenship, however, there is nothing to suggest that this would have made any difference. Again and again, in legislative, bureaucratic, and judicial actions, federal authorities affirmed the national will, treating emancipated blacks as a separate and inferior group of inhabitants, whose identity derived from their color rather than their free status. In 1810 Congress excluded blacks from the U.S. Postal Service. Gideon Granger, Jefferson's postmaster general, had sent Congress a confidential message some years earlier, expressing the administration's opposition to black mail carriers. Just as enabling blacks to become literate represented a potential threat, so did employing them in the postal service, Granger warned. Anything that afforded African Americans "an opportunity of associating, acquiring, and communicating sentiments, and of establishing a chain or line of intelligence ought to be avoided."[39] Congress eventually accepted Granger's recommendation and passed legislation mandating that "no other than a free white person shall be employed in conveying the mail." Ten years later, it authorized the voters of Washington, D.C., to choose a white city government and enact black codes to control the city's blacks, both slave and free. The State Department also regularly refused to grant passports to emancipated blacks, unless they could prove that they enjoyed the rights of free citizens in their home state or had a white person with sufficient influence sign their petition.[40]

Though the question of black citizenship remained unresolved until 1857, when the Supreme Court ruled against it in *Dred Scott*, a series of attorneys general, the nation's chief legal officers, consistently agreed that free blacks failed to qualify as citizens. In 1821, William Wirt, who served in both the James Monroe and John Quincy Adams administrations, advised Virginia officials that emancipated blacks in the port of Norfolk could not act as captains on trading vessels, because federal regulations limited the senior command position to American citizens. Citing Virginia statutes denying emancipated blacks fundamental civil rights, Wirt argued that the state had chosen to exclude them from citizenship and thus they failed to meet the federal requirement for ships' captains.[41] Wirt's ruling applied only to Virginia, but its reasoning guided subsequent federal decisions for thirty-six years, until *Dred Scott*.

In 1843, Attorney General Hugh Legare attempted to clarify federal policy governing the rights of emancipated blacks to acquire public land. As
things stood, citizens could claim a homesteading right to the newly opened
western territory, a prerogative denied to aliens. Addressing the riddle of
black rights in the public domain, Legare agreed with Wirt that blacks were
not citizens, but neither could they be classed as aliens. The plain intention
of federal law was to exclude foreigners from the acquisition of public land,
and though blacks were not citizens they ought to be granted homesteading
rights as members of a previously unrecognized class of permanent inhabitants. "Free people of color are not aliens," Legare insisted. Instead, they
"enjoy universally . . . the rights of denizens" and their "civil status" was "that
of a complete denizenship."[42]

Though Legare's successors rejected his reasoning, dismissing it as an
erroneous argument engendered "by a generous disposition," his effort to
establish a separate category for emancipated blacks may well represent the
most perceptive contemporary analysis of one aspect of America's racial
predicament in the first half of the nineteenth century. Though we have been
taught to think of slavery as the single great dilemma of the antebellum period,
whites had also begun to struggle with a second vexing question: the nation's
future as a mixed society. How could white America absorb a significant
population of free blacks who not only were personally repellent but also
threatened to pollute the purity of the white race? Even before segregation
provided an answer in the early years of the twentieth century, the dim
beginnings of Jim Crow and "separate but equal" emerged in Legare's designation of free blacks as "denizens"—a special category of native inhabitants
with rights and privileges of their own, which were consistently inferior to
those enjoyed by whites.

CHAPTER 6

THE RISE OF INTERREGIONAL TENSION

I am in earnest—I will not equivocate—I will not excuse—I will not retreat a single inch—AND I WILL BE HEARD.

—WILLIAM LLOYD GARRISON, 1831

From morning to night, day after day, and week after week, nothing can get a hearing that will not afford an opportunity to lug in something about negro slavery. It is negro in the morning, the poor negro at noon—and at night again this same negro is thrust upon us. . . . I beg, gentlemen, to remember there are some white people in this country, and these white people are entitled to some consideration.

—OHIO CONGRESSMAN WILLIAM SAWYER, 1848

Hostility between the North and the South had remained muted in the Republic's early years, primarily because of George Washington's imposing presence. The nation's first chief executive had inspired deferential awe, giving him remarkable power to govern by example, and characteristically he chose to ignore the slavery question, hoping to allow the constitutional compromise time to take root and grow into established law. In spite of this policy of benign neglect, interregional controversy over the slavery question occasionally erupted. In 1790, when Benjamin Franklin submitted his "mal-apropos" memorial to Congress urging it to consider emancipation, that relatively cordial body of northern and southern politicians turned into a seething cauldron of mutual hostility. Thomas Tudor Tucker of South Carolina accused Franklin of asking

Congress to act in violation of the new Constitution, which threatened to plunge the nation into civil war.[1] After a rapid exchange of insults, a committee dominated by northerners and moderates from the upper South formed to study the powers vested in Congress in regard to the abolition of slavery. The committee's report heartened southerners, for it determined that Congress was prohibited from eliminating the slave trade before 1808 and had no current powers to pass an emancipation act. But the report also concluded that the prohibition against emancipation did not apply to slaves born after the end of the African trade. In other words, in less than twenty years the power to free slaves would gradually begin to accrue to the national government, and the southern states would lose their absolute prerogative to control the future of their bondsmen. Ultimately, the report resulted in no congressional action, but Congress included it in its permanent record despite strenuous objections by most southerners and a few northern representatives concerned by the ill will that the document generated. Of minor importance itself, the report remains noteworthy because it prefigured the overt resentment that would soon overtake the Congress and the nation at large.

In November 1800, after ten years in cosmopolitan Philadelphia, the national government moved to a primitive site along the Potomac. Symbolically, many construed the move as a shift in power away from the commercial, Federalist North in favor of the agricultural, slaveholding South, but northern congressmen had agreed to the move in exchange for the South's approval of the federal government's assumption of state war debts. Many northerners were distressed by the removal of the government to a location where no prohibition existed against slavery and a visitor could observe from the Capitol steps "a procession of men, women, and children, ... bound together in pairs, some with ropes, and some with *iron chains*," mournfully trudging along on their way to the auction block.[2]

A month later, Thomas Jefferson managed to eke out a narrow victory over the incumbent John Adams in the presidential election—an election decided by the representation bonus from the three-fifths compromise. Without the fifteen extra electoral votes derived from slaves, the Federalists—who captured nearly three-quarters of the vote in the North—would have soundly defeated Jefferson's Democratic-Republican Party.[3] Northern leaders groused that the presidency had been stolen due to an undemocratic technicality, delivering the office to a southern planter who believed that the federal government had no power to interfere in the ownership of slaves and that any such attempt was unconstitutional.

Jefferson's presidency started out quietly enough, but in 1803 a historic opportunity presented itself which carried not only substantial personal political risk but the potential to undermine the already shaky constitutional arrangement between North and South. After a final, unsuccessful attempt to restore Gallic hegemony over Haiti, Napoleon abandoned his dream of a colonial empire in the Americas and offered France's enormous, ill-defined holdings west of the Mississippi to Jefferson's envoys for the ridiculously low price of $15 million, about a quarter of which would be paid to U.S. citizens to discharge their claims against France.[4] The vast extent of land, the opportunity to close out any foreign threat to the Mississippi, and the terms of the payment were irresistible. With a stroke of the pen, Jefferson could double the nation's size and reshape its destiny.

Serious questions existed, however, which Jefferson had to rationalize before the sale could be completed. Though he had long believed in the efficacy of local government and the ideal of democracy based on the virtuous yeoman farmer who resolved his problems in a community of neighbors, he was also not immune to dreaming of the United States as a great international power—a "nest from which all America, North and South, is to be peopled."[5] A second problem was the Constitution itself, which made no provision for a situation like the purchase of Louisiana. Having repeatedly stated his commitment to a presidency constrained by constitutional limits, Jefferson found himself in the embarrassing position of needing to carve out a whole new area of power that the founding fathers had ignored. The Constitution contained not a word about the acquisition of new territory, and if Jefferson chose to buy Napoleon's western lands and managed to win congressional approval, he not only would be expanding the size of the nation beyond anything that could be considered a cohesive community, but he also would be violating the constitution by asserting executive and legislative power in an area where none existed.

In the end, legal technicalities gave way to a bargain that was too good to pass up, and the nation acquired the Louisiana Territory, taking an enormous stride in its inevitable expansion to the Pacific. Jefferson excused playing fast and loose with the Constitution by arguing that he had never intended to enlarge the power of his office; rather, Louisiana represented a once-in-a-lifetime "fugitive occurrence," which he had pursued only to "advance the good of [the] country," and he deftly threw himself on the mercy of his fellow Americans "for doing . . . unauthorized what we know they would have done for themselves had they been in a situation to do it."[6]

Fortunately for Jefferson, his political instincts proved flawless. The acquisition of the vast central plains stretching from the Mississippi to the Rocky Mountains was popular, and most Americans rejoiced in the expansion of their nation into an empire—a term Jefferson seized on and regularly employed from that point forward. The nation had not only gained control of the mouth of the Mississippi, creating a host of new economic possibilities for the center of the continent, but had also acquired an enormous amount of land, which opened new—and to some, frightening—possibilities.

In the North, a number of dissenters objected to the acquisition of this new, unbounded domain. Some, like Josiah Quincy, mayor of Boston, recognized the danger that Louisiana posed to the fragile relationship between North and South. The acquisition of millions of acres of western territory, he wrote in a letter to the southern Federalist Oliver Wolcott Jr., former secretary of the treasury, would threaten the Republic by destroying "the political equipoise contemplated at the time of [the Constitution]."[7] Though Congress had managed to craft a provision for the future of the territories east of the Mississippi, it had avoided the question of new acquisitions, perhaps fearing that any attempt to define how they might affect the power balance would ruin the hoped-for agreement.

With the purchase of Louisiana, the looming certainty of several additional states left everyone on edge, unsure of what it meant in relation to slavery. Northerners feared that states in the West would want slaves to make up for their shortage of manpower. A new militancy, matching the obduracy the South had exhibited from the beginning in Philadelphia, crept into northern rhetoric. Without a constitutional amendment to protect the balance of power, the uncontrolled acquisition of the Louisiana Territory would dissolve the North's obligation to remain loyal to the United States, Quincy warned. As it was the right of all states, so it was "the duty of some . . . to prepare for separation, amicably if they can, violently if they must."[8]

Destabilizing the sectional agreement on slavery had never been part of Jefferson's plan, but as an unintended consequence of the Louisiana Purchase it represented the pivotal event that moved the nation onto the high road to civil war. The opening of the West would energize the power struggle between the North and the South, increasing their mutual anger and bitterness as the years passed, but in 1803 it seemed to some southerners, Jefferson included, that Louisiana might offer at least a partial solution to the slavery problem. Convinced that blacks and whites could never live together, Jefferson had advocated some form of colonization for nearly twenty years. Now, with the acquisition of the Louisiana Territory, an opportunity presented itself—one that would not entirely eliminate the imposing black presence in America but would reduce it by spreading blacks throughout a series of new states.

Diffusion, as this plan came to be called, had first been suggested by two Virginians, Republican senator William Giles and professor of law George Nicholas, in 1798, when Congress considered the question of slavery in the Mississippi Territory. Jefferson and his supporters had adopted the idea, and as William Plumer, United States senator and later governor of New Hampshire, noted, it was obvious in the congressional debates over the Louisiana Purchase that southerners wanted "to encrease the means of disposing of [the slaves] who are most turbulent & dangerous to them" and, at the same time, "raise the[ir] price . . . in the market."[9] Diffusion not only would reduce the threat of servile rebellion but promised to spread blacks throughout the West, which would mean more slave states entering the power struggle in Washington on the southern side. Nor did it hurt matters when Jefferson exercised his presidential power over the territories by refusing to allow whites in Louisiana to buy blacks imported from abroad. The prohibition insured that all bondsmen in Louisiana, except those who had lived there under the French and their descendants, would come from the Old South, where their departure would create a less threatening ratio between the races.

In his annual message of December 1806, Jefferson also moved to end the African trade at the earliest possible date.[10] Of all the states, only South Carolina still allowed the importation of slaves from outside the country, and after gauging the strength of their opponents, which included a substantial number of votes from the upper South, even its representatives seemed resigned to the death of the foreign slave trade. Negotiations between the two sides faltered, however, over two questions: first, whether the federal government or the states would dispose of smuggled slaves seized as contraband; and second, which of the governmental entities would regulate the coastal shipping that carried slaves between states. In both cases, southerners objected to the bill that finally passed, insisting that the federal government had invaded the states' right to oversee slavery. Committed to local control, a number of representatives from the upper South who had originally supported the bill now switched sides, making the final vote largely sectional. Though the act lacked any real enforcement procedures and southerners continued to smuggle blacks into the country, at least on paper the North's legislative victory handed the Old South a monopoly on the sale of slaves, ensuring it an uncontested market through which to diffuse its slaves into the West.

States like Virginia and Maryland wasted no time in selling slaves to western buyers, but the effects of diffusion on the political struggle between North and South would not be felt until the federal government began dividing up the Louisiana Territory. Since the 1790s, Congress had adhered to an informal protocol for admission to the Union, an arrangement that kept tension between the two regions at a minimum. States entered the Union alternately, one in the North and one in the South, preserving the balance of power between the sections as the nation expanded: first Vermont (1791), then Kentucky (1792); Tennessee (1796), then Ohio (1803); Louisiana (1812), then Indiana (1816); Mississippi (1817), then Illinois (1818). At last, in 1819, with all the opportunities to create new slave states east of the Mississippi exhausted, Congress had to face the momentous question of expansion in the West. Statehood for Missouri was the immediate issue, and as the House debate on Missouri opened, northerners and southerners viewed one another warily. Though it was above the Mason-Dixon Line, the traditional boundary between slave and free states, Missouri had become home to about fifty-five thousand whites and ten thousand enslaved blacks, and it was generally understood that left to their own devices Missourians would choose to align themselves with the South and become a slave state. When a measure was introduced authorizing the establishment of a state government for the territory, New Yorker James Tallmadge promptly offered an amendment that challenged southern expectations and indicated that northerners were not about to surrender the West without a fight. Tallmadge asked for a prohibition on the further introduction of slavery into Missouri and for the establishment of a plan to emancipate the children of the slaves already living there. As the House reporter recorded in his official minutes, the proposal immediately provoked "an interesting and pretty wild debate."[11] Both northerners and southerners offered a variety of arguments relying on precisely the same source, the Declaration of Independence. Northerners claimed that the nation's original principles had been set aside at the constitutional convention in order to accommodate the South, saddled as it was with the existing system of slavery; but for new states, whose unsettled societies could still be shaped by republican values, Congress was obligated to return to the ideals of the Declaration. Nonsense, southerners replied; it was exactly the principles of the Declaration which demanded that Missourians be allowed to choose for themselves whether their state would be slave or free. What more important principle was there in the nation's founding ideals than the right of self-government? Congress was careening toward an ideological impasse, and that was precisely where their mutual intransigence finally carried them. "A fire which all the waters of the ocean could not extinguish" had been lit, according to the Georgian Thomas W. Cobb, and it could be drowned "only in blood." "An opportunity is now presented," New Hampshire's Arthur Livermore responded, ". . . to prevent the growth of a sin which sits heavy on the soul of every one of us. By embracing this opportunity, we may retrieve the national character, and in some degree, our own." In the House, where the North held a substantial majority, representatives narrowly approved the amendments prohibiting slavery in Missouri and establishing a system of gradual emancipation, but both measures were defeated in the Senate, where a handful of northern Democrats chose party loyalty over antislavery and voted with the South. The two houses declared themselves officially deadlocked; on its first try, Congress had failed to resolve the explosive issue of slavery in the West.[12]

No politician raised the Missouri question again for almost a year. In the intervening months, Congress admitted Alabama as the twenty-second state, restoring the balance in the Senate between slave and free states at eleven each, and established the Arkansas Territory to the south and southwest of Missouri. Meanwhile, Maine announced its intention to break away from Massachusetts and apply for separate admission to the Union. By coupling Missouri's fate with Maine's desire for statehood, the South's bargaining position became much stronger. It could offer northerners a straightforward political quid pro quo to retain the Senate's existing balance: the paired admission of a proslavery Missouri and a new free state, Maine.[13]

At the same time, the North had been weakened in a subtler, less obvious way. When Alabama sought admission to the Union, even James Tallmadge had offered no objection, acknowledging that it would have been next to impossible to deny slavery to an area surrounded by slave states, where 40,000 blacks, a third of the population, already lived and worked in chains. Soon after, when Congress formed the Arkansas Territory, Tallmadge did try to outlaw slavery there but could not find sufficient votes to approve the measure even in the House. With sixteen northern members defecting, southern congressmen managed to stymie Tallmadge and his antislavery supporters, though only by the barest of margins, 89 to 87. The failure of the North to act together on Arkansas signaled a resolve far weaker than it had seemed in the earlier Missouri debates. Even more than Missouri, Arkansas represented an unformed community; only some 1,600 slaves lived there, and it was a perfect opportunity to stop slavery dead in its tracks had the North felt truly committed to halting its western advance. Instead, many northerners apparently viewed Arkansas simply as a western extension of the South. The message appeared plain enough: The North would not hew to its high-minded crusade of national redemption and would focus instead on preserving its own power by insuring that slavery remained confined below the Mason-Dixon line.

And indeed, for northerners the significance of the traditional boundary between the two regions was the crux of the Missouri controversy. The Mason-Dixon line, which followed the Ohio River from the Appalachians, joined the Mississippi at Missouri's southern border, and northerners wanted to preserve the demarcation between freedom and slavery at that same latitude (36°30') across the West. To admit Missouri as a slave state would have breached the time-honored line between the regions, and without it, northerners would lose perhaps their most important guarantee of future security. At bottom, they feared that slavery simply would be too enticing to western settlers and that without a clear and unequivocal line of separation, the West might be transformed into a solid bloc of slave states wedded to the South.

A year earlier, when Missouri had first come before Congress, its future was debated as a classic disagreement over states' rights and the authority of the federal government. Did Missourians have the right to decide for themselves whether or not they wanted slaves, or could Congress put conditions on their admission to the Union, forcing them to give up slavery? Nothing could be mediated between these two extreme positions: to support one meant denying the other. By 1820, however, a number of congressmen, most of them from the South, stepped forward under the pragmatic leadership of House Speaker Henry Clay of Kentucky, seeking a realistic solution to the Missouri stalemate by providing both regions with balancing equivalents. The paired admissions of Maine and Missouri represented one set of matched advantages for the two regions, but the really critical point concerned the 36°30' boundary. Obviously, the South badly wanted Missouri as a slave state, but what equivalent could it offer the North? As it worked out, the South would give an apparently ironclad guarantee, written into the Maine-Missouri statehood bill, forever prohibiting slavery above 36°30' in the remaining territory of the Louisiana Purchase. Initially, northerners balked at even considering a compromise that breached the continuation of the Mason-Dixon line, but ultimately they consoled themselves with the promise of binding assurances from the South that Missouri would be the one and only exception. As John Quincy Adams pointed out, northerners really had no choice. Half the states in the Union supported the Missourians' desire for slaves. Far better, Adams maintained, to accept the southern compromise and focus on restricting the spread of slavery beyond Missouri.[14]

Though southerners had gotten what they wanted—statehood for Missouri—and had engineered the compromise that made it possible, to Jefferson the whole episode represented "the most portentous [crisis] which ever yet threatened our Union," an unqualified disaster that left him depressed and fearful for the nation's future.[15] In a letter to John Holmes of Massachusetts, written a few weeks after the House had approved the Maine-Missouri admission bill, Jefferson observed that the momentous question of Missouri had startled him "like a fire-bell in the night, tolling the knell of the Union." Though Congress had managed to find a momentary solution, it represented "a reprieve only, not a final sentence. . . . A geographical line, coinciding with a marked principle, . . . once conceived and held up to the angry passions of men, will never be obliterated," Jefferson warned, "and every new irritation will mark it deeper and deeper."[16] Clay and his southern cohorts had shied away from the states' rights argument, a principle with which the vast majority of them surely agreed but which left them no bargaining room with the North. To Jefferson, however, their willingness to settle the Missouri debate on practical terms instead of insisting on the underlying principle of self-determination had sold out the nation's most fundamental value, the bulwark protecting the South's freedom to practice slavery. The new southern leaders, Jefferson feared, had become as contemptible as the northern "dough-faces," turncoat members of Congress who voted on the basis of expediency and often supported legislation that worked against the interests of their constituents at home.[17] Jefferson believed, correctly, that the real issue in Missouri turned on political power and that the Federalist leaders of the North had outwitted the South. "The Missouri Question is a mere party trick," he insisted to Charles Pinckney. Having failed to dominate the South in the three decades since adoption of the Constitution, "the leaders of federalism ... have changed their tack and thrown out another barrel to the whale."[18] Southerners had been enticed by the prospect of gaining Missouri to grant the North the right to limit the expansion of slavery, which Jefferson saw as a preliminary step to outlawing it entirely. His tone wavering between hysterical and elegiac, Jefferson wrote to Holmes that he would now return to the bosom of Abraham believing that the sacrifices of the Revolutionary fathers had been "thrown away by the unwise and unworthy passions of their sons." The modern generation's thoughtless indifference to the God-given right of self-determination represented an "act of suicide on themselves, and of treason against the hopes of the world."[19]

What came to be known as the Missouri Compromise had an overwhelming impact on Jefferson, arousing the old warrior from his retirement and forcing him, at last, to make a choice. For nearly forty years, he had avoided committing himself, unwilling to take a stand either as a champion of antislavery or as a true Virginian. Now, believing that the South faced imminent danger, Jefferson moved to implement a radical scheme he had long harbored—to train southern minds in a southern university.

Though Jefferson had always questioned northerners' ability to empathize with the South, Missouri confirmed for him that their crass, mercantile natures prevented them from understanding either the southern way of life or its aristocratic principles of honor and loyalty. He became convinced that southerners had to watch out for themselves, by creating their own leaders to protect what he believed were *the* authentic American values. As a young man, Jefferson had formulated plans for democratic, tax-supported schools that would give Virginia the chance "to bring into action that mass of talents which lies buried in poverty . . . for want of the means of development."[20] But the Virginia legislature had repeatedly failed to provide money for a system of primary schools, and now Jefferson focused all his efforts on the creation of a state university. To Jefferson's mind, Missouri had demonstrated how woefully unprepared fledgling southerners were to appreciate or defend their homeland. For the young gentlemen of Virginia, a stay in the North at an elite university like Harvard or Princeton had become an expected rite of passage, in which they put the finishing flourishes on their formal education and established friendships that would last throughout their lives. Unfortunately, from Jefferson's point of view, many of them also came home full of opinions and principles in opposition to those of the South, espousing the malevolent northern vision of a "single and splendid government . . . founded on banking institutions and moneyed corporations."[21] He viewed the situation as akin to a state of war: "if not arrested at once [it] will be beyond remedy"; and he appears to have declared what amounted to a personal state of emergency.

Jefferson got state approval for his university from the General Assembly in 1819 and then set out to acquire funds. He also drew up the architectural plans himself, oversaw the construction, and recruited five faculty members from Europe, which he thought had the best professors. He opened what he called his "academical village" on March 7, 1825, having supervised not just the new school's construction but its curriculum. At least in the fields of law and politics, in which the youthful members of Virginia's slaveholding class needed to be trained, freedom of thought and openness to a variety of viewpoints would not be tolerated. Only the true constitutional doctrine of states' rights and local control over slavery would be taught, and Jefferson himself became the grand inquisitor, choosing faculty that he felt certain would never stray from orthodoxy and going as far as to rewrite classical texts, such as Hume's *History of England* and Blackstone's *Commentaries*, in order to "republicanize" them by removing the faintest whiff of heresy.[22] "Enlighten the people generally," Jefferson had written many years earlier, "and tyranny and oppression . . . will vanish like evil spirits at the dawn of day." Nevertheless, at the end of his life, stripped of his faith that the Revolution had ushered in a new era of human history and doubting whether the nation would survive beyond his death, Jefferson chose to curtail "the illimitable freedom of the human mind" in order to teach southern orthodoxy to the young men of Virginia. Left with only his lifelong attachment to his native state, Jefferson capitulated, surrendering his belief in free speech and open discourse to a narrow, misguided local loyalty—his last, fading connection to the world of his youth.

*   *   *

Jefferson had been correct in believing that the Missouri Compromise in no way solved the larger issues of slavery's future and the division of power in the national government. Disillusioned with their partnership and its future, northerners and southerners angrily eyed one another, awaiting the next skirmish. Southerners, certain that they were being persecuted, drew together, retreating into a fortress mentality, which they hoped would isolate their slaves and preserve the southern way of life. The proslavery argument took on a new, more aggressive tone, and began to identify northern treachery rather than servile rebellion as the primary threat to the South. Unlike the wretched hirelings of New England, whom no one really cared for, slaves ranked among the happiest people in the world, slaveholders insisted, with all the comforts of life provided for them by their faithful owners.[23] Naturally content with their carefree existence, slaves became rebellious only when free blacks or northern agitators took advantage of their innocence and stirred them to hate their masters. After Missouri, the South's fixation on isolating its bondsmen increased tenfold, as slave owners tried to close off every possible threat that might incite them to rebellion.

In 1822, the specter of Haiti reappeared in Charleston, South Carolina, in the person of Denmark Vesey, an ex-slave who had bought his freedom with money he won in a lottery.[24] The South Carolina militia arrested Vesey and charged him with being the leader of what many in the nineteenth century considered the most elaborate insurrectionary plot ever devised by American slaves.[25] Proud of his heritage and unwilling to bow to any man, Vesey had been the property of a sea captain in the slave trade, and in nearly twenty years of service he had traveled the world, learned several languages, and educated himself not only through practical experience but by learning to read and devouring books of every kind, including one on the Saint-Domingue revolution in the 1790s. Even after he had given up seafaring, he still sought out blacks from the ships in Charleston Harbor, anxious for news from whatever ports they had visited around the world. After winning his freedom, Vesey had taken up the carpenter's trade, and Charleston's blacks recognized him as a natural leader—stern, impeccably honest, and intent on persuading his fellow blacks to suffer no more indignities at the hands of white people.

According to witnesses at his trial, Vesey's scheme had grown into a broad conspiracy, enlisting thousands of local slaves, including an armorer who went about secretly turning farm implements into pike heads and bayonets, as well as a secretary who wrote to the president of Haiti asking for assistance in the coming insurrection. Vesey planned first to attack arsenals and armories on July 14, 1822, the anniversary of the French Revolution and the darkest night of the month, and then lay siege to the entire city. Betrayed by an informer, a house servant, the plot fell apart before the middle of June, and in less than a week Vesey and the other prominent conspirators—nearly 100 members of the black community, all of whom "were considered faithful, honest fellows"—went on trial for their lives. Ultimately, 27 were acquitted, 34 were transported, and 35 hung, Vesey among them, within a few weeks—proof, as the *Charleston Times* noted, that South Carolinians would not hesitate to mete out swift, merciless justice to "the Jacobins of the country . . . the anarchists and the domestic enemy; . . . the barbarians who would . . . become the destroyers of our race."[26] South Carolina leaders feared a broader conspiracy, reaching who knew where—to the North? perhaps to Haiti?—but surely aided and abetted by black seamen, whom they suspected of holding advanced views and who were perfectly positioned to serve as couriers for the antislavery movement. State legislators had already passed laws limiting the movement of free blacks and preventing those who left the state from returning; now they moved to eliminate another potential threat by passing a series of Negro Seaman Acts, aimed at prohibiting African American sailors from communicating with local African Americans. Straightforward in their intent, the laws required that all blacks serving on ships calling at South Carolina ports be arrested and jailed until their captain gave the signal to weigh anchor and depart. A problem naturally arose from the reaction of the ships' owners and captains, who not only lost the use of their crew members while in port but also had to pay the costs of their confinement. At least one English trading vessel had nearly its entire crew locked up and the British government filed a formal protest in Washington in 1824, which was referred to Attorney General William Wirt. Though Wirt concluded that the statute violated the Constitution, South Carolina defied the federal government, stubbornly refusing to give up imprisoning black sailors, and the practice became law in several other southern states. In 1831, after Andrew Jackson had replaced John Quincy Adams as president, a new attorney general, John Berrien, whose sympathies lay with the South, reversed Wirt's decision, affirming the "general right of a State to regulate persons of color within its own limits." In Berrien's view, South Carolina had not only the right but an obligation to protect its citizens from the "moral contagion of rebellion."[27]

Berrien's ruling represented a small victory at a moment when the nerves of southern whites were badly frayed. The Nat Turner insurrection broke out in Virginia in the same year, following closely on two other unsettling developments in the North: the appearance of the free Negro David Walker's *Appeal in Four Articles*, which exhorted blacks to rise up against their oppressors, and the initial publication of William Lloyd Garrison's antislavery newspaper, *The Liberator*, both of which were suspected of inciting Turner and his followers. The inviolable fortress that slaveholders hoped to erect appeared dangerously porous, threatened even by the U.S. mail, which, despite its lily-white carriers, had brought the "fanatical" mischief of Walker and Garrison into the South. The first issue of *The Liberator* appeared on New Year's Day, 1831, and contained what amounted to a declaration of war against southern slaveholders: "I *will* be as harsh as truth. On this subject I do not wish to think, or to speak or write, with moderation. . . . I am in earnest—I will not equivocate—I will not excuse—I will not retreat a single inch—AND I WILL BE HEARD."

Garrison's newspapers, letters, and pamphlets, the Washington, D.C., *National Intelligencer* complained, represented crimes as "diabolical" as poisoning the South's water supply.[28] In Charleston, a white steward on a ship out of Boston had already been sentenced to a year in prison and fined $1,000 for circulating copies of Walker's *Appeal* in the city, and southerners hoped to discourage antislavery sympathizers from using the postal system with the threat of similar punishment. In the District of Columbia, Georgetown passed a municipal ordinance sentencing free blacks to thirty days in jail and a $25 fine for carrying *The Liberator* out the door of a post office; in Columbia, South Carolina, a local vigilance committee offered a substantial reward for the identification of anyone distributing Garrison's paper or other inflammatory material.[29]

As the slaveholders' determination to close off the South grew, an antithetical resolve to open it to the message of abolition gathered strength in the North. Though true abolitionists would never represent more than a minuscule percentage of the northern population, an antislavery movement had finally developed that matched the South in its fervor and commitment to a set of principles from which it was unwilling to retreat. Harriet Martineau noted that the American Colonization Society, if it had accomplished nothing else, had "originated abolitionism" by arousing free blacks and white opponents of slavery.[30] Certainly, abolitionists had existed before the society's founding, particularly among the Quakers, but it was a fertile spawning ground for the new breed of militants that appeared in the 1830s. Garrison himself had begun his antislavery career in the colonization movement, signing on as an assistant to Benjamin Lundy, editor of *The Genius of Universal Emancipation*, a one-man newspaper favoring a gradual program of manumission for slaves and their subsequent removal to Africa. Similarly, the Tappan brothers, Arthur and Lewis, wealthy New York businessmen, had flirted with colonization before finding their true calling as allies of Garrison and financial angels for the radical abolitionists. Their money was critical in transforming Lane Theological Seminary in Cincinnati into a hotbed of radical action, where several young men who would later become abolitionist leaders first encountered Garrison's ideas. Many had favored colonization but were converted through a series of seminars led by the noted abolitionist Theodore Weld, eventually one of Garrison's closest allies.[31]

In 1832, Garrison published his only book-length work, *Thoughts on African Colonization*, a denunciation of the colonization movement as a fraud inadvertently aiding slave owners. The American Colonization Society claimed that it wanted to end slavery, Garrison observed, but its scheme raised so many difficulties that it made the idea appear impossible. In place of the interminable gradualism supported by colonizationists, Garrison proposed *immediatism*: that abolitionists should strive for nothing less than the unconditional immediate emancipation of all slaves and the complete acceptance of blacks into American society. Working through the government was a waste of time because the Constitution was so bloodied and corrupt that it could never be reformed. The only answer, Garrison insisted, was to make the nation realize that slavery was not merely a sin but the worst of sins, and to establish "in the hearts of men a deep and widespread conviction of the *brotherhood of the human race*."[32]

A year later, in 1833, in order to consolidate the New England and New York branches of the abolition movement, Garrison founded the American Anti-Slavery Society in Philadelphia—the city, he pointed out, where the Declaration of Independence had been signed. The New Yorkers, led by the Tappan brothers, tended to be more restrained than Garrison and his followers—particularly on the issue of immediatism—but a compromise was reached by including in the society's manifesto statements conceding that under the Constitution the federal government had "no right to interfere with . . . the slave states" and that the society would never "in any way, countenance . . . resorting to physical force." In its "Declaration of Sentiments," written by Garrison himself, the American Anti-Slavery Society also pledged to wage an aggressive campaign to wear down and ultimately defeat slaveholders through moral persuasion. Agents of the society would be ceaseless in lifting up "the voice of remonstrance, of warning, of entreaty, and rebuke, and will circulate unsparingly and extensively antislavery tracts and periodicals."[33]

From the abolitionists' point of view, Garrison had founded the American Anti-Slavery Society at the perfect time. By 1835, printing had undergone a technological revolution, making the mass production of written material faster, easier, and cheaper than anyone could have dreamed ten years earlier.[34] With new steam-driven presses, stereotyped plates, and inexpensive rag paper, all underwritten by the Tappan brothers, the Anti-Slavery Society set out to swamp the country with pamphlets, tracts, newspapers, handkerchiefs, emblems, and even candy wrappers carrying the abolitionists' message. In the previous year, the society had circulated 122,000 pieces of literature; in 1835 the number rose to more than a million, and in July alone the society mailed 20,000 pamphlets and tracts throughout the South.[35] As one might expect, southerners quickly became enraged. Denouncing the abolitionists as irredeemable incendiaries, they took their case to the great majority of northerners, who had little active interest in reforming the South and were sure to be uncomfortable with anything that threatened civil disruption. Southerners insisted that responsible northerners had an obligation to police their own community and "beat down the firebrands and false philanthropists" among them either legally or extralegally, by doing whatever it took to silence them. The Virginian John Tyler, who would later become the nation's tenth president, publicly blasted the Anti-Slavery Society: "Arthur Tappan [and] Mr. Somebody Garrison might enjoy patting the greasy little fellows [slaves] on their cheeks and giving them lovely kisses" but their endless provocations threatened to revive the Missouri issue "in a new and terrifying form" and "blow the union into atoms."[36]

Aroused northerners took the South's complaints seriously and put together numerous public meetings, questioning what could be done. In the end, however, while northerners willingly offered military aid to quell slave rebellions, they were reluctant to abridge free speech and avoided taking any concrete action to silence Garrison and his followers." 'Words, words, words' are all we're to have, and they will not at all restrain Tappan and his associates," a disappointed southerner wrote after attending a meeting in New York. Needless to say, the outcome satisfied no one and only increased the two regions' mutual frustration and division. To southerners, it seemed that northern leaders ignored their serious concerns, dismissing them with "set phrases and taffety xpressions [sic]," while northerners took offense at the South's "braggart style" and insisted that the "right to discuss the question of slavery, or any other question under heaven [cannot] be denied."[37]

As they had earlier, southerners turned to local post offices to stem the flow of abolitionist literature, but this time they garnered far greater support, not only from postmasters in individual southern stations but from the head of the service in Washington and from President Andrew Jackson, himself a Tennessee slaveholder. Southern postmasters refused to deliver abolitionist mail, claiming that handling it endangered postal buildings and individual mail carriers by eliciting violent reactions from supporters of slavery. Amos Kendall, the postmaster general, agreed, acknowledging that while no one had a legal right to exclude abolitionist literature from the mail, southerners were responding on the basis of a higher law of self-preservation, which made their actions a form of patriotism rather than a crime. Jackson went further, ruing the abolitionists' destructive behavior and calling on Congress to pass a law prohibiting "under severe penalties, the circulation ... of incendiary publications, intended to instigate the slaves to insurrection."[38]

The Anti-Slavery Society had a second major project on its action agenda, a petition drive aimed at wiping out slavery in the District of Columbia. By 1836, three years after its founding, the society had doubled in size and established more than five hundred local chapters spread across fifteen states. Its members, both men and women, began actively buttonholing their neighbors, asking them to sign petitions to make the nation's capital free. They intended their petitions for northern representatives in Washington, who then would present them to the House, where it was hoped that the hundreds of thousands of signatures would force a debate on the question. The abolitionists were anxious to confront slavery in Washington because many northerners felt a lingering resentment that slavery in the seat of the national government had been presented to them as an accomplished fact. Southerners stood firm in their belief that the District, having been carved out of Maryland and Virginia, remained more southern than northern, and they demanded that Congress refuse to accept the petitions. Acceptance, they argued, would violate the constitutional guarantee that the federal government would never meddle with slavery. Though he was a senator, the South Carolinian John C. Calhoun, who had served as vice president under John Quincy Adams and Jackson, became the leading strategist for southerners in the House. Congress should follow normal parliamentary procedure, he insisted, and simply let the petitions be read and then table them, which would cut off any further discussion. The petitions represented a grave insult to the South and were so loaded with abusive terms that they must be decisively rejected to repel further agitation.[39] For nearly six months, the House debated whether to receive the petitions or refuse to act on them. They finally permitted their reading but placed them on the table without referring them to committee; the House would take no further action whatsoever. The *gag rule*, as it came to be called, effectively ended citizen antislavery protests to Congress until it was repealed eight years later.[40] In the intervening years, John Quincy Adams, who in 1831, as a representative from the Plymouth district of Massachusetts, became the only former president to take a seat in Congress, doggedly carried on a lonely battle against the gag rule, repeatedly introducing one antislavery petition after another, all of which Congress rejected without a word—a protest that continued into Adams's seventy-eighth year and finally forced frustrated southerners in the House to try to censure him. A petition, in essence, was "a prayer," Adams insisted, "a supplication to a superior being which the Creator of the universe did not deny to the lowest, the humblest, and the meanest," and rather than rejecting petitions on slavery the House ought to accept them with the "added incentive" that they represented the only means available for "those low in the estimation of the world" to have their views expressed.[41]

Even as they stanched the flow of petitions to Congress, southerners undermined themselves with the great majority of ordinary northerners. Most northern whites would have been happy to find a way to live amicably with the South, and most were probably willing to overlook slavery, but when southerners began opposing basic freedoms like the right to petition and the right to open discussion, northerners grew increasingly impatient. What gave the South the right, after all, to dictate to the North, when it was slaveholders who clearly were in the wrong?

Garrison and his abolitionist followers also aroused deep resentment among northern whites, however. As Harrison Gray Otis, former senator from Massachusetts and ex-mayor of Boston, told an antiabolitionist rally at that city's Faneuil Hall in August 1835, the abolitionists were nothing less

than a "*revolutionary society*," intent on creating enough trouble and discontent
to spell the ultimate end of the Union. They not only sought to recruit men
to their "holy crusade" but they also wanted women "to turn their sewing
parties into abolition clubs and even tried to teach little children when they
meet to eat sugar plums or at the Sunday schools ... that A B stands for abolition."[42] But the northern resentment ran deeper than anger at the abolitionists' desire to include women and children in their movement. Among
working-class whites, there was a constant fear that millions of emancipated
slaves would destroy the value of free white labor—a fear that exacerbated
the stress of their always precarious economic situation. William Leggett,
editor of the *New York Evening Post*, warned that if freed slaves could not raise
themselves to the white man's level, "they might pull the latter down ... and
thus lower the condition of the white laborer by association, if not by amalgamation."[43] Abolition threatened powerful economic interests, and its success would be felt at every level of American society. "Millions upon millions
of dollars [are] due from the Southerners to [northern] merchants and
mechanics . . . , the payment of which would be jeopardized by a rupture
between the North and the South," a New York business leader told the abolitionist Samuel J. May. "We cannot afford, sir, to let you and your associates
succeed in your endeavor to overthrow slavery. It is not a matter of principle
with us. It is a matter of business necessity."[44]

Abolitionists became targets for an epidemic of white violence in the
North. In 1833, angry crowds had surrounded the founding meeting of the
Anti-Slavery Society, threatening to drive the abolitionists out of
Philadelphia.[45] The South was essentially off-limits to abolitionists because
nearly all the southern states had passed laws against freedom of speech in
relation to slavery, and authorities would give any individuals espousing abolition substantial prison sentences—if they managed to survive the torture
and beating that would likely accompany their arrest. In the North, even in
New York and Boston, the authorities seemed powerless to guarantee the
safety of abolitionist leaders. In 1834, an antiabolitionist crowd broke up a
mixed meeting of blacks and whites at the Chatham Street Chapel in New
York City and then ransacked Arthur Tappan's home nearby, starting a bon-
fire with furniture that was carried into the street.[46] The following year, an
angry mob assaulted Garrison at an antislavery rally in Boston, chanting in
unison, "Lynch him! Lynch him!" Not long afterward, mobs burned down
the printing offices of two abolitionist newspapers, *The Philanthropist* in Ohio

and the *Alton Observer* in Illinois. Elijah P. Lovejoy, the courageous editor of the *Observer*, had been burned out on three previous occasions; he died from a gunshot wound, which he suffered while trying to protect his new press that had been unloaded from a riverboat and was being stored in an Alton warehouse.⁴⁷

The abolitionists' moral crusade intensified the strife between the North and South, but the emerging shape of the nation and the struggle for power, which would be decided in the territories, remained the flash point of contention between the regions. After the rancor engendered by Missouri, the admission of new states had been pushed to the side for sixteen years, but in 1836 Congress returned to the principle of paired admissions, matching Arkansas and Michigan in order to preserve sectional parity. In general, the two separate admission bills met with little opposition, except for an unusual provision in the Arkansas constitution that denied the state the power ever to emancipate slaves. From the southern point of view, the citizens of Arkansas were asking nothing more than equality with northerners, whose constitutions declared that slavery would never be allowed in northern states. Men like John Quincy Adams, however, bridled at the Arkansans' attempt to put slavery beyond the reach of the state's future citizens, if someday they had a change of heart. Though the Arkansas bill eventually passed, Adams and his allies mounted a spirited protest, another landmark in the career of the septuagenarian ex-president as the antislavery conscience of the House.

Though the admissions of Arkansas and Michigan proceeded with relative ease, 1836 also marked the establishment of the independent Republic of Texas, reopening the volatile question of westward expansion. Fifteen years earlier, Moses Austin, a miner and trader who had fallen on hard times in Missouri, traveled to what was then the Eastern Interior Province of Mexico and received permission from the Spanish to settle three hundred families there. Austin died before he could put together a company of pioneers, but his son, Stephen F. Austin, carried through with the plan and in 1822 founded the first settlement of U.S. citizens in Texas, primarily white southerners accompanied by a substantial complement of slaves. Events moved swiftly for the new Texans. Mexico's national independence movement, which had started in 1811, finally succeeded in ousting the Spanish

royalists, and in 1828 Vicente Guerrero became president of the newly independent country. As one of his first official acts, he abolished slavery, which
had obviously not been in the southern settlers' plans. Hoping to retain their
slaves, they petitioned for an exemption from the emancipation decree;
when that failed, they decided they had no other choice and declared their
independence from Mexico on March 2, 1836. Overwhelmed at the Alamo,
the Americans soundly defeated the Mexican army six weeks later at San
Jacinto, essentially ending the Mexican government's bid to suppress their
rebellion. As Stephen Austin noted, Texas was meant to be "slave country."[48]

Though Mexico never recognized the independent political existence of
the Republic of Texas, the United States sanctioned it a year later. The
Mexican government issued a stern warning that it would consider any
attempt to annex Texas an act of war. Naturally, southerners favored immediate annexation, confident that Texas would enter the Union as a slave
state, but the abolitionists had different ideas. Pamphleteering, an aggressive
petition campaign, and Adams's unbending opposition in the House to both
the extension of slavery and the prospect of war with Mexico created major
roadblocks to annexation. Lewis Tappan and Stephen Pearl Andrews, a former New Englander who had emigrated with Austin, worked out a scheme
for the British government to finance the purchase of Texas from Mexico
through the London Anti-Slavery Society and make it a British colony free
of slavery. When the plan became known in the South, it inspired an angry
wave of protest from slave owners, and Andrews was attacked by a proslavery mob and sent packing back to Massachusetts. Nevertheless, the abolitionists succeeded in stopping annexation, at least for the time being.

The presidential campaign of 1844 produced a textbook example of the
quandary over morality and politics: Should one vote on the basis of conscience, or was it right to support a candidate with whom one disagreed in
order to achieve immediate political goals? The question turned on statehood for Texas and the possibility of war with Mexico. The Democrats
chose James K. Polk, a Tennessee slaveholder who supported immediate
annexation; the Whigs responded with the venerable Henry Clay, another
slaveholder but an opponent of annexation; and the Liberty Party, created in
1840 by abolitionists who favored political action, selected James Birney of
Ohio, the editor of the antislavery newspaper The Philanthropist, who had
managed to capture only a few thousand votes as the party's candidate in the
previous presidential election.[49] Texas was the major issue in the campaign,

and antislavery voters had to make a choice between an uncomfortable vote for the slaveholder Clay, which would block annexation, or a vote for Birney, which would likely help elect Polk, who favored the acquisition of Texas and the expansion of slavery. As one might expect, both black and white abolitionists were deeply divided on the question. When the ballots were counted, Birney had received sixty-two thousand votes—only about 3 percent of the total but enough in crucial states to insure Polk's victory. "If the fruit of electing Mr. Clay would have been to prevent the extension of slavery," Abraham Lincoln, an obscure Illinois lawyer and politician, asked, "could the act of electing have been evil?"[50]

To the chagrin of abolitionists, particularly the Birney voters, Polk proved to be even more aggressively proslavery and expansionist than they had expected. In short order he not only annexed Texas but moved American troops into Mexican territory to extend the Texas border 150 miles south to the Rio Grande. He clearly intended the troop movement as a gesture of provocation and quickly got what he wanted: an armed confrontation in which eleven Americans died and five were wounded. When word of the incident reached Washington, Polk declared war, falsely portraying Mexico as the aggressor, "which had invaded American territory and ... shed American blood upon ... American soil."[51] Both the South and West roundly applauded Polk's actions, but the North vigorously opposed the war and continued its strong dissent throughout the conflict. Mexico had been made "the victim of Anglo-Saxon cupidity and love of dominion," the black abolitionist Frederick Douglass roared, "in a disgraceful, cruel, and iniquitous war waged to extend slavery."

In spite of his critics, Polk remained firm in prosecuting the conflict, finally accepting a Mexican surrender only after American forces had taken control of Chapultepec and began entering Mexico City. While many expansionists wanted to seize all of Mexico, Polk contented himself with the northern half, an area less populated than the South and ripe to be turned into a land for Anglo-Saxons. In March 1848, the Senate ratified the Treaty of Guadalupe Hidalgo, garnering for the United States the territory that would become New Mexico, Arizona, California, Nevada, Utah, and portions of Colorado and Wyoming. The treaty excluded Texas because the Americans insisted that it already belonged to the United States, having been granted statehood in 1845 immediately following its annexation. Nevertheless, it, too, should be counted as part of the spoils of the Mexican

War, which opened the way to the next bitter confrontation between the North and the South.[52]

With the Treaty of Guadalupe Hidalgo, the nation had strong-armed its way to a real-estate bonanza rivaling the Louisiana Purchase, one that again created a volatile set of opportunities sure to reignite the power struggle over slavery and the future of the territories. In 1845, prior to Polk's taking office, the Senate had passed a bill based on the Missouri Compromise, excluding slavery from whatever portion of Texas lay north of 36°30'. Slaveholders objected, and when Polk became president two months later the new Congress overruled the previous one, deciding that everything within the new territory should be construed as a single area that rightfully belonged to Texas. The amount of actual ground involved made the dispute a minor one, but it indicated that southerners would insist that the Missouri Compromise applied only to the area within the Louisiana Purchase, and that a new understanding would have to be worked out for the land taken from Mexico.

A year later, in 1846, the Pennsylvania congressman David Wilmot fired the first shot in the battle to establish new rules for expansion to the Pacific. Polk had asked Congress for $2 million, hoping to mend relations with the Mexican government by portraying the Texas annexation as a purchase, and Wilmot attached an amendment to the appropriation bill designed to block the expansion of slavery into the Far West. "I have no squeamish sensitiveness upon the subject of slavery, no morbid sympathy for the slave," Wilmot assured his congressional colleagues; instead, the Pennsylvanian wanted to save the West for his own people and give them what they already had lost in much of the eastern two-thirds of the United States. "I plead the cause and rights of white freemen," he declared. "I would preserve to free white labor a fair country, a rich inheritance, where the sons of toil, of my own race and own color, can live without the disgrace which association with negro slavery brings upon free labor."[53] The Wilmot Proviso excluded slavery in any territory that might be acquired from Mexico, but after the House repeatedly passed the bill, southern senators brought it to a halt.

By 1848, with Polk unwell and another presidential race looming in which slavery and the West would set the agenda, a variety of conflicting viewpoints emerged to frame the issues for the coming election. Among the abolitionists, there had been a split as early as 1840 between the Garrisonites, who believed that their case could be made only through moral suasion, and more practically oriented men like the Tappans, who felt that to be effective the abolitionists had to enter the public arena and achieve whatever they could through political action. James Madison's diary detailing the proceedings of the Constitutional Convention was published the same year, and for Garrison it revealed a design to unite the North and South so terribly flawed that nothing short of a moral rebirth could save the nation. In 1848, the politically active abolitionists who had formed the Liberty Party and backed Birney in 1844 split over whether they should limit the party platform to the single issue of slavery or take positions on a wide range of questions that might attract more voters. In the end, many left the party, seeking a more broadly based political affiliation, and those who remained renamed themselves the National Liberty Party but never again came close to the sixty-two thousand votes Birney had received four years earlier.

To attract southern voters, both major parties nominated candidates who appeared to have strong proslavery leanings. The Whigs chose General Zachary Taylor, a Louisiana slaveholder and hero of the Mexican War who earlier had battled Seminoles and fugitive slaves in Florida. The "Bloodhound candidate leading the Bloodhound Party," Garrison sneered, recalling the tracking dogs that Taylor had used to run down his adversaries in the Florida swamps.[54] The Democrats nominated Lewis Cass of Michigan, who had gained recognition in the slavery debate as an advocate of popular sovereignty—or squatter sovereignty, as its foes called it—which many in the South favored. Popular sovereignty left the question of whether a state would be slave or free to its original settlers to decide, without interference from Congress.

Finally, defectors from the Liberty Party and dissident Whigs and Democrats, who deserted after both their conventions chose proslavery candidates, formed the Free-Soil Party. Reaching into the past, the Free-Soilers selected as their nominee former president Martin Van Buren, who had lost his bid for a second term in 1840. A New Yorker, Van Buren had opposed the annexation of Texas and the expansion of slavery; and the Free-Soil Party succeeded, at least temporarily, in bringing together men as disparate as the New England abolitionist Charles Sumner and Wilmot, the champion of the white race who hoped to purify the West. The new party adopted the motto "Free Soil, Free Speech, Free Labor, and Free Men," but it quickly became clear that the majority of Free-Soilers could not be counted as friends of African Americans. While the party platform demanded that the federal government block slavery's entry into the West, it silently accepted its presence in the South, promising not to meddle in the affairs of existing states. Several black abolitionists, including Frederick Douglass, attended the Free-Soil Convention, and organizers even allowed Douglass to speak, but would not seat any of them as delegates, since many whites objected. After struggling with an uneasy conscience, Douglass went on to endorse Van Buren, but he made clear that the endorsement represented a temporary alliance to block slavery in the West and that the Free-Soilers lacked the high standards and liberal views of true abolitionists.[55]

When Polk heard that Taylor had won the election, he dismissed his successor as "wholly unqualified, uneducated, and exceedingly ignorant of public affairs."[56] Most observers agreed that "Old Rough and Ready" had won because his position on slavery remained vague enough to avoid alienating voters on either side of the Mason-Dixon line. Northerners had voted for him as a war hero and southerners trusted him as one of their own, a plantation owner with a substantial number of slaves. A political innocent, Taylor stood poised to leap into the intersectional struggle, where the heat would more than match anything he had experienced on the battlefields of Mexico. Slavery had pushed aside all other business in Congress, "appropriating to its own use the time which properly [belongs] to the people—the white people . . . who constitute this great nation," William Sawyer of Ohio complained. "From morning to night, day after day, and week after week, nothing can get a hearing that will not afford an opportunity to lug in something about negro slavery. It is negro in the morning, the poor negro at noon—and at night again this same negro is thrust upon us. . . . I beg, gentlemen, to remember there are some white people in this country, and these white people are entitled to some consideration."[57]

Frustrated southerners saw their situation fast becoming hopeless. European immigrants had swelled population counts in the North and West, leaving the South with a shrinking percentage of votes in the House of Representatives, and though the Senate remained equally divided between the regions, it appeared that southerners would soon become a permanent minority unless all the territory taken from Mexico entered the Union as slave states. Even before Taylor took office, the implacable John C. Calhoun called for a caucus of southern congressmen from both parties to consider their predicament and what might be done. Though opposed by moderates who wanted to give Taylor a chance before taking the offensive, Calhoun dominated the meeting, boldly laying out the South's grievances in a defiant speech later known as the Southern Address. At the root of every problem, he observed, lay the northerners' sanctimonious unwillingness to treat southerners as equals. Convinced of its moral superiority, the North refused to grant the same legal protection to southern property—in the form of slaves—that it routinely gave to the belongings of its own citizens. In the territories, Calhoun insisted, southerners should "not be prohibited from migrating with their property," because the land belonged equally to the two regions.[58] Calhoun went on to catalog an entire list of constitutional violations against the South: What had been said about the territories also applied to Washington, D.C., where southerners had as much right to their property as northerners. In addition, northern states had passed liberty laws, which prevented owners from recovering runaway slaves, even though the Constitution guaranteed interstate cooperation in returning fugitives to their masters. These grievances, coupled with an endless flow of abolitionist agitation, which the North refused to make any serious effort to halt, threatened to destroy slavery, and southerners faced the horrifying possibility of being reduced to a powerless minority whose fate would be in unsympathetic hands. For many of his colleagues, Calhoun's address represented an ultimatum calling for drastic action, even secession.

When Taylor took office, he quickly moved to end the conflict over the territories by resolving the two most pressing questions in the West: the futures of California and New Mexico. In his final address, Polk had announced the discovery of gold in California, an event that would alter the perception of its future and immeasurably strengthen the position of Free-Soilers. With the gold rush already under way, no one could continue to regard California as simply another area in which to extend the western advance of cotton, and most of the territory's whites wanted to reserve its mining wealth for free white labor. Acting on advice from his secretary of state, John M. Clayton, Taylor believed that the best way to end the squabbling over California and New Mexico was to "skip the territorial stage and organize [them] as states . . . with such constitutions as they adopted." Taylor sent emissaries to both territories, encouraging political leaders to apply immediately for statehood, while at the same time he assured northerners that they "need have no apprehension of the further extension of slavery."[59] Barely six weeks later, Californians were asked to vote on a constitution prohibiting slavery forever, and by the beginning of 1850 the document had reached Washington, along with a formal application for admission to the Union. Southerners exploded, aghast not only at the prospect of California as a free state but also at their betrayal by Taylor, who they had hoped would ultimately feel the tug of his southern roots and protect them from their enemies.

Months of heated debate followed—a wildfire raging through Congress that would burn hot for a time, then cool temporarily, only to burst forth again just when it seemed it might be controlled. In February, only weeks after California petitioned for statehood, Henry Clay—back in the Senate after the Whigs had bypassed him as their presidential candidate in favor of Taylor—stepped forward once again with a compromise solution designed to rescue the Union. Adopting the same strategy he had used in relation to Missouri, Clay proposed a series of balancing resolutions, which he hoped would satisfy both North and South. Clay proposed that Congress allow California to enter the Union as a free state but deny admission to New Mexico and any other prospective western states until they had gone through the normal territorial process without prior restrictions on slavery. Second, in the District of Columbia the trading of slaves would be forbidden, but the southerners' right of ownership would be guaranteed. Third, a border dispute over the Texas–New Mexico line would be settled by the nation's assuming $10 million of Texas debt. And finally, southerners would be given assurances that Congress had no intention of prohibiting the interstate slave trade, and a new, more stringent fugitive slave law would be enacted.

For two days Clay defended his resolutions, calling on both northern and southern members to put aside sectional concerns and accept his compromise to preserve the Union. The time for extremism had passed, he argued, and more than ever the nation needed moderation and patriotism. Clay spoke out for selflessness rather than self-interest; but for many of his colleagues—on both sides of the debate—entirely different principles seemed to be at stake. To John Calhoun, the issue was "a full and final settlement, on the principle of justice." Almost universally, southerners had lost faith that the North would ever fulfill the guarantees of equality promised in the Constitution. In fairness to itself, Calhoun insisted, the South had nothing to give to reach a compromise. It simply wanted justice and the law to prevail, which meant nothing less than a full restoration of the rights that southerners had been promised. Anything short of that would end in "disunion."

Northerners, too, relied on principles to reject Clay's call for compromise, invoking higher, universal law to respond to Calhoun's argument that the South's constitutional rights had been violated. Horace Mann of Massachusetts, a newcomer to Congress, heaped scorn on the South's belief that it had a right to spread slavery into the territories. Nothing could be justified that violated "not only the teachings of Christianity, but the clearest principles of natural religion and of natural law." People should be allowed to carry what legitimately belonged to them anywhere, he acknowledged, but men and women did not constitute property, and to call them such seemed nothing more than a cheap trick, for which any juggler or mountebank would be hooted off the stage. Slavery represented a perpetual state of war that citizens had to resist, and thus Mann reluctantly would accept "disunion, even a civil or servile war"—anything, in fact, "that God in his providence shall send, [rather] than an extension of the boundaries of slavery."[60]

An old-fashioned dogfight threatened to tear Congress apart, but President Taylor stood firm, seeking to impose his own views on the nation's future. Unwilling to ally himself with northerners or southerners, or even with the implicit sectionalism in Clay's compromise, he wanted simply to grant statehood to California as a valuable addition to the consolidated Union, without making it a question about slavery. In the Senate, the New Yorker William Seward, one of Taylor's closest confidants, lectured his colleagues on the reality of change and the need for an expanded vision. Admitting that as a northerner he personally opposed slavery, Seward questioned the southern belief that the Constitution guaranteed the South equality with the North. The founding fathers had not organized the United States as a joint stock association, in which the two sections each held 50 percent of the shares. Instead, it functioned as a political state, providing peace and continuity for its citizens by dealing with the inevitable changes that came with time. As an institution, one could characterize slavery only as "temporary, accidental, partial, and incongruous," while people experienced their desire for freedom as "perpetual, organic, [and] universal." In the end, slavery must give way, Seward predicted; but in the short term, both northerners and southerners needed to realize that they were not teetering on the brink of disunion, only struggling with the agony "resulting from the too narrow foundations of both and of all parties."[61]

President Taylor's insistence that people view the United States as a single, consolidated nation represented a noble vision of what America ought to be, but his confidence that he could simply order Congress to deal with the present crisis on that basis revealed his political naïveté. As Polk had suggested, Taylor lacked political preparation for the presidency; he was more comfortable giving orders in the style of a general than in seeking consensus, as politicians must. Congress, in contrast, understood the practical art of decision making and realized that ultimately they would have to choose between compromise or disunion, which made the pressure to arrive at a negotiated settlement overwhelming. Still, with the president threatening to hang anyone who tried to impeach him and Calhoun convinced that the standoff would end in disunion, powerful voices were raised to block any solution based on mutual concessions.

When Clay had presented his compromise at the beginning of February, Calhoun was ill, too sick to attend. A few days later, however, given the chance to respond, Calhoun appeared wrapped in a blanket, pale and drawn, regretting his inability to speak at length but asking to have his sentiments read by a colleague. The leader of southern militancy was dying, a consummation that followed barely two months later, on the last day of March. Calhoun's departure represented only the beginning of the nation's season of death. On the Fourth of July, after having consumed copious amounts of ice water and cherries at an Independence Day gala, Taylor fell ill with a stomach ailment, and five days later he, too, succumbed.[62] Fate had removed the two most imposing obstacles to a political compromise. In February, shortly before his death, Calhoun had urged the Mississippi legislature to call for the slave states to assemble at Nashville in early June. When the time for the convention arrived, nine states sent delegates, and Calhoun's old conservative allies, led by the South Carolinian Ronald B. Rhett, assumed that the meeting would be an opportunity to drum up additional support for secession. But without Calhoun's imposing presence, most of the delegates felt inclined to be conciliatory, and at the meeting's end they issued a statement rejecting disunion and indicating their willingness to accept an extension of the 36°30' boundary to the Pacific as the basis for an intersectional compromise.

Just as Calhoun's demise damped much of the fire of the southern secessionists, Taylor's death reversed the position of the nation's chief executive. His successor, the New Yorker Millard Fillmore, a loyal friend to northern business—in Garrison's words, "as pliant a piece of dough as ever was handled"—had quietly supported a peaceful compromise from the beginning of the controversy.[63] Taking office, Fillmore moved swiftly, enlisting Stephen Douglas of Illinois, a leading spokesman for popular sovereignty, as his mouthpiece in the Senate. In short order Douglas crafted a new set of bills designed to ease specific objections of both North and South, and by the middle of September he had won approval for the entire package, which contained the essential elements of Clay's earlier proposals: the admission of California as a free state, the organization of the New Mexico Territory without prior restrictions on slavery, $10 million for the settlement of the Texas border dispute, the prohibition of the slave trade in the District of Columbia, and a new fugitive slave law.[64]

Compromise supporters rejoiced that the nation had once again retreated from the brink of chaos and perhaps found a cure for the running sore of intersectional strife. "There is . . . peace now prevailing throughout our borders," Clay announced shortly after Congress had reached agreement. "I believe it is permanent." Equally upbeat, Fillmore proclaimed in his annual congressional message that the compromise represented the final settlement of a perilous question that had been threatening to destroy the Union since its inception.[65] Inevitably, however, the compromise did not satisfy everyone. In the North, men with strong abolitionist leanings—like Ohio senator Salmon P. Chase, who had made a name for himself as a lawyer defending runaway slaves—dismissed the compromise as an abdication of responsibility by the federal government. "The question of slavery in the territories has been avoided," Chase observed, "not settled." Southerners also expressed skepticism, feeling vanquished by the North and doubting that their adversaries would honor the assurances they had given. A "circle of fire approaches us on all sides," the *North Carolina Standard* warned. If the North refused to drop the "question of slavery by taking it out and keeping it out of Congress," the paper predicted, "the BONDS" of Union surely would be "DISSOLVED!"[66]

The Compromise of 1850, as it came to be called, achieved only a fragile peace, and as the practical consequences of the agreement became clear they shattered the momentary calm. Before 1850, when southerners had complained that the North denied them equitable treatment in relation to runaways they could point to both the Constitution and the Fugitive Slave Act of 1793 to show that the law backed them up. Northerners, however, refusing to regard men and women as mere chattel, felt that a higher law protected Negroes; consequently, most northern states had enacted liberty ordinances blocking the enforcement of federal statutes. State laws gave blacks the right to have their cases heard by judges rather than justices of the peace, for example, which raised the standards of evidence, and severe penalties for illegal seizure discouraged slave catchers bent on simply kidnapping blacks—slave or free—and sending them South. Even after 1842, when Supreme Court Justice Joseph Story, a New Englander with impeccable antislavery credentials, ruled in *Prigg v. Pennsylvania* that states had no power to interfere in the slaveholders' federal right to recover their fugitive property, most northern jurisdictions continued to enforce liberty laws and treat slave owners who tried to evade them as criminals.[67] The Compromise of 1850, with its revamped fugitive slave law, provided southerners with the justice they felt they had previously been denied. The Fugitive Slave Act stiffened the 1793 law by making the recovery of runaways strictly a federal matter, in which the states could not interfere. Rather than having to make their case in the North, as local liberty ordinances forced them to do, slave owners went before a court in their home state, from which the fugitive had fled, and obtained a certificate authenticating their right to recover the runaway. Carried to a free state, this document wound up not with the local authorities but with a special federal commissioner, who would issue a warrant for the fugitive's arrest. Following the individual's capture, federal marshals prepared a second certificate, confirming the runaway's identity. At no point in the proceedings did courts allow prisoners to present evidence or even to testify in their own defense; the original southern certificates were treated as binding judicial decisions. The escapees had only one recourse: to appeal to the southern courts in which the judgments had originated.

Northerners reacted to the new law immediately and in many cases violently. Even before it passed, Horace Mann denounced it as "so worthy of abhorrence, so truculent, so fiendish," that its equal could not be found "upon the statute book of any other civilized nation on the globe."[68] The measure also inspired consternation among blacks in the North—even those who had been legally emancipated—because it effectively put them at the mercy of southern justice, by depriving them of the legal protection that the northern states had provided. A number of blacks fled immediately to Canada, unwilling to wait and see what would happen. In Cleveland, the *True Democrat* reported that panic spread by the Fugitive Slave Law caused Negroes to leave in droves. The *Pennsylvania Freeman* estimated that as many as 40 percent of Boston's nine thousand blacks had departed within twenty-four hours after passage of the law. To many black leaders, the situation demanded a greater degree of militancy, and they pledged themselves to armed resistance. "The only way to make the Fugitive Slave Law a dead letter is to make a half a dozen or more dead kidnappers," Frederick Douglass told a rally of abolitionists and others sympathetic to the cause at Faneuil Hall in October 1850. "Every colored man should sleep with his revolver under his head, loaded and ready for use," and newly arrived fugitives should be armed and taught that "it is no harm to shoot any man who would rob them of ... [their] liberty."[69]

Calls for armed self-defense created a serious dilemma for many of the abolitionists. Though Garrison had not hesitated to condemn the Fugitive Slave Law as "an edict so coldblooded, so inhuman and so atrocious, that Satan himself would blush to claim paternity to it," he counseled abolitionists to resist the law only by nonviolent means. Over the next two years, however, events persuaded even Garrison of the need for militant resistance. In September 1851, at Christiana, Pennsylvania, a Maryland slave owner named Edward Gorsuch led a party of friends, relatives, and federal officers to the farm of William Parker, a leader of the local black community, hoping to recover four of his runaway slaves who had escaped two years earlier. Parker's farm served as a station on the Underground Railway to the North. A prolonged and deadly fight took place over the next several days, attracting as many as two hundred blacks from the surrounding area. Gorsuch was killed and his son was wounded. President Fillmore, fearing that the violence would spread, dispatched a contingent of marines to help round up the unruly blacks. The federal courts moved swiftly, charging thirty-six blacks and five whites with treason, not one of whom was ever convicted. Parker escaped to Canada.[70] Despite the government's preposterous overcharging, the Christiana incident was salutory in one respect: as Douglass pointed out, it demonstrated that "the frequency of arrests and the ease with which they were made quickened the rapacity, and invited the aggressions of slave-catchers." Armed resistance, he added, "checked these aggressions and [brought] the hunters of men to the sober second thought." Garrison saw the truth in Douglass's analysis, and by April 1852 he, too, argued that people of conscience had to overthrow the Fugitive Slave Law by whatever means necessary. "If the Revolutionary fathers were justified in wading through blood to freedom and independence," he observed, "then every fugitive slave is justified in arming himself for protection and defense, in taking the life of every marshal, commissioner or other person who attempts to reduce him to bondage."[71]

*   *   *

The second great concern for southerners was, of course, access to the territories with their slaves. Southerners believed that their constitutional rights were being ignored, but with the arrival of a new, opportunistic administration in Washington, the chance to reopen the entire West to slavery soon presented itself. Fillmore's truncated presidency ended in 1852, when northern members of his own party, the Whigs, disillusioned by his support for slaveholders and the Fugitive Slave Law, refused to nominate him for a second term. Instead, they chose General Winfield Scott, another hero of the Mexican War and a Virginian with a strong sense of loyalty to the Union and deep reservations about slavery. Scott lost to the Democrat Franklin Pierce of New Hampshire, one of his subordinates in Mexico, who won by a landslide, capturing the majority of northern votes and persuading the South that he would defuse the slavery issue with an evenhanded administration of justice and a return to constitutional principles.

Pierce harbored powerful expansionist ambitions—a trait he had in common with Stephen Douglas, who was the chairman of the Committee on Territories in the Senate. Both men shared a vision of a transcontinental railway tying the nation together by connecting either Saint Louis or Chicago to California. How could the nation "develop, cherish and protect its immense interests and possessions" in the West, Douglas asked, without "Railroads and Telegraphs from the Atlantic to the Pacific, through our own territory?"[72] Pierce and Douglas agreed that the first step in making the nation truly transcontinental was to encourage emigration over the plains by creating the Nebraska Territory from a part of the Louisiana Purchase north and northwest of Missouri, above 36°30'. Winning approval in Congress posed a serious difficulty, however. In 1845 both Florida and Texas had been admitted to the Union, giving the South a critical advantage of two states in the Senate. Iowa had been admitted in 1846, followed by Wisconsin in 1848, which reestablished parity, but then in 1850 California had swung the advantage to the North. With southerners primed for resistance, Douglas needed to find a way to stop them from voting against the organization of the Nebraska Territory. Failing to gain enough southern votes by appealing for their patriotic support for expansion, he turned to the Compromise of 1850 and formulated a questionable interpretation of its meaning aimed at wooing the South by reopening Nebraska to the possibility of slavery. In 1850, Congress had created not only the New Mexico Territory but the Utah Territory, in a separate bill spelling out requirements for statehood that read essentially the same as New

Mexico's. In relation to slavery, Congress had given both territories the right to follow the principle of popular sovereignty, leaving it to the settlers to decide whether their societies would be slave or free. Pointing to New Mexico and Utah, Douglas now argued that the actions by Congress superceded the Missouri Compromise and made popular sovereignty the accepted national policy. The 36°30' rule no longer applied to the Louisiana Territory, he insisted, and in January 1854 he introduced a bill for the organization of Nebraska which left the slavery question to be decided by the territory's pioneers.[73] Hoping to satisfy the South without inspiring the wrath of northerners, Douglas's proposal followed the precedent he had deduced from the 1850 compromise without ever mentioning Missouri. Southerners understood how desperately Douglas wanted their votes, however, and they quickly showed their dissatisfaction with his initial bill, insisting that popular sovereignty for Nebraska was not enough to gain their support. They demanded a larger prize: a specific repeal of the ban on slavery north of 36°30'. With no other direction in which to turn, Douglas rewrote the proposal, this time including a repeal of the entire Missouri Compromise and the division of Nebraska into two territories, Kansas to the west of Missouri and Nebraska to the northwest, which gave him the southern support he needed to pass the measure.

In the past, Douglas had called the Missouri Compromise "a sacred thing, which no ruthless hand would ever be reckless enough to disturb," and by dividing Nebraska into two territories, one which seemed almost certain to remain free even if the other embraced slavery, he hoped to calm the North. But the bone he threw to northerners must have seemed a sorry replacement for what had been taken from them, and Douglas realized he was about to face "a helluva storm." When the bill's supporters first read the proposal repealing the Missouri Compromise aloud in Congress, Free-Soilers, led by Salmon P. Chase, immediately issued an appeal to the nation, denouncing it as "a criminal betrayal of precious rights, . . . part and parcel of . . . a plot to exclude from a vast unoccupied region" European immigrants and free white labor, and make it a home for despots, populated by masters and slaves. Chase distributed his *Appeal of the Independent Democrats to the People of the United States* to newspapers throughout the North, and mass meetings and petition campaigns protested the Nebraska infamy, blaming Douglas and his dough-faced northern allies for opening the door to slavery's reentry into areas where it had been prohibited forever.[74]

Believing that the "storm" would soon expend its "fury," Douglas badly misjudged the intensity of the North's reaction. Though he remained in the Senate until his death in 1861, the ill feeling he engendered among northerners for his part in the organization of Nebraska destroyed his chances as a presidential candidate. After having barely missed out in 1852 when his popularity was on the rise, he was unable to muster the support he needed to capture the Democratic presidential nomination in 1856. Four years later he would finally succeed in being nominated, but only as the candidate for the National Democratic Party, which had split with southern Democrats and gave him no real chance of winning. Nebraska had raised Douglas to his zenith: "I passed the Kansas-Nebraska Act myself," he later claimed; and for a time he exercised a kind of dictatorial power in both houses of Congress. But in the end he failed to recognize how deeply betrayed his fellow northerners would feel by his pandering to the South.[75] Nebraska spelled his downfall.

Douglas's decline represented a personal tragedy, but more important for the nation, the repeal of the Missouri Compromise set in motion decisive realignments in both the Whig and the Democratic Parties which greatly increased the likelihood of a violent confrontation between the North and the South. The Democrats had been the party of Jefferson, and the Whigs first appeared in the 1830s when widespread resistance to the Democratic leadership of Jackson and Van Buren had led to the creation of a new opposition party. Though both parties had managed to forge coalitions between northerners and southerners, giving them national scope on many questions, it also was the case that on sectional issues southerners usually united to defend slavery, while northerners were more likely to take into account party loyalty and seldom voted as an antislavery bloc. When the Senate repealed the Missouri Compromise, the vote once again reflected both the united strength of the South and the failure of northerners to hang together. Whatever political arm-twisting went on, the final tallies showed that in the House and Senate combined, nearly 90 percent of southerners had supported repeal and only 64 percent of northerners had voted against it. Among northern Democrats, just 56 percent had cast ballots to save the prohibition of slavery above 36°30'.[76]

Resentment among voters in the North at the undoing of the Missouri Compromise took its toll on the Democratic Party. In the next two congressional elections, voters angry over the Kansas-Nebraska fiasco took their revenge, turning northern Democrats out of office. In the House, Democrats lost well over 70 percent of the seats they had held before repeal of the Compromise, and the number of northern Democrats dropped from 91 to only 25. Southern Democrats held their own, occupying 63 seats in 1856, only 4 fewer than they had in 1854. Though the balance between northern and southern Democrats in the Senate remained relatively close, southerners had taken control of the party in the House, where they outnumbered northerners by more than two to one.[77]

The Kansas-Nebraska controversy also brought about the demise of the Whigs. Northern members of the party had unanimously opposed Douglas's bill, while nearly all the southern Whigs supported it. Faced with overwhelming evidence of their inability to agree with the southern wing of their own party, northern Whigs rebelled, choosing to leave en masse in order to form new political alliances rather than remain "forever the vassals of imperious taskmasters." As one Illinois Whig concluded soon after the repeal of the Missouri Compromise, "Whig, Democrat & free soil are now all 'obsolete ideas' . . . and what shall we do next? What but unite on *principle* instead of *party*."[78] In spite of old differences and a period of hesitation as new coalitions formed, runaway Whigs, Free-Soilers, and a substantial number of disgruntled Democrats finally united around the obvious, overriding imperative they shared: the need to contain the *Slave Power* and block its expansion wherever possible. "This war with slavery is too radical, too long, too big for success without a power constructed especially for it," a Maine Free-Soiler explained. "Cromwell needed a better army and so do we."[79]

The struggle between North and South had entered a new, more perilous phase. In the past, men from both regions had shared the major political parties, managing to work together on many issues apart from slavery— and even more important, developing relationships that brought them in contact with one another in spite of their differences. After 1855 and the repeal of the Missouri Compromise, the political climate would grow excruciatingly contentious, as pro- and antislavery advocates separated into two primarily single-issue parties that seldom could agree on anything. The battle over slavery had been muted as long as the combatants believed the Union was worth preserving. The transformation of the two parties into opposing camps based solely on their commitment to freedom or slavery signaled that faith was rapidly waning on both sides of the Mason-Dixon line. The national spirit that had held the Union together was succumbing to the mutual bitterness of northerners and southerners.

CHAPTER 7

THE ADVENT OF THE CONFEDERACY

It is high noon, thank God!

—WILLIAM LLOYD GARRISON, 1860

We have just carried an election on principles fairly stated to the people. Now we are told in advance the Government shall be broken up unless we surrender to those we have beaten. . . . In this they are either attempting to play upon us or they are in dead earnest. Either way, if we surrender, it is the end of us and of the government. They will repeat the experiment upon us ad libitum.

—ABRAHAM LINCOLN, 1861

The first important test for proslavery Democrats and antislavery Republicans was the national election of 1856. In February, the leaders of the new Republican Party met in Pittsburgh to prepare for their nominating convention and outlined a remarkably restrained preliminary platform. Hoping to attract as many converts as possible, particularly among slaveless southerners, the platform simply called for the early admission of Kansas as a free state without mentioning any of the other problems antislavery radicals had hoped to address. Disappointed, Frederick Douglass complained that "[n]othing [was] said of the Fugitive Slave Bill, . . . of Slavery in the District of Columbia, . . . of the slave trade between States, . . . of securing the rights of citizens from the [North], or the constitutional right to enter and transact business in the slave states."[1]

By spring, however, events had emboldened Republican leaders to take a

more radical stance. When Stephen Douglas split Nebraska into two territories, he had hoped to reduce the possibility of violence between settlers by
separating northerners and southerners, but a battle for Kansas began
almost immediately after it gained territorial status. Backed by southern
slave owners and supported by federal troops, emigrants from Missouri set
up a territorial government, intending to make Kansas a slave state.
Unwilling to concede territory north of 36°30' to the South, northerners—
supplied with arms and money by the New England Emigrant Aid
Society—established a separate government, dedicated to keeping Kansas
free. By the middle of 1855, two angry, antagonistic populations existed in
the territory, and in May 1856, after a series of minor skirmishes, an
armed struggle ignited. Seven hundred "Border Ruffians" from Missouri,
formed into a posse by the territory's federal marshal, overran and destroyed
Lawrence, the major settlement of the free Kansans, firing cannons at the
Free State Hotel, demolishing two newspaper offices, and burning to the
ground two dozen houses. Within the space of a few hours, the posse had
wiped out most of the money, supplies, and equipment the aid society had
provided. Having pledged to their eastern backers not to resist federal
authorities, the inhabitants of Lawrence had been caught off guard, and
northerners reacted with anger and disbelief, astonished by the slaveholders'
duplicity and outraged that the national government had been a party to
such a plan. "Bleeding Kansas," the New York Tribune thundered, "bound hand
and foot by the administration who will not let her go free."[2]

On May 22, after Missourians had finished sacking Lawrence, northerners
were presented with a second major calamity, back in the nation's capital.
Charles Sumner, one of the Republican leaders in the Senate, had taken the
floor two days earlier and begun a marathon indictment of the South and the
Pierce administration for their crimes against Kansas. The Missourians had
conspired with the federal government in the "rape of a virgin territory," he
lamented, and the men who had carried it out were in thrall to the "harlot, slavery." In the North, Sumner's attack won immediate praise: "[T]he greatest voice
on the greatest subject that has ever been uttered since we became a nation," the
poet Henry Wadsworth Longfellow declared.[3] From southerners, of course, it
drew universal recrimination, and in Preston Brooks, a young House member
from South Carolina, it provoked something more.[4] Sumner's diatribe had
included personal attacks on key congressional figures, like Douglas and the
South Carolinian Andrew P. Butler, whom Sumner had called the Sancho

Panza and Don Quixote of slavery. Brooks, related to Butler and apparently feeling that not only the South but his family had been insulted, approached a seated Sumner and, without warning, clubbed the older man into unconsciousness with a heavy wooden cane. The vicious assault left blood on the floor of the Senate and kept Sumner from returning to the chamber for more than three years. "Bleeding Kansas and Bleeding Sumner" became the new rallying cry of frustrated northerners. The violence that hung over "the frontiers of Kansas like a storm cloud charged with hail and lightning" had found its way into the Senate chamber, William Cullen Bryant, the editor of the *New York Evening Post*, wrote. Violence had become "the order of the day," he warned, and if the North wanted to avoid being bullied, people of the free states would have to meet fire with fire.[5]

By the time the Republican Party held its nominating convention in June, antislavery activists had gained the upper hand, and the party quickly adopted a far more aggressive platform than it had been willing to accept four months earlier in Pittsburgh. The Republicans promised to tighten the collar around slaveholders by insuring that the federal government would use its constitutional power to eliminate slavery wherever it could and prohibit its expansion into the territories. They chose John C. Frémont, a Free-Soiler who had become a national hero as a western scout and served as a California senator, as their presidential nominee, setting the stage for the first national contest in which the candidates for the two major parties represented the opposing views of their pro- and antislavery constituents: Frémont and the "Black Republicans" versus the Democrats' James Buchanan, a Pennsylvanian, who preached that southerners had been abused long enough as a minority and that their rights needed to be protected as a first step toward national reconciliation.

A compromise selection at his party's convention, Buchanan's middle-states roots saved the election for the South. Almost exactly, the electoral votes divided geographically, with Frémont capturing eleven of the northernmost states and Buchanan winning every southern state except Maryland, which gave its eight votes to Millard Fillmore on a third-party ticket. Buchanan's victory was assured when he carried his home state of Pennsylvania and neighboring New Jersey, along with Illinois, Indiana, and California. While the Republicans had shown remarkable strength in their first national outing and their future appeared bright, the party of the South held on to the presidency for four more years.

In his inaugural address, Buchanan expressed his desire to resurrect a mutual sense of harmony and friendship between the North and the South. Denouncing abolitionist agitation and the struggle for Kansas, he urged all citizens to unite and cheerfully accept the Supreme Court's ruling in a case currently before it—whatever the decision might be—as a final solution to the slavery question. Buchanan's studied sense of fair play was a sham, however, since letters written to him in secret by two justices, John Catron and Robert C. Grier, revealed exactly what the court's findings would be. Emanating from a body heavily weighted with southerners and Democrats, *Dred Scott v. Sandford* would deliver a vindication to slave owners and a troubling rebuke to the North.[6]

The circumstances of the case were straightforward. In 1834, the slave Dred Scott, who lived in Missouri with his master, Dr. John Emerson, an army surgeon, had been taken first to Illinois and then to the Wisconsin Territory, both of which were free, when Emerson was transferred there. After 1838, Scott accompanied his master to a number of other posts, eventually returning to Missouri, and from 1840 to 1846 Emerson hired Scott out to a variety of people. When Emerson died, Scott sued his deceased master's wife for his freedom in a Missouri court, having discovered that in a number of previous cases the principle had been established that once a slave resided in free territory he automatically gained his freedom. Based on Scott's stay in Illinois and Wisconsin, a jury of Missourians emancipated him, but Mrs. Emerson appealed to the state supreme court, where the case took on a larger dimension than the simple question of an individual slave's status. The higher court ignored its own precedents and rejected Scott's plea for freedom, citing as its reason overriding political issues, which had grown in importance and weighed heavily on a case such as the one before it. "Times are not as they were when former decisions on this subject were made," the court explained. "Not only individuals but States have been possessed with a dark and fell spirit that aimed at the overthrow and destruction of our government." Setting aside judicial impartiality in order to champion slavery, the state court reversed the earlier decision, giving not "the least countenance to any measure which might gratify" the anarchic, rebellious spirit of Missouri's enemies.[7]

Even before it reached the U.S. Supreme Court, *Dred Scott* had been transformed into a political case, and its resolution by the highest court in the land reflected the sectional loyalties of its members, particularly its leader. The chief justice, Roger B. Taney of Maryland, had already revealed himself as a partisan supporter of slavery when, as Andrew Jackson's attorney general, he maintained that whatever privileges blacks enjoyed were "a matter of kindness and benevolence rather than right." Later, though he insisted that states had the power to refuse to obey federal law, he ruled against northern attempts to defy the Fugitive Slave Act. Of the other eight justices, each wrote separate opinions, with six supporting Taney and two in dissent, but it was the chief justice's views that became the official position of the court and that even now are thought of as the *Dred Scott* decision.

On March 6, 1857, Taney rejected Scott's petition for freedom on two grounds. First, he reviewed not only the nation's history but the Constitution as well and concluded that the founding fathers had never intended American blacks to enjoy "the privileges and immunities of citizens." Instead, blacks had been "justly and lawfully reduced to slavery" for the benefit of whites: "bought and sold and treated as . . . ordinary article[s] of merchandise . . . whenever profit could be made." In short, African Americans were a form of property rather than human beings and "had no rights which the white man was bound to respect." As for Dred Scott, he was a citizen neither of Missouri nor of the United States, and thus he had no standing to institute a court proceeding in either jurisdiction.

Even if Scott had had a legitimate right to be heard, Taney maintained, a second, equally imposing barrier existed that invalidated his claim. Scott had based his suit on the belief that his extended residence in free territory had gained his freedom, a mistaken assumption on two grounds. First, the Constitution gave Congress explicit power only over the territories already in existence at the time of the document's writing; thus, it had no authority to prohibit slavery in the Louisiana Territory, and consequently Scott's stay in Wisconsin had not been on free ground after all. Second, his claim violated the Fifth Amendment, which guaranteed that no citizen could be deprived, without due process, not only of life and liberty but of property, which for southerners had always included slaves. "Upon these considerations," Taney wrote, "it is the opinion of the court that the act of Congress which prohibited a citizen from holding and owning property of this kind in the territory . . . is not warranted by the Constitution, and is therefore void." Dred Scott's travails amounted to nothing that would set him free.

The decision was a source of bitter frustration for antislavery leaders, like Frederick Douglass, who assailed it as "judicial . . . wolfishness" that reflected the biased views of the Supreme Court's "slaveholding wing."[8] Clearly, *Dred Scott* reopened a number of critically important questions that northerners believed had already been decided in their favor. Taney and the six justices who voted with him had agreed that as a slave Scott was mere property without any standing as a citizen, and consequently Missouri law determined his status once he had gone back to Saint Louis. Did this mean that any black American, going from a free to a slave state, now could lose his freedom on the basis of local law, which in effect turned him into a piece of property? Similarly, the court ruled that the Fifth Amendment protected a slaveholder's property rights and thus slavery could not be barred from the territories. As Abraham Lincoln would ask in his debates with Stephen Douglas in 1858, could the court extend the principle it had enunciated in relation to territories and also declare that "the Constitution . . . does not permit a *state* to exclude slavery from its limits?" Were northerners at the mercy of a court that had claimed for itself the power to undo all of the North's antislavery legislation overnight and make the entire nation a union of slaveholding states?

Dred Scott also undermined the North's position in relation to the territories. Knowing full well what the court would say, James Buchanan had suggested in his inaugural address that the decision would "speedily and finally settle the one difference of opinion" over the Kansas-Nebraska Bill still creating friction between the regions. Though northerners and southerners alike had accepted popular sovereignty, which left the settlers of a territory "perfectly free to form and regulate their domestic institutions in their own way," they still differed on *when* the question of slave or free should be decided. If the settlers of a new territory made a choice at the beginning of the territorial process, it would determine whether the flow of immigrants would come from the North or the South. If they delayed the choice until just before the time when the territory became a state—that is, after immigrants from both sections had arrived—slavery would already be established, which would make it almost impossible to eliminate. Naturally, the North wanted the vote at the earliest possible time, while southerners favored waiting until statehood was imminent. The *Dred Scott* ruling came down solidly and unequivocally on the side of the South. Since the Supreme Court had concluded that Congress did not have the authority to exclude slavery from a territory not in existence at the time the Constitution was written, no power existed to address the question of whether it would be slave or free until it was prepared to enter the Union and its settlers wrote their state constitution.

Horace Greeley, the editor of the *New York Tribune*, dismissed the *Scott* decision as a judgment carrying no more moral weight than the opinion "of a majority of those congregated in any Washington barroom," but it still came as a seismic shock to many northerners. *Dred Scott* made it clear that although the North was home to several million more people than the South, it was nevertheless at a disadvantage in terms of power. The executive and judicial branches of the federal government had lined up against it, and in Congress a critical number of northern Democrats loyal to the Buchanan administration made it impossible to put together a consistent antislavery majority.

Buchanan had relied heavily on the South to get elected, and as president he repaid his obligation by appointing a number of southern leaders to his cabinet and faithfully supporting their interests against their northern adversaries. The immediate point of contention remained Kansas. After the destruction of Lawrence, northerners had responded with brutal violence of their own, particularly the massacre and mutilation of five proslavery settlers at Pottawatomie Creek, a raid engineered and executed by the strident abolitionist John Brown and his sons, who were intent on instilling "a restraining fear" in slaveholding Kansans lest they should think the sack of Lawrence had given them the upper hand.[9]

A bitter struggle was under way between southerners, supported by Buchanan and the federal authorities, and northerners, whose immigrant population was outstripping the South's. In the first territorial elections of 1854 and 1855, residents of Missouri had crossed the state line into Kansas to intimidate northern voters and cast illegal ballots, which resulted in a proslavery territorial legislature that refused to seat free staters, set up a territorial capital in the southern stronghold of Lecompton, and handpicked a governor sympathetic to slavery. Northerners responded by establishing rival institutions in Topeka, but they remained at a disadvantage because the Pierce administration had recognized only the Lecompton government. In 1857, with President Buchanan's approval, proslavery leaders scheduled a convention for September in Lecompton to draft a constitution for the admission of Kansas to the Union. Knowing the meeting would be rigged in favor of southerners, antislavery supporters boycotted the election of delegates, and of the nine thousand registered voters in the territory, only two

thousand cast ballots, almost all favoring proslavery representatives.[10] Before
the convention began, Buchanan had sent a new governor, Robert J. Walker,
a stalwart Mississippian—originally from Pennsylvania—who had demonstrated his political and personal loyalty to both the Democrats and the
president. Assured that the administration wanted "the actual *bona fide* residents of the Territory, by a fair and regular vote, unaffected by fraud or violence . . . to decide for themselves what shall be their social institutions,"
Walker acted almost immediately to throw out hundreds of questionable
ballots in the recent territorial election, shifting power in the legislature from
southerners to antislavery moderates. When the rigged statehood convention met in September, its members—accustomed to having their own way
and exasperated by what they took to be Governor Walker's naive interference in the territory's affairs—responded by drafting an uncompromisingly
aggressive constitution reflecting their unwillingness to loosen their grasp on
Kansas. The right to own slaves was "inviolable," the document announced,
standing even "before and higher than any constitutional sanction." Nor
could the slaveholders' right to their property be easily changed, since the
state's constitution could not be altered or amended for at least seven years.
Finally, rather than submitting the document to the territory's settlers for
approval, the convention members called for a referendum allowing voters to
decide only one question: whether they preferred the constitution with slavery or without. If the latter option won, no more slaves would be imported,
but in either case the bondsmen who were already in Kansas, and their
descendants, would be allowed to remain.

Free staters refused to cast ballots in the initial referendum, and among
fewer than seven thousand voters, more than six thousand chose the constitution with slavery. Having boycotted the election, northerners questioned
the size of the turnout, however, and a congressional committee declared at
least three thousand of the ballots illegal, coming either from Missouri residents who had crossed the line to vote or Kansans who had died or had
never existed. In January 1858, the committee held a second referendum,
closely supervised by the new antislavery territorial legislature, and this time
voters were allowed to pass judgment on the entire constitution. With most
proslavery voters staying home, only 138 approved the constitution with
slavery, 24 approved it without, and over 10,000 rejected it altogether.
Surveying the vote, Governor Walker acknowledged the obvious: the
Lecompton constitution represented a last-ditch effort by southerners to

save Kansas for slavery. Still trusting that Buchanan sincerely wanted a fair vote, Walker, supported by moderate northern Democrats, recommended that the president throw out the Lecompton constitution. "I doubt if three hundred men wish to fasten slavery on Kansas," he wrote. "No party stands for slavery; [and] the people will fight before they let this cheating document, which means slavery both ways, go through."[11]

Buchanan had cast his lot with the South, however, and he refused to repudiate his support for either the proslavery Kansans or the Lecompton constitution, a tactical error for which he and the Democrats would pay dearly. After the vote overwhelmingly rejecting the document, William Seward, now a leader of the Republican Party, declared the battle for Kansas all but over. Some southerners, unable to countenance the "barefaced lying and cheating" of the Lecompton leadership, were prepared to accept defeat, but for the more militant a victory in Kansas had become a test of their will. The South needed to stand up "for the maintenance of a principle, barren, it is true, but indispensable for our future protection," Louisiana's Senator John Slidell insisted.[12]

Buchanan and his southern advisers had erred badly in judging their support. From the beginning of his presidency, proslavery forces had managed to dominate Congress with a majority composed of the solidly Democratic South supported by a smaller number of dough-faced northerners with stronger loyalties to their party than to their region. Buchanan's determination to shove the outrageous Lecompton swindle down the throat of antislavery Kansans finally became too much for many northern Democrats to accept, and they rebelled, shattering the regional coalition that had given the Buchanan administration control of the House and Senate. Buchanan tried to win back his northern followers with cajolery, threats, and even bribery, but the rift could not be healed as long as the president refused to back down on Kansas. Even Stephen Douglas, who had engineered the reopening of the West to southerners and faithfully supported the territorial policies of Fillmore, Pierce, and Buchanan, turned against the president, unwilling to stand idly by while Buchanan made a travesty of the principle of popular sovereignty to please the South. Calling the initial referendum on the Lecompton constitution nothing more than "trickery and jugglery," Douglas swore that if Kansans were to be given a constitution "in violation of the fundamental principle of free government, under a mode of submission that is a mockery and insult, I will resist it to the last."[13]

With Douglas's help, congressional Republicans managed to block acceptance of the Lecompton constitution. Though it carried in the Senate by a comfortable margin, House Republicans joined by twenty Douglas Democrats succeeded in stalling it by requiring the Kansas legislature to resubmit the constitution to voters in a third, strictly controlled referendum. Buchanan and his congressional allies attempted to influence the vote by including a provision stating that failure to accept the document would mean that Kansas had to wait several years, until its population reached ninety thousand, before it could reapply for statehood. Nevertheless, in August of 1858 Kansans again rejected the proslavery constitution, this time by a margin of six to one.

The defeat brought peace to Kansas, clarifying its future as a free state. Though its loss represented a serious setback for southerners, it ultimately proved less important than the political disaster it visited on the Democratic Party. In the 1858 congressional elections, insurgent Douglas Democrats fought bitterly against party regulars in the North, attacking their readiness to sell out the region's interests for political appointments and personal gain. Only two years earlier, when Buchanan was elected, fifty-three free-state and seventy-five slave-state Democrats had been carried into the House. But with many northerners feeling betrayed by the administration's stand on Kansas, Democrats above the Mason-Dixon Line were turned out in astonishing numbers. When the dust had settled, sixty-nine southern Democrats remained in office, but among northerners the number had fallen to thirty-one, and twelve of those had voted against the Lecompton constitution. Republicans, on the other hand, had gained seventeen seats, which meant not only that they would control the House but that they had picked up a substantial number of voters whose support they could expect in the coming presidential race.[14] The question now was whether they should dilute their principles to unite with the Democrat Douglas and his allies—who had joined the Lecompton struggle not to oppose slavery but to protect popular sovereignty—or retain their distinctive identity as the antislavery party. Just as in 1855, when the Missouri Compromise was dismantled, the lines between traditional political positions had become blurred and the chance for new alliances presented itself; but before they could be seriously considered, John Brown's rebellion distracted the nation, driving a wedge between Republicans and Douglas Democrats.

*   *   *

On October 16, 1859, John Brown, who had already demonstrated his anti-slavery zeal at Pottawatomie, attacked the federal arsenal at Harpers Ferry, Virginia, with an "army" of about twenty men, including two of his sons and five blacks.[15] Taking over the armory, he hoped to distribute weapons to slaves and foment a revolution that would spread throughout the South. The following day, a wildly exaggerated report of the attack reached Washington. Hundreds of abolitionists aided by "a gang of negroes," all heavily armed, had occupied the town, authorities claimed. President Buchanan responded by sending one hundred marines, led by Colonel Robert E. Lee, to crush the rebels, but before they arrived the local militia had cornered Brown and his followers, killing several and leaving nothing for Lee to do but the final mopping up, which he accomplished by beating down the arsenal door and apprehending Brown and seven surviving members of his band.

Two weeks later, the rebel leader was tried and sentenced to be hanged at the beginning of December; before he died, a startling tale of conspiracy unfolded. Brown apparently had not acted on his own but had been supported throughout by the "Secret Six," a group of prominent eastern abolitionists that included Gerrit Smith, a New York philanthropist and one of the nation's largest landholders.[16] Several senators—abolitionists like Seward and Henry Wilson of Massachusetts—had also been told of the plan. Frederick Douglass, who fled to England to avoid prosecution, had been briefed by Brown himself only two months before the attack, when Brown had asked Douglass to join him in order to attract slaves to his cause, like bees to a hive.

To different people, Brown represented wildly different things. To radical thinkers like Henry David Thoreau, Harpers Ferry was "the best news America ever had . . . for no man in America has ever stood up so persistently and effectively for the dignity of human nature," and he declared that when Brown was hung, the gallows would become a symbol as sacred as Christ's cross. Others who shared Brown's abolitionist views reacted more cautiously, reluctant to speak out in favor of what they saw as rash fanaticism. Brown's actions had been "utterly repugnant" and "fatally wrong," the Republican press insisted, not wanting to alienate ordinary northern voters. "An appeal to slaves" was something Republicans "never [had] made, and never will make," the New Hampshire senator John P. Hale assured the nation.[17]

In the South, of course, Brown's raid stoked the fires of hatred and distrust already raging in the hearts of slaveholders. Brown's butchery of defenseless, unarmed settlers in Kansas in 1856 had shown him to be a fiend incarnate; at Harpers Ferry he had hoped to drench the soil in human blood and make the South another Saint-Domingue. And how did the North react? Had Brown robbed a bank, no one would have argued against his execution, but since he chose instead the "robbery of slave property" he had been transformed into a hero and martyr, whose desperate adventure had demonstrated the depth of the abyss between two nations masquerading as one.[18]

Of all the reactions to Harpers Ferry, William Lloyd Garrison's proved the most insightful. The abolitionist leader understood that the importance of Brown's raid lay not in the act itself but in what it showed about the nation's consciousness. In a speech to the Massachusetts Antislavery Society in May of 1860, Garrison pointed out that if Brown had attacked Harpers Ferry twenty years earlier, nearly everyone would have agreed that he died as a lunatic and a fool. Even ten years ago, most northerners still sympathized with the South's objections to abolitionist agitation. But now, Garrison said, most people had no trouble "swallow[ing] John Brown whole, and his rifle in the bargain." The commotion at the U.S. arsenal had simply sounded the time of day, Garrison concluded. "It is high noon, thank God!"[19]

Brown's raid represented a defining event for the nation's politicians. Prior to Harpers Ferry, it at least seemed possible that Republicans and Douglas Democrats might unite in opposition to James Buchanan and the southern wing of the Democratic Party. But Stephen Douglas reacted to Brown's raid by tying it to the Republicans, calling it the "natural, logical, inevitable result of the[ir] doctrines and teachings," and he proposed new antisedition laws aimed at abolitionist groups, which would have given federal authorities power to quash conspiracies threatening the southern states. The shock waves emanating from Brown's raid jolted men, forcing them to revisit their deepest convictions, which accentuated political differences and made cross-party coalitions impossible to form.

As the election season of 1860 began, the two factions of the Democratic Party girded for a fight at the national convention in Charleston, South Carolina, a hotbed of southern radicals. Still in control of the Democrats in Congress, Buchanan had taken his revenge on Douglas by removing him as chairman of the Committee on Territories, but the Illinois senator retained a power base in the local Democratic leadership of the northern states, and his support ran deep enough for him to arrive at the convention with a slim majority of the delegates prepared to back him rather than Buchanan. Though he lacked the two-thirds majority needed to secure the nomination, Douglas had enough votes to control the party platform, and a fight quickly broke out over the slavery plank.

In his 1858 debates with Abraham Lincoln, Douglas had asserted that in spite of the *Dred Scott* ruling giving southerners an inviolable right to slave property in the territories, settlers should feel free to pass their own laws barring slavery. Before coming to the convention, a number of delegates from the Deep South, led by Jefferson Davis of Mississippi, had called for a federal slave code for the territories to protect owners from unfriendly legislation such as Douglas had envisioned and for a statement repudiating his position altogether. When the matter was put to a vote, the Douglas supporters prevailed by a margin of 165 to 138, prompting a southern walkout by 50 delegates from eight states. Even after the slaveholding militants had withdrawn, however, Douglas still lacked the votes to capture the presidential nomination, and when no compromise candidate appeared on whom the separate factions could agree, the delegates decided to adjourn and reconvene two months later in Baltimore. On the second try, Douglas managed to win the nomination, with the Georgian Herschel V. Johnson as his running mate. Douglas's victory was made possible because a second group of southerners had defected, choosing to go instead to Richmond, where the earlier breakaway radicals had assembled to monitor the proceedings in Baltimore. When the news arrived that Douglas would head the regular party ticket, the dissidents chose their own nominees, John C. Breckinridge of Kentucky and Joseph Lane of Oregon, as their presidential and vice presidential candidates. The disagreement over Kansas had splintered the national Democratic Party into a northern and southern wing, with separate tickets and declining prospects in the coming election.[20]

On the Republican side, William Seward appeared to be the likely presidential candidate when the party's convention met in Chicago in May, but he failed to win the nomination on the first two ballots, and Abraham Lincoln emerged as a compromise choice. Seward had entered politics in the 1820s and had established himself as a powerful foe of slavery, but he had also made a considerable number of enemies in more than thirty years on the national scene. Lincoln had the advantage of being relatively unknown, having gained nationwide attention only two years earlier in the seven debates with Douglas in Illinois during their contest for the Senate. Though

Douglas had won the election, Lincoln's oratorical skills and his ability to speak to the slavery issue had raised his stature in the minds of many Republicans. In Illinois Lincoln had refused to back away from the unresolved conflict between the regions. "I believe this government cannot endure permanently half slave and half free," he asserted. Either slavery would be arrested and placed "in the course of ultimate extinction" or it would become lawful throughout the Union. Lincoln steered clear of any suggestion of a radical solution. The federal government should not "directly or indirectly . . . interfere with . . . slavery in the states where it exists," he had declared in the initial debate. "I have no purpose to introduce political and social equality between the white and black races. There is a physical difference between the two, which in my judgment will probably forever forbid their living together upon the footing of perfect equality." Nevertheless, though Negroes were not equal in many respects to whites—"certainly not in color, perhaps not in moral or intellectual endowment"—they were entitled to all the "natural rights enumerated in the Declaration of Independence." In the final debate, in Alton, Lincoln summarized his position on slavery. The fight over slavery represented another chapter in the eternal struggle between right and wrong—a battle by the weak and powerless against what he called the "tyrannical principle" that allowed a despot or a race of men to say, "You work and toil and earn bread, and I'll eat it."[21]

During the debates, Douglas had complained that Lincoln adopted a different set of principles for every locality: in the northern part of the state, they were "jet black," in the center the "color of a decent mulatto," and in southern Illinois "almost white." Without question, Lincoln's critique of slavery contained ideas that sometimes seemed impossible to integrate, allowing different audiences to arrive at a variety of meanings, and his nomination inspired a wide range of reactions. Among southerners, his insistence that the nation could not remain a "house divided" and that either freedom or slavery ultimately would destroy the other showed that he was a fanatic, more dangerous even than Seward. In the North, while Frederick Douglass seemed willing to give Lincoln the benefit of the doubt and praised him for his "cool well-balanced head and firmness of will," other black abolitionists, like H. Ford Douglass (no relation to Frederick), who had dealt with Lincoln in Illinois, dismissed him as a tool of the Slave Power. At best, H. Ford Douglass maintained, Lincoln wanted to stop the extension of slavery in the territories, but he clearly had no interest in doing anything for slaves in the existing states.[22]

H. Ford Douglass had it right—not just about Lincoln but about the entire antislavery Republican Party, which made the territories the central issue in its platform position on slavery. Rejecting the new dogma of *Dred Scott* as dangerous political heresy, the Republicans declared that freedom was the "normal condition" in the United States, and that no one—not Congress, the territorial legislatures, or any individual—could make slavery legal in the territories. But they assured the South that this doctrine spelling the end of slavery in the West did not apply to the existing states. The 1860 Republican platform affirmed "the right of each state to order and control its own domestic institutions according to its own judgment exclusively, essential to that balance of power on which the perfection and endurance of our political fabric depends."

As the election of 1860 drew near, southern Democrats, who insisted on the freedom of slave owners to emigrate with their property anywhere they wanted, and Republicans, who were equally determined to make the territories free once and for all, were poised for a confrontation that never materialized. By now the North and the South had drifted so far apart that instead of a true national election, the country essentially held separate contests on each side of the Mason-Dixon line. In the North, Democratic Party loyalists left the southern candidate, Breckinridge, off the ballot in several states; voters there chose between Lincoln and Douglas. Similarly, the South limited the contest to Breckinridge and John Bell, of Tennessee, the candidate of a new party called the Constitutional Unionists, primarily a collection of old southern Whigs who wanted to put aside slavery as a political issue in order to preserve the Union. Lincoln's name appeared on the ballot of only the northernmost southern states and was excluded altogether in the ten states of the Deep South. In the end he carried only about 40 percent of the nation's popular vote—a total of about 1,850,000, nearly all from the North—but he won in an electoral college landslide, receiving 180 votes from eighteen free states. The other northern candidate, Douglas, finished second in the popular vote, with about 1,300,000, but managed a mere 12 electoral votes, winning only Missouri and 3 electors from New Jersey. Of the southern candidates, Breckinridge won 72 electoral college votes from eleven slave states, and a popular vote of about 850,000. Bell won in three border states—Kentucky, Tennessee, and Virginia—capturing 39 electoral votes and a popular total of about 600,000.[23]

* * *

Lincoln's election was generally well received in the North—even among the abolitionists, a group usually quick to criticize Republicans as too cautious and slow-moving in relation to slavery. A Lincoln presidency, in and of itself, might not offer much, Frederick Douglass noted in November 1860, but "in light of its relations and bearings," it signaled a monumental step forward. "For fifty years the country has taken the law from the lips of an exacting, haughty, and imperious slave oligarchy." Lincoln's election had "vitiated their authority, and broken their power" by uncovering the North's strength and the South's weakness. Even more important, Douglass added, "it has demonstrated the possibility of electing, if not an Abolitionist, at least an *anti-slavery* reputation to the Presidency of the United States."[24]

For the first time since John Quincy Adams, the nation had a president firmly committed to antislavery principles and, even more important, one who owed no political debt to the South. Recognizing that the tide had shifted in national politics, many southerners seemed ready to agree with Frederick Douglass, doubting only that Lincoln would prove to be merely an empty reputation rather than a full-blown abolitionist. Even the relatively moderate *Atlanta Confederacy*, a newspaper that had backed Stephen Douglas in the election, despaired at the prospect of a Lincoln presidency: "Let the consequences be what they may—whether the Potomac is crimsoned in human gore, and Pennsylvania Avenue is paved ten fathoms in depth with mangled bodies, or whether the last vestige of liberty is swept from the face of the American continent, the South will never submit to such humiliation and degradation as the inauguration of Abraham Lincoln."[25] Not all southerners reacted so violently. Particularly in the upper South, with far fewer slaves and only half as many slave owners, a strong contingent of Constitutional Unionists counseled patience and restraint. The time for rebellion would come when "the Constitution is trampled upon, the Lexington *Kentucky Statesman* suggested; until then, the South needed to "wait, wait, wait." But the Unionists were arguing from a decided disadvantage, asking southerners simply to sit still until they were slapped in the face again, while secessionists could play on their frustration and announce that the time had come to defend their dignity and honor.

The most militant of the southern states, South Carolina, with a population nearly 60 percent black, had already decided upon radical action. In November, when the state legislature met to pick its representatives to the electoral college and Lincoln's victory seemed a foregone conclusion, it called for a constitutional convention in December to consider secession. On December 20, citing their belief that Republicans intended to wage war "against slavery until it shall cease throughout the United States," the 169 delegates in attendance, nearly all slave owners, voted unanimously to leave the Union.

As the South Carolina radicals hoped, their precipitate departure set off a firestorm that spread swiftly across the lower South. In a little over a month, with the intimidating help of secessionist mobs, six other states left the Union: Georgia, Florida, Mississippi, Alabama, Louisiana, and Texas. In February 1861, all except Texas—which insisted on a popular referendum before it could finally approve secession—met in Montgomery, Alabama, to form a provisional Confederate government. As Alexander H. Stephens, who had been a Georgia senator and would become vice president of the Confederacy, explained, the rebel government's foundations rested upon a single great truth: that "the negro is not the equal of the white man; that slavery, subordination to the superior race, is his natural and normal condition." The secessionists framed the outline of a new nation, but they desperately needed other southern states to join them to have any real chance for success. The white population of the states that met at Montgomery barely exceeded 2.6 million—less than a third of the total for the entire South. If the Confederacy hoped to stand on its own—not only against the North but as an independent nation—it would need the manpower of states like Virginia, North Carolina, and Tennessee, as well as their wealth and natural resources.

Hoping the secessionists could be brought back into line simply by waiting them out, Lincoln reacted calmly to the challenge. A confrontation might drive states that were still wavering—sympathetic to the rebels but hesitant to leave the Union—into the Confederate camp. Maintaining a public silence prior to his inauguration, Lincoln communicated privately with southern friends, making clear that he had no intention of pursuing an abolitionist agenda. Specifically, he assured them that slavery would not be threatened anywhere in the existing states or in the District of Columbia. He also promised to leave untouched the domestic slave trade and vigorously enforce the Fugitive Slave Law, in part by pressuring northern states to repeal their liberty ordinances. Finally, he offered his support for a constitutional amendment permanently guaranteeing slavery's existence, an idea southerners had floated in the past.[26]

On March 4, 1861, in his inaugural address, Lincoln made his views public, bitterly disappointing northern abolitionists. Flatly stating that the North would not start a war, Lincoln aimed to solidify the wavering southern states' support for the Union, which he hoped would force the rebels' return. To Frederick Douglass, the new president appeared just as ready to kneel before the Slave Power as any of his predecessors. Analyzing Lincoln's address in his *Monthly*, Douglass observed that the president had pronounced himself willing to pursue slaves "if they run away, to shoot them down if they rise against their oppressors, and to prohibit the Federal Government *irrevocably* from interfering for their deliverance." It remained to be seen, Douglass angrily observed, whether Lincoln would be "able to do more than hand over some John Brown to be hanged, suppress a slave insurrection, or catch a runaway slave—whether [he is] powerless for liberty, and only powerful for slavery."[27] He found Lincoln's unwillingness to contest the South's constitutional right to slavery outrageous, but he nevertheless acknowledged that the president had made two important points with no concessions to the southern rebels. First, it was Lincoln's duty as president to maintain the Union, and he had assured the nation that it would remain inviolable. Second, he had promised not to retreat from the Republican Party's goals in the territories. Moderates in Congress had explored several schemes to defuse the crisis between the regions, the most notable being the Crittenden Plan, which would have reinstated 36°30' as the dividing line between slave and free territory, but in his inaugural address Lincoln rejected any compromise, insisting that the territories would be free.

Lincoln's speech disappointed the rebels more than it did Douglass. The president had been cool and conciliatory, rather than threatening. As the moderate editor of the Raleigh *North Carolina Standard* observed, "*It [was] not a war message* but a plea for harmony," which the "Disunionists" could not have approved. What would have made them "shout for joy" was a speech breathing "violence and war" that would have guaranteed "the permanent and final disruption of the Union."[28] Instead, Lincoln had chosen the path of "masterly inactivity," as the *New York Times* put it, aimed at gently converting "the Southern people from Secessionism." Force could never restore the Union or permanently preserve it, the *Times* observed. Southerners would have to "*come* back,—not be driven back" to their partnership with the North, and in the meantime the government needed to "avoid everything which will change the issue and prevent [them] from exercising their calm judgment on the subject."[29]

Part of Lincoln's solemn inaugural pledge to preserve the Union was a promise "to hold, occupy, and possess the property and places belonging to the government."[30] Across the Deep South, rebel forces had already taken over federal forts and arsenals, and only two installations, both offshore, remained in federal hands: Fort Sumter, at Charleston, South Carolina; and Fort Pickens, at Pensacola, Florida.[31] Pickens had been secured through a formal truce negotiated with the rebels in Florida, making Sumter the only remaining federal installation that Lincoln was committed to protect. As such, it became a symbol for northerners and southerners alike. On the one side, it embodied the federal government's determination not to allow the rebels to quit the Union; on the other, it represented the continuing unwillingness of northerners to recognize the South's legitimate constitutional rights—in this case, the right to secede. Even though it had no real strategic value, Fort Sumter carried heavy symbolic meaning, making it a likely place for trouble to start. A few days before Lincoln's inauguration, the outgoing Buchanan administration had received word from the fort's commander, Major Robert Anderson, that his supplies were nearly exhausted and that at best he and his men would be able to hold out for only six more weeks. Anderson suggested that twenty thousand to thirty thousand troops would be required to storm the batteries trained on Sumter, if the government meant to defend it. Lincoln, as the new president, received these dispatches the day after his inaugural, as Buchanan and his advisers retired to the sidelines, leaving a nonplussed chief executive with an unexpected and critical problem demanding his attention.[32] Lincoln had been given to understand that Sumter was well provisioned and maintained a large store of supplies, allowing him time to wait out the rebels. Anderson's dispatches threw his entire policy into disarray. Either he would have to surrender the fort, a vital symbol of the government's resolve, or he needed to act decisively to relieve it, dropping the policy of "masterly inactivity" with which he had hoped to gain the support of southern moderates. Quite naturally, Lincoln vacillated, realizing the importance of his choice but uncertain what it should be. Could he rely on Anderson, he asked his subordinates. Might the major be a southern sympathizer, looking for a peaceful way to hand over the fort to the rebels? Uncertain, Lincoln sought the counsel of his newly appointed cabinet and military leaders, and for nearly a month the evacuation of Sumter seemed imminent. To Simon Cameron, the secretary of war, it appeared certain that armed intervention would initiate a long and bloody conflict. For Secretary of State William Seward no military advantage could be gained, and the federal government likely would lose the wavering border states. Even military leaders like Winfield Scott believed that the fort was not worth holding and that the greater wisdom was in evacuation, which would "give confidence to the eight remaining slave-holding states, and render their cordial adherence to the Union perpetual."

Sometime near the end of March, Lincoln told the House Republican leader Francis P. Blair Sr. that almost without exception his cabinet favored the evacuation of Sumter and he believed that "such would be the result." Still, the president seemed reluctant to commit himself absolutely—no doubt because he was wary of the reaction in the North. Though evacuation represented sound policy in relation to the Confederacy and the border states, at home people had begun to grumble about Lincoln's likely capitulation; on April 1, Republicans in Ohio had been badly beaten in a state election, a loss that party leaders attributed to the continuing stalemate at Sumter. As one Ohio Republican wrote, the state had spoken "in thunder tones" against the surrender. "It is to us a Waterloo defeat, and all know that the supposed evacuation . . . is what did it."

Lincoln delayed a final decision, and with time running out, opinion all around him seemed to be shifting. Not only had his friend and fellow Republican Lyman Trumbull introduced a resolution in the Senate calling on the president to "use all the means in his power to hold and protect" the nation's property, but by the beginning of April most of his cabinet members had reversed their position, with only Seward and Caleb Smith, the secretary of the interior, still favoring evacuation. In the end, Lincoln was left to make the decision essentially on his own, and as he often would throughout the Civil War, he attempted to steer a middle course, which meant rejecting both evacuation and a military defense of Sumter. He decided instead to reprovision the fort, sending Anderson news of his intention on April 4 and writing the South Carolina governor two days later, indicating that only essential supplies, no additional troops or weapons, would be inserted into Sumter—peacefully he prayed, but with force if necessary. By creating as little disturbance as possible, Lincoln aimed to salvage his original strategy of placating southerners while preserving Sumter as a symbol of the North's resolve. Politically, he had come to believe that the fort could not be surrendered without serious repercussions for the Republican Party, and he hoped that by carefully limiting the government's role to resupplying Anderson and his men, he could place the responsibility squarely on the shoulders of the rebels if the mission deteriorated into an armed encounter.[33]

On April 8, the South Carolina governor received Lincoln's notice that he had dispatched a naval expedition to provision Sumter. The governor turned the matter over to P. G. T. Beauregard, the Confederate general in charge at Charleston, who only two months earlier had resigned as superintendent of West Point. Beauregard in turn relayed the message to Jefferson Davis, the Confederate president, who demanded the surrender of the fort before the relief ships arrived. On April 11, Anderson refused to surrender, and 4:30 the following morning the first shots sounded in an artillery bombardment that took no lives but would continue for thirty-three hours. Finally, on April 14, Anderson raised the white flag, surrendering Sumter to the Confederate forces.[34]

With the genie of war out of the bottle, both sides moved quickly, anxious to prove that the other lacked the necessary resolve for a long and bitter struggle. On April 15, Lincoln issued a proclamation requesting seventy-five thousand state militia men to quell an insurrection "too powerful to be suppressed by the ordinary course of judicial proceedings." Lincoln's call not only brought a flood of exuberant volunteers, it also precipitated the departure of four of the states that had vacillated between the Union and the Confederacy. The defections of Virginia, Arkansas, North Carolina, and Tennessee brought the rebels to their full strength, more than doubling their white population and vastly improving their chances not only for military victory but for an independent future. With hymns in praise of freedom and not the slightest hint of irony, young southerners left their homes and took to the field, confident that they could not fail in a cause so just. Across the battlefields were other young men—in many ways, their mirror images— with as deep a belief in their own cause and equally willing to die for it. The gathering armies of the North were the "instruments of God's vengeance, to execute His judgment," Alexander Randall, the Wisconsin governor, said. "His flails wherewith on God's great Southern threshing floor, He will pound rebellion for its sins."[35] Over the next four years, the nation would be shrouded in darkness, and an ocean of blood would flow in America's cruelest, most costly war.[36]

*   *   *

Perhaps no question from the American past has been more widely discussed than the causes of the Civil War. Certainly, slavery, the great human issue dividing the North and the South, lay at the root of the conflict. Nevertheless, most northerners had no interest in going to war to emancipate southern blacks and would have been willing to allow slavery to stand if an agreement could have been reached confining it to the nation's southern tier. Only three years after the war ended, Alexander H. Stephens, the Confederacy's vice president, published *A Constitutional View of the Late War Between the States*, in which he argued that slavery had been "a drop in the ocean compared . . . with other considerations."[37] Though the rejection or acceptance of slavery was the defining question separating the two societies, that alone did not bring them to war. Rather, the conflict arose from a variety of causes, the most fundamental being the power struggle engendered by westward expansion, which destroyed the fragile constitutional agreement the founding fathers had reached in 1787.

From 1820 on, the struggle between North and South had escalated as each sought to expand its way of life into the new western states and gain control of the national government. Both the Louisiana Purchase and the Treaty of Guadalupe Hidalgo added millions of acres of virgin territory to the nation, creating tremendous opportunities for expansion, but also increasing regional tension. By 1860, northerners and southerners appeared ready to agree that the balance of power envisioned in 1787 no longer worked—but each thought that the other side had taken advantage of them. In the South, slaveholders believed an absolute constitutional guarantee existed that slavery would remain a state matter in which the national government had no right to interfere, and they felt betrayed not only by the northern states' specific refusal to obey the Constitution but by their failure to honor its spirit. In their eyes, northerners had made no real effort to muzzle the abolitionists, to enforce the Fugitive Slave Law, or to open the territories to all the nation's citizens by granting southerners the same constitutional protections they gave to their own property.

Northerners were vexed by the Slave Power's stranglehold on the federal government, which it had managed to maintain since the nation's beginning. Between the election of George Washington and 1850, the presidency had been held by slave owners for fifty years. Both the Speaker and the chairman of the Ways and Means Committee in the House had been southerners for more than forty of those years. In the Supreme Court, of the thirty-one justices appointed over the same period, eighteen came from the South; and of the five two-term presidents—Washington, Jefferson, Madison, Monroe, and Jackson—all were southerners.[38] Since the signing of the Constitution, the North had enjoyed a substantial population advantage—by 1860, nearly 19 million whites lived above the Mason-Dixon line and barely 8 million below it—but still the South controlled the government in Washington. Quite naturally, northerners had a difficult time accepting their minority position when an imposing majority of American citizens lived in the North.

Lincoln's election in 1860 precipitated a crisis that shattered the nation. Buchanan's ill-advised insistence that Kansas had to become a slave state destroyed the coalition of northerners and southerners that had enabled proslavery Democrats to hold the presidency, and Lincoln had emerged as the angry North's response to the arrogance of the Buchanan administration. Throughout the 1850s, the South had put together a string of important legislative and judicial victories—a new Fugitive Slave Law, the repeal of the Missouri Compromise, the reopening of the West to slavery, and *Dred Scott*—but southerners believed that Lincoln's election blighted their hopes. The prospect of a new and possibly vindictive northern president with strong antislavery beliefs was enough to convince southern radicals that they could no longer find a home in the Union. To them, secession appeared as the only alternative, and they insisted that the individual states retained the right to withdraw from the Union based on the Tenth Amendment of the Constitution, which guaranteed that all powers not delegated to the federal government remained in the hands of the separate states. The principle of states' rights had been established at the Constitutional Convention—over the objections of James Madison, Gouverneur Morris, and others—but precisely how far it extended remained unclear.

Talk of secession had arisen before on at least three occasions, and on both sides of the Mason-Dixon line. In the 1790s, southerners, led by Jefferson and Madison, had formulated resolutions in the Kentucky and Virginia legislatures objecting to the recently instituted Alien and Sedition Acts, maintaining that only the states could pass laws limiting free speech and a free press. In 1814, New Englanders had met at the Hartford Convention to protest the War of 1812, threatening to withdraw from the Union and negotiate their own peace with the British.[39] In 1832, the southern nullifiers, led by John C. Calhoun, had insisted that each of the separate states had the right to repudiate federal legislation inimical to its interest—in this case, a series of new tariffs that fell more heavily on the South than on the North. As expounded by Calhoun, the principle of nullification rested on the constitutional recognition of two levels of government, the state and the nation. New laws had to be approved by a majority at each level before they became valid, and each individual state retained the right to secede, because the Union represented a compact of independent states that had never agreed to give up their sovereignty.[40] In the past, secession represented the ultimate threat that dissidents used to express their unwillingness to accept the hegemony of the federal government, but the leaders of the Confederacy had gone a step further by not merely talking about it but actually attempting it.

The South's position made war unavoidable because Lincoln took seriously his duty to preserve the Union. Even before his inauguration, he recognized that the southern radicals had left him without choices. "We have just carried an election on principles fairly stated to the people," he wrote Representative James T. Hale of Pennsylvania in January 1861. "Now we are told in advance the Government shall be broken up unless we surrender to those we have beaten. . . . In this they are either attempting to play upon us or they are in dead earnest. Either way, if we surrender, it is the end of us and of the government. They will repeat the experiment upon us *ad libitum*."[41]

Though the South had no way of realizing it, in Lincoln it had finally come up against a northern politician who, when the moment of truth arrived, could not be pushed into giving slave owners unreasonable concessions. As the new president told a Pennsylvania audience in 1861, southerners had "a Constitution under which we have lived over seventy years, and acts of Congress of their own framing, with no prospect of their being changed; and they can never have a more shallow pretext for breaking up the government, or extorting a compromise, than now."

What caused the Civil War? Surely it never was a crusade by the North to set blacks free. Slavery did represent the fundamental, irreconcilable difference separating the North and the South, but the problem they finally were willing to fight over arose from the challenge presented by westward expansion to the uneasy partnership hammered out at the Constitutional Convention—which, in the final critical hours, became a contest of wills between southern radicals and Abraham Lincoln.

CHAPTER 8

THE TOILS OF RECONSTRUCTION

Nigger voting, holding office, and sitting in the jury box, are all wrong, and against the sentiment of the country. Nothing is more certain to occur than that these outrages upon justice and good government will soon be removed, and the unprincipled men who are now their advocates will sink lower in the social scale than the niggers themselves.

—COLUMBUS (MISSISSIPPI) DEMOCRAT, 1869

A revolution is taking place—by force of arms—and a race are disenfranchised— they are to be returned to a condition of serfdom—an era of second slavery.

—ADELBERT AMES, 1875

On April 9, 1865, Robert E. Lee surrendered at Appomattox. Five days later, Lincoln's assassination would leave the nation with no clear plan for the reconstruction of the South. Lincoln once said that he never controlled events but instead had been controlled by them. As the newspaper editor and northern Democrat John Forney put it, perhaps explaining the president better than he had explained himself, Lincoln moved "in conjunction with propitious circumstances, not waiting to be dragged by the force of events or wasting strength in premature struggles with them."[1] In the final months of his life, with the war winding down, Lincoln watched as the force of events and circumstances unfolded, searching for the best way to rebuild the Union.

In his annual message to Congress on December 6, 1864, he had urged the members to pass the Thirteenth Amendment outlawing slavery. Two months later, after much wrangling, the amendment was approved, and on February 3 Lincoln met with representatives of the Confederate president, Jefferson Davis, to explore the possibility of peace. Lincoln indicated that he could delay emancipation perhaps until 1870, providing the Confederate legislatures would agree in advance to ratify the amendment. Rebuffed by Davis, Lincoln buttonholed General Benjamin F. Butler in early April to solicit his views on colonization, an idea that Lincoln had found attractive since before the Civil War and one that he still hoped would solve the dilemma posed by white unwillingness to integrate with blacks.[2] The president had economic reasons as well: in an address to Congress in 1862, he had argued that reducing the nation's supply of black labor would increase the demand and the wages for a white labor force. An American entrepreneur named Ambrose W. Thompson had acquired 2 million acres in what is now Panama and was offering to sell coal to the government at half price if it would provide him with Negro colonists to work as miners. Lincoln appointed Senator Samuel Pomeroy of New Jersey as the United States colonization agent to round up prospects and arrange transportation, but William H. Seward, the secretary of state, questioned the validity of Thompson's title to the land and persuaded the president to drop the Panama idea. Soon afterward Lincoln was attracted by a similar business venture, this one on a small island off the coast of Haiti known as Ile à Vache. This time, he signed a contract with several American businessmen to provide Negro colonists as lumberjacks, and in May 1863, 435 Negroes left Washington, D.C., for the island. The project failed miserably and quickly turned into a disaster: in its first several months 100 blacks died of smallpox or starvation, and in February 1864 Lincoln rescued the remaining blacks and brought them back to the mainland. A few days after his conversation with General Butler—who was discouraging on the subject of any colonization plan—Lincoln suggested in his last public address, April 11, 1865, that blacks who had served in the Union Army, as well as the most intelligent among them who had remained civilians, should be given the right to vote.

Many misread Lincoln as weak and vacillating, but he had become a master at weighing his options and choosing the best opportunities that circumstances presented. Early in the war, he had indicated that what he did in relation to "slavery, and the colored race" would depend on how it affected the reuniting of the North and the South. "If I could save the Union without freeing *any* slaves, I would do it," he wrote on August 22, 1862, to Horace Greeley, the Republican editor of the *New York Tribune*, who had demanded in an editorial that the president free the slaves, "and if I could save it by freeing *all* the slaves I would do it; and if I could save it by freeing some and leaving others alone I would also do that."[3] For Lincoln, the resurrection of the prewar Union represented a sacred duty, and every step he took throughout the war, including freeing the slaves, he conceived as a means of achieving that goal.

Lincoln unveiled his Emancipation Proclamation in September 1862 with the intention of putting it into effect at the New Year. Hoping to entice slave owners to rejoin the Union, Lincoln gave the Confederates one hundred days to cease their rebellion or face not only the loss of their bondsmen but the possibility that they might revolt or run away to join the Union forces. If the Confederate states did not capitulate, Lincoln would free "all persons held as slaves within any state, the people whereof shall then be in rebellion against the United States." A stunning practical maneuver that undermined the South's control over its slaves while at the same time tapping into a new source of manpower for the Union Army, the Emancipation Proclamation—as William Seward observed—emancipated slaves only beyond its reach and left them in bondage where it might have had an effect.[4] In Kentucky, Missouri, Maryland, and Delaware, which had never left the Union, as well as in occupied areas of Louisiana, Virginia, and Tennessee, over seven hundred thousand blacks remained enslaved, untouched by what Lincoln himself called "a fit and necessary war measure." Most of them would have to wait until the war's end and passage of the Thirteenth Amendment before gaining their freedom.

In spite of its limitations, most abolitionists praised the Proclamation, willing to concede that as far as it went, it represented an act of immense historic consequence. Still, they remained less than enthusiastic, troubled because the Proclamation was obviously a strategic act aimed at prosecuting the war rather than a moral choice in favor of black freedom; and at year's end, when Lincoln issued his wartime reconstruction plan for areas occupied by the Union Army, Radical Republicans, the abolitionist wing of the party, were doubly distressed by the lax terms he set for the readmission of conquered states to the Union.

To be granted a pardon, former Confederates had merely to swear future loyalty to the national government and formally accept the end of slavery. Certain groups were prohibited from taking the oath—Confederate officials, high-ranking military officers, and anyone guilty of mistreating prisoners of war—but everyone else would have their property restored, with the exception of their slaves, immediately upon reaffirming their allegiance to the United States. A state became eligible to reenter the Union when the number of individuals signing the loyalty pledge reached 10 percent of the votes that the state had cast in the national election of 1860. At that point, the recently converted supporters of national unity—those who had signed on the dotted line and represented no more than one in twenty of a state's population—could elect delegates to write a new state constitution, which would lead to the return of full statehood once Congress had approved it. The new state constitutions had to contain a statement abolishing slavery, but they could also include a temporary pauper's code for blacks, consistent "with their present condition as a laboring, landless, and homeless class."

As with all his war moves, Lincoln baited his hook with an easy peace, hoping to divide the Confederate states and lure at least some of them back into the Union. To the Radical Republicans, however, his conciliatory attitude and apparent willingness to leave the future of freed slaves in the hands of southern whites indicated a lack of moral commitment and will to guide the nation through the critical period of postwar reconstruction. Lincoln seemed ready to cap the North's victory and make the nation whole again as quickly as possible by establishing local governments in the rebellious states, which would restore power to essentially the same people who had turned their backs on the Union in 1860.

At the war's beginning, Lincoln had not foreseen the emancipation of the slaves, and though he rejoiced in having lifted the moral burden of slavery from the nation's back, he had no clear idea of what should become of the 4 million blacks who gained their freedom. Resurrecting the Union had been the focus of everything he did for four long years; but with peace in sight, a troubling future, filled with alarming questions he had barely considered, presented itself. In February 1865, when the House approved the Thirteenth Amendment, Lincoln declared it "a King's cure for all the evils that winds the whole thing up."[5] Rather than a cure, however, the end of slavery raised a series of new questions that in many ways the nation would find harder to deal with than anything it had faced during the war.

*   *   *

Having been granted their freedom, blacks presumably became citizens, but what exactly did that mean? Southerners still clung to their belief in black inferiority and remained as opposed as ever to the two races intermingling. In the North, although many whites had favored emancipation (if for no other reason than to punish the South), they, too, still harbored deep prejudices and had no interest in opening their communities to blacks. Only the Radical Republicans, a small minority, believed in racial equality at least in some form, but their numbers would shrink as halfhearted supporters, exhausted by the war, fell away when they realized that the struggle for racial justice had only just begun. With no national consensus in favor of admitting them into white society, what would become of the newly freed slaves?

Lincoln and most northern whites appeared ready to savor their victory and return things to normal as quickly as possible by restoring traditional institutions in the South. Having saved the Union, chastised southern slave owners, and—as a kind of moral bonus—ended slavery, their triumph seemed complete. Now they were willing to offer a just and lasting peace, followed by a policy of national reconciliation that promised "malice toward none [and] charity for all." In practical terms, this meant a return to power for the old landholding aristocracy, which had been shorn of its slaves but could be counted on to maintain order in southern society, just as it had in the past. Northerners had always preferred to see slavery as a southern issue, and now many of them were willing to turn the problem of how to treat emancipated slaves over to former slave owners—a strategy that would leave the North free of responsibilities in regard to the freedmen. The Radicals alone objected, offering their own fiercely contentious interpretation of what needed to be done to rebuild the South. To their way of thinking, the real issue underlying the war had always been the question of black equality rather than Union solidarity, and the North's victory had created a historic opportunity to reshape southern society.

The Radicals wanted to convert the failed Confederate rebellion into a social revolution by restructuring the southern states as a requirement for their readmission to the Union. With the Confederacy on its knees, the time was right for a compensatory program that would shatter the foundations of the Old South and give former slaves a foothold as free citizens. "The infernal laws of slavery" had prevented blacks from acquiring even a rudimentary education to manage the ordinary affairs of life, Thaddeus Stevens, the Radical leader in the House, observed, which obliged Congress "to provide for them until they can take care of themselves. If we do not furnish them with homesteads and hedge them about with protective laws; if we leave them to the legislation of their late masters, we had better have left them in bondage."[6]

At the root of the disagreement between Lincoln and the Radicals lay differing views of the Confederate rebellion. Seeking to pave the way for an easy peace, Lincoln argued that the seceding states had never left the Union; instead, the rebellion had been carried out by individuals, who would be held accountable—at least until they admitted their error and renewed their loyalty to the nation. But the *states themselves* had never lost the right to reclaim their places in the Union with their basic institutions intact—except for slavery, which had been permanently and irrevocably destroyed. The Radicals, by contrast, insisted that the southern states had voluntarily removed themselves from the Union and by virtue of their rebellion had committed what Charles Sumner, who had joined the Radicals at the start of the war, called "state suicide," forfeiting all their rights and protections under the Constitution and putting themselves in the same position as any other territory belonging to the United States. Having recklessly thrown away statehood, they had no choice but to meet whatever conditions Congress set before being restored to the Union.

Though Lincoln tried to dismiss his disagreement with the Radicals as an argument over a "pernicious abstraction," the difference was significant for two reasons: First, if the states had never left the Union, they retained their constitutional rights and thus were protected from any sweeping new requirements for readmission to statehood which Congress might impose in order to break the old aristocracy's stranglehold on southern society. Second, in terms of jurisdiction, the executive branch could insist that it retained the power to set policy for the rebels if they remained states, but as territories their fate would be in the hands of Congress.

When Lincoln was assassinated, many Radical Republicans looked upon his death as a blessing.[7] No longer saddled with an apparently weak leader, they had high hopes for his successor, Andrew Johnson, who, as the Union's provisional wartime governor in his home state of Tennessee, had seemed intent on a thorough housecleaning to destroy the old order based on slavery. "The tall poppies must be struck down," he proclaimed in a nominating speech at the Republican convention in 1864, swearing vengeance against the leaders of the Confederacy. More of a Free-Soiler than an abolitionist, however, Johnson proved a bitter disappointment to the Radicals. Though he stood fast as an enemy of the slaveholding aristocracy, he identified with the white laboring classes and had no interest in promoting black equality. In a remark to Lincoln that spring he had noted that colonization might yet provide the answer for "two races [that] cannot get along together."

Reiterating Lincoln's contention that only individuals had rebelled, President Johnson maintained that the rights of the rebel states had been suspended but not destroyed, and he moved swiftly to restore them to the Union with a minimum of difficulty. He established a policy for amnesty much like Lincoln's, which allowed most Confederate sympathizers to regain their rights as citizens merely by pledging their future loyalty to the United States. He also invited the rebel states to hold constitutional conventions at which anyone could serve as a delegate who had signed a loyalty oath and was eligible to vote on the day the state seceded—a provision that conveniently excluded African Americans.

Johnson stonewalled Congress, refusing to support critical measures needed to establish blacks as independent citizens. The Massachusetts abolitionist Wendell Phillips declared that before the nation could leave ex-slaves to fend for themselves, they ought to be "on [their] own soil, . . . with the right of the ballot and the school-house within reach."[8] Land, the vote, and education were the three specific areas in which blacks wanted help in order to defend themselves against southern whites. Johnson insisted, however, that the federal government's responsibility extended no further than simply protecting the persons and property of the freed slaves, and he balked at allowing them to vote, arguing that the question of suffrage ought to be left to the individual states to decide. Blacks, Johnson insisted in his December 1867 annual address to Congress, had "less capacity for government than any other race of people. No independent government of any form has ever been successful in their hands. On the contrary, wherever they have been left to their own devices they have shown a constant tendency to relapse into barbarism."

Johnson not only opposed black voting rights but also rejected the nascent policy of confiscation and redistribution that the Radicals had hoped would establish blacks on their own land. Throughout the war, the expectation had been building among southern blacks that the government would grant them "forty acres and a mule" to start them on the way to economic independence. There had been sporadic efforts at land redistribution during the war, particularly on the sea islands off South Carolina, which the U.S. Navy occupied at the end of 1861, and later along the Georgia coast, after William Tecumseh Sherman's march to the sea. Sherman's army had attracted thousands of freed slaves, who abandoned their former plantations to accompany the liberating troops. At least in part because he wanted relief from the burden of supplying thousands of camp followers, Sherman exercised his power as the region's military commander to issue a special field order enabling freed blacks to take possession of the land abandoned by slave owners on Georgia's offshore islands—between Charleston, South Carolina, and Augusta—and on adjacent coastal plantations up to thirty miles inland. Each family would receive possessory title to forty acres of land for the duration of the war, with the understanding that Congress would make their ownership permanent once peace arrived. Soon forty thousand ex-slaves had been settled on more than four hundred thousand acres of rich farmland, where they quickly set to work building independent black communities, with constitutions and laws regulating schools, churches, roads, and other matters associated with their daily lives.

Unfortunately, Sherman's Special Field Order #15 represented the high point in land distribution to former slaves. Two months later, Congress formed the Bureau of Refugees, Freedmen, and Abandoned Lands, under the supervision of the War Department, to deal with emancipated blacks and displaced whites. Along with providing rations and medical aid to those in immediate need, the bureau took charge of eight hundred thousand acres of land that had been abandoned, seized for taxes, or taken from slave owners for their part in the rebellion. Congress dramatically weakened the bill authorizing the bureau, however, and turned the proposed massive land redistribution into a hollow promise. Instead of outright grants of land, the bureau gave blacks the right to lease forty acres for three years at an annual rent of 6 percent of the value of the land, with an option to purchase when the lease expired. Even more discouraging, the government set aside for blacks only a small portion of the land it held; the rest it sold at public auctions, where the bulk of it fell into the hands of speculators or large plantation operators.[9]

Conservative Republicans and Democrats in Congress had gutted the ex-slaves' dream of land ownership, but Johnson gave it its final interment. In September 1865, the president reversed the policy of the Freedmen's Bureau, ending confiscation and ordering the restoration of all land to its original owners, providing they signed loyalty oaths and their property had not been ordered sold by a court decree. Johnson sent out federal marshals to seize from blacks nearly all the area covered by Sherman's field order, along with thousands of additional acres in the Carolinas, Virginia, Louisiana, and Mississippi. A few months later, he vetoed the renewal bill for the Freedmen's Bureau, putting it out of business and effectively ending the ex-slaves' hopes for land of their own.

Johnson professed to believe that the South "would treat the negro with greater kindness than the North if it were let alone and not exasperated," and he encouraged the rebel states to hold conventions to draft new constitutions while at the same time providing them with only the broadest hints at what those documents should contain. Other than exacting a repeal of the articles of secession, adoption of the Thirteenth Amendment, and a pledge of allegiance to the United States, he left it to the all-white delegates at the southern conventions to fill in the details of their new state governments. The conventions responded with defiance, making sure that the old white order would remain in charge throughout the South. As the Republican *North Carolina Standard* noted, "disloyalty had crouched and sniveled at the feet of the victorious national forces" a few months earlier, but Johnson's "leniency and mercy had warmed it into life [and] treason [had] become bold and defiant."[10] Though the delegates reluctantly accepted the president's relatively mild demands in relation to secession, slavery, and the loyalty oath, they left no doubt that little had changed in the way that southerners intended to live, and that their blacks would continue to be denied most of the privileges of citizenship, such as the right to vote, hold office, sit on juries, and attend public schools.

Elections followed in November 1865 as the next step in Johnson's rush to resurrect the South, and with blacks unable to vote, southerners overwhelmingly returned former Confederate leaders to power, both at the state level and as members of the House and Senate, who presumably would assume their long-vacant seats in Congress. The seventy-odd southern electees who headed to Washington formed a rogue's gallery of unreconstructed rebels, many of whom had never even bothered to take the oath of allegiance to the national government. Along with Alexander H. Stephens, the Confederate vice president, who had been charged with treason and paroled, the South's representatives on their way to Washington included fifty-eight former Confederate congressmen, six members of the cabinet, and a number of high-ranking military officers and former state legislators.[11]

In January 1866, in his State of the Union address, Johnson tried to pass off the South's restoration of civil government as a fait accompli. Order had been restored, he assured Congress, and elected officials had taken the reins of power. Nothing more needed to be done, except to admit southerners to their rightful places in the national government. More than a little skeptical, the Republicans, led by the Radicals, stood their ground, anxious to contest the president's unseemly haste in returning the southern states to the leaders of the slavocracy. "Neither the rebellion nor slavery is yet ended," Charles Sumner wrote to friends in Massachusetts, and he and his congressional allies slammed the door, refusing to seat the southerners. The Republicans swiftly went on the offensive, intent on wresting control of Reconstruction from the president. Determined to make a new start at rebuilding the South with themselves rather than Johnson in charge, they quickly passed the nation's first Civil Rights Act and sent legislation to the White House restoring the Freedmen's Bureau. Interpreting the Thirteenth Amendment as not only abolishing slavery but guaranteeing free institutions, the Civil Rights Act conferred citizenship on anyone born in the United States; promised them such rights as the ability to conduct economic transactions, undertake litigation, and testify in court; and made violation of those rights a federal crime—though, significantly, the act said nothing about political rights or suffrage. To no one's surprise, Johnson vetoed both measures, claiming that the Civil Rights Act amounted to discrimination in favor of "the colored and against the white race" and that the Freedmen's Bureau, whose continuation he had already blocked once, no longer served any purpose, since civil institutions had been restored in the South and the nation had never intended the federal government to provide food, clothing, shelter, and education to African Americans.[12]

Congress responded with remarkable unity. For the first time in the nation's history, it overrode a presidential veto on a major issue, not once but twice. Both Congress and Johnson had reached a point from which neither would back down, and their mutual bitterness grew as the sharp-tongued president took to the stump for the upcoming congressional elections. Likening himself to the beleaguered Christ and casting the Republican leaders as a band of Judas Iscariots, Johnson roused his followers by asking whether the Radicals Wendell Phillips and Thaddeus Stevens ought not to be hanged. He had finally overreached, however, and northern voters had grown weary of both his eagerness to welcome evidently unrepentant south-erners back into the Union and his arrogant unwillingness to consider any views other than his own. To the great joy of Republicans, who believed that everything the nation had fought for hung in the balance, the 1866 election brought a stunning reversal of power, giving the Radicals veto-proof majori-ties in both houses of Congress and effectively stripping the president of control over Reconstruction. "I was a conservative in the last session of this Congress," Stevens joked to colleagues, "but I mean to be a radical hence-forth."[13]

After their earlier successes with the Civil Rights Act and the authoriza-tion bill for the Freedmen's Bureau, the Congress had approved the Fourteenth Amendment, a relatively mild measure that avoided specifics, instead broadly prohibiting the states from abridging the "privileges and immunities" of every citizen or depriving any person of "equal protection" under the law. With no power to stop its submission to the states, Johnson had passed it along after briefly registering his disapproval. With a firm grip on power, the Republicans took charge, determined to overthrow the presi-dent's lenient Reconstruction policy with their own more stringent demands. As George Julian of Indiana explained, instead of Johnson's "hasty restoration" and oaths inviting the rebels to commit perjury, the South needed "*government*, the strong arm of power, outstretched from the central authority . . . in Washington."[14]

In March 1867, Congress passed two bills limiting Johnson's power: one that protected members of the government who sided with the Radicals from being dismissed by the executive branch, and a second, which routed all military orders from the president through the General of the Army and the Senate before they could be sent. Next, the Congress passed the first of three Reconstruction Acts that would appear over the next several months, detailing its plan for the transformation of the rebel states. Declaring that "no legal . . . governments or adequate protection for life and property" existed in the South, the law brushed aside Johnson's civil apparatus and divided the remaining ten rebel states (Tennessee had reentered the Union in 1866 by ratifying the Fourteenth Amendment) into five military districts, each headed by a wartime Union general.

Hoping for a short military occupation, the Radicals began an activist program, designed to prepare the Confederate states for readmission to the Union. As a first step, military commanders would register all adult males, black and white, except for those disenfranchised for their association with the Confederacy. Hoping to end the dominance of slaveholders, the Radicals expanded the grounds for the disqualification of ex-rebels, denying the right to vote or hold office to thousands Johnson had welcomed with open arms. Among those able to register, members of both races would vote for delegates to write their state's new constitution, which had to include a provision enfranchising African Americans. When a state had ratified its constitution as well as the Fourteenth Amendment, the House and Senate would consider admitting its representatives to Congress.

Having dropped the demand for black land ownership, Radicals focused on suffrage as the only other measure drastic enough to reshape the old social order and create a new stability in the South. In the summer of 1866, whites had rioted in both Memphis and New Orleans, raising havoc in black neighborhoods and killing nearly one hundred African Americans between the two cities. As Carl Schurz, Lincoln's ambassador to Spain and a Union general at both Chancellorsville and Gettysburg, noted after touring the Confederacy, "the Southern States" were turning into "a vast slaughter pen for the black race." "Emancipation . . . is submitted to only in so far as chattel slavery in the old form could not be kept up. . . . The people boast that when they get the Freedmen's affairs in their own hands, to use their expression, 'the niggers will catch hell.' "[15]

The Radicals believed that empowering blacks in the political process would establish their substance as citizens and make them a force to be reckoned with by anyone seeking office. "Give the negro a vote in his hand, and there is not a politician . . . who would not do him honor," Wendell Phillips observed. "Give a man his vote, and you give him tools to work and arms to protect himself."[16] The Radicals' demand that blacks be allowed to vote was undermined, however, by the North's own rejection of black suffrage. In most states above the Mason-Dixon line, African Americans lacked the franchise; and nothing suggested northern attitudes were likely to change. Between Lee's surrender and the end of 1866, four states—Wisconsin, Connecticut, Minnesota, and Nebraska—cast votes to make the denial of black suffrage statutory, a trend that would continue in New Jersey, Ohio, Pennsylvania, and Michigan over the next two years.[17]

Fear of African Americans going to the polls even reached into the abolitionists' ranks. Many—Garrison included—doubted blacks were ready for the responsibility of voting as free citizens. "Chattels personal may be instantly translated from the auction-block into freemen," he noted in *The Liberator* in 1867, "but when were they ever taken at the same time to the ballot-box, and invested with all political rights and immunities? According to the laws of development and progress, it is not practicable." Even the ultraradical Stevens questioned whether African Americans should be given the vote immediately. Though he was ready to disenfranchise southern whites to "revolutionize their feelings and principles," he worried that blacks ought to wait before they voted. "Four or five years hence," he maintained, "when the freedmen shall have been made free indeed, when they shall have become intelligent enough, and there are sufficient loyal men there to control representation from those States," would be the right time to give African Americans the vote.[18]

For southerners, no clearer proof of northern hypocrisy existed than the Radicals' demand that blacks be given the franchise in the South while they were not allowed to vote in most northern states. Northerners could not deny the contradiction, but they argued that the two cases differed vastly. While the Constitution had always guaranteed the individual states the freedom to set their own voter qualifications, southerners had forfeited that right when they rebelled, and Congress now had the power to impose new conditions on them as requirements for reentry into the Union. The issue was critical for northerners because they realized that, for them, Reconstruction could not conclude successfully without black suffrage in the South. Not only was the ballot a potent tool that blacks could employ to defend themselves after federal troops had departed, but even more important, northerners needed enfranchised southern blacks to vote along with them to salvage a victory in the congressional power struggle between the two regions. Though the North had triumphed in the war, without the freed slaves' votes southern whites would end up the winners in the battle for political representation.[19] With blacks as bona fide citizens, the census would count each as an individual, rather than as three-fifths of one, boosting the South's population count and its number of representatives in the House. With southern blacks able to vote, many of those added House seats could be expected to go to candidates allied with northern Republicans; with blacks disenfranchised, however, conservative whites would likely fill all the southern seats. "Shall the death of slavery add two-fifths to the entire power which slavery had when slavery was living?" Roscoe Conkling of New York asked his fellow congressmen, expressing the frustration of Republican leaders, who feared the net result of the North's battlefield victory would be the loss of power in the House.[20]

Earlier, when they had passed the Fourteenth Amendment in Congress, Republicans had tried to address the problem of African American suffrage in the manner Stevens preferred, determining the number of a state's representatives by the number of adult males given the franchise, rather than by total population. Instead of the federal government mandating black suffrage, the scheme left it to the southern states to decide whether to allow African Americans to vote. The drawback for the states, of course, was that by limiting the franchise to whites, they would reduce the number of registered votes and, thus, have fewer representatives in the House.

While Johnson remained in charge, the rebel states, except for Tennessee, had defiantly refused to ratify the Fourteenth Amendment, leading Republicans to mandate black suffrage in the Reconstruction Acts. Southern obstinacy had forced Congress not only to take the question of black suffrage out of the hands of the individual states, but to go further in empowering African Americans than they likely would have on their own. Over the next two years, Johnson continued to obstruct Congress in any way he could, which led to his nearly being removed from office after having been impeached for flouting the restrictions the Radicals had imposed on him. In spite of their difficulties with the president, however, Republicans pressed forward, enlisting the resurrected Freedmen's Bureau and the army to register blacks; and by the middle of 1867, voting rolls were completed throughout the South. In the final tally of registered voters, African Americans totaled slightly more than 700,000 along with about 660,000 whites.[21] Over 100,000 former rebels had been disenfranchised. In five states—Alabama, Florida, Mississippi, Louisiana, and South Carolina—African American registrants outnumbered whites, even though blacks represented the majority of the population in just the last three. Only about 25 percent of registered voters supported the white supremacist views of the planter aristocracy, giving African Americans and their allies a powerful majority dedicated to remaking southern society.

In the fall of 1867, the states held their elections, enabling voters to call for constitutional conventions and to select delegates. Though many whites boycotted the elections, blacks "voted their entire walking strength," as one Alabama Republican put it, "no one staying at home that was able to come to the polls." Carpetbaggers—northerners who had come South either in some

capacity related to Reconstruction or looking for economic opportunities—
and scalawags—native southerners who opposed the old order and were
willing to participate in racial coalitions—joined with blacks, anxious to create a new southern social order. Almost everywhere the black turnout hov-
ered around 80 percent. Out of 1,000 state-convention delegates elected, 265
were black, 107 of them born into slavery. With the ex-rebels in retreat, the
first open and honest elections in southern history—and as W. E. B. Du Bois
would later observe, perhaps the last—were a rousing victory for the advocates of black equality and the Republican Party.[22] In short order, conventions
met in all ten former rebel states and drafted new constitutions guaranteeing
equal rights for both races, establishing universal suffrage, and disenfranchising
a substantial number of whites branded as disloyal. Though the conventions
disappointed some blacks by failing to provide the hoped-for land distribution, a new political order appeared to have taken hold in the South.
"Government by mere *numbers*," the North Carolina conservative John Worth
called it, "universal suffrage that undermined civilization."

Meanwhile in the North the 1867 midterm elections had shaken the
confidence of the Republican leadership. Across the North, Democrats
scored impressive victories, eroding the gains Republicans made in 1865 and
reducing their congressional majority by roughly three-quarters. One of the
chief reasons for the party's heavy losses, *The Nation* explained, came from its
fidelity to the cause of equal rights. If Republicans wanted to retain power,
a constituent warned Schuyler Colfax, the Speaker of the House, judicious
party leaders needed to tell the Radicals that the party could go no further
with them: "You see the disasters which have happened to our cause in the
fall elections, from . . . adopting [their] views."[23] Having championed black
suffrage, however, Republicans could hardly reverse themselves. The elections of 1867 had also made it clear that the futures of Reconstruction and
the Republican Party had become mutually dependent. In the North,
Democrats controlled 45 to 50 percent of the popular vote, and with the
support of white southerners, who almost universally detested the
Republicans, Democrats would wind up in the majority in Congress once
the southern states were readmitted to the Union, if blacks were not allowed
to vote. The Republicans needed a strong southern black turnout to hold
their own, and thus they were forced to play a dangerous political game,
encouraging blacks to go to the polls while at the same time trying to retain
their white supporters in the North.

By the spring of 1868, most of the southern states had approved their new constitutions, ratified the Fourteenth Amendment, and elected a state government and representatives to Washington. Satisfied that seven of the states had met the conditions for their return to the Union, the House and Senate voted to readmit Alabama, Arkansas, Florida, Georgia, Louisiana, and the Carolinas at the end of June. Mississippi, Texas, and Virginia remained in limbo, still unwilling to make their peace with Congress. On July 27, before adjourning, the House and Senate seated the seven states' representatives and, on the basis of their votes, declared the Fourteenth Amendment ratified.

The Republicans welcomed the return of the reconstructed rebel states just in time for the presidential election, and with the nearly unanimous support of the South's black voters, swept the war hero Ulysses Grant and his running mate, Schuyler Colfax, into office. The victory insured that congressional Reconstruction would continue, but as Republicans weighed the future, whatever enthusiasm they felt was tempered with apprehension. In the days leading up to the election, the Democratic vice presidential candidate, Frank Blair, had campaigned openly as a white supremacist, attacking the Republicans for having turned the South over to "a semi-barbarous race of blacks" and insisting that the army should be sent to declare the new state governments "null and void" and return the region to white rule.[24]

Blair reflected the feelings of a great number of whites. In fact, Grant had not won a majority of the white vote, and for the supporters of black equality Blair's outspoken racism raised troubling questions: How long could Reconstruction survive? And given the peculiar two-tiered nature of American governance, could the South be adequately reformed so that when control reverted to local authorities, they would be unable to destroy everything that the Republicans had set out to accomplish?

The problem, of course, lay in the resurrection of states' rights. When Congress readmitted the southern states to the Union, they automatically regained the rights and privileges they had enjoyed before the Civil War. With a return to home rule, the qualifications for black voting and whatever form of state government southerners chose for themselves were no longer legitimate federal concerns. States' rights, beloved for the protection it had given slavery, would allow southerners once again to take charge of local issues. "The miserable evasion, that the protection of personal rights and liberty for every citizen . . . belongs entirely to the State and in no case to the

United States," the *Boston Commonwealth* complained, had nearly cost the nation its life, and now the South would use it again to institute a new reign of white supremacy.

When Ulysses Grant took office on March 4, 1869, he set out to accomplish three goals to preserve Reconstruction and the Republican Party: First, he wanted to solidify black suffrage in the South to make sure that blacks developed sufficient political power to protect themselves and send Republicans to Congress; second, he hoped to reach out to southern whites and persuade his former foes to accept a racially mixed society; and finally, he wanted to encourage support for the Republicans in the North with moderate Reconstruction policies that would not alienate northern voters.

Needless to say, Grant faced gargantuan difficulties. Though he admonished the nation to address Reconstruction "calmly, without prejudice, hate, or sectional pride," the reality remained that southern whites, their northern counterparts, and African Americans had spent over two hundred years locked in battle with one another, and it appeared unlikely that their differences could be resolved by appealing to their shared heritage as Americans. Nor could they agree upon a common future. Embittered southerners remained stuck in the past, dreaming that they might somehow restore the South's golden age. Blacks wanted to rewrite the social contract and launch a more equitable society. And most northern whites had grown increasingly impatient with the whole notion of Reconstruction and wanted to leave the Negro problem in the hands of southerners who had created it in the first place.

On all sides, conflicting events bombarded and befuddled Grant, making it nearly impossible for him to act decisively. Though blacks had voted in impressive numbers in the presidential election, southern whites made it clear that the future of black voting remained uncertain. Only two months after Georgia had been readmitted to the Union, its state legislature had voted to expel its black members, insisting that the new state constitution lacked any provision allowing them to hold office. Three African American members of the senate were dispatched along with twenty-five of the twenty-nine blacks in the Georgia house; of the four permitted to remain, all had light skin and appeared white. Even worse, in the weeks before the presidential election, southern whites had created an atmosphere of violence and intimidation aimed at discouraging blacks from going to the polls. A number of white supremacist groups had formed after the war: Knights of the White Camellia, the White Brotherhood, the Council of Safety, the Constitutional Union Guard, and the Pale Faces. The most powerful and certainly the most frightening was the Ku Klux Klan, organized in 1866 in Tennessee. Led by ex-Confederate officers and dedicated to the restoration of white rule no matter the cost, klaverns, as the local organizations called themselves, spread quickly to every southern state. In northern Alabama, the Klan had instilled "a *nameless terror* among negroes, poor whites," and anyone else standing in the way of the South's traditional leaders. "Save us if you can," a black veteran implored the state's governor, William H. Smith, who chose instead to look the other way.[25] In the small town of Camilla, Georgia, a band of four hundred white supremacists under the command of the local sheriff opened fire on a parade of blacks who were celebrating the possibility of going to the polls for the first time. Masked and hooded whites moved through the black crowd wielding knives, axes, and guns, injuring and killing scores of black men, women, and children. In various places large and small in Louisiana, angry white mobs roamed the streets, breaking up Republican rallies and attacking, sometimes murdering, blacks. They destroyed newspaper offices and ran platoons of men through plantations, randomly butchering black men and women. Around Saint Landry Parish alone, whites killed two hundred black plantation workers. Frightened that their activities to get out the black vote would result in further deaths, Republican officials in Louisiana and Georgia had turned aside from Grant's presidential campaign. Though many freed slaves braced themselves and bravely went to the polls anyway, white intimidation in parts of Tennessee, Alabama, and South Carolina suppressed the Republican vote sharply from the extraordinary levels of 1867, and a number of Georgia counties with black majorities cast not a single vote for the Republican ticket. With the readmission to the Union of most Confederate states, the federal government had removed not only the army but the military judicial structure, where blacks had taken their grievances, eliminating the first line of federal defense for African Americans. Under home rule, blacks had no other choice but to turn to local law enforcement and courts, which often felt intimidated themselves or acted complicitly to maintain white control.

Recognizing that nothing more than the power of the new southern constitutions, which could be changed at any time, guaranteed the black vote, congressional Republicans and President Grant agreed that only a federal amendment could put the vote beyond the reach of white supremacists. The Republican platform of 1868 had called for just such an amendment for southern voters, but party leaders balked at extending the idea to the North, knowing that their constituents wanted no part of African Americans voting at home. For northerners, the Republicans maintained, suffrage properly belonged to the people of those states. But as Grant himself admitted, the imposition of black suffrage in the South without extending it throughout the country defied common sense, and within days of the election Republicans in Congress declared that they would move forward with a constitutional amendment ensuring African Americans everywhere the right to vote.

When Congress first took up the matter, it appeared that they might pass a truly revolutionary amendment. Though Democrats objected that blacks belonged to an inferior race and lacked the necessary competence to vote, and that such a constitutional amendment would infringe on states' rights, Republicans offered a broad measure banning discrimination in both the right to vote and the right to hold office. As Henry Wilson of Massachusetts proposed, no citizen would be denied "the exercise of the elective franchise or . . . the right to hold office in any State on account of race, color, nativity, property, education, or creed."[26] The Wilson version of the amendment afforded exactly the sort of hard-edged protection that southern blacks needed, but ultimately Congress lost its nerve and delivered what one Republican leader described as a half loaf, rather than the whole one necessary to guarantee suffrage for African Americans.

Debating the amendment, Connecticut senator James Dixon pointed out that he and his colleagues needed to consider not one issue but two: Who shall have the vote, and who shall create the voter?[27] In its final form, which dropped the question of holding office and merely insured that the right to vote could not be denied or abridged "on account of race, color, or previous condition of servitude," the Fifteenth Amendment answered the first question but ignored the second. African Americans would have the vote, Congress agreed, but it refused to address the equally important issue of who would decide voter eligibility. Republicans, no doubt leery of the angry reaction that federally mandated universal suffrage would provoke among voters in the North, diluted the Fifteenth Amendment by allowing the individual states to set voter qualifications, such as literacy, education, or property.[28] Though Grant and congressional Republicans tried to portray the amendment's passage as a victory that "conferred on the African Race the care of its own destiny," in fact it offered no real protection for the black vote.[29] With unfettered freedom to establish registration requirements for black voters, northern and southern whites quickly realized that the Fifteenth Amendment did not require whites to open the polls to blacks.

Similar frustrating obstacles blocked many of Grant's other efforts to mediate between the conflicting interests of his northern constituents, white southerners, and African Americans. Though he hoped to attract southern support through conciliation, he could do little to satisfy the region's whites without jeopardizing the rights of the freedmen. After Georgia expelled its black legislators, the state refused to ratify the Fifteenth Amendment, and Congress responded by revoking its readmission to the Union until the state accepted the amendment. Grant sent the military back to Georgia and forced the legislature ultimately to reinstate its black members and pay them for the time they had not been allowed to serve.[30]

Nothing short of federal intervention would have protected the rights of Georgia's black officeholders, but Grant nevertheless believed that he could gain the confidence of southerners by dealing with them gently. Three additional states—Virginia, Mississippi, and Texas—still remained outside the Union, and Grant tried to win the support of their white leaders by easing the requirements for readmission to statehood. The majority of voters in those states had balked at provisions in their new constitutions that denied former Confederates the right to vote and hold office. Approached by a delegation of white Virginians who showed some willingness to support black equality, including suffrage, provided that the federal government remove its proscriptions against ex-rebels, Grant agreed to allow the state to vote again on a new constitution, with the measures barring former Confederates addressed separately. The president passed the proposal on to Congress, urging its acceptance on the grounds that Virginians now seemed ready to "adopt and maintain" a constitution and laws that would "effectually secure the civil and political rights of all persons within their borders."[31] Though the Radicals objected, moderate and conservative Republicans favored the idea, and with Grant's assent they agreed that the proposal should also be extended to Mississippi and Texas, adding the additional requirement that the states would have to ratify the Fifteenth Amendment.

In terms of support for Grant and the Republicans, election results in the three laggard states produced, at best, mixed results. All the proscriptions against ex-rebels, voted on separately, went down to defeat, restoring not only the vote but the right to hold office to a class that represented the states' most fervent foes of Reconstruction. But for what it was worth, Grant had accomplished the ratification of the Fifteenth Amendment, prompting Jacob D. Cox, his interior secretary, to comment that the North could bid "a last affectionate farewell to Reconstruction."[32] At the state level, although Grant's allies managed to gain control of the legislatures in Mississippi and Texas (they lost ground in Virginia), the elections' most noteworthy development was the coming together of Democrats and conservative Republicans in anti-Reconstruction coalitions, creating larger, better organized opposition parties, a result diametrically opposite to the one Grant intended.

Grant's effort to build centrist political support never really had a chance. Its success would have required the nation's deeply divided citizenry to overcome the long-standing racial and sectional antagonisms that had caused the war and that Reconstruction inflamed daily. Though Grant's second year in office appeared to be a time of reconciliation, as Congress permitted Virginia, Mississippi, Texas, and Georgia to rejoin the Union, the divisions in the nation remained as bitter as ever. The black vote in 1868, which had carried not only Grant but numerous blacks into state offices, had galvanized southern whites, who swore to do whatever it took to resist the destruction of their society.

Whether within the law or outside it, southerners were ready to raise the "white man's flag," the crowing cock emblazoned above the slogan "White Supremacy—For the Right," which survived on the Democratic Party's Mississippi ballot until the 1950s. The Columbus, Mississippi, *Democrat* ran an editorial in March 1869 that typified public sentiment in the South: "Nigger voting, holding office, and sitting in the jury box, are all wrong, and against the sentiment of the country. Nothing is more certain to occur than that these outrages upon justice and good government will soon be removed, and the unprincipled men who are now their advocates will sink lower in the social scale than the niggers themselves."[33] Southern conservatives had passed the point where they actively resisted federal authority; instead, they had learned to accept Washington's demands quietly and wait until the troops departed, when they could return to running the South in whatever way they chose.

By 1870, the Ku Klux Klan had become the underground military arm of the Democratic Party in the South. Though not formally linked, the two organizations shared the same goals: the return of blacks to their subservient role as the South's labor force and the political destruction of the Negro's supporters in the Republican Party. Without visible ties, the two organizations nevertheless enlarged one another's image among southerners: the Klan gained a degree of respectability from its informal association with the Democratic Party and gave the Democrats, in return, an aura of frightening power that helped to intimidate blacks and southern Republicans. Generally led by seasoned Confederate veterans, the klaverns in effect took over the political process and enforced rigid social standards that strictly separated the races, spreading terror to keep southern blacks in their place. Southern publishers increased the fervor for Klan justice by turning out scores of books and pamphlets aimed at proving Negro inferiority, among them *The Negro Race: Its Ethnology and History* (1866), by the physician Josiah Nott, who believed that Negroes had evolved at a different time and from a more degenerate genealogical line than whites; *White Supremacy and Negro Subordination* (1868), by John Van Evrie, a racist anthropologist; and a book titled *Nojoque*, by a North Carolinian named Hinton Rowan Helper. Ten years earlier, Helper, who had migrated to the North, wrote an antislavery book, *The Impending Crisis of the South*, which Republicans distributed during the 1864 presidential campaign. Helper believed that slavery represented a ruinous system for the South and wanted a serious, damn-the-expenses effort at colonization to rid the country of all blacks. By the time he wrote *Nojoque* in 1867, his hatred of African Americans had intensified and he prayed for a future when "the negroes, and all other swarthy races of mankind" will have "completely fossilized" and disappeared from America. In Helper's mind, the nation had to go through a series of purifying steps, starting with the denial of all civil and social rights to blacks. Then the federal government had to remove them from the cities and transport them to reservations, in anticipation of the third and final step, deportation to Africa. "America and all the other continents and islands, for white men!" Helper declared. "Erebus for the negroes! Limbo for the mulattoes! Hades for the Chinese! And Tophet for all the other swarthy and copper-colored ghouls!"[34]

Helper and his like enjoyed a vast audience in the South, where, by the end of the 1870s, political assassination, murder, lynching, whipping, rioting, home burning, and the slaughter of livestock had all become commonplace tactics in the Klan's repertoire of violence, which extended as far as the sick imaginations of its leaders could reach. For Klan members, nearly any type of violence could be justified; the more horrible the act, the greater the fear it inspired. In 1869, in Alabama, Klansmen came to the home of the freedman Albert Moore, viciously beat him, ravished a young girl visiting his wife, and wounded a neighbor, explaining they all were being punished for voting "the radical ticket." The next year, in Laurensville, South Carolina, a racial confrontation a month after Republicans had won a close election race turned into a "negro chase," in which rioting whites drove 150 blacks from their homes and murdered 13, including the newly elected white probate judge, a black legislator, and other prominent political figures.[35]

Klan violence extended beyond politics: terror also functioned to define blacks' status in society, particularly when they succeeded in raising themselves above the level of wholly dependent laborers. The Klan did "not like to see the negro go ahead," a white Mississippian observed, presumably because successful blacks provided bad examples for others to emulate. The Klan brutalized African Americans for owning land or even a few pigs or a cow. Whites who aided them by distributing homesteads to former slaves or trading with black tenants also became targets of white terror. James L. Alcorn, who later served as governor of Mississippi, had several plantation buildings torched for having rented land to former slaves.[36]

Addressing Congress in March 1870, Grant requested increased federal power to protect life and property that the Klan had rendered insecure. The "free exercise of the franchise has by violence and intimidation been denied to citizens in several of the states lately in rebellion," the president stated, sending the House and Senate documentary evidence of more than five thousand cases of white terrorism. Between May 1870 and April 1871, at Grant's insistence, Congress passed a series of Enforcement Acts, enlarging federal power to cope with white violence. The first established "a criminal code upon the subject of elections," which empowered the president to appoint election supervisors throughout the South to bring federal charges against local officials who interfered with black voters. The second act focused primarily on large cities in the North, where Democrats also sought to keep blacks from polling places. And the third—often called the Ku Klux Klan Act, and by far the most comprehensive—addressed a wide range of crimes committed by individuals, turning them into federal offenses if they went unprosecuted by the states.[37]

In the meantime, Congress had responded to the skepticism of some of its members by forming its own joint committee of inquiry into southern violence, which held hearings in Washington. Additional meetings were planned throughout the South, but as it happened, the five-member Committee on Outrages, headed by the Republican senator John Scott of Pennsylvania, held hearings in only one southern state, North Carolina. The committee examined fifty-two witnesses during January and February 1871, including two blacks and six Klansmen. Three victims of Klan violence also testified; one of them, a white teacher in a black school, had been given thirty lashes, he said, "for teaching niggers and making them like white men." The Scott committee eventually published thirteen volumes of testimony, exhaustively portraying the viciousness and brutality of the Klan's campaign against southern blacks.[38] James E. Boyd, a lawyer, former Confederate soldier, and Klansman, boasted of membership in three secret societies besides the Klan: the White Brotherhood, the Invisible Empire, and the Constitutional Union Guards. He answered the committee's questions without hesitation or hedging. When Senator Scott asked how many Klansmen had been Confederate soldiers, Boyd answered, "Really, now! The majority."

What was the purpose of the Klan?

"Their object was the overthrow of the Reconstruction policy of Congress and the disenfranchisement of the Negro."

What methods did the Klan use?

"Almost any means that were necessary. If it was necessary to whip a man to break down his influence against us, they would do it. If necessary to kill him, they would do it."[39]

With the Enforcement Acts, Grant attempted to pierce the shield of states' rights that had enabled southerners to escape prosecution for terrorist activity condoned by local officials. Prior federal action, like the 1866 Civil Rights Act, had applied only to public officeholders; crimes committed by individual Klansmen remained local matters, and federal authorities had no way of addressing them. Grant's close adviser, Benjamin F. Butler, summed up the president's frustration perfectly: It made no sense that the Constitution guaranteed citizens fundamental rights but left the federal government powerless to protect them.[40] With no fear of consequences, the Klan night riders galloped through the states' rights loophole. In the Enforcement Acts, Grant asked for and was given extraordinary powers—military intervention, federal prosecution, and the suspension of habeas corpus—to end their reign of violence." These are momentous changes," *The Nation* noted, "[that] not only increase the power of the central government, but . . . arm it with jurisdiction over a class of cases of which it has never hitherto had, and never pretended to have, any jurisdiction whatever."[41] Naturally, Democrats objected to Grant's power grab, but there were rumblings of discontent even among some members of his own party. Though House Speaker James G. Blaine insisted that the reaction to the Ku Klux Klan Act followed party lines, other Republicans— like Lyman Trumbull and Carl Schurz—questioned whether the president had gone too far. The states were the "depositories of the rights of the individual," Trumbull declared, and the establishment of a federal criminal code that punished crimes like murder and assault rendered state criminal codes almost meaningless.[42]

Headed by Attorney General Amos T. Akerman, the newly established Justice Department went on the offensive in the second half of 1871, occupying South Carolina with military troops and indicting hundreds of whites throughout the South. In court cases, Akerman allowed many lesser Klansmen to go free in exchange for their cooperation, but he ultimately secured prison terms for a substantial number of Klan leaders. While rejoicing "at the suppression of KuKluxery," Akerman later wrote, he felt "greatly saddened by the perversion of moral sentiment among . . . Southern whites which bodes ill to that part of the country." Though the Klan Act succeeded in temporarily quashing southern violence, it also revealed the tragic flaw at the center of Reconstruction. As the carpetbagger Albert T. Morgan observed, state authorities lacked the strength, or were unwilling, to enforce the law, and only *"steady, unswerving power from without"* could guarantee the survival of local Republican regimes.[43]

Encouraged by members of his administration who had extensive land holdings there, Grant also became involved in an ill-advised scheme to annex the Dominican Republic, in hopes that it could play a crucial role in the future of American blacks. Strategically Grant wanted a Caribbean naval base, but he knew that the South needed labor—cheap black labor—to rebuild its economy, and he reasoned that if blacks had somewhere else to go, southern whites would begin to appreciate their value. Moreover, they might be willing to pay a premium to have black workers remain in the states. Grant hoped that the annexation would give blacks greater economic leverage in their dealings with southern whites. Even if that plan failed, the

Dominican Republic could become an escape hatch for them; it seemed large enough and sufficiently rich in resources to provide a haven for "the entire colored population of the United States, should it choose to emigrate."[44] Though the worn-out fantasy of colonization lurked in the background of Grant's plans, even Frederick Douglass, who traveled to the Dominican Republic as a member of a presidential fact-finding commission in 1871, returned favorably impressed. Not only would it offer American blacks an alternative to life in the South but annexation would also uplift the poverty-stricken Dominicans, Douglass wrote in his report, "transplanting within her tropical borders the glorious institutions" of the United States.[45]

Grant's scheme for the Dominican Republic failed, primarily because of opposition from Charles Sumner, who had become the chairman of the Senate Foreign Relations Committee. Other congressional leaders, like Nathaniel Banks and Benjamin Butler, along with such influential figures as Horace Greeley and Henry Adams, approved the plan, but Sumner balked, worried that annexation would threaten the independence of Haiti, still the only black republic in the Western Hemisphere, which shared the island of Hispaniola with the Dominicans. Grant personally appealed to Sumner for support, but the Radical leader rebuffed him, opening a bitter rift between the two that only grew deeper when the treaty, which required a two-thirds majority, stalled in the Senate. Grant took his revenge by asking the Republican caucus to relieve Sumner as chairman of Foreign Relations, replacing him with the wealthy coal, oil, and railroad investor, Lincoln's former secretary of war Simon Cameron, which, in the words of the New York World, amounted to "swapping an eagle for a toad."[46] More than anything, perhaps, the incident illustrates the difficulty Grant faced in acting decisively without alienating at least one of the groups he had hoped to unite when he declared that Americans needed to come together and seek "the greatest good [for] the greatest number."

By 1872, as he began his campaign for reelection, Grant faced the open hostility not only of Democrats in both the North and the South but of many Republicans. Relationships had frayed so badly that the Republican Party appeared on the verge of splintering. Seven years had passed since the war's end, and resistance by southern whites had blocked every attempt to produce a stable alternative to the old aristocratic order. For frustrated Republicans, many of whom shared their constituents' urgent desire to leave the Negro question behind, the bright hope for a southern society in which blacks could participate fully had turned into a millstone, dragging down the administration's efforts to meet its obligations to its other, increasingly impatient citizens. Worn down by intractable southern resistance and anxious for closure on the rebellion and its aftermath, many Republicans appeared ready to forswear their commitment to black equality. When Congress finally reported its findings on Klan violence in the spring of 1872, it declared that revolutionary conditions—intimidation, whippings, rape, and murders—characterized the South, resulting from a "conspiracy against Constitutional law and the Negro race."[47] Nevertheless, the report's recommendations remained surprisingly conciliatory. Though the committee favored the continuation of Grant's emergency powers to suppress the Klan, it also included a provision that suggested a new tack for Congress in dealing with the South. At least partly accepting the southern assertion that Klan activity offered a reasonable response to "bad legislation, official incompetency, and corruption," the report proposed that Congress restore the right to vote and hold office to all former Confederates. Congress had taken a turn to the right and apparently reconsidered the root cause of the South's problems. As Jacob Cox, who had left Grant's cabinet in 1870, wrote, the time had come to recognize that southerners "can only be governed through the part of the community that embodies the intelligence and the capital."[48]

In May 1872, the split among Republicans became official, as dissidents gathered in Cincinnati to hold their own convention. Calling themselves Liberal Republicans, disgruntled party members, including leaders like Trumbull, Schurz, and Greeley, met to formulate a new direction—a move away from the president's self-destructive preoccupation with the South. "Reconstruction and slavery we have done with," E. L. Godkin, the editor of *The Nation*, noted; "for administrative and revenue reform we are eager." Outlining a platform concentrating on broad societal issues like tariff reduction, lower taxes, and the reformation of civil service, the Liberal Republicans also spelled out a new southern policy: political amnesty, no more federal intervention, and the restoration of local government led by men of money.[49] With Schurz, the Liberal Republicans' leading spokesman, disqualified by foreign birth, and a number of individuals with as many liabilities as assets vying for the nomination, Horace Greeley eventually emerged as the new party's presidential candidate. Greeley had flaws of his own that called into question his judgment, having supported peaceful secession in the months prior to Fort Sumter and, in 1864, having launched a quixotic private effort to negotiate an end to the war.[50] In his favor, however, he enjoyed wide popularity, and his position as the nation's leading newspaper editor had made him a familiar voice in national politics. Though most people knew Greeley as a consistent supporter of black equality and suffrage, his transformation into a presidential candidate brought an adjustment in his thinking. Blacks had to be realistic, he now insisted, adopting the Liberal Republicans' position and sounding for all the world like one of the unrepentant southerners he had frequently railed against. "Political equality is far off. Social equality will remain forever out of reach. Don't expect free gifts of land. Segregate yourselves; employ each other. Who are your best friends?— Sound, conservative, knowing white Southerners."[51]

The Democratic National Convention also endorsed Greeley, but Grant managed to survive, winning reelection in spite of the Liberal Republicans' opposition on one side and his estrangement from Sumner and the Radicals on the other. Party loyalists and blacks, who still revered the president as a war hero, carried him back into office, but Grant and his policies had taken a hit that called into doubt the future of Reconstruction. Across the South, Klan violence—"bloody deeds [teaching] the negroes that to vote against the wishes of their white employers and neighbors was to risk death"—had reappeared to suppress the black vote, giving white supremacists power in Georgia, Texas, Tennessee, Maryland, Kentucky, Missouri, and Virginia.[52] In three other states—Louisiana, Alabama, and Arkansas—two opposing slates, one supportive of blacks and the other committed to white supremacy, contested the election's outcome; and though Republicans ultimately won control of the local governments in all three of those states, they did so only after federal authorities either threatened to intervene or actually did. In New Orleans, street battles erupted when backers of the Democratic candidate tried to evict his Republican adversary from the governor's mansion. Similar events occurred in Alabama, where white supremacists forcibly took over the statehouse, and in the Arkansas capital of Little Rock, where supporters of white and black Republicans fought each other. In Colfax, Louisiana, in the bloodiest massacre of Reconstruction, sixty-one blacks who had barricaded themselves in the town's courthouse fearing for their lives were killed by artillery fire. The local militia took thirty-seven more as prisoners and executed them in the town square.

In his second inaugural address, in March 1873, Grant continued to insist on the protection of Negro rights as a major goal of his administration, but his resolve had weakened noticeably. The president had joined with Congress to approve the restoration of the right to vote and hold office for ex-Confederates, and the election results made him even more circumspect in relation to black equality. Noting that blacks still did not enjoy "the civil rights which citizenship should carry with it," Grant promised to work to secure those rights, "so far as Executive influence can avail." But he also wanted no misunderstanding about the limits of his commitment: "Social equality is not a subject to be legislated upon, nor shall I ask that anything be done to advance the social status of the colored man."[53]

Grant had not yet given up hope that he could secure the rights of African Americans while at the same time reconciling white southerners to an integrated society, but he had grown increasingly impatient with Republican regimes in the South that seemed unable to win local support and had to call on Washington for help every time violence erupted. Two years earlier, Governor William Woods Holden of North Carolina, a recent convert to black enfranchisement, had asked Grant for troops to secure peaceful elections and the president had dispatched a military regiment. After the assassination of several Republican officeholders and black supporters, Grant sent more troops and armed the state militia. Each time he intervened, however, Grant realized that he only undermined the prospects for better relations with the South's white majority, and by January 1874 his irritation with Republican "monstrosities that exhausted the life of the party" had become palpable. "I am tired of this nonsense," he wrote. "I am done with them, and they will have to take care of themselves."[54]

A severe economic crisis overtook the nation in 1873, triggered by a decline in the price of gold that led to the collapse of several leading financial institutions, including Jay Cooke & Company, which had marketed the Civil War loans of the federal government. By 1874, the deepening depression cast a pall over Grant's efforts to aid African Americans. With financial worries of their own, both northerners and southerners resented their tax dollars being spent on blacks, and Democrats quickly seized the issue, faulting the president and his administration not only for the nation's financial troubles but for the betrayal of their own race. Nor did Grant win many friends by vetoing a congressional measure that he regarded as inflationary which aimed at providing at least some relief for white workers.

Grant recognized that even among his closest followers an aggressive policy of intervention no longer enjoyed anything more than tepid support, and in an attempt to restore order he returned to trying to reconcile white southerners to black civil and political rights. He pardoned many of the Klan members who had been convicted under the Enforcement Acts and limited future prosecutions to the most "flagrant cases of murder &c."; at the same time, he publicly expressed his opposition to integrated schools, convinced that southerners would shut down public education rather than allow white children to be taught alongside blacks. No matter what Grant did, however, his efforts to woo white southerners were doomed. Though moderates like Tennessee's Gideon Pillow, an old battlefield foe, assured Grant that "Kindness and confidence . . . and manifestations of sympathy and respect" would win him the "support [of] the great body of the intelligent southern white population," most southern whites remained steadfastly determined to regain control of their homeland.[55] Meanwhile, in the North, popular support for Reconstruction had fallen away to practically nothing.

The elections of 1874 were a political disaster for the Republican Party. Saddled not only with economic depression and unpopular Reconstruction policies but with charges of rampant corruption, the Republicans were forced out of office, giving control of the House of Representatives and a number of state governments to the Democrats. Grant found particularly troubling the rout of congressional Republicans in the South, where widespread violence by the Klan and a new supremacist group, the White League, kept blacks from the polls and dictated the election of eighty-nine Democrats and only seventeen Republicans. Republicans remained in charge in just four southern states: Mississippi, Louisiana, South Carolina, and Florida. In Louisiana, Grant had been forced to send troops to New Orleans to put down an insurrection by 3,500 White Leaguers, who had launched a fierce attack on local police and black militia with the aim of taking over the city and installing their own governor. Republicans and Democrats both claimed victory in Louisiana's state legislative elections, and at the beginning of 1875 Democrats—backed by the White League—tried to take control of the state assembly by forcibly installing their candidates in a number of disputed seats. Anticipating trouble, Grant dispatched General Philip H. Sheridan to New Orleans, directing him to restore order. The general brought a contingent of his troops to the legislative hall, expelling the Democratic claimants "at the point of the bayonet." Having completed his mission, Sheridan wired Washington, noting that the White Leaguers who had hatched the scheme were no better than common bandits and ought to be executed.[56] Northerners had had their fill of intervention, however, and criticized both Grant and Sheridan for arrogance and their complete disregard of civil authorities. One Republican observer noted that Sheridan had doubtless told the simple truth when he likened the leaders of the White League to ordinary criminals, but the people had grown "tired [of] this worn out cry of 'Southern outrages'!!! Hard times & heavy taxes make them wish the 'nigger, everlasting nigger,' were in——or Africa."[57] How long would it be, Carl Schurz asked the Senate, before federal troops interfered "in Massachusetts and in Ohio? How long before the constitutional rights of all the states and the self-government of all the people may be trampled under foot?" Like the South, northerners now seemed ready to ignore white terrorism, excoriating Grant for trying to set himself up as an American Caesar and insisting that the people of Louisiana be left alone to work out their problems among themselves.

Grant went before the Senate to explain his actions, reminding the assembled lawmakers that "lawlessness, turbulence, and bloodshed [had] characterized the political affairs of [Lousiana] since its reorganization." A series of horrendous episodes, particularly in the last two years, had marked its unhappy history: the Colfax massacre, in which "bloodthirstiness and barbarity were hardly surpassed by any acts of savage warfare"; the 1874 assassinations at Coushatta, in which six Republican officeholders, both black and white, had been "seized and carried away from their homes and murdered in cold blood"; and recent events in New Orleans, where troops had been withdrawn to placate white conservatives, who then tried to overthrow the elected government with an army of their own. "It is a deplorable fact that political crimes and murders have been committed in Louisiana, which have gone unpunished," Grant continued, "and which have been justified or apologized for," and would remain "as a reproach unto the State and country long after the present generation has passed away." As long as he remained in office, Grant pledged, he would tolerate "neither Ku Klux Klans, White Leagues, nor any other association using arms and violence to execute their unlawful purposes." Nor would he concede that "Union men or Republicans could be ostracized, persecuted, and murdered on account of their opinions," as happened too often throughout the South.[58]

Grant's forthright stand silenced his northern critics but did nothing to restore the power he had lost in the 1874 elections. The House, now dominated by Democrats and conservative Republicans, severely curtailed the president's ability to intervene in the South. A do-nothing policy clothed in moral platitudes took hold in Congress. "There is a social, and educational, and moral reconstruction of the South needed that will never come from any legislative hall, State or national; it must be the growth of time, of education, and of Christianity," the Republican congressman from Connecticut and ex–Union general Joseph Hawley observed. "We cannot put justice, liberty, and equality into the hearts of a people by statute alone."[59]

The barrenness of the congressional policy soon revealed itself in Mississippi. With state elections scheduled for 1875, white Mississippians, fancying themselves redeemers of the old utopian South, were finally free to work out their own problems. Realizing that federal intervention had essentially ended, the Democratic state convention went through the formality of adopting a platform that recognized black rights and then colluded with White Leaguers and other supremacist groups to embark on a campaign of murderous violence meant to intimidate blacks by demonstrating that local authorities lacked the power to protect them. Newly formed white rifle clubs paraded through the towns of the Black Belt, where the high concentration of African Americans gave Republicans a majority of the state's registered voters, disrupting political meetings and attacking party leaders. In early September, in Yazoo County, a company of Democratic militia broke up a Republican rally, wounding several members of the audience and forcing the local sheriff to flee for his life. Taking control of the area for several days, whites lynched many of its most prominent black citizens. Equally savage attacks took place in Louisville, Macon, Clinton, Utica, Satartia, and Coahoma County, all part of a coordinated campaign of terror that came to be called the Mississippi Plan. The embattled Republican governor, Adelbert Ames, wrote to a colleague in November 1875 that a *"revolution* is taking place—by force of arms—and a race are disfranchised—they are to be returned to a condition of serfdom—an era of second slavery."[60]

For southern whites, the Mississippi Plan demonstrated the effectiveness of massive violent resistance. In 1873 there had been as many as 6,000 scalawag votes supporting Republicans throughout the state; intimidation all but eliminated them in 1875. Among blacks, though many risked death to go to the polls, the turnout fell sharply, particularly in places where violence had taken the lives of many of their leaders and destroyed the Republican infrastructure. In Yazoo County, Adelbert Ames had enjoyed an 1,800-vote margin of victory two years earlier, but in 1875 Democrats triumphed in legislative races by a lopsided 4,044 to 7. Throughout the Black Belt, Republican votes dropped precipitately, creating an electoral landslide that gave conservatives 80 percent of the seats in the state legislature.

In the weeks leading up to the election, Mississippi officials had begged Grant to send federal troops, but the president had hesitated and ultimately acted too late, advised by those around him that intervention would dampen Republican prospects in the presidential and congressional races of 1876. "The whole public are tired out with these annual, autumnal outbreaks in the South," Grant conceded to John Lynch, the only Republican congressman from Mississippi, and "the great majority are ready now to condemn any interference on the part of the Government." Later, when the extent of the Democratic triumph became clear, Grant acknowledged that he had made a mistake in choosing to follow his head rather than his heart. Still, he maintained, it was unlikely that Mississippi could have been saved, and he had wanted to avoid damaging the Republicans' chances for success in the coming elections in the North.[61]

With Democrats firmly in charge of the House and few Republicans still willing to back intervention, Grant had become a lame duck doubly wounded. He had no real power to affect the South, not just because he had decided to bow out of the upcoming election but also because he had lost control of Congress. Perceived as a liability by his own party, he played no role in the selection of Ohio governor Rutherford B. Hayes as the Republican presidential candidate to oppose the Democrat Samuel J. Tilden, of New York. With little separating Hayes and Tilden on other issues, southern policy became an important campaign issue. While both parties repudiated Grant's aggressive intervention in the South, the Republicans warned that Democrats wanted to return to power the same unreconstructed leaders who had guided the Confederate states out of the Union.

Democrats tried—with limited success, particularly in South Carolina—to restrain white supremacist violence, recognizing that unbridled terrorism would probably lose them as many votes in the North as they would gain in the South. White Leaguers and Klan members, buoyed by the triumph of the Mississippi Plan, now wanted a victory on their own terms, one that would restore, according to one Klansman, "the eternal fitness of things—a white man in a white man's place and a black man in a black man's place" and wash away the bitter taste of frustration and defeat. Throughout the South, continual outbreaks of violence marred the campaign of 1876, the worst of which erupted in Hamburg, South Carolina, a predominantly black town, where whites claimed they had suffered frequent indignities at the hands of African Americans. A confrontation between black militia and white troops under the leadership of General Matthew C. Butler, one of the area's leading Democrats, arose over a minor disagreement, when a local white farmer demanded that some blacks step aside to make way for his carriage at the town's Fourth of July parade. In the ensuing fight, whites killed Hamburg's black marshal and took twenty-five blacks prisoner, five of whom they summarily executed. The next morning, whites rioted through the town, destroying black homes and businesses. "How long these things are to continue, or what is to be the final remedy, the Great Ruler of the universe only knows," Grant mourned, admitting his own impotence. When southerners complained of lost rights, he added, they really meant the freedom "to kill negroes and Republicans without fear of punishment and without loss of caste or reputation."[62]

To most observers, Tilden's election appeared a foregone conclusion, and with early triumphs in New York, New Jersey, Connecticut, and Indiana, there seemed little doubt that the nation would have a Democratic president after sixteen years of Republican rule. But as the evening progressed, though Tilden maintained an insurmountable lead in the popular vote, Hayes rallied. By morning the election appeared to have produced a virtual dead heat in the electoral college, with the outcome still contested in three southern states, where Republican officeholders threw out returns from counties that had denied blacks the right to vote. Rival Democratic governments had formed in Louisiana, South Carolina, and Florida, and they in turn selected separate slates of presidential electors, all of whom insisted that their votes represented the will of the people and should be validated by Congress.

In Washington, the Constitution muddied the situation even further. Though the Twelfth Amendment directed the "President of the Senate to open all certificates in the presence of both houses of Congress," it did nothing to clarify how the votes should be counted. Was it up to the Senate president, a Republican, to decide the legitimacy of the competing slates, which likely would have made Hayes the winner, or was it the job of the House and Senate—the former Democratic, the latter Republican—to choose the electors, almost certainly creating a deadlock? With no clear constitutional direction, the two parties ultimately agreed to appoint a fifteen-member commission consisting of five representatives from the House, five senators, and five Supreme Court justices; seven commission members would come from each party and the fifteenth would be chosen from the court by the other four justices, two of them Democrats and two of them Republicans.[63]

Controversy erupted immediately over the selection of the fifth judge when the justices' first choice, the independent-minded David Davis, stepped aside in favor of a Republican, Joseph P. Bradley. Though Davis later insisted that he never doubted that Hayes had won the election, Democrats complained loudly when the commission repeatedly voted eight to seven to confirm the Republican electors and make Hayes the president. Feeling that they had been shamefully cheated, congressional Democrats set out to block the new president's inauguration by paralyzing the House and preventing a final count of the electoral votes. With the situation rapidly deteriorating and firebrands in both parties calling for the use of force, Hayes's representatives met with Democratic leaders at a Washington hotel, Wormley House—owned, ironically, by the city's wealthiest African American—and over a period of a few days worked out a deal allowing Hayes to become president. Though the exact terms of the "Bargain of 1877" never became public, its general intent seemed clear immediately. In the words of the leader of the Kansas Republican committee, the new administration's policy would "conciliate the white men in the South. Carpetbaggers to the rear, and niggers take care of yourselves."[64]

Hayes took the oath of office a few days later and swiftly began the final surrender to southern redemption. The Tennessee senator David M. Key was installed as postmaster general, joining William Evarts, the new secretary of state, who had served as Andrew Johnson's counsel at his impeachment trial, and Carl Schurz, Hayes's choice to head the Interior Department, who had led the Liberal Republican revolt of 1872. In the following months, Hayes withdrew federal troops from Louisiana and South Carolina, where they had been sent to protect embattled Republican regimes, leaving the Republicans at the mercy of the white supremacist wolves. "To think that Hayes could go back on us when we had to wade through blood to place him where he is now," lamented an ex-slave who had put his life on the line to vote. As the editors of *The Nation* observed, the time had come for "the negro to disappear from the field of national politics. Henceforth, the nation, as a nation, will have nothing more to do with him."[65]

A number of voices spoke out against the government's capitulation, but in the popular mind they represented men whose day had passed. Hayes's "policy of compromise, of credulity, of weakness, of subserviency, of surrender upheld might against right . . . the rich and powerful against the poor and unprotected," William Lloyd Garrison fumed. And Wendell Phillips, fearful for blacks denied the protection of federal troops, warned, "The whole soil of the South is hidden by successive layers of broken promises. To trust a Southern promise would be fair evidence of insanity."[66] Only the remnants of the abolitionist movement—dismissed as overwrought, even hysterical— and blacks themselves appeared willing to look honestly at the reality of the North's surrender and what it portended for the future. As W. E. B. Du Bois would note some sixty years later, "the slave went free; stood a brief moment in the sun; then moved back again toward slavery."[67]

Though southern conservatives were defeated in their effort to dissolve the Union, their militant refusal to let the North dictate the terms of peace provided them with a victory that offset their losses on the battlefield. They no longer owned their slaves, but they were already on their way to developing a new labor system that would enable them to continue dominating black workers. Moreover, with the reassertion of home rule and the doctrine of states' rights, they once again felt confident that the impassable color line in southern society would remain in place. Perhaps even more important, by counting blacks as full-fledged citizens, they had expanded their representation in the national government, giving traditional southern leaders far more power than they had when the war began. By 1880, nine out of ten southerners in Congress had served the Confederacy, either in the army or in government, including eighteen ex–Confederate generals and the former commander of a prisoner-of-war camp. At least on the issue of race, the Democratic majority had evolved, in the words of Joseph Hawley, into a "motley compound of all the don'ts, won'ts, shan'ts, hates, [and] prejudices of the times."[68]

CHAPTER 9

"SEPARATE BUT EQUAL": JIM CROW BECOMES THE LAW OF THE LAND

The destinies of the two races, in this country, are indissolubly linked together, and the interests of both require that the common government of all shall not permit the seeds of race hate to be planted under the sanction of law. . . . [The court's decision would] not only stimulate aggressions, . . . [but would] encourage the belief that it is possible, by means of state enactments, to defeat the beneficent purposes [of the Constitution].

—JUSTICE JOHN MARSHAL HARLAN (IN DISSENT), 1896, PLESSY V. FERGUSON

Weel about and turn about and do jis so,
Eb'ry time I weel about I jump Jim Crow.

—MINSTREL PERFORMER THOMAS "DADDY" RICE, C. 1830

When federal troops withdrew from Shreveport, Louisiana, in 1877, marking the end of Reconstruction, a local black leader named Henry Adams noted that African Americans lost all hope, realizing that they "had got [back] into the hands of the very men that held [them] as slaves, and there was no way on earth they could better [their] condition."[1] Violence against blacks, already commonplace in areas where the power of outmanned federal authorities had seldom reached, now erupted everywhere, as whites reclaimed absolute control over southern society. "Colored men are daily being Hung, Shot, and otherwise murdered and ill-treated because of their complexion and politics," the black lawyer John Mardenborough of South Carolina reported. "While I write a colored woman comes and tells me her husband was killed last night . . . by white

men and her children burned to death in the house; . . . her person was outraged . . . and then she was whipped—such things as these are common
occurrences."[2]

Perhaps nothing indicates the post-Reconstruction desperation of
southern blacks more clearly than their sudden interest in colonization. For
a hundred years most blacks had resisted every scheme for their wholesale
removal to Africa, the Caribbean, or South America, citing their native birth
and avowing that the United States was the only home they had ever
known.[3] But in 1877, groups of African Americans began contacting the
American Colonization Society, seeking transportation and aid to resettle in
Liberia.[4] Financially strapped and all but moribund, the society managed to
send only a few hundred blacks to Africa in the 1870s and 1880s, but
African Americans continued to search for ways to escape the return to the
past envisioned by southern redeemers. A group of over three thousand
black men led by Henry Adams, who with their families amounted to perhaps ten thousand people, petitioned Congress either to provide adequate
protection for their rights or to appropriate funds to send them to Africa or
some other place where they could live in harmony, free from white oppression. As the home of John Brown, Kansas held a particular attraction for
blacks, inspiring the exodus of 1879, in which emigrants mainly from the
border states of Kentucky, Tennessee, and Missouri—the so-called
Exodusters—increased the number of black Kansans by more than 150
percent.[5] Between 1890 and 1910, a steady migration totaling some one
hundred thousand blacks left the South for the Oklahoma Territory, looking to stake claims for free land under the terms of the federal Homestead
Act. Though whites tried to run the blacks out of the territory, the latter
succeeded—in places like Langston, Boley, Rentiesville, Vernon, and
Clearview—in creating their own towns, insulating themselves from the
surrounding hostility. When Oklahoma became a state, whites passed laws
disenfranchising African Americans and segregating most public facilities,
leading a number of blacks to pack up and move again, many farther west
and at least one group of two hundred to Saskatchewan.[6]

Uncertain how northerners would respond to the curtailing of black
rights, southern leaders moved cautiously in the beginning. Nevertheless,
from the waning years of Reconstruction to 1903, every southern state
passed legislation restricting black suffrage. Across the South, legislatures
enacted laws that the *Richmond Dispatch* candidly admitted had no other pur-

pose but "to perpetuate the rule of the white man."[7] Though in certain states—Virginia and Tennessee, for example—blacks continued to play an active role in politics until the beginning of the 1890s, their voting declined sharply in most southern states, where barely half the number of black voters registered in 1880 still went to the polls in 1888.

Though most southerners would have been willing to disenfranchise African Americans in their state constitutions, the Fifteenth Amendment, which outlawed the abridgment of voting rights on the basis of race, gave them pause. Rather than directly prohibiting blacks from casting their ballots, state election officials chose instead a series of race-neutral qualifications and voting procedures that effectively excluded blacks without mentioning them directly. Local election officials eliminated many blacks in the registration process because they could not provide a proper address, had been convicted of a crime, or had breached some technicality that officials invented on the spot. Those who survived this initial personal screening had cleared only the first hurdle. Each of the southern states also required either a poll tax or a literacy test, or in some places both. In most instances, the poll tax had to be paid anywhere from six months to a year in advance, with interest accruing on unpaid amounts. While legislatures set the general standards, enrollment officers determined actual eligibility, and they freely flunked nonliterate blacks while passing their white counterparts. Because blacks were the least educated part of the population, they usually had trouble proving their ability to read and write—or proving it, at any rate, to the satisfaction of local officials. An alternative measure allowed applicants to demonstrate their knowledge of the state constitution verbally in place of the ability to read, giving local officials even wider latitude in deciding who passed and who failed.

Blacks who succeeded in meeting all the registration requirements still faced serious obstacles at their polling places.[8] Registrars employed arcane procedures like the multibox system and the secret ballot to confuse black voters, who, without directions or assistance from white election workers, often invalidated their votes by casting them incorrectly. The multibox system, adopted by South Carolina in 1882, Florida in 1889, and North Carolina in 1900, asked voters to use different ballots for every office or issue being contested in an election and then deposit them in separate boxes. To further confuse the process, election officials frequently shifted the boxes, so that black voters could not memorize the order while waiting to mark their ballots.

Similarly, registrars introduced the secret ballot, often portrayed as a reform measure to protect privacy but instituted primarily to weed out poorly educated voters. Before 1888, political parties printed their own ballots throughout the United States, which enabled an individual to vote simply by recognizing his party's distinctive format. The secret ballot was used first in the North, but southerners quickly seized on it as another way to curtail black voting.[9] Shifting to a single, publicly printed ballot that listed all the candidates for an office in an ornate, unfamiliar script, often leaving out any indication of party affiliation, southern officials forced semiliterate blacks to make confused, frequently incorrect choices—or else to give up in frustration and make none at all. By 1910, southern blacks had been effectively excluded from the franchise, and along with it nearly any form of political office. In every state except Virginia, where registration requirements were less stringent, fewer than 10 percent of blacks remained on the voting rolls.

The formidable barriers that whites erected to keep African Americans from the polls not only excluded them from voting but created a sense of hopelessness. Many blacks simply gave up trying to cast ballots, either because they wanted to avoid the humiliating registration process or because they thought no one represented their interests or deserved their vote. Almost every question that the electorate would eventually vote on was resolved before election day, in white-only primaries. Since political parties operated as private organizations, they could limit their membership to whites, who understood that by banding together in the Democratic Party, they could resolve their differences among themselves, hold harmonious primaries and unanimous elections, and never again face the deplorable situation in which one faction of white men called upon blacks to defeat another faction. Josephus Daniels, editor of the *Raleigh News and Observer*—he later would become Woodrow Wilson's secretary of the navy—noted that the resolution of differences at the primary level provided a guarantee of "permanent good government by the party of the White Man."[10]

Whites now enjoyed unlimited power to take whatever steps they deemed necessary to purify southern society. Almost immediately, white leaders focused on miscegenation and school integration, two particularly sensitive issues. From 1870 to 1884, nine of the eleven southern states moved to outlaw miscegenation and to segregate schoolchildren, either by passing constitutional provisions or enacting laws. Defeat in the war, the humiliating occupation by federal troops, and the spectacle of former slaves who took their equality for granted had left southern males desperate for redemption, and they turned first to antimiscegenation laws and segregated classrooms in large part out of a need to reassert themselves as guardians and defenders of their women and children. Other forms of segregation—in public transportation, hiring practices, restaurants, hospitals, orphanages, and public drinking fountains—were enacted after 1890, when states restored earlier statutes or formulated even stricter measures. These came to be known as Jim Crow laws, after a popular Negro stereotype in minstrel shows.

White violence had flourished during Reconstruction, but more often than not it had been politically motivated, aimed principally at intimidation. By the 1880s, the elimination of black voters through legal measures made political intimidation and violence unnecessary. In their place, angry whites took up lynching, a ritualistic form of slaughter carried out by mobs of supposedly respectable whites who tortured, maimed, burned alive, dismembered, and hanged blacks—ostensibly on the basis of rumors that they had offended a white woman—without affording the victims an opportunity to defend themselves. The savagery of these events defies description, but many lynchings have been preserved in photographs sold as postcards to commemorate what one observer at a 1902 hanging called "the answer of the Anglo-Saxon race to black brutes who would attack the womanhood of the south."[11]

According to statistics compiled by the National Association for the Advancement of Colored People (NAACP), hangings began to accelerate in the second half of the 1880s, and by the next decade white mobs had lynched more than 1,100 blacks throughout the South. In the central Piedmont area of North Carolina, the Republican jurist and Ohio native Albion W. Tourgee counted the crimes that whites committed against blacks in his judicial district over that period: 12 blacks murdered, 9 raped, 14 cases of arson, and over 700 beatings, including that of a 103-year-old black woman bludgeoned to death by Klansmen. Over an eighty-year period ending in the mid-1960s, some 3,500 southern blacks fell victim to racial vigilantes. Ida B. Wells, the crusading black journalist who exposed the atrocities of spontaneous southern justice, refuted the idea that lynching existed as a punishment for rape, and indeed found that less than 30 percent of lynchings involved even the charge of rape. In 1892, she published a remarkable pamphlet titled *Southern Horrors* (intended to mock the phrase "Southern Honors"), which examines the psychological link between the loss of southern manliness and the rise of lynching.[12] Far more white men raped African American women than the reverse, Wells pointed out, but whites took no notice of such crimes. The reason lay in their perception of the victims. Black women were seen as wanton and naturally licentious, while white women were virginal and pure, indulging in sex only for the noble goal of procreation. Black and white men reflected the attitudes of their female companions: African American males were lustful and used to having their way with compliant, promiscuous women; whites, in contrast, admired and respected the high-minded morality of white womanhood and had taken on the role of their protectors as a sacred duty. In their own self-justifying minds, white men believed that it was "not the same thing for a white man to assault a colored woman as for a colored man to assault a white woman."[13] Black females "had no finer feelings nor virtue to be outraged," while the black rapist represented nothing less than the sullying of white purity by darkness and evil. Lynching, Wells recognized, arose from the collective insecurity of defeated white men, who tried to reaffirm their sense of superiority by using black women freely and punishing black men who lusted after chaste white women.

Deep in their hearts, most southern whites still longed for some kind of final solution to cleanse the South of blacks. As Thomas P. Gibbs, a member of the Georgia Senate, wistfully predicted in 1889, "the time will come . . . when the white people will rise as one man and demand emigration or extermination." Blacks, the populist *Progressive Farmer* agreed, marred the body politic like "a running festering sore, whose peaceful departure would be hailed with delight and rejoicing."[14] Nevertheless, practical economic considerations made it clear that blacks would remain a necessary part of southern life. Southern whites found themselves caught in a familiar bind: wanting to exclude blacks from their society as absolutely as they had in the days of slavery but also recognizing the need for black labor to provide the manpower for the South's agrarian economy.

Landowners needed a reliable workforce they could depend on from year to year, but they also wanted to pay as little as possible for it; consequently, black workers lacked sufficient economic incentives to stay put if a better opportunity presented itself. The problem turned less on a shortage of labor than on the unequal distribution of ex-slaves: certain states, particularly in the Cotton Belt, cried out for more workers, while places like Virginia, swamped with blacks, had huge unemployment rates. During Reconstruction, the Freedmen's Bureau had attempted to solve this problem by establishing an employment service, which not only found jobs for blacks but negotiated their contracts and relocated them across the South. The bureau gave tens of thousands of ex-slaves transportation assistance in an effort to shift "the surplus negroes from . . . overstocked districts to places where they could procure employment and subsistence and support themselves and thus relieve the government" of the responsibility for their care. Though not always happy with the wages arranged by federal officials, landowners who needed workers received a valuable service. Whites in areas that lost blacks, however, complained that the labor market had tightened, forcing them to pay higher wages. With the states on their own again, many revisited the question of black labor, searching for ways to preserve local resources by restricting the ex-slaves' mobility and keeping them at home. Several states enacted three types of laws limiting the freedom of blacks to move at will: laws aimed at blacks themselves, those directed against employers who took another man's workers, and measures restricting the rights of labor agents.

The earliest laws directly affecting black workers were contract-enforcement statutes that penalized them for violating labor agreements. In 1875 in Tennessee, blacks who willfully broke a contract "without good and sufficient cause" had to forfeit any payments "due for service already rendered, and be liable for such other damages" as the landowner might reasonably claim. States also enacted vagrancy laws to intimidate blacks, who could be arrested simply for being out of work. Frequently, the punishment included a term at hard labor, which in effect returned them to slavery: the state, which provided little or no oversight, leased the convicted vagrants out to landowners, who could treat them in any way they pleased. Black workers were also bound to their employers by debt so that they would never be free to pursue other opportunities. No matter whether they worked as tenant farmers (who provided their own stock, farm implements, and other provisions) or sharecroppers (who supplied only their labor), blacks frequently required cash or seed loans, which landlords carried as continuing accounts. Eventually the Supreme Court outlawed this practice—which it termed *peonage*, the perpetual "holding of persons in servitude" by means of indebtedness—as a violation of the Thirteenth Amendment. But the desire to ensnare blacks in agreements that effectively deprived them of their freedom remained strong, and southern landowners continued to invent variations on the idea, enabling them to control blacks as debtors until each of the new schemes was overturned in the federal court system.[15]

States also passed laws against employers who lured another man's workers away, and against labor agents, resented as outside agitators threatening the landowners' hold on black workers. Enticement laws made it illegal to hire anyone "under contract or in the employ of another" and made violators liable for damages to the original employer. If an individual hired a black person without realizing that he or she still remained under contract, the new employer had to fire the worker immediately when the prior commitment became known or face a claim for damages. By 1890, every southern state except Texas and Virginia had either enacted new measures against enticement or stiffened existing laws, and in places like Alabama and North Carolina enticement was made a criminal offense as well as a civil one.

A limited number of labor agents who hired blacks for jobs outside the South had been in business during Reconstruction, but the end of the federal effort to find work for blacks opened new opportunities for private recruiters, many of whom had worked for the Freedmen's Bureau and stayed in the South to hire laborers willing to move to the North or West for better wages. Courts had enacted measures to control labor agents in the 1860s, establishing nominal licensing fees, but by the end of the 1870s the growing number of northern recruiters intent on luring away the South's workforce were seen as a threat to the region's economic health. State legislators limited their activities by greatly increasing the cost of licenses and imposing jail terms on agents who tried to recruit without having paid their fees. In 1891, North Carolina established a licensing fee of $1,000 for every county in which a recruiter operated and set penalties for violators that ran as high as $5,000 in fines and two years in jail.

Embracing blacks as laborers while at the same time rejecting them as members of their communities, white southerners rapidly constructed a schizophrenic post-Reconstruction society. No longer slaves, blacks had achieved what appeared to be undeniable legal equality, but whites still refused to accept them as equals. Once again, the nation faced essentially the same dilemma that had dogged white America since the Declaration of Independence: Either white Americans had to accept equality with blacks, or the racial apologists who believed in white superiority needed to show that equality somehow was not what it seemed and blacks deserved nothing more than what they already had been given.

In 1896 in *Plessy v. Ferguson*, the U.S. Supreme Court took up the question of exactly where the boundaries of black equality lay.[16] No band of southern radicals, six of the eight justices who heard the case came from the North and relied on the attitudes and customs of their home states as well as previous case law to arrive at their decision. In 1892, Homer Adolph Plessy, who had one-eighth African blood, bought a first-class ticket on the East Louisiana Railway and took his seat in a whites-only compartment, an action the railroad itself supported, wanting to save the cost of an additional car on each of its trains. As had been prearranged, the conductor ordered him to move to the black section. Plessy refused, and a police officer took him into custody and locked him up in the New Orleans parish jail for violating an 1890 Louisiana statute that called for "equal but separate accommodations" for blacks and whites traveling on railroads within the state.

Plessy's lawyer was Albion W. Tourgee, a close friend of Ida B. Wells; he had founded the national Citizens' Rights Association during Reconstruction to push for black civil rights and had a high profile in the South as an outspoken advocate for black causes. Tourgee opened his argument with the flat assertion that government did not have the power to determine the racial identities of its citizens. He then took his argument in a different direction, contending that the perception Plessy had of himself as a white man constituted a property right, "with an actual pecuniary value," that no one could take away without due process, concluding that "the reputation of being white. . . is the most valuable sort of property, being the master-key that unlocks the golden door of opportunity."[17]

A Louisiana district court presided over by John H. Ferguson, a Massachusetts carpetbagger who had remained in the South after Reconstruction, heard the case. Only a few months earlier, Ferguson had presided over a similar trial involving the railroad, in which another black, Rodolphe Desdunes, had remained in the car reserved for whites after the train's conductor ordered him to leave. Ruling against the railway, Ferguson had supported Desdunes's right to sit wherever he pleased. But one important difference separated that case from Plessy's: Desdunes's train traveled between states and consequently fell under the jurisdiction of the federal government, which regulated interstate commerce. Plessy's train traveled from one point to another within Louisiana, which made it, southerners insisted, subject only to state law.

Based on his belief that a state had jurisdiction over travel that took place entirely within its borders, Ferguson ultimately ruled against Plessy. On appeal, the case made its way to the Supreme Court, which ruled against Plessy seven to one. Justice Henry Billings Brown of Michigan wrote the opinion for the majority, affirming the states' right to pass Jim Crow—or separate but equal—laws as long as they did not conflict with specific constitutional powers that belonged to the federal government. Reviewing past cases, Brown argued that *separate but equal* represented an established principle that had been affirmed again and again in both the North and the South. "Laws forbidding the intermarriage of the two races may be said in a technical sense to interfere with the freedom of contract," he wrote, "and yet have been universally recognized as within the police power of the State." Similarly, in Massachusetts, the establishment of separate schools for white and black children had been held "a valid exercise of the legislative power" as early as 1849.

Though the government secured black political rights, Brown observed, it could not guarantee their social equality. "Social prejudices cannot be overcome by legislation," and equal rights would never be gained through "the enforced commingling of the two races." If blacks and whites hoped "to meet upon terms of social equality, it must be the result of natural affinities, a mutual appreciation of each other's merits and a voluntary consent of individuals." The fallacy in Plessy's argument, he explained, lay in the "assumption that the enforced separation of the two races stamps the colored race with a badge of inferiority. . . . If this be so," he disingenuously concluded, it was "not by reason of anything found in the act, but solely because the colored race chooses to put that construction on it."[18]

Brown's opinion gave comfort to white supremacists. Narrowly construing the Fourteenth Amendment, he held that the federal government lacked the power to provide blanket protection for the rights of African Americans. The amendment's equal-protection clause applied only to the actions of the states and not to those of private individuals; consequently, blacks had no other recourse if they desired social equality but to hope that whites would have a change of heart and embrace them as equals. In the meantime, they had been granted political equality, which was all the government had the power to provide; rather than complaining about the presumed unfairness of private enterprises like the railway, they ought to rejoice in the political rights they had been granted.

Six of his fellow justices agreed with Brown's claim that "separate but equal" was a legally justifiable response to what the court described as the natural distinctions between the races, but John Marshall Harlan, one of two southern members of the court and the lone dissenter in the *Plessy* decision, refused to cave in to pressure from his colleagues.[19] "If enforced according to their true intent and meaning," he declared, the Thirteenth and Fourteenth Amendments protected "all the civil rights that pertain to freedom and citizenship." Harlan brushed aside Brown's contention that blacks had reacted out of heightened sensitivity and that nothing inherent in "separate but equal" suggested inferiority. "Everyone knows," he wrote, that the "statute in question had its origin in the purpose, not so much to exclude white persons from railroad cars occupied by . . . blacks, as to exclude colored people from coaches . . . assigned to white persons." Though privately owned, a railroad was a public highway; thus Louisiana had attempted to compel the separation of the races aboard a public conveyance on the basis of white prejudice. The Constitution, however, remained "color-blind and neither knows nor tolerates classes among citizens." With respect to civil rights, Harlan wrote, the humblest stood alongside the most powerful as peers, and he found it deeply troubling that the Supreme Court, "the final expositor of the fundamental law of the land," had concluded that a state could "regulate the enjoyment by citizens of their civil rights solely upon the basis of race." To Harlan, the decision in *Plessy v. Ferguson* seemed as pernicious and irresponsible as the outcome of *Dred Scott*. Though the recent amendments to the Constitution were supposed to have eliminated the legal inferiority of blacks articulated in *Scott*, *Plessy* made it clear that there still existed "in some of the States, a dominant race—a superior class of citizens," for whom color was the defining difference between themselves and their social inferiors. "The destinies of the two races, in this country, are indissolubly linked together," Harlan warned, "and the interests of both require that the common government of all shall not permit the seeds of race hate to be planted under the sanction of law. . . . Sixty millions of whites surely are in no danger from the presence here of eight millions of blacks," but the Court's decision would "not only stimulate aggressions, more or less brutal and irritating, upon the admitted rights of colored citizens, but . . . [would] encourage the belief that it is possible, by means of state enactments, to defeat the beneficent purposes" of the Constitution. What could more certainly "create and perpetuate a feeling of distrust between the races," he asked, than local laws, "which, in fact, proceed on the ground that colored citizens are so inferior and degraded that they cannot be allowed to sit in public coaches occupied by white citizens? . . . That, as all will admit," he concluded, was "the real meaning of such legislation as was enacted in Louisiana."

Harlan laid out a remarkably accurate road map of the nation's future, but most whites were unwilling to recognize the "indissoluble link" between themselves and black people, and Brown's opinion entered case law as the standard for the next half century, a prolonged era of stagnant race relations in which little happened to give African Americans comfort or hope. Before the Civil War, they could still put their faith in a great day coming, when divine justice, abetted by the abolitionists, would strike down the evils of slavery and blacks at last would go free. But with "separate but equal" decreed by the nation's highest court, the hope for black deliverance disappeared. The promise of equality had been hollowed out by white insincerity and semantic trickery.

Even if whites had wanted to take the principle of separate but equal seriously, it represented an impossible standard to meet. How could the equality of schools and other public facilities be accurately measured, particularly when they were bound to change over time—and for that matter, who would do the measuring? Separate but equal was nothing more than a subterfuge, enabling whites to distance themselves from blacks. Once the gulf between the races had passed muster with the Supreme Court, few whites cared whether anything approaching equality existed for African Americans. *Plessy v. Ferguson* produced disastrous results for blacks because it meant that in relation to the services and facilities that whites enjoyed, they constantly came up short. In education, the individual states—not only in the South but throughout the country—were now free to make their own decisions about black schooling, and with the equal-protection clause of the Fourteenth Amendment blunted by *Plessy* they consistently favored white schools and white children at the expense of black ones. The influence of separate but equal neatly balanced the legal requirement for black equality and the nearly universal refusal of whites to have anything to do with African Americans. Even among northern humanitarian organizations that aided black schools in the South, the patronizing assumptions of separate but equal served as the theoretical underpinnings for attempts to improve the lives of African Americans through education.

By the time *Plessy* was decided, Booker T. Washington had emerged as the leading black spokesman for industrial training, perhaps the most fundamental issue in the debate over African American schools. Born a slave, Washington had obtained an education through sheer will power and strength of character, graduating in 1875 from Virginia's Hampton Normal and Agricultural Institute, the leading school for blacks in the postbellum South. Hampton admitted its first students in April 1868 and quickly became the model for many of the southern normal schools in the training of black teachers. Its white founder, Samuel Chapman Armstrong, had been a brigadier general in the Civil War and led the Eighth and Ninth Regiments of the United States Colored Troops; in full uniform at the school's inauguration, he announced, "I can say to any noble, aspiring, whole-souled colored youth of either sex in the South—'Here you can come ragged and poor as you are, and become the men and women you wish to become.' "[20]

Armstrong paid special attention to students who demonstrated a penchant for politics. In the 1880s, every black delegate to the Virginia legislature with more than a grammar school education was a Hampton graduate. The most politically astute of them all, and Armstrong's decided favorite, was Booker Taliaferro Washington. The first graduate to return to Hampton as a teacher, Washington proved himself remarkably talented in the classroom—so much so that Armstrong recommended him in 1881 as the principal of Tuskegee Institute, a new school for blacks in Tuskegee, Alabama. Among whites, with Armstrong as his public relations adviser, Washington soon became the most widely admired African American in the country. An adviser to three presidents—Theodore Roosevelt, William Howard Taft, and Woodrow Wilson—he preached the importance of manual labor and the need for blacks to take pride in their work no matter how humble it might be. The African American's greatest danger, Washington declared, was that "in the great leap from slavery to freedom we may overlook the fact that the masses of us are to live by the production of our hands. . . . It is at the bottom of life we must begin, and not at the top." Blacks needed to integrate their "industrial, commercial, civil, and religious life [with whites] in a way that shall make the interests of both races one," Washington maintained, but the desire for social equality was extreme folly: "In all things that are purely social we [must] be as separate as the fingers, yet one as the hand in all things essential to mutual progress."[21]

Though whites regarded the second-class status of black Americans as a permanent condition, to Washington it was merely the starting point from which blacks would begin their ascent to full citizenship. Still, his view of blacks as the socially segregated laborers of American society, even if only temporarily, made him a black man whites could trust. "Hampton and Tuskegee have done great good," the president of Harvard, Charles W. Eliot, observed. "I know of no educational or philanthropic object which should more commend itself to American patriots."[22]

Most black leaders and their white supporters, however, had a hard time buying Booker T. Washington's desire to make industrial training the dominant form of black education. In 1898, when President William McKinley praised Washington for instructing students in practical industry rather than attempting the unattainable by teaching a regular college curriculum, William Hayes Ward, the editor of the New York Independent, angrily requested a clarification of exactly what was unattainable to the Negro and at what schools it might be taught. W. E. B. Du Bois joined Ward: "So far as Mr. Washington preaches thrift, patience, and industrial training for the masses, we must hold up his hands and strive with him.... But so far as Mr. Washington apologizes for injustice, North or South, does not rightly value the privileges and duty of voting, belittles the emasculating effects of caste distinction and opposes the higher training and ambition of our brighter minds—so far as he, the South, or the Nation does this—we must unceasingly and firmly oppose them."[23]

The great sticking point between Washington and Du Bois centered on the education that the most promising black youths—in Du Bois's phrase, the Negro population's "talented tenth"—ought to receive. Both men believed in the need to create leaders, but for Washington that meant an industrial education to train teachers to "reach the masses and show them how to lift themselves up" through hard work and accommodation to white social institutions. According to Du Bois, blacks needed strong leaders who had honed their intellects through higher education and developed the sophistication needed to fight aggressively for Negro rights with confidence and even a touch of arrogance. Each man attacked the other repeatedly in public: Du Bois criticized Washington's refusal to "teach anything higher than the three R's," while Washington insisted that Du Bois lacked any understanding of the needs of ordinary blacks.

The two men vowed to resolve their differences at a conference at Carnegie Hall January 6–8, 1904. The industrialist Andrew Carnegie and a number of other northern businessmen and philanthropists underwrote the affair. After much political jockeying, Washington and Du Bois agreed on twenty-eight prominent black leaders they would invite to discuss, among other subjects, industrial education for the black masses. The conference's first two days were taken up by polite discussion among the two principals and the invited guests; the third day devolved into two opposed and unyielding groups—one favoring Washington, supported by Carnegie, and another made up of black intellectuals, who backed Du Bois.[24] In his *Autobiography* Du Bois describes the pall that Carnegie and his associates cast over the meeting by continually showering Washington with what Du Bois termed "fulsome praise." After the white delegation's departure on the afternoon of the third day, the black attendees finally spoke freely to one another, no longer concealing their personal rancor. Eventually, both groups focused on a narrow range of issues that allowed them to reach some kind of agreement, and they formed the Committee of Twelve for the Advancement of the Negro Race, headed by Washington, Du Bois, and one of Washington's supporters, Hugh M. Browne, the principal of a state industrial school for blacks in Pennsylvania. The committee met once, without Du Bois, and promptly folded.

From Du Bois's point of view, Washington had become an Uncle Tom, allowing himself to be taken advantage of by northern industrialists who, under the guise of philanthropy, used his message of hard work and humility to encourage blacks to accept their inferior economic and social status quietly. Though Washington surely believed sincerely in the value of industrial training, the attraction for many of his white supporters lay in the promise of racial calm, which they believed would follow if African Americans learned to patiently accommodate themselves to second-class citizenship. Beginning in 1898, northern philanthropists and white educators from the South, seeking to promote racial harmony, had begun meeting annually in Chicago to discuss black education. Agreeing on the need to teach respect for racial hierarchy, they favored a commonsense program for black education, essentially the same as Washington's. Black laborers needed "to be taught to work, to submit to authority, [and] to respect their superiors," George T. Winston, the president of North Carolina's College of Agriculture and Mechanic Arts declared. "The saw, the plane, and the anvil must take the place" of Latin, Greek, and the other traditional elements of the liberal arts curriculum. The group won the support of many of the North's leading industrialists, who established a series of eleemosynary trusts that over the next thirty-five years would contribute vast sums to help open new schools for blacks in the South. In 1902, for example, John D. Rockefeller, of Standard Oil, at the urging of his son, John D. junior, gave $1 million to create the General Education Board for "the promotion of education within the United States of America without the distinction of race, sex or creed." Over the next thirty years, Rockefeller contributed an additional $128 million to the organization. Andrew Carnegie endowed Tuskegee with $1 million in 1906, and only a few years later Julius Rosenwald, the president of Sears Roebuck, established a similar fund in his family's name dedicated to the training of blacks in industrial subjects "designed to adjust the worker to the society in which he lives and therefore to make him a more desirable and worthy member of the community." These same trusts denied funding to black colleges like Fisk and Howard, which taught traditional liberal arts courses, because those institutions refused to fall in line and train their students for menial occupations such as agricultural worker, laborer, and porter, in which whites thought they belonged.

In 1945, W. E. B. Du Bois explored the inequities that fifty years of separate but equal legislation had created in Atlanta schools. Atlanta had "one school for every 855 white children," he wrote, and one "for every 2,040 Negro children." Over the years, local authorities had invested $2,156 in land and buildings for every pupil at white schools, while for blacks the equivalent figure was $887. Similar inequities existed in every comparison Du Bois made: Annual student expenditure for whites was $108.70 and for blacks about a third of that. Whites attended school six and a half hours a day; African Americans—relegated to "the black market of public education," the split session—attended three and a half hours per day, losing "at least 2,700 class hours" through the first six years of school. Black students had a shortage of teachers, almost no library facilities, and no kindergartens, resulting in many of the same problems educators bemoan today: "unsupervised leisure hours," "irregular attendance," "retardation," "delinquency," and the "reduced efficiency of overburdened teachers."

With statistics, Du Bois captured only the most apparent forms of discrimination, but he was unable to calculate how deeply racism had seeped below the surface and infected the traditional academic disciplines. In 1859 Darwin's *Origin of Species* had begun overturning accepted scientific beliefs. Coinciding as it did with the end of slavery and the coming of legal equality, it was inevitable that whites would employ a theory that could be interpreted to provide a model of scientific predestination—in disciplines like psychology, sociology, and economics—to explain the superiority of whites over blacks as the inevitable result of evolutionary laws. In 1876, William Graham Sumner, a Yale professor of political science and a leading proponent of social Darwinism, taught the first sociology course in the United States. Praising the competitive advantages of the Protestant ethic of hard work, frugality, and temperance, Sumner identified the American male as a peerless example of the well-equipped survivor, bound to triumph in the evolutionary struggle. To Sumner, human competition was a natural law that could "no more be done away with than gravitation." Just as species struggled against one another in the natural world, human beings competed for survival in an economic contest bound to be won by those with the largest endowment of business and financial virtues. To anyone who complained that his sociology bore harshly on the weak, Sumner responded that *strong* and *weak* were merely terms for "the industrious and the idle, the frugal and the extravagant." The laws of nature allowed people only a narrow freedom of choice. If they did not like the survival of the fittest or the law of civilization, they could pursue the only other alternative—"the survival of the unfittest," which was the "law of anti-civilization." People could choose the first or go on "vacillating between the two, but a third plan—the socialist desideratum—a plan for nourishing the unfittest and yet advancing in civilization, no man will ever find." Though "eighteenth-century notions about equality, natural rights, classes and the like" had produced states and legislation "strongly humanitarian in faith and temper," such ideas were relics of the past, which had to give way to science. "The *mores* of the twentieth century will not be tinged by humanitarianism as those of the last hundred years have been," Sumner assured his students.[25]

Sumner rarely addressed racial issues directly, but a number of his intellectual peers applied social Darwinism to the struggle between blacks and whites. In 1892, the renowned geologist Joseph Le Conte, who had graduated from Harvard and taught at the University of California, published his views on race problems in the South. Born in South Carolina, Le Conte saw the conflict between blacks and whites in starkly Darwinian terms. "Laws determining the effects of contact of species, races, varieties, etc. among animals" also applied to "the races of men," he wrote. Weaker varieties like the Negro, a race "still in childhood that had not yet learned to walk alone in the paths of civilisation," were destined either to "extinction [or] relegation to a subordinate place in the economy of nature." Blacks had to choose between a return to slavery or inevitable extinction through "extermination or mixture." If blacks refused to submit to white control, the law of self-preservation, which took precedence over all others, would make their destruction unavoidable. Nor could amalgamation save blacks. Interbreeding between pure racial types like the Teuton and the Negro produced the worst results, Le Conte warned: degraded and often infertile mulattoes, whose failure to multiply would result in the slow withering away of the black race, overcome by "the pitiless laws of organic evolution."[26]

Social Darwinism enabled whites to ground black inferiority in the irrefutable laws of nature; but they also were busy interpreting the nation's struggle over slavery and its subsequent spiral into war, in order to heal the division between northerners and southerners and reunite the white race. By the 1890s, a thriving community of historians, favoring national reconciliation, portrayed slavery and the war years as a national disaster in which both regions had suffered mightily. In the meantime, they pointed out, black Americans had failed to make anything of their freedom. Worse than that, they had become a threat—one that whites needed to face together. Men who thirty years earlier had fought one another to the death were transformed into tragic brothers who had gone to war reluctantly to defend their homes and their clashing cultures. James Ford Rhodes, a northerner who taught at Columbia University, became the nation's first recognized authority on slavery. In his multivolume history, he maintained that northerners and southerners alike had contributed to the moral wrong of slavery and shared responsibility for the war. New Englanders had made fortunes financing the ships that carried the Africans that southerners had purchased, and the frank recognition of one's own sins would make forgiveness between the regions possible. Dedicated to bringing the North and South together, Rhodes invoked the Christian principle of "judge not, that ye be not judged" to admonish both regions to seek forgiveness from their former adversaries. Though Rhodes attacked slavery, criticizing many of the harshest practices of the plantation owners, the slaves themselves represented the real villains of his story. Black females lacked chaste sentiments, he observed, and yielded "without objection, except in isolated cases, to the passion of their masters." What caught his eye when he watched a group of field hands at work was not the brutality of slave labor but the "besotted and generally repulsive expression" of the blacks themselves: "their brute-like countenances, on which were painted stupidity, indolence, duplicity, and sensuality; their listlessness; their dogged action; the stupid, plodding, machine-like manner in which they labored." When Rhodes met President Theodore Roosevelt in 1905, the president suggested that blacks lagged some "200,000 years behind" whites in their development. From his own experience, Rhodes responded, the difference seemed more like a million years. Only individuals like Booker T. Washington, he insisted, could "save the negro from being forced to the wall in competition with . . . whites."[27]

In 1893, only a year after James Rhodes's views on slavery first appeared, a young Princeton professor, Woodrow Wilson, published a book titled *Division and Reunion* that whitewashed slaveholders and blamed the North for the Civil War.[28] Born and raised in Virginia, Wilson portrayed the South as an idyllic, deeply conservative society that had wanted nothing more than to preserve its honor and principles, but had been betrayed by northerners. With "broad acres" and many slaves, he wrote, the southern planter pursued "an easy, expansive life of neighborly hospitality, position, and influence, inspired by a truly democratic instinct and sentiment of equality." In dealing with slaves, southern gentlemen had been bound by the responsibility that comes with ownership and their own "noble and gracious type of manhood" to cultivate truly patriarchal relationships. "Constantly under their master's eye," field hands found themselves "comfortably quartered, and . . . kept from overwork both by their own laziness and by the slack discipline to which they were subjected." Though masters now and then harshly punished or even brutalized their slaves, such episodes Wilson regarded as exceptional; most stories of mistreatment represented exaggerations or outright fictions that ignored the plantation's "characteristic spirit and method." When the Civil War came, it pitted the rich, powerful North against an underdog

South that managed to sustain itself through "sheer spirit and devotion." Southerners had always "resolutely, almost passionately, resisted change," and in their minds the "national idea had never supplanted . . . the original theory of the Constitution," which recognized that the Union had been formed as a confederation rather than as a consolidation. To Wilson's way of thinking, southerners had gone to war as defenders of the Constitution to protect the doctrine of states' rights, a doctrine that unprincipled northerners wanted to destroy not only to end slavery but to terminate the South's right to secede.

Wilson expounded southern history as high tragedy with a happy ending. Though the South had lost its innocence with the coming of war, and its "leisure and . . . old-time culture" had been irrevocably destroyed, it had survived, transformed "as if by a marvel, into likeness to the rest of the country." Freed from "the incubus of slavery, the South had sprung into . . . new life; and the days of inevitable strife and permanent difference had grown strangely remote." Still harboring a sentimental allegiance to the gallant South, Wilson refused to apologize for southerners having held slaves, but he rejoiced in the reintegration of the two regions as "the old alienation of feeling" died out and a new community of shared interests developed between North and South.

Wilson went on to serve as the first nonclerical head of Princeton University and then as governor of New Jersey. In 1912, running as a Democrat, he became the first southerner since Zachary Taylor to win the presidency. Though he had run as a progressive reformer and corruption fighter, Wilson proved, in relation to blacks, more a southerner than a progressive. Though he had sworn during the campaign that blacks could "count upon . . . absolute fair dealing . . . and everything by which I can assist in advancing the interests of their race," he quickly allowed the rule of separate but equal to penetrate the entire federal government, where it had not existed before. By mid-1913, segregated work areas, toilets, and lunchrooms had appeared in a wide variety of government offices, along with new, racially separate job assignments—particularly in instances where African American men had previously supervised white women. Even Booker T. Washington noted after a visit to the nation's capital that he had "never seen the colored people so discouraged and bitter as they are at the present time."[29]

Except in rare instances, Wilson declined to appoint blacks to federal positions of any consequence. Previously, certain jobs had been reserved for

African Americans: diplomatic posts in black nations, registrar of the treasury, recorder of deeds and customs collector for the District of Columbia, and several others. When Wilson took office, blacks held thirteen midlevel-appointee posts and eleven positions in the diplomatic and consular corps. Five years later, only one black judge and six black diplomatic officers remained, and Wilson had made only two significant black appointments—one as minister to Liberia and the other as a District of Columbia municipal court judge. The president was under considerable pressure from southern conservatives in his own party, who joined with the National Democratic Fair Play Association, which supported racist legislation, and much of the white population of Washington, D.C., in lobbying for a segregated national government. As the New York Evening Post noted, the capital was "essentially a Southern city" that held a "Southern view of the negro." Whites in government had long "resented being compelled to associate with the negroes," but never before had there been "an Administration that dared to cater to this feeling, except in surreptitious ways. . . . There had always been . . . a wish to do it, but not the courage."[30]

Wilson also revealed his racist tendencies in his support for D. W. Griffith's The Birth of a Nation. Based on Thomas Dixon's antiblack novel The Clansman, the movie presented a romanticized southern interpretation of white supremacy, black savagery, the evils of Reconstruction, and the heroic redemption of the South by the Ku Klux Klan. Unfortunately, many moviegoers accepted the film as an accurate picture of the Civil War and its aftermath, and it confirmed their belief in the unrestrained wildness of blacks and the essential nobility of the southern cause. At its first public showings, the film met with substantial resistance from African Americans and a fair number of northern whites, but Wilson held a private screening for his cabinet, and allowed his approval of the film to be made public, assuring that it would be widely viewed throughout the country. When black leaders complained, the president replied through his secretary that the White House showing had been merely "a courtesy extended to an old acquaintance," and that the president was entirely unaware of the "character" of the film before it was shown.[31]

The extension of the doctrine of separate but equal throughout the federal government represented the final step in the post–Civil War exclusion of

African Americans, shunting them into a racial netherworld essentially disconnected from contact with whites. The South formalized two distinct societies for blacks and whites with an elaborate system of state laws requiring separate facilities in every conceivable situation—schools, railway stations, lunch counters, drinking fountains, bathrooms, and so on. Though the two races often worked alongside one another, frequently in white homes, in public they had to hide any signs of friendship or intimacy and instead carried on an elaborate ritual of avoidance, sacrificing human relationships to preserve racial separation. In the North and West, where the number of blacks remained small, most whites had little or no contact with African Americans. Their most intimate impressions of them were gleaned from popular entertainment or stereotypes created to advertise commercial products. From the blackface minstrel shows to Aunt Jemima, the grinning purveyor of pancakes, to Niggerhair Chewing Tobacco, which promised to be thick and tightly packed, commercial advertising reduced African Americans to insignificance as "darkies," "pickaninnies," "Uncle Toms," and "mammies," filled with good-humored ignorance but lacking the intelligence to learn from their often outlandish mistakes.[32]

During slavery, whites had ignored the humanity of African Americans, treating them as property. With blacks as free citizens, whites begrudgingly acknowledged them as human beings but invented new forms of humiliation, sometimes subtle but often audacious, to hammer out the constant and consistent message of black inferiority. Though the day-to-day insults of separate but equal often caused blacks excruciating mental torment, the psychic damage they suffered from even more glaring examples of white insensitivity can hardly be comprehended. In 1906, for instance, the New York Zoological Park exhibited a Pygmy in the monkey house, in the same cage as an orangutan. Billed as a "purely ethnological exhibit," Ota Benga—"Age, 23. Height, 4 feet 11 inches. Weight, 103 pounds"—became wildly popular, drawing large crowds that roared with laughter as man and ape frolicked together. When a group of black clergymen protested the African's imprisonment, William T. Hornaday, the park director, enigmatically replied that the Pygmy had been housed in the monkey cage because it represented "the most comfortable place we [could] find for him."[33] A few days after the exhibit opened, the New York Times noted that Benga and the orangutan were about the same height, giving one an opportunity to study their obvious points of resemblance. "Their heads are much alike," the newspaper observed, "and both grin in the same way when pleased."

The Ota Benga exhibit represented a particularly offensive example of the humiliation of blacks, but the Senate of the United States came close to matching it with a plan they debated in 1923 to erect a monument in Washington honoring "The Black Mammy of the South." White southerners claimed innocent intentions: both to honor their heritage and to commemorate an African American figure they admired and respected, who embodied for them the qualities of love, fidelity, and loyalty. Blacks and their supporters doubted white sincerity, seeing in the statue the desire to keep alive memories of white domination and African American inferiority. As the board of directors of the Phillis Wheatley YWCA in Washington declared in 1923, blacks "do not like to be vividly reminded of the unfortunate condition of some of our ancestors." However well the mammy "may have performed . . . as a foster mother to many of the progeny of the South," she represented "the shadows of the past." "Such irritants," the board concluded, "are not conducive to the harmony of citizenship."[34]

The mammy project ultimately died a quiet death, but not without self-righteous protestations from white southerners. The *Baltimore Sun*, conceding the failure of the idea in Washington, argued that it had never occurred to white proponents of the statue that "the present generation of colored people would be ashamed of the mammy. The last thing in [white] minds was to wound sensitive feelings or to remind her descendants that they came from a race of slaves." If the mammy were alive today, the newspaper declared, she likely "would give her learned and superior grandchildren a sharp piece of her very sharp mind." Though she lacked "much book learning, she could be scornful of persons who 'put on airs' and certainly wouldn't stand any nonsense from any person of color, free or slave."

Forced to accept humiliation instead of equality, blacks grew increasingly restive, longing for the unfulfilled promise of fair play that they had expected to accompany emancipation and citizenship. Still heavily concentrated in the South, many blacks looked to the North as the promised land, where the burden of discrimination would be lifted and they could enter into American society, at least partially. Within a few years, purely by chance, two unrelated disasters occurred in quick succession, which for blacks had the welcome effect of encouraging them to flee the South and head for the big cities of the North. By 1916, World War I had choked off immigration from Europe, creating a shortage of workers in the North, while business orders had increased to make up for the falling production of war-torn Continental industries.[35] At the same time, the boll weevil had arrived from Mexico, destroying millions of acres of cotton as it spread gradually across the South, temporarily ruining the region's agricultural economy. In the Sea Islands of South Carolina, where in 1918 the state had produced 1,688 bushels of cotton, the number fell to only 167 the following year.[36] Lenders and merchants withdrew their support from farmers, many of whom were forced to file for bankruptcy and let their workers go. Unskilled agricultural workers flocked to southern cities, swelling labor pools, depressing wages, and making work difficult to find. Obvious incentives for departure existed on both ends, and African Americans, particularly experienced urban workers, left the South—well over a million between 1916 and 1930, bound for New York, Chicago, Philadelphia, Detroit, Cleveland, Pittsburgh, and any other northern destination where it appeared that opportunities existed.

The Great Migration was a major demographic shift in the nation's black population, and for many blacks newly removed from the South, escape—at least in the beginning—proved exhilarating. "I don't have to master every little white boy comes along. I haven't heard a white man call a colored a nigger . . . since I been in the state of Pa.," a new arrival to Philadelphia wrote home sometime between 1916 and 1918. "I can ride in the electric street and steam cars where I get a seat. . . . I am not crazy about being with white folks, but if I have to pay the same fare I have learn to want the same accommodation."[37] But while blacks no longer had to deal with the smothering segregation that confronted them at every turn in the South, they would soon discover that they were hardly more welcome in the North than they had been at home.

Blacks arrived in cities like Chicago and New York hoping to find jobs with higher wages, but with little or no savings and desperate for work they had to take whatever they could get, usually at about the same or lower pay than they had received in the South. Largely rejected by white union members, who not only wanted to keep their organizations lily-white but hoped to limit competition, blacks were taken up by employers seeking strikebreakers in their struggles with organized labor. "The Negro had [only] one-half of a bad chance to get a job," a New York official commented, and owing no loyalty to white workers, many blacks accepted whatever they could find with little thought of what the effect would be on white union members.

Along with strikebreaking, African Americans accepted jobs that whites refused to do—dynamiting and loading coal deep in the mines of West Virginia, pouring molten metal in the steel mills of Pittsburgh, cleaning up blood and animal parts in the Chicago stockyards. Grueling and frequently dangerous, these jobs seldom offered any possibility of advancement, leaving blacks once again at the bottom of the social ladder, their lowly position extending beyond work into every aspect of their lives. Before the Great Migration, blacks had lived in small pockets scattered throughout northern cities. As their numbers grew, whites became more and more uncomfortable—the novelist James Weldon Johnson remarked that whites fled "as if from a plague"—and increasingly blacks were isolated in inner-city ghettos. Landlords grossly inflated rents in black areas, and two or even three families often made do by sharing a small efficiency apartment without a stove, a private bath, or running water. Malnutrition, disease, a soaring infant mortality rate, and frequent arrests for public drunkenness, gambling, and other petty crimes inevitably followed from their straitened circumstances, confirming the white belief that blacks were irresponsible, antisocial outsiders who could never live alongside whites.

While lynchings in the rural South declined, the arrival of large numbers of unwanted migrant blacks shifted the epicenter of violence to the cities in the North. In 1917 in East Saint Louis, the first in a series of violent race riots broke out. Continuing for days, the turmoil left forty-eight dead, several hundred injured, and more than three hundred buildings ransacked or destroyed. Recalling the last half century, readers may think of race riots as events set off by blacks to vent their anger, but whites were the instigators of most of the earlier riots, which began over rumors or relatively petty incidents and exploded into expressions of racial hostility and a warning to blacks to stay in their place. In mid-1919—the "Red Summer," as James Weldon Johnson called it—rioting against blacks spread across the United States.[38] In a period of only a few months, race riots broke out in twenty-six cities, including Chicago and Washington, D.C. The Chicago riot began when a seventeen-year-old black who had gone swimming with friends in Lake Michigan drifted into an area reserved for whites. Whites and blacks shouted obscenities at each other on the beach, which led to fighting and stone throwing, including some aimed at the youngster in the water, who drowned. The incident touched off a race war throughout the city which became the worst racial confrontation in the nation's history, lasting day and night for almost two weeks.

Just as in Chicago, the immediate cause of the Washington riot masked deeper resentments. A series of lurid newspaper articles about rapists, presumed to be black, inflamed local whites, particularly servicemen, and when the *Washington Post* ran headlines of another rape on its front page, soldiers, sailors, and marines took to the streets in roving bands, accosting blacks, dragging them off streetcars and out of restaurants, and beating them mercilessly. With little interference from the D.C. police, white mobs took over the city, and after four days federal troops had to be mobilized to restore order. Rioting against African Americans followed in the earlier, sinister tradition of southern vigilante violence and in fact has been called "a magnified, or mass, lynching" by the Swedish economist Gunnar Myrdal, who in 1944 published his monumental study of racism in the United States, *An American Dilemma: The Negro Problem and Modern Democracy*. A reflection of the intense emotional hostility of urban whites toward the growing number of blacks in their cities, the riots served a practical purpose, intimidating blacks by reminding them of the white community's power and clarifying what would and would not be tolerated. As an extralegal sanction employed by whites to control African Americans, the race riot became the weapon of last resort when legal means to keep blacks in line failed.

The riots of 1919 caught the attention of the federal government's investigative agencies, who chose to overlook the fact that in nearly every instance whites had initiated trouble and insisted instead that Bolshevik or socialist propaganda had incited blacks to violence. Labor strife before World War I, and the war itself, had led to the establishment of a national surveillance network to guard against foes of the American system. The General Intelligence Division of the Justice Department's Bureau of Investigation (headed by an ambitious young attorney named J. Edgar Hoover), the army's Military Intelligence Division, and the Postal Service were all granted broad emergency powers under the Espionage Act of 1917 to pursue radical labor leaders, foreign agitators, and members of disaffected groups like African Americans, who might hinder the war effort.[39]

Along with W. E. B. Du Bois, who by then had helped found the NAACP and was editor of its publication, *The Crisis*, there was a new generation of younger African American intellectuals, whose views were closely scrutinized by civilian and military officials. Du Bois had arrived at a temporary truce with the government during the war, when he suggested that the races ought to put aside their differences and unify against a foreign enemy. When the war ended, however, he immediately demanded a shift in tactics, maintaining that blacks would be cowards and jackasses unless they returned from the fighting ready for a new battle. With peace at hand, African Americans had to "marshal every ounce of our brain and brawn to fight a sterner, longer, more unbending battle against the forces of hell in our own land."[40] The Postal Service, which considered refusing to deliver the edition of The Crisis in which Du Bois's views appeared, judged them "unquestionably violent and extremely likely to excite a considerable amount of racial prejudice (if that has not already reached its maximum amongst the Negroes)." After a week's delay, however, the magazine was distributed, in part at least because postal officials had a long list of black publications— The Messenger, The Negro World, and The Crusader—that they regarded as even more dangerous.

Originating in New York, nearly all these journals were run by members of the "New Crowd Negroes," as one of their leaders called them—a group of tough-minded young blacks whose orientation tended to be radical and socialist but whose primary loyalty was to their race.[41] The Messenger was founded in 1917 by A. Philip Randolph and Chandler Owen, two young men who had migrated to New York City from the South and were unrelenting in their criticism of white America. In an early wartime editorial titled "Pro-Germanism among Negroes," they addressed white fears that black discontent resulted from foreign subversion. Randolph and Owen agreed on the deep dissatisfaction of American blacks but placed the blame squarely on domestic issues: "peonage, disenfranchisement, Jim-Crowism, segregation, rank civil discrimination, injustice of legislatures, courts and administrators." It struck them as ludicrous that the nation had gone to war "to make the world safe for democracy," while at home it denied black citizens "economic, political, educational, and civil equality." Dismissing the charge that African Americans stood on the sidelines rooting for a German victory in the war, they explained that blacks, innocent of pro-German feelings, were guilty of plain old anti-Americanism, which meant simply that they were "anti-lynching."[42]

As socialists, Randolph and Owen tended to view the nation's problems in terms of class even more than race. Thus they believed that blacks needed to join the labor movement along with whites, preferably as members of the radical Industrial Workers of the World (IWW). Both The Crusader and The Negro World, in contrast, were black nationalist publications and held that whites were unreliable allies who would ultimately remain loyal to their own race. *The Negro World* began publication in 1918 as the voice of Marcus Garvey's Universal Negro Improvement Association, which aimed to instill racial pride, to foster black economic growth, and to develop a repatriation plan to build a black-led nation in Africa. A Jamaican by birth, Garvey became a blunt, unflinching spokesman for a back-to-Africa movement that would include not only African Americans but blacks whom slavery had scattered all over the world. "All races," he observed, "look forward to the time when spears shall be beaten into agricultural implements," but until then, "oppressed peoples need to avail themselves of every weapon that may be effective in defeating the fell motives of their oppressors. . . . In a world of wolves one should go armed, and one of the most powerful defensive weapons within the reach of Negroes is the practice of RACE FIRST in all parts of the world."[43] Particularly frightening to government officials, Garvey's call for blacks to unite internationally inspired surveillance not only by Hoover and his men but by the British, who feared that his message would lead to trouble in the Caribbean. Hoover finally nailed Garvey for using the mails to defraud people by soliciting money for his steamship company, the Black Star Line. Between 1919 and 1921, Garvey and his wife had collected an estimated $10 million. In 1923, a federal judge found him guilty, and two years later he began serving a five-year sentence. President Coolidge pardoned Garvey and deported him in 1927 to Jamaica as an undesirable alien.

While Marcus Garvey's hope of uniting blacks around the world inspired fears of a global confrontation, *The Crusader*, edited by Cyril V. Briggs, suggested a more immediate threat. Like Garvey, Briggs came from the Caribbean (the island of Nevis), and he shared Randolph's and Owen's belief that blacks should not take sides in a war between imperialist powers. In the October 1919 issue of *The Crusader*, Briggs advertised the formation of the African Blood Brotherhood. Militaristic in tone, the announcement offered membership by enlistment, without dues, fees, or assessments, the only requirement being that recruits were "willing to go the limit!" Purposely vague, Briggs seemed to be advocating the formation of a paramilitary organization committed to extreme measures to defend African Americans. Blacks were morally superior to whites, he maintained, because "the Negro has not had the opportunity to be mean, brutal, cruel and inhuman that the white[s] have had for several centuries." The time had come, however, for blacks to mobilize to protect themselves from further injustice. As Herbert

Boulin, Briggs's spokesman, explained, the African Blood Brotherhood intended to "allow those who attack us to choose the weapons. If it be guns, we will reply with guns."[44]

The emergence of these militant black leaders coincided with an era in which domestic and foreign adversaries were being closely watched. President McKinley had been assassinated in 1901 by an anarchist, and shortly before May Day in 1919 thirty-eight government leaders, most of them prominent foes of radicalism, had been sent mail bombs. But in lumping blacks together with militant labor unionists, foreign agitators, anarchists, and enemy aliens, government investigators were led astray by a mixture of paranoia and prejudice, demonizing American blacks as part of a vast international conspiracy rather than recognizing them as disgruntled citizens with legitimate complaints. Black radicalism aimed to promote "Pan-Negroism and a combination of the other colored races of the world," a crack investigator for the Military Intelligence Division, Captain John B. Trevor, warned in 1919: "As a colored movement it looks to Japan for leadership; as a radical movement it follows Bolshevism and has intimate relations with various socialistic groups throughout the United States. With this latter connection it naturally sympathizes with and has relations with the Irish, the Jews, and Hindus."[45] Ironically, with all their agents and informants, government officials overlooked the fact that Garvey, Briggs, Randolph, Owens, and other black radicals constantly feuded among themselves and appeared incapable of getting along with one another, much less uniting as members of an international conspiracy.

Throughout the 1920s, the stagnation of separate but equal, the intimidation of race riots, and the government's monitoring of radicals kept blacks on the defensive. In 1921, Tulsa experienced several days of racial violence after a white girl accused a black elevator operator of attempting to rape her. Whites completely destroyed a well-to-do section in Tulsa known as the "Black Wall Street," using machine guns and bombs to attack black homes and businesses. The National Guard eventually restored order, but not until fifty whites and perhaps two hundred blacks had been killed and more than $1.5 million worth of property had been destroyed by fire.[46] In 1927 blacks were dealt another blow, this time by the Great Mississippi Flood, the worst inundation in the nation's history. All along the river, water breached the levees, submerging the surrounding lowlands. Local inhabitants from both races suffered terribly; but even in the midst of catastrophe, landowners maintained the discipline of segregation. Not only were the races separated in refugee camps, but white officials kept blacks on the levees against their will, demanding their labor and refusing them transportation that would have carried them to safety.[47]

In 1929 the arrival of the Great Depression made matters even worse. As the last hired and first fired, blacks everywhere, but particularly in the South, found themselves in desperate economic straits.[48] By the end of 1930, farm income throughout the South had fallen by half, taking with it any hope for prosperity in southern cities. Manufacturing in Atlanta and New Orleans declined by 50 percent; in Birmingham by at least 70 percent. Throughout the country, jobless rates soared: among white males it reached 25 percent; for African Americans it averaged 40 percent, and in some cities with large black populations, like Detroit, it approached 60 percent for male blacks and 75 percent for female blacks. Herbert Hoover, the Republican president, stubbornly resisted direct government aid to individuals, preferring instead programs intended to stimulate the economy from the top down. By the fall of 1931, however, with the nation showing no signs of recovery, voters had grown disillusioned and turned to the Democratic governor of New York, Franklin Delano Roosevelt, who promised aggressive and innovative action to reverse the decline. It was the task of his party, Roosevelt told the Democratic convention in Chicago, to break with "foolish traditions" and provide the American people with what they needed, "work and security." Though not a program likely to inspire conservative support, Roosevelt's promise of radical change—a New Deal for the nation's citizens—was embraced even by individuals like Edward O'Neal, the head of the reactionary American Farm Bureau Federation, who feared "a revolution in the countryside" unless something was done quickly.[49]

Inaugurated on March 4, 1933, Roosevelt embarked on the nation's longest presidency, slightly more than twelve years that spanned the Great Depression and the Second World War. In both instances, he faced the need for an unprecedented national mobilization to ensure America's survival. Other issues quite naturally became secondary, and Roosevelt dealt with them in the context of the greater emergency. Under his guidance, America recovered its economic health and rose to preeminence as a world power. But confronted by two momentous crises, the president had little time for divisive racial questions, emphasizing instead the common bond blacks and working class whites shared and maintaining that the two races had essentially the same fundamental problems: hunger, inadequate housing, unemployment, disability, and old age.

Roosevelt's relations with African Americans are particularly difficult to assess. Philosophically, he believed in equal opportunity, and indeed, he filled his administration with innovative young intellectuals who favored radical governmental action to provide social and economic justice for ordinary citizens. But Roosevelt was also a realist, who faced a difficult political landscape throughout his presidency. Coming out of the 1932 election, he felt no specific obligation to blacks, who generally had not voted for him. Despite Hoover's glacial insensitivity—among other things, he had sent black Gold Star mothers to Europe on a segregated ship to visit their sons' graves— black voters had remained loyal to the party of Lincoln.[50] Roosevelt had won the election with the backing of white southerners, becoming only the second Democratic president since before the Civil War. But unlike Wilson, he came from the North—automatically arousing suspicion—and continually needed to shore up his southern support.

By 1933, favored by the longevity in office that a one-party region could give to its representatives, conservative southern Democrats had a commanding grip on Congress, and Roosevelt desperately needed their votes for his economic recovery plan. In the first hundred days of the New Deal, an impressive battery of activist legislation would never have passed without the support of the vice president, the majority leaders of both the House and the Senate, and the chairmen of several key congressional committees, all of whom were southern Democrats. The price of passage, however, was compromise that resulted in the effective exclusion of African Americans. Though programs like the National Recovery Administration (NRA), the Civilian Conservation Corps (CCC), and the Tennessee Valley Authority (TVA) all gave lip service to racial equality, in practice they favored whites at the expense of blacks.[51] At the insistence of southern conservatives, the NRA, which set wage standards, excluded farm workers and domestic servants, about three-quarters of the black workforce, and allowed for "traditional" geographic variations in the minimum wage. Blacks quickly recognized the government was conducting business as usual and ruefully noted that NRA stood for "Negro Removal Act," "Negroes Ruined Again," or "Negro Run Around." The TVA, headed by David Lilienthal, had similar problems. Though it trumpeted its decentralization and freedom from federal control, independence simply meant that local officials, who enforced southern attitudes toward blacks, ran the program. African Americans not only received the dirtiest, lowest-paying jobs; they also represented a mere 1 percent of the workers hired, and when the chance to purchase homes in the model town of Norris, Tennessee, came along, the opportunity was restricted to whites.

The marriage between administration liberals and conservative Democrats in Congress put enormous pressure on the president. Conservatives recognized that Roosevelt's economic recovery program threatened states' rights and undermined the South's social traditions, and they continually sought to put limits on it. Liberals, on the other hand, faulted the president for doing too little, arguing he should take the lead in the struggle for social justice, particularly in relation to African Americans. Within the administration, men like Harold Ickes, the secretary of the interior, and Harry Hopkins, the federal emergency relief administrator, supported African American aspirations, along with a coterie of forceful black intellectuals who had joined the New Deal not only to fight the depression, but to advance their own race. Robert C. Weaver, John Preston Davis, William Hastie, and Ralph Bunche had known one another as graduate students at Harvard, and they accepted positions in Washington, hoping Roosevelt would use the power of the federal government to begin a second Reconstruction in the South.[52]

The president's wife, Eleanor, also became a militant advocate for African Americans. Remarkably independent, Mrs. Roosevelt embraced the fight for racial equality, refusing to temper her own opinions when she disagreed with her husband and serving as a White House conduit for the views of black leaders, which the president often would have preferred to avoid. On at least one occasion, in 1934, she badly embarrassed Roosevelt, when she arranged a meeting with Walter White, the executive director of the NAACP, who was seeking presidential support for a federal anti-lynching law. Unable to refute White's arguments, Roosevelt finally admitted that he simply could not afford politically to speak out in favor of antilynching legislation. If he did, he explained, southern conservatives would block every bill he needed passed "to keep America from collapsing."[53]

Perhaps realizing she had gone too far, Mrs. Roosevelt uncharacteristically deferred to her husband when the issue came up again. Following the lynching of an Alabama man a few months later, she was asked to speak at a rally in Carnegie Hall, but decided against it when the president indicated that her appearance would increase his difficulties with Congress. White continued to fight unsuccessfully for anti-lynching legislation, asking Roosevelt to condemn a Southern filibuster against it in 1935, which the president refused to do. He also avoided any further direct contact with the NAACP leader, employing his wife as a messenger to express his sympathy for the bill, though he would never take an active role in its passage.

The uneasy relationship between Roosevelt and southern Democrats fell apart in the wake of the Supreme Court crisis of the mid-thirties. In 1935, the court had begun overturning key elements of the New Deal, restricting "the government's right to regulate the economy . . . , to tax and spend for the general welfare, and to interfere with the freedom of contract," Roosevelt complained.[54] African Americans switched to the Democratic Party in the presidential election the following year, buoyed by the number of blacks in the administration and by the president's continued assurances that the benefits of the New Deal should extend to everyone. Winning in a landslide, Roosevelt tried to realign the Court, which had taken under review two more crucial New Deal programs, Social Security and the Wagner Act that gave workers the right to organize and bargain collectively.

The president wanted Congress to liberalize the Court by adding six or more new justices; but southern Democrats, who favored the Court's conservative direction, led a bipartisan revolt, defeating Roosevelt's plan. The struggle opened a rift that could never be healed, and later that year Democratic and Republican foes of the administration joined together to issue a "Conservative Manifesto" repudiating the New Deal and calling for tax reductions, a balanced budget, strict attention to states' rights, and respect for private property.[55]

The alienation of southern Democrats drove Roosevelt in search of fresh supporters for the New Deal agenda. A Gallup poll indicated that in contrast to their representatives who followed the dictates of the region's ruling landowners and business interests, a majority of southerners approved Roosevelt's plan to make over the Court. Having lost the region's conservative political leaders, the president tried to go directly to the people, personally campaigning in the South for liberal candidates. Though he had little success in the 1938 midterm elections, Roosevelt opened the door for a grassroots movement that represented the first step in reforming the region's white-only political process.

New Deal leaders had come to realize that the key to southern progress was to reform the electorate. Though conservatives had nearly absolute local control, the South nevertheless represented fertile ground in which a new political movement could develop for precisely the same reason that one was needed: The right to vote had been so severely restricted that only a few whites could cast ballots, and their handpicked candidates would become vulnerable by the addition of a relatively limited number of new voters. Important House members like Georgia's Eugene Cox, the chairman of the Rules Committee, had been elected again and again with only a little over five thousand votes in a district with a population that exceeded a quarter million.[56]

With Roosevelt openly battling southern conservatives in Congress, the administration's relationship with poor whites and blacks took on a new significance. The president actively pursued their votes throughout the South, where nearly two-thirds of the adult white population was disenfranchised along with an even greater percentage of African Americans. The potential existed among the poor to remake southern politics; and of all the measures concocted to limit the right to vote, none was more widely used than the poll tax. In the early 1930s, the populists Huey Long and Claude Pepper had managed to eliminate the tax in their home states; and in both cases, the effect of repeal had been startling: voting rolls increased by 90 percent in Louisiana and by 140 percent in Florida.[57]

In November 1938, a conference was held in Birmingham, Alabama, that brought together labor organizers, New Deal administrators, dispossessed whites, black leaders, and southern liberals as well as Eleanor Roosevelt and Supreme Court Justice Hugo Black. Violating a city ordinance that made integrated meetings illegal, the conference members sat together and organized a political movement to support a federal antilynching law, demand equal pay for black and white teachers, and plan a voting rights campaign. The Birmingham police, led by Theophilis Eugene "Bull" Connor, interrupted the meeting and ordered blacks and whites to segregate themselves on opposite sides of the auditorium. Mrs. Roosevelt arrived precisely at that moment, placed a chair in the middle of the center aisle, sat down, and refused to budge, forcing Connor to retreat in frustration.[58] The incident highlighted the founding of the Southern Conference for Human Welfare (SCHW), which would lead the campaign for federal legislation to outlaw the poll tax.

With help from Lee Geyer, a California member of the House, the SCHW brought together a number of organizations like the NAACP, the National Negro Congress, the American Federation of Labor, the Congress of Industrial Organizations, the National Farmers Union, and the League of Women Voters to form the National Committee to Abolish the Poll Tax (NCAPT). Though the NCAPT intensely lobbied Congress, southerners resisted efforts to outlaw the tax, which for them represented a renewal of northern attempts during Reconstruction to take over the South's electoral process. African Americans, labor radicals, and the Communist Party were trying to subvert the Constitution, Mississippi senator Theodore Bilbo warned. How dare they "tell the southern states [with] three-fourths of all the Negroes . . . how they should treat, control, and handle the race problem."[59] Southerners fought a prolonged battle in Congress, threatening to blow apart the Democratic Party; and ultimately, they delayed the poll tax repeal until the 1960s, when it finally was banned by the Twenty-fourth Amendment. Though the New Deal reformers' immediate campaign failed, they succeeded in creating a durable coalition that would continue the fight for social justice and an expanded franchise.

The bill to repeal the poll tax was killed by a Senate filibuster several months after the United States entered World War II. With the wartime emergency, everything in Washington changed. Roosevelt could no longer wait for a long-range political strategy to alter the electorate in the South in order to remove his conservative opponents. Instead, he shifted his own priorities and once again began cooperating with southern Democrats, who had put new pressure on him by threatening to withhold support for national mobilization.

Clark Foreman, a staunch supporter of African Americans, who had joined the administration as "special adviser on the economic status of Negroes" in 1933 and later held a variety of jobs that brought him into conflict with southern conservatives, became the first victim sacrificed to placate the South. Southerners demanded his resignation, and the president reluctantly agreed, recognizing he had lost an accomplished administrator and loyal friend. Under the aegis of the Joint Committee for the Reduction of Non-Essential Federal Expenditures, conservatives also gutted many of the New Deal's core programs, including the Civilian Conservation Corps, the National Youth Administration, the Works Progress Administration, the National Resource Planning Board, and the Farm Security Administration.[60]

Supporters of the poll tax repeal shifted their attention to a Soldiers' Vote Act, which they tried to pass in 1942 and again the following year. The bill would have given all members of the military the vote, including more than four hundred thousand African Americans. Southerners objected that it took the right to establish voter qualifications away from the states and put it in the hands of the federal government; and once again, a bitter standoff ensued. To Joseph Guffey, chairman of the Senate Democratic Campaign Committee, southerners had joined together in an "unpatriotic and unholy alliance" to block men and women in the services from voting. Threatening a walkout that would leave northern Democrats high and dry, an angry Josiah Bailey of North Carolina replied that southerners were losing patience and might form their own "Southern Democratic Party," which would control the electoral college and hold the "balance of power" in the country. Ultimately, southerners won out with a substitute bill that simply encouraged states to pass legislation allowing members of the armed forces to vote.[61]

Despite the rollback of New Deal programs and the vehement resistance of southern whites, World War II represented a time of accelerating progress for African Americans. Just as in the past, the wartime emergency created unique opportunities for blacks, whose manpower once again was urgently needed. On the home front, the enormous migration of African Americans, who left the South for defense-related jobs in the North, gave many blacks a new level of economic security and relief from the most oppressive practices of the intensely segregated South. In addition, nearly a million African Americans served in the armed forces, expanding their horizons of opportunity and reestablishing ties between northern and southern blacks separated by the Great Migration that began in 1916 and continued through the 1920s.

Progress was also made in the courts and by the growing readiness of black leaders to confront the national government. In 1941, A. Philip Randolph, who had become president of the Brotherhood of Sleeping Car Porters, threatened an African American march on Washington unless the armed forces and defense industries were opened equally to blacks as well as whites. Though the military remained segregated, a compromise on the home front resulted in the creation of the Fair Employment Practices Committee, which prohibited discrimination in defense-related companies and federal agencies. In 1944, in *Smith v. Allwright*, African Americans also enjoyed a significant victory in the Supreme Court, when eight justices appointed by Roosevelt voted to end the all-white primary.[62] The decision had a profound effect, giving new life to registration and voting drives throughout the South.

The increased mobility of African Americans and their growing assertiveness met with rising resistance from whites, of course. In both the North and the South, violence against blacks, particularly against soldiers and civilians working for change, rose dramatically. Nearly all African American recruits went to the South for basic training, and hostile whites responded to their presence with a new round of race riots and lynchings. In the North, competition created tension between blacks and working-class whites, who resented the growing number of African Americans entering the job market and looking to find housing, often in previously all-white neighborhoods.

Black leaders made no effort to hide their disappointment at the reaction of southern liberals and moderates to the new African American assertiveness. Since Reconstruction, whites in the South who portrayed themselves as friends of African Americans had maintained that the educated "better class" of their community favored black equality, but that it had to proceed slowly and not disrupt southern society. Faced with a new urgency among blacks, however, liberals and moderates hastily qualified their support for African Americans, emphasizing the need for southerners to defend their traditional way of life. Blacks had to realize, the southern journalist John Templeton Graves wrote in 1942, that "segregation . . . is not going to be eliminated. This is a fact to be faced, but it does not preclude a constant improvement in the Negro side of jim crow."[63]

Responding in *The Negro Quarterly*, the black essayist Thomas Sancton acknowledged the support liberals and moderates had given African Americans in the past, but could not accept that in the midst of a war for freedom and democracy they would suggest that "the Negro must always expect to be jim crowed. . . . Deep down in his white soul," the southern liberal feared that "the race of serfs which he hoped to lead gradually to a higher plane of freedom and welfare" would slap his hand away and say "the hell with you; I want democracy and I want it now." Unless the federal government somehow "got the political will and moral guts to make the race problem . . . the concern of the nation, the Negro faces hopeless odds," Sancton concluded. Without a forceful push from Washington, southerners would remain "chained to the deadly ideology of another century."[64]

An exhausted Roosevelt died on April 12, 1945, leaving much unfinished business. Though the war was not over, it clearly was winding down and would end within a few months. On the home front, however, many of the fundamental goals of the New Deal still had not been achieved. The war had created a boom that swept away the depression; but the conversion to a peacetime economy would still present difficult challenges for the ordinary citizens Roosevelt had championed. In relation to blacks, the New Deal had given them a burgeoning sense of optimism and hope, but race remained a monolithic problem that kept the nation divided and sick at its core.

On the positive side, hundreds of thousands of black veterans with worldly experience and a confident sense of their own worth were returning to join the struggle for racial equality, which already was under way in northern cities and throughout the South. In 1944, Roosevelt had passed the Servicemen's Readjustment Act, or GI Bill, giving veterans chances for education and homeownership, two of the primary tools for advancement blacks had sought since the end of the Civil War. African Americans obviously were on the move, determined that a new era was coming and that the old days of separate but equal were essentially over.

Still, many whites remained adamantly opposed to change. Efforts to end the poll tax continued to meet a stone wall throughout the South, and in Mississippi, information on voting, elections, and any kind of political activity was systematically excluded from textbooks in black schools.[65] Campaigning for governor of Georgia in 1946, Eugene Talmadge exploited white fears, rousing voters with lurid descriptions of what would happen if Jim Crow were overthrown and African Americans were allowed to vote. White politicians would have to kiss black babies, and "pretty white children will be going to school with Negroes, sitting in the same desks." Though Talmadge lost the popular vote, which he dismissed as "Moscow-Harlem zoot suiters trying to take over Georgia," he easily won election, triumphing by a margin of two to one in the county elector system designed to perpetuate white rule.[66]

During the war, Roosevelt had instituted the "V for Victory" campaign as a symbol for the triumph America hoped to achieve overseas. Black leaders had responded with their own "Double V Campaign," declaring that the nation needed to win peace at home as well as abroad. America and its allies had succeeded in Europe and Asia, but the domestic struggle for black equality had been only fitfully waged. At war's end, with the rest of the world essentially in ruins, triumphant America seemed poised for a decisive battle between the opposing armies of racism and the "democracy of opportunity for all people" that Roosevelt had envisioned in 1932.

CHAPTER 10

CIVIL RIGHTS VICTORIES;
CIVIL RIGHTS BACKLASH

No memorial or eulogy could more honor President Kennedy's memory than the earliest possible passage of the civil rights bill for which he fought so long.
—LYNDON B. JOHNSON, NOVEMBER 27, 1963

They all hate black people, all of them. They're all afraid, all of them. . . . That's it! They're all southern! The whole United States is southern!
—GEORGE CORLEY WALLACE, OCTOBER 7, 1968

The New Deal and Roosevelt's wartime leadership produced fundamental changes in American attitudes, profoundly altering the struggle between blacks and whites. Throughout the 1930s, the president's concern for the common man and his accompanying scorn for "economic royalists" encouraged a belief in the equal rights of all Americans, regardless of class or race. In 1941, the war effort was undertaken in defense of freedom and justice—national values that Americans presumably held sacred at home as well as abroad. Just as during the Revolution when the nation's leaders invoked natural rights, Roosevelt brought the country together with rousing, idealistic appeals that tacitly promised a new era of fair play and decency for America's black citizens. Seeking to transform that idealism into action, Roosevelt made the government into an agent for social change, redistributing resources through relief programs, encouraging workers to organize in order to assert their rights, and providing jobs for people unable to find employment in a depressed economy.

The New Deal demonstrated the potential of federal action to remake American society, and its possibilities were not lost on blacks and their allies, who hoped that it would lead to a second Reconstruction. Following the president's death, the question of whether or not succeeding administrations would continue down the liberal path Roosevelt had chosen became the overriding issue in the struggle for black advancement. For southern conservatives and their liberal opponents, control of the government in Washington meant the difference between the continued expansion of federal powers and a resurgence of the old doctrine of states' rights. The ultimate question, of course, was to what degree the Roosevelt years had changed the racial attitudes of working-class whites in both the North and the South. Would they at last be willing to accept the expansion of African American rights in postwar America?

Harry Truman, Roosevelt's successor, was a bitter disappointment to conservative Democrats—though he owed his presidency to them. At the 1944 party convention, Henry A. Wallace, the incumbent vice president and leader of the party's liberal wing, was favored to win renomination as Roosevelt's running mate. Wallace, an Iowan, had joined the New Deal to head the Agricultural Adjustment Administration in 1933 and had become increasingly radicalized after 1936, when he traveled through the South and witnessed the crushing poverty of sharecroppers and tenant farmers. Rejecting any form of white privilege, he frequently spoke out in favor of racial equality and full citizenship for blacks, arguing that they were among the country's "oldest families" and had made "vast contributions in labor and loyalty" to the rest of America.[1] Though he received an enthusiastic welcome from the convention delegates and led on the first ballot, the party leadership, dominated by southerners, had decided in advance that he would be denied renomination. Roosevelt's health was obviously failing, and conservatives wanted to control the future direction of the party by choosing his successor; in need of southern support for the war effort, Roosevelt had agreed to leave the vice presidential choice to the convention, and it went to Harry Truman, a two-term senator from Missouri and a proven party loyalist, on the second ballot. Truman was recognized as a good team player from a border state rather than the Deep South, a region that was still anathema to northern voters.

But when Truman became president, he immediately made it clear that he intended to lead the nation as its chief executive, rather than serve as a surrogate for southern Democrats. Now that the war was winding down, conservatives had begun talking about abolishing the Fair Employment Practices Committee (FEPC), which had more than tripled the number of black civil servants and had forced similar changes in defense-related companies with government contracts. Congressional Republicans and their southern allies wanted to let the agency die by allowing bills for its continuation and funding to expire in the House Rules and Appropriation Committees. After consulting with black leaders, President Truman wrote to the chairman of the Rules Committee, calling the FEPC's termination "unthinkable." Job discrimination led to labor strife as well as substandard living conditions for a substantial number of Americans, he argued. Fair employment needed to be established "permanently as part of . . . national law."[2]

It was expected that the new president, having come from the Senate, would enjoy better relations with Congress than Roosevelt had, but Truman's directness and his determination to dictate policy quickly created a wall between him and his former colleagues. His defense of the FEPC was the first in a series of moves emphasizing his independence from the conservative leadership that had made him vice president. Roosevelt had dealt with his adversaries by becoming a political virtuoso, playing the legislative branch in any way he could to enact his programs. With neither Roosevelt's patience nor his political skill, Truman found himself at odds with conservative Democrats in Congress and powerless to pass legislation without their support. As he had with conservatives, he also lost favor among New Deal liberals. Though he took a strong stand on federal questions like the FEPC, he publicly stated that the poll tax was "a matter for the southern states to work out," disillusioning Roosevelt reformers, who believed that the only hope for economic and racial justice was an expansion of federal powers.[3] When city leaders in Washington prevailed on him to block FEPC chairman Charles Houston's attempt to force the Capitol Transit Company, which ran Washington's public transportation system, to end discriminatory hiring practices, the president withdrew his support of Houston, who quit, setting off a wave of resignations and firings that in a short time removed most of the liberal reformers from the Truman administration. Men like Harold Ickes, Robert Weaver, and Henry Wallace (whom Roosevelt had appointed secretary of commerce) were all either let go or walked away, disgusted by Truman's evident reluctance to carry on the

New Deal. By 1946 Truman had isolated himself from both the left and the right and relied on a narrow base of support composed mainly of party hacks and longtime personal allies.

Surprisingly, a degree of relief came with the rise of domestic anticommunism, which followed the split with the Soviet Union and the beginning of the cold war. Conservative politicians mercilessly exploited the loyalty issue to discredit their rivals, forcing a split among liberals between those who refused to turn on old friends in the American Communist Party and those who moved closer to the administration to demonstrate their patriotism. At the beginning of 1947, the House Un-American Activities Committee brought about the demise of the activist Southern Conference for Human Welfare, vilifying it as the nation's "most deviously camouflaged communist front organization," which sent many of its anticommunist members—Eleanor Roosevelt and the historian Arthur Schlesinger Jr. among them—scurrying to join the newly created Americans for Democratic Action, a haven for mainstream liberals willing to exchange the confrontational tactics of the SCHW for the tepid liberalism of the Truman administration.[4]

Bolstered by the support of former New Dealers who had been transformed by the latent Red Scare into centrists, Truman relied more and more on his independent powers as chief executive. Though the activism of the Roosevelt years had faded, the president vowed to carry on the fight for racial justice. "We must make the federal government a friendly, vigilant defender of the rights and equalities of all Americans," he told the NAACP's annual meeting in 1947. The nation could no longer wait for "the growth of a will to action in the slowest states or the most backward community."[5]

With the 1948 election looming, Truman seemed likely to lose the presidency, trailing the Republican candidate, Governor Thomas E. Dewey of New York, by a substantial margin. At the same time, the Democratic Party itself seemed on the verge of disintegrating. At its convention in February, Democratic stalwarts from both the left and the right walked out, vowing to form independent parties as an expression of their dissatisfaction with the president. Southern conservatives adjourned to Birmingham, where they created the States' Rights Party (the "Dixiecrats") and selected J. Strom Thurmond, the governor of South Carolina, as their presidential candidate on a platform that rejected the "totalitarian" government in Washington and insisted on the southern states' right to practice segregation.[6] The liberals, dismayed by what they perceived as the president's caution on civil rights, chose their old favorite, Henry Wallace, to lead the newly formed Progressive Party.

With Dewey apparently on his way to an easy victory, Truman moved boldly, hoping to win back liberal and black voters who had switched or were considering switching to Henry Wallace. Acting on recommendations from fact-finding commissions he had set up the previous year, the president issued Executive Orders 9980 and 9981: The first established a color-blind fair employment policy at every level of the federal government and instituted oversight procedures to ensure that it would be enforced; the second promised "equality of treatment and opportunity" throughout the armed services "as rapidly as possible."[7] Acting entirely on his own as the nation's chief executive, Truman had bypassed Congress and integrated both the federal civil service and the military.

The president's aggressive use of executive power temporarily silenced his black critics, and with the support of urban blacks—particularly in California, Illinois, and Ohio—he defeated Dewey in a stunning upset. The Democrats also took control of Congress, although Republicans and conservative southerners retained enough votes to filibuster civil rights legislation. The next two years were frustrating ones for the proponents of civil rights, as bills to revitalize the FEPC, raise the minimum wage, establish national health insurance, provide low-income housing, ensure an equitable distribution of federal aid to education, eliminate the poll tax, crack down on lynching, and grant home rule to Washington, D.C., all failed to win passage. Congress was paralyzed, the venerable Harlem-based *Amsterdam News* observed. The Republican Party was "the party of archconservatism, opposed to social change," while Democrats claimed to favor "liberal reform" but were also "the party of the reactionary South"—and Truman was their "prisoner."[8] Still, the president persisted in his independence, claiming to want nothing to do with Dixiecrat votes. Though he achieved little legislative success, his use of executive power roused others to action on civil rights: By 1949 nine states had established fair employment practices committees, and the number of black voters had risen from perhaps 250,000 ten years earlier to nearly 1 million.[9] Truman also focused increasingly on the courts, appointing liberal and black judges to the federal bench and employing Attorney General Tom Clark and the Justice Department to challenge discriminatory practices that violated the Constitution.

In housing, restrictive covenants—agreements that stopped owners from selling their homes to anyone other than a member of their own race—were widely used to make sure that neighborhoods remained lily-white. In 1948, when *Shelley v. Kraemer*, a suit attacking the practice, reached the Supreme Court, Clark and Solicitor General Philip Perlman filed an amicus curiae brief, arguing that such covenants were illegal because "judicial enforcement" amounted to "governmental action" against rights protected by the Constitution. In a unanimous decision, Chief Justice Frederick M. Vinson agreed that no court could legally enforce contracts written to protect segregated housing. Though it took several more years to eliminate the practice, *Shelley v. Kraemer* inspired a series of related reforms benefiting blacks and other minorities. The Federal Housing Administration was pressured to eliminate racial distinctions from its underwriting rules and to end segregation in federally sponsored public housing. And private landlords and developers were discouraged from discriminating, by the denial of government financing and insurance for segregated projects. Working with civil rights advocates, the Justice Department participated in a series of increasingly important Supreme Court cases, including *Henderson v. U.S.*, which challenged the separate seating of black passengers in railway dining cars, and *Sweatt v. Painter* and *McLaurin v. Oklahoma State Regents*, which attacked discrimination in Texas and Oklahoma schools. But while the plaintiffs won in all three cases, each was decided on narrow grounds that left *Plessy v. Ferguson* and the overarching legal principle of separate but equal intact.

Truman announced at the beginning of 1952 that he would not seek reelection, but enough time remained to open the way for his administration's most important civil rights victory—one for which he is seldom given sufficient credit. Early in the year, the Supreme Court agreed to hear a series of cases concerning school segregation in Kansas, South Carolina, Virginia, and Delaware. Though arguments were postponed until after the presidential election, Truman instructed his new attorney general, James P. McGranery, to submit a brief reflecting the views of the administration. Short and to the point, McGranery argued that the time had come to strike down school desegregation. Not only was it harmful to America's image abroad, raising doubts "even among friendly nations as to the intensity of our devotion to the democratic faith," but it was also "wrong as a matter of constitutional law, history, and policy." Separate but equal, McGranery argued, represented an "unwarranted departure" from American principles "based upon dubious assumptions of fact combined with a disregard of the basic purposes of the Fourteenth Amendment."[10]

Perhaps reluctant to take on such a volatile issue, the Supreme Court ignored the school desegregation suits until June 1953, when it asked for more information from the two sides in *Brown v. Board of Education of Topeka* and requested that the newly formed Eisenhower administration submit a brief and prepare oral arguments. Matters were furthered delayed by the death of Chief Justice Vinson in September, and the case was put off until Vinson's replacement, California governor Earl Warren, was confirmed in March of the following year. When *Brown v. Board of Education* was finally heard, the brief prepared by Eisenhower's Justice Department came under intense scrutiny. Influenced not only by the surprising strength that Republicans had shown among southern whites in the recent election but by the president's own ambivalence toward desegregation, Attorney General Herbert Brownell and his staff had prepared what they called "an objective nonadversary discussion" of the issues—a review of relevant case law that refused to take a stand of any kind. As Dorothy Fleeson of the *Washington Post* reported, Brownell had simply done a "sidestep." Though he told the Court that it had the power to decide the case, "he did not—in contrast to Attorney General McGranery for the Truman administration—tell them they ought to decide it against segregation."[11]

On May 17, 1954, Earl Warren announced the Court's unanimous decision, making school segregation illegal and effectively scuttling *Plessy* and the mandated separation of blacks and whites in American society. In reaching their conclusion, the justices relied on both McGranery's spirited assertion of the unconstitutionality of separate but equal and on a brief submitted by the NAACP providing data on the policy's harmful psychological effects. Much of the NAACP's brief had been assembled in 1950 by Truman's Mid-Century White House Conference on Children and Youth.[12] Segregation could not help but be detrimental to a child's education, the Court held, because it convinced black children that they were inferior, which adversely affected their motivation to learn. Separate educational facilities were "inherently unequal" and had no place in public education. *Brown v. Board of Education* gave back to African Americans the legal right to full citizenship that had been taken from them nearly sixty years earlier in *Plessy*. It was also a blow to the doctrine of states' rights. Rejecting the southern belief that the individual states had wide latitude to treat blacks in whatever way they wished, the Court ruled that every citizen enjoyed the same constitutional privileges, which it was the responsibility of the federal government to protect. Truman's determined use of executive power had led to a historic decision that would put whites on the defensive and fuel the civil rights movement of the 1960s and 1970s.

Only a few days before leaving the White House, President Truman addressed Congress on the state of the Union and reviewed the administration's civil rights record. A "great awakening of the American conscience" was tearing down the barriers that had blocked the way to equal freedom for African Americans, Truman declared.[13] There were surprising accomplishments on many fronts. Only about 4 percent of black workers were unemployed, and between 1947 and 1952 the median income of black families had grown from $1,600 to $2,300. A shift in the kinds of jobs that blacks held had also occurred: Only 12 percent had been white-collar workers in 1940; ten years later the figure had risen to 21.4 percent. Skilled workers rose from 3 percent to 5.5 percent, and semiskilled workers from 10.3 percent to 18.3 percent. In addition, blacks were benefiting from liberalized social welfare measures like a higher minimum wage—up from its beginning rate of 25 cents an hour in 1938 to 40 cents an hour in 1945—the expansion of Social Security, and a growing number of public health facilities. Together these measures had increased the life expectancy of black men from fifty-three years in 1940 to sixty-two years in 1953, and from fifty-six to sixty-five years for black women in the same period. The percentage of black children in public schools had risen from 69 to 75 percent between 1940 and 1950, and the number of blacks in college had grown from 23,000 to more than 113,000. In housing, black ownership had increased from 24 percent to 35 percent, and between 1949 and 1953 the percentage of African American men in the air force had risen from 5 to 9 percent, and in the Marine Corps from 2 to 7 percent.[14]

Truman had no illusions that the job was finished. Though change was under way, pressure from the top was still needed to carry out policies that whites continued to resist. In the nation's capital, though the restaurants had been opened to blacks, hotels remained rigidly segregated. Officials of the Veterans Administration opposed the integration of its hospitals—fearing, among other things, that the same plasma might be used for members of both races. The Winstead Amendment had been introduced in the House to allow whites the option of transferring out of integrated military units.

And Confederate flags appeared on bases around the world as symbols of protest against Truman's desegregation order. The struggle for equality remained "far from complete," the president warned, concerned that his successor, Dwight D. Eisenhower, lacked the commitment to carry on a federally led civil rights revolution. Eisenhower's talents as a leader and manager were undeniable; nevertheless, he was a southerner by birth and apparently lacked any clear-cut political leanings. Truman also remembered that Eisenhower had opposed the integration of the military when he testified before the Senate Armed Services Committee in 1948, maintaining that blacks would never be able to compete successfully with whites and that legislation could not make people like one another.[15]

Truman acknowledged that the new president would not be stymied by the congressional stonewalling he had faced, but would the abandonment of civil rights be the price of a more amicable relationship? In his first press conference of the presidential campaign, Eisenhower had expressed his agreement with a 1950 Republican declaration of principles which stated that liberty versus socialism was the nation's overriding domestic issue. The same day he had also rejected federal fair employment oversight, saying that such matters had to be left to the states to handle. Truman had learned the hard way that states' rights was the most powerful weapon that enemies of civil rights had, and in a speech on June 13, 1952, to the graduating class of Howard University, he fired back that neither the states nor "the efforts of men of goodwill" were enough to win the battle for racial equality. Only the "full force and power of the federal government" could guarantee the constitutional rights of every individual.[16]

When Dwight Eisenhower took office, he immediately announced his intention to discontinue his predecessor's aggressive use of executive power in relation to civil rights. Convinced that discrimination represented a failure of individual feelings rather than a societal problem, Eisenhower insisted that its solution lay in "persuasion, honestly pressed; and . . . conscience, justly aroused" rather than in edicts that forced people into social arrangements that violated their beliefs.[17] Truman's program of coerced integration had provoked unnecessary resistance, Eisenhower believed; his job was to restore order and allow the nation to function as it always had.

Eisenhower's low-key approach to desegregation quickly ran into trouble.

Truman's Executive Order 9980 had mandated equal opportunity in the federal government, and the Fair Employment Board (FEB) had been established as a watchdog committee to provide oversight. Eisenhower replaced the FEB with his own Committee on Government Employment Policy, while at the same time reducing the agency's size and curtailing its budget. Its function also changed from investigation and enforcement to simply providing information and guidelines for supervisors and workers—a move that immediately reduced the number of complaints it received. The net result, of course, was a continuing failure to provide equality for blacks, not only in federal employment but ultimately in services. In the Farmers Home Administration, which processed home loans at the county level, African Americans were excluded throughout the country from local boards that qualified loan applicants, and as late as 1960 minorities were given a mere 4 percent of farm housing loans. In several states, they received none at all.[18] In nearly every case where whites faced desegregation—in government agencies, the military, schools, companies involved in interstate commerce, housing, or public recreational facilities—there were always individuals or groups determined to preserve white privilege, and the government needed to exert the full force of its legal powers to make it clear that federal law would be upheld.

Nevertheless, Eisenhower remained committed to local control and minimal involvement by Washington, even when he was confronted by the assault on segregated schools set in motion by *Brown v. Board of Education*. In the aftermath of the Supreme Court's decision, the president lamented the appointment of Earl Warren as "the biggest damn fool mistake" he had ever made. Obviously he would have preferred school desegregation to have been left in limbo—that is, in the hands of individual communities and their local school boards.[19] To Eisenhower, whites who vowed to block integration remained respectable members of American society despite their refusal to accept the judgment of the nation's highest court. Another system had been "upheld by the Supreme Court for sixty years," he reasoned, and throughout that time southerners had been law-abiding citizens, obeying the Constitution by supporting the hallowed doctrine of separate but equal.[20]

When the Supreme Court announced the *Brown* decision, it had said nothing about implementation, wanting to allow whites a cooling-off period before deciding how quickly integration would take place and who would be responsible for overseeing it. Nearly a year after the original decision, the

Court set a date for oral arguments on implementation and asked interested parties to file briefs. Southerners, of course, argued that desegregation ought to be left up to local school boards. The NAACP maintained that it should begin immediately and be completed within eighteen months. The solicitor general, Simon E. Sobeloff, reflecting the president's desire to create as little disruption as possible, recommended a strikingly nonspecific "middle-of-the-road concept of moderation with a degree of firmness."[21]

In its original order the Court had broken new ground, radically altering the racial boundaries of American society; but faced with the difficulties of implementation and the president's reluctance to use the federal government's powers of enforcement, it retreated. Rather than aggressively promoting implementation, the justices extended a conciliatory hand to the South. They ordered the desegregation plans of local school boards to be approved and monitored by federal district courts, and they avoided setting a specific timetable for integration. Much to the relief of southern officials and segregationist leaders, judges from their own communities rather than outsiders would oversee desegregation, and there was no limit on the time it might take—other than the vague admonition that it should proceed "with all deliberate speed."[22]

The Supreme Court's ruling in *Brown II*, as it came to be called, gave southerners hope that desegregation might be avoided after all. They were further encouraged by a decidedly southern interpretation of *Brown I* offered by John J. Parker, of the Fourth District Court of Appeals. The first desegregation case, *Briggs v. Elliott*, which had originated in South Carolina, was remanded to Parker's court on July 15, 1955. "The Constitution . . . does not require integration," Parker concluded. Nor does it "forbid such discrimination as occurs as the result of voluntary action. It merely forbids the use of government power to enforce segregation."[23]

Parker's assertion that the Constitution offered no objection to voluntary segregation became the basis for a series of schemes by local boards throughout the South to evade integration. Allowing students "freedom of choice" rather than assigning them to schools resulted in classrooms that almost always remained segregated, without requiring school boards to have an official policy mandating separation of the races.[24] Pupil placement laws, which assigned students on the basis of complicated psychological and moral criteria, also became popular: as late as 1968, 68 percent of black children were still attending all-black schools, and 82 percent were still attending schools that were at least 95 percent black.[25] Though the "Parker Doctrine" was eventually rejected by the federal courts, it and similar tactics assuming that the Constitution prohibited only government-sanctioned segregation were used to delay integration for extended periods as cases worked their way through the court system.

Eisenhower was content to keep his distance and allow the lawyers and judges to settle the problems of school desegregation, but his aloofness grew increasingly difficult to maintain as more and more southerners joined white supremacist groups advocating violent resistance to school integration. In the summer following *Brown I*, the first White Citizens' Council was organized in Mississippi, and in Virginia local leaders created a number of chapters of the Defenders of State Sovereignty and Individual Liberties and the National Association for the Advancement of White People. In 1956, when a mob stopped Autherine Lucy from enrolling at the University of Alabama and again when unruly whites denied twelve blacks entry to the high school in Clinton, Tennessee, the president maintained that he had no intention of interfering as long as a state did "its best to straighten [the problem] out." Clarifying his position at a press conference, Eisenhower declared that he could not imagine any circumstances that would induce him "to send federal troops . . . into any area to enforce the order of a federal court."[26]

The president's assurances that he would never use the army to protect blacks in their attempts to integrate schools were bound to embolden segregationists. Though he surely had not intended to, Eisenhower set the stage for the climactic confrontation that took place when schools opened in September 1957. By the end of summer, a segregationist group calling itself the Mothers' League of Little Rock had run out of court maneuvers to block the integration of the city's Central High School. Encouraged by Arkansas governor Orval Faubus, who called out the state's National Guard to surround the school, the Mothers' League and a mob variously estimated at between five hundred and several thousand turned away nine black children attempting to enroll at Central High. With the situation out of control, Woodrow Mann, Little Rock's mayor, without the support of the local citizenry or Faubus's approval, wired the White House and pleaded with the president to provide federal troops. Blaming extremists generally and Faubus in particular, who had personally misled the president by assuring him that he would not allow the situation to get out of hand, Eisenhower restored order by sending in 1,000 soldiers, half of them members of the elite 101st Airborne Division from Fort Campbell, Kentucky.[27]

Though Eisenhower had decided it was time to restore order, ultimately he believed that his face-off with Faubus had accomplished little and in fact might have caused more harm than good. At a press conference in early October he stated that at the core of his political thinking it was "the sentiment, the goodwill, the good sense of a whole citizenry that enforces the law."[28] Central High had been desegregated, but at the cost of rising southern anger and Arkansas's further alienation from much of the country. All of this was true, of course, but at bottom the president's views reflected an unacknowledged racism that placed the immediate well-being of whites above equality for African Americans and refused to see both races simply as citizens, deserving of the same rights and privileges. Little Rock convinced Eisenhower to stay as far away as he could from school desegregation, an issue that threatened to inflame the entire South. Publicly he refused to respond to reporters' questions about it, claiming that whether he agreed or disagreed, he did not want to influence public opinion. The Justice Department was instructed to concentrate on the process of desegregation rather than on expanding it. Controlling violence would take precedence over legal efforts to force more southern schools to integrate. Eisenhower also directed the administration to refocus its civil rights efforts on promoting black voter registration rather than school integration, in hopes that after blacks had acquired more political power they would be able to look out for themselves—thus eliminating the need for federal intervention to protect them. Early in 1955, when the Justice Department proposed a civil rights bill aimed at increasing the number of black voters, Eisenhower and senior members of the cabinet had responded skeptically. But after Little Rock the idea gained new momentum, both because the president wanted to pull back from school desegregation and because of growing efforts by conservative whites to consolidate their power in the Deep South. In Mississippi, the White Citizens' Council embarked on a campaign to intimidate blacks into withdrawing their names from voters' rolls, and by the end of 1955 fourteen Mississippi counties no longer had any registered black voters. A year later, only 20,000 of Mississippi's 497,000 voting-age blacks were registered, and in Alabama and Georgia the numbers were only slightly better: 53,000 of 516,000 and 163,000 of 633,000.[29]

By the middle of 1957, a broad civil rights bill was being debated in Congress. The bill created an investigative commission with subpoena powers to examine civil rights problems, expanded the Civil Rights Section of the Justice Department into a division, extended conspiracy prosecutions to individuals as well as groups, allowed citizens to sue for civil redress when they were denied the right to vote, and empowered the attorney general to seek injunctive relief for civil rights violations. Though Eisenhower approved the creation of the Civil Rights Commission and the structural changes in the Justice Department, he balked at the expansion of federal prosecutorial powers, so they were presented to Congress simply as suggestions by the attorney general.[30] The bill eventually passed, but only after two changes had been made by conservative southerners: the elimination of many of the attorney general's expanded powers, which they opposed as threats to state sovereignty, and the addition of a jury trial provision, which meant that civil rights violators would be tried before members of their own communities, likely to be sympathetic to the southern cause. Though the enforcement provisions of the original bill had been effectively crippled, what remained allowed the administration to claim a legislative victory in relation to civil rights.

In practice, the 1957 Civil Rights Act accomplished little, in terms of either prosecutions or increasing the number of black voters. In the following two years, the Justice Department initiated a mere three cases charging southern officials with discriminatory practices that interfered with voter registration. The department's legal actions, investigators from the Civil Rights Commission (CRC) declared, were "disappointing in number, nature, and results."[31] The act's only noteworthy success, in fact, was the devastating report filed by the CRC in September 1959. Though some African Americans were politically apathetic, the report stated, there could be little doubt that the greatest barrier to black voter registration was obstruction by white officials. Across the South, sixteen counties where blacks constituted the majority of the voting-age population had no registered African Americans; in an additional forty-six counties that were primarily black, fewer than 5 percent were registered. African Americans were denied access to the voting rolls, the report concluded, through trickery or intimidation, which took a number of different forms, including unfair administering of literacy tests, extended processing time for black applicants, purges of voting lists, violence, and economic intimidation. Though an effort was made in 1960 to streamline the registration process, it was largely unsuccessful, leaving disenfranchised blacks in about the same position they were before. Paul Douglas, a liberal Democratic senator from Illinois, noted after the follow-up act of 1960 that blacks still faced "an elaborate obstacle course" before being allowed to register.[32]

As Eisenhower left office, he could contemplate, perhaps with some satisfaction, a lot of things that had not happened. Southern whites had not been forced to adjust to massive social change. Nor had they been made to share political power by allowing blacks to vote. Most white children still were not required to sit next to black youngsters in school. What Eisenhower chose to ignore, of course, was that blacks continued to suffer from the deprivation of their constitutionally guaranteed rights, and their misery had been compounded by the president's caution and moderation. During the Eisenhower administration, a period of relative national prosperity, the rate of black unemployment rose to between 7.5 and 12.6 percent, as opposed to between 2.2 and 4 percent for whites in the same period. Violence and intimidation against blacks escalated throughout the South. Lynching returned in 1955, Mississippi accounting for three that year, including the brutal death of Emmett Till near the town of Money. The following year, the White Citizens' Council boasted over 300,000 members. Eldon Lee Edwards, a paint sprayer at the GM plant in Atlanta, resurrected the Klan of the 1920s and in late September 1956 staged a cross-burning ritual on Stone Mountain; 1,500 people attended, the largest such turnout since the end of World War II. In 1957, the council savagely beat a black clergyman for attempting to enroll black children in an all-white school in Birmingham, while down the road in Montgomery, white segregationists exploded four bombs in local churches, injuring scores of parishioners. Meanwhile, inner-city ghettos decayed as whites departed for the suburbs, taking with them most of the mortgage money loaned by federal and state agencies.

For blacks, the price of Eisenhower's passivity and reluctance to use federal power to bring racial justice to the South was simply too high. Martin Luther King Jr. would later remark that the kind of moderation practiced by men like Eisenhower led African Americans to "the regrettable conclusion that the Negro's great stumbling block . . . is not the White Citizens' Counciller or the Ku Klux Klan, but the white moderate, who is more devoted to 'order' than justice; who prefers a negative peace which is the absence of tension to a positive peace which is the presence of justice."[33]

* * *

John F. Kennedy's election in 1960 was expected to put an end to the Republican era of passivity on civil rights. Handsome, engaging, liberal, and above all young, the new president was primed to restore excitement and innovation to a government that had grown staid and unimaginative. Before becoming a presidential candidate, however, Kennedy had shown only a lukewarm interest in civil rights. In 1955, he had written a book titled *Profiles in Courage*, in which he described Reconstruction as "a black nightmare the South could never forget" and maligned Thaddeus Stevens as "the crippled, fanatical personification of the Radical Republican movement."[34] He had also been sharply criticized by the NAACP for his voting record on the 1957 Civil Rights Act, particularly his support for the South's jury trial amendment. But after he became a national candidate, he worked hard to mend fences with black leaders, opening a personal channel of communication with Roy Wilkins, the NAACP's chief operating officer; and in October 1960, only a few weeks before the election, he scored a significant public relations victory among blacks by using his personal influence to come to the aid of Martin Luther King Jr.

In mid-October, King, who was on probation for driving with an expired license in De Kalb County, Georgia, had been sentenced to four months of hard labor as a parole violator, after having been arrested for trespassing during a demonstration in Atlanta. King's supporters first called the Richard Nixon camp asking for help but were told there was nothing the vice president could do and that only President Eisenhower could intervene. They next approached Kennedy, who arranged two calls, one by members of his staff to the state's Democratic governor and a second, personal call to Mrs. King, offering sympathy and support. The civil rights leader was released within a few days, and though the event was barely reported in the mainstream press, it received considerable attention in black newspapers. Kennedy workers also made sure the story did not go unnoticed, distributing 2 million flyers in black communities before election day.[35]

As a Democratic president, Kennedy faced the same problem that Roosevelt and Truman had. With a record 68.8 million voters going to the polls, he beat Richard Nixon by only 100,000 votes, and he owed his victory to a strong showing by southern Democrats and urban blacks. Two antagonistic constituencies had saved him from defeat, but to satisfy one on civil rights meant offending the other. His brother Robert, the attorney general and the president's closest adviser, warned him that civil rights was a dangerous political issue that could not be addressed by taking sides but had to be finessed.

Though the Democratic convention had called for new efforts to strengthen fair employment and cut down on discrimination in housing and education, Kennedy rejected any attempt to pass legislation on these matters a few months after becoming president. Following Truman's example, he decided instead—as his aide Harris Wofford explained before the National Civil Liberties Clearing House in March 1961—on "a quiet, steady campaign of executive action" rather than a "loud fight for a congressional civil rights bill" that was likely to fail and would poison his relationship with southerners in Congress.[36] Black leaders were naturally upset, but they reacted calmly, characterizing their disapproval as a difference with the administration rather than a quarrel. Kennedy had already begun courting blacks through various gestures and meaningful appointments to governmental and judicial posts. The White House press and photographers' pool was desegregated. African Americans became regular guests at the White House and at Robert Kennedy's Virginia home, and the president withdrew his membership in Washington's elite Cosmos Club when it refused to admit Carl Rowan, a black deputy assistant secretary of state. In terms of appointments, Kennedy chose a number of African Americans for important federal positions, including Thurgood Marshall, the principal attorney in the *Brown* case, who became a justice on the Second Circuit Court of Appeals in New York. But he also was criticized for restricting his black judicial nominees to the North and cooperating with congressional conservatives in the appointment of white segregationists to federal courts in the South.

Under Eisenhower, the Justice Department had retreated from the courts, voluntarily surrendering its responsibility to initiate civil rights suits in favor of a more passive role as a referee, seeing that order was maintained and the law obeyed in face-offs between blacks and whites. Kennedy adopted a similar policy, intervening in disputes to head off violence but trying to avoid taking sides. The difficulty, however, was that by standing on the sidelines the federal government ceded to African Americans the power to choose where the next encounter would be, and as younger, more militant individuals came to the fore in the civil rights movement, their actions became increasingly confrontational. In May 1961, Freedom Riders from the Congress of Racial Equality (CORE) and the Student Non-Violent Coordinating Committee (SNCC) traveled across the South on Greyhound buses, testing segregation in interstate transportation. The year before, in *Virginia v. Boynton*, the Supreme Court had outlawed segregated bus terminals, and the riders intended to integrate waiting rooms, bathrooms, and cafeterias wherever they stopped. In Anniston, Alabama, their bus was burned, and when they proceeded to Birmingham they were beaten by a mob and locked up by the city's notorious police chief, Bull Connor. Attorney General Robert Kennedy intervened, and the riders were allowed to depart for Montgomery, where, once again, they were attacked and jailed by local police. Undaunted, they voted to move on to Mississippi, but this time Robert Kennedy worked out an agreement in advance with the governor, Ross Barnett, which guaranteed that the civil rights activists would not be assaulted but would be jailed as soon as they arrived in Jackson.[37] Though no one was entirely satisfied with the arrangement, the Justice Department succeeded in defusing the situation without completely alienating either southern whites or the Freedom Riders' supporters. The riders had brought to the nation's attention the denial of legal rights to blacks engaged in interstate travel; southern whites had been allowed to arrest the activists who had violated local laws; and the federal government had acted only to maintain public order, not to force integration.

Earlier that year, a black air force veteran named James Meredith had applied to the University of Mississippi, and at the end of May the university officially rejected his application. Meredith brought suit in the federal district court, and Judge Sidney C. Mize eventually found in favor of his legal right to matriculate. On September 25, 1962, Meredith traveled to Oxford, Mississippi, accompanied by a chief U.S. marshal, to register at the university. Personally turning Meredith away, Governor Barnett vowed that he would rather go to jail than allow a black man to enter Ole Miss. When Robert Kennedy tried to persuade him to change his mind, Barnett invoked the timeworn doctrine of nullification, questioning whether the federal government had the right to force its views on states unwilling to accept them. A night of rioting ensued on the university campus, and the Mississippi National Guard was federalized. The president chose to wait the situation out, however, and Barnett, who had been convicted of contempt and ordered to pay $10,000 for each day Meredith was unable to register, capitulated.

Intent on mending frayed relationships, President Kennedy worked hard to soothe southern feelings. In a nationally televised address on the evening before Meredith was to register at Ole Miss, Kennedy stated that individuals had the right to "disagree with the law but not to disobey it." The federal government had played no part in bringing Meredith's suit, he pointed out, but once the courts had decided the case, he was obliged to carry out their orders. All the appeals court judges were southerners, he reminded his audience, and their decision in no way represented the imposition of northern values on Mississippi. Finally, he declared that the southern states could not be blamed individually for "the accumulated wrongs of the last hundred years of race relations." Responsibility had to be shared by the entire nation.

Kennedy had kept another explosive confrontation from growing into something larger and more dangerous, but as his experience in the South grew he was becoming increasingly frustrated by his inability to solve problems rather than just control them. In the midterm elections, Democrats picked up four seats in the Senate while sustaining only minimal losses in the House, and though his advisers remained divided, by the beginning of 1963 Kennedy was seriously considering civil rights legislation. On February 28, he sent a message to Congress asking for enhanced powers to protect black voting rights and speed school desegregation.

Less than two months later, Birmingham erupted, confirming Kennedy's belief that the federal government needed to take a more active role in the South. Hoping to create a situation so critical that it would force the city fathers to negotiate, Martin Luther King Jr. had begun a concerted campaign of sit-ins and demonstrations to integrate the Deep South's most segregated city. King sent wave after wave of marchers into the city center, where they were quietly arrested, and the protests continued in spite of a court injunction against demonstrations. When most of the men had been locked up, Birmingham's black women and children joined the marches, enraging the local police, who used fire hoses and dogs to round them up on their way to jail—appalling images that were shown on national television. The home of Martin Luther King's brother and the motel that housed the protesters' headquarters were bombed, and blacks rioted in retaliation, raging throughout the city, looting and destroying property. Order was finally restored when the president threatened to call out the Alabama National Guard, and a truce was brokered by Justice Department officials which included promises by local leaders that many of the city's facilities would be desegregated within ninety days.[38]

Events in Birmingham angered people throughout the nation, and the president addressed them on television, stressing the urgent need for civil rights legislation. As things stood, he declared, no laws existed giving the federal government power to intervene when local authorities brutalized demonstrators, as had happened in Birmingham. The nation was facing a "moral crisis" that could not be solved by repressive police, more demonstrations, or token agreements by city officials, and the time had come for legislation in Congress. Though he perhaps overstated the impotence of the federal government, Kennedy had been frightened by Birmingham, and he and his advisers hoped that with a forceful response they could discourage widespread violence in other cities around the nation.

The first rejoinder to the president's message was the assassination of Medgar Evers, the NAACP's field secretary in Jackson, Mississippi, only a few hours after Kennedy had spoken. Undeterred, the president sent his civil rights bill to Congress in a matter of days. In it he proposed fair employment legislation, additional powers for the attorney general to initiate suits for individuals denied admission to segregated schools, a ban on discrimination in privately owned interstate commerce facilities, discretionary power to cut off federal aid to schools that continued to discriminate, and the creation of a federal mediation board to resolve racial disputes.[39] Southerners in the House and Senate reacted with fierce resistance to the president's bill, immediately moving to block it and much of the other legislation Kennedy had proposed earlier in the year, including a tax reform measure that the president and Congress had agreed was urgently needed. Kennedy was also under pressure from a chorus of southern governors and J. Edgar Hoover, a closet segregationist, who informed him that King and the entire Southern Christian Leadership Conference (SCLC) were controlled by Communists intent on destroying the American way of life. On the other side, African American leaders arranged a march on Washington in August, which brought a quarter of a million people, black and white, to the capital to demand federal action on civil rights.

Having been overtaken by events, Kennedy finally seemed ready to play a more active role in the black struggle, but he was never allowed the opportunity. In the South, his approval rating had fallen sharply, and at the urging of Texas Democrats he set off in the middle of November with Vice President Lyndon Johnson to meet with party officials and woo the state's voters. On November 22, 1963, Kennedy was assassinated in Dallas, leaving a nation in mourning and his civil rights legislation buried beneath an avalanche of conservative resentment in the Senate Judiciary Committee.

*   *   *

Lyndon Johnson's accession to the presidency dismayed the inner circle of Kennedy advisers, many of whom had been opposed to his selection as the vice presidential candidate, a political choice that Kennedy had made to appease the South. As vice president, Johnson had been ostracized— particularly by Robert Kennedy, who regularly excluded him from Justice Department meetings on civil rights, treating him like an uneducated Texas bumpkin. But there was a good deal more to Johnson than the Kennedy people realized. He had first joined the House in 1938 from poverty-stricken Gillespie County in the Texas Hill Country, where in the 1860s people had voted twenty to one against joining the Confederacy. There were no "plantation and darkies," Johnson acidly recalled, and he had never "sat on . . . my parents' or grandparents' knees listening to nostalgic tales of the antebellum South." Both his father and his grandfather were old-time populists: His grandfather helped organize the local interracial People's Party in the 1890s, and thirty years later his father was one of the prime movers when the Texas legislature passed an anti-Klan bill making it a crime "to parade or otherwise . . . operate in masks."[40]

Johnson had joined the House of Representatives as an ardent believer in the New Deal, but he quickly realized that loyalty to the Democratic leadership in Congress was the key to success and he fell in line as a southerner defending the region against northern liberals. He later explained in his 1971 memoir, *The Vantage Point: Perspectives of a Presidency, 1963–1969*, that until he became the Senate majority leader in 1955 he had no choice but to vote with the other southern Democrats: "One heroic stand and I'd be back home, defeated, unable to do any good for anyone, much less the blacks or the underprivileged."[41]

Just five days after Kennedy's death, Johnson went before Congress and spoke to the nation. Movingly, he expressed America's loss and offered his sympathy to Jacqueline Kennedy and her two small children. He also recognized the monumental opportunity he had been given, and he was too astute a politician to let it slip away. Before Kennedy's death, the civil rights bill had been bogged down in Congress, but with the nation mourning its dead hero, how many southerners would dare to block it now? "No memorial or eulogy could more honor President Kennedy's memory," Johnson declared, "than the earliest possible passage of the civil rights bill for which he fought so long."[42] Johnson understood that if he hoped to secure his presidency and lead the nation, it was imperative to solidify his support among liberals and minorities, who regarded civil rights as the nation's most pressing problem. "I knew that if I didn't get out in front on this issue they would get me," he later recalled. "They'd throw up my background against me [and] use it to prove I was incapable of bringing unity to the land." As Lawrence O'Brien, an adviser to both men, noted, "Johnson believed the Kennedy people were going to try to deny him the nomination in '64," and his concern for civil rights represented "a fit between his personal feelings and his political needs."[43]

As Senate majority leader, Johnson had built a reputation as a political strategist and arm twister who could deliver votes when others would be ready to admit defeat. As president, he began a furious lobbying effort to round up the support he needed for civil rights legislation. First, he addressed African Americans, inviting to the White House not only older, established figures like Martin Luther King Jr., A. Philip Randolph, and Roy Wilkins, but James Farmer of CORE, one of the leaders of the Freedom Rides. "I am going to get this job done," the president told Farmer, "and what you need to do is tell Republicans if they vote for this bill, you'll tell your people to vote for them. And I think you should, too." Farmer later noted that he realized he was being "buttered up," but knowing what the president was doing "did not lessen its effectiveness."[44]

Johnson next turned his attention to white leaders in business, labor, and the churches, presenting essentially the same case again and again: that an end to discrimination was a moral imperative that could wait no longer. Finally, having marshaled his forces, he turned to Congress, confident that he was ready for a sustained battle on familiar turf. Just as with all civil rights legislation, his bill faced a crucial procedural question: whether its opponents could successfully block it with a filibuster. Making it clear that he had the necessary majority to bring congressional business to a standstill until the civil rights legislation was voted on by both the House and the Senate, Johnson convinced the Republican leadership to desert the southern Democrats, depriving them of the votes to sustain a filibuster. On June 10, after fifty-seven days, 44 Democrats and 25 Republicans voted for cloture on the longest filibuster in Senate history, sending the civil rights bill to the Senate floor. Nine days later, it passed by a vote of 73 to 27. Two weeks later, the House gave its approval 289 to 126, capping a historic legislative campaign in which Johnson's brilliant leadership had steered the Congress to enact the first forceful civil rights legislation since Reconstruction. The bill not only outlawed many types of discrimination in private businesses but also established a new federal administrative structure to ensure compliance and gave the government power to withhold federal funds from violators.

Johnson had been "hurling himself about Washington like an elemental force," the *New Republic* noted, but he was by no means ready to rest.[45] Already he had begun planning for the months ahead, and during the signing ceremony for the Civil Rights Act he startled Nicholas Katzenbach, the attorney general, by asking him what they ought to do in relation to civil rights the following year. "Let's get a voting rights bill," Johnson insisted.

First, however, he needed to win the nomination and be reelected. Late in August 1964, the Democrats met in Atlantic City. Despite a potentially divisive row when the president refused to support an effort by the Mississippi Freedom Democratic Party to unseat the state's regular delegation, the convention quickly turned into a celebration of Johnson's War on Poverty, comprehensive social welfare legislation intended to eliminate poverty throughout the country. "America is One Nation, One People," the Democratic platform announced. "The welfare, security and survival of each of us resides in the common good—the sharing of responsibilities as well as benefits by all the people."

Most polls indicated an easy victory for Johnson in the general election, but in spite of—or perhaps in part because of—his successful battle for passage of Kennedy's Civil Rights Act and his initiation of the War on Poverty, a backlash was in the making. Ever since the New Deal, liberal Democrats had been widening federal programs to include African Americans. By the mid-1960s, many working-class whites had outgrown government assistance, thanks to an extended period of national prosperity, and they had begun questioning whether what they were receiving under Johnson represented a raw deal rather than a continuation of the New Deal. The Great Society was providing medical insurance to the elderly, school aid to children, and civil rights to blacks but, it seemed, almost nothing for ordinary white people like themselves, who went off to work every morning, paid taxes that constantly rose, and seldom received anything from Washington in return. Their changing attitude toward welfare was a bellwether of their discontent. In the

1930s, many of the government's programs were designed to protect whites while ignoring blacks. Social Security had initially excluded agricultural workers and domestic servants because southerners objected to the additional cost of providing benefits for black workers. Similarly, Aid to Dependent Children (ADC), the original form of welfare, was intended for widowed mothers rather than women with children who had no husband at home, because whites believed that blacks were sexually promiscuous, and to include them would not only make the program's costs skyrocket but would reward them for immorality. ADC was expected to decline and ultimately disappear as more and more people began receiving coverage under the death benefit provision of Social Security. The number of families on ADC did continue to shrink until the 1950s, but then the trend reversed itself.[46] By 1957 more people were receiving ADC than any other form of welfare, and the profile of the typical recipient had changed. No longer simply a program for widows and their dependent children, ADC now provided support primarily to single mothers who had been deserted by, or had never lived with, the father or fathers of their children.[47] Overlooking the fact that federal welfare programs had originally been constructed to exclude African Americans, whites complained that the number of blacks on ADC had risen sharply and that they now constituted the majority of recipients. Rather than recognizing that many of the causes of illegitimacy are rooted in poverty—lack of education, hopelessness, family instability, etc.—whites tended to blame black moral depravity. In 1960, Louisiana governor Jimmie Davis attempted to cut off payments to women living in what he termed "unsuitable homes" and to those who had an illegitimate child while on welfare or were cohabiting with a man "without benefit of formal marriage." Ninety-five percent of the homes that local social workers found unsuitable belonged to blacks, and the Department of Health, Education, and Welfare stepped in and blocked Davis's plan.[48]

By the beginning of the 1960s, the complaint that the federal government accorded blacks special treatment had spread to the North as well. In Newburgh, New York, a welfare revolt broke out in 1961, led by the town manager, Joseph Mitchell. Newburgh's welfare system, in which 50 percent of the recipients were black, had collapsed under the weight of "a steady influx of outsiders principally from Southern states, who apparently have no desire to take root and become part of community life," Mitchell wrote in a report to the city council.[49] The answer, he suggested, was to require newcomers to show a legitimate job offer that brought them to Newburgh before they could become eligible for welfare.

Many northern whites were growing increasingly disillusioned, which opened them to the racial message of the Alabama demagogue George Corley Wallace. When he was elected governor in 1962, Wallace confided to his political cronies that he intended to make race the basis of politics not only at home but throughout the country.[50] A few months later, when two black students, Vivian Malone and James Hood, tried to enroll at the University of Alabama, Wallace had his first opportunity for national exposure, playing the familiar role of southern governor blocking the schoolhouse door. Though the standoff between Nicholas Katzenbach, the towering assistant attorney general, and the diminutive governor had been carefully choreographed to avoid any real violence, it made for riveting television footage that validated the resentment of many whites across the nation. Once again, representatives of the federal government were siding with blacks against their own kind. Wallace read a lengthy proclamation attacking the "usurpation of power by the central government" and vowed to forbid its "illegal and unwarranted action" as a violation of states' rights guaranteed by the Constitution. While a few might applaud the federal government's actions, he concluded, millions would "gaze in sorrow upon the situation existing at this great institution of learning."[51] And indeed they did. Within a week, Wallace had received more than one hundred thousand letters, over half of them from northerners and 95 percent expressing approval of what he had done. Surprised at first by the northern reaction, Wallace soon realized that it signaled a monumental shift in national sentiment. Northern whites no longer felt that race played an insignificant role in their own communities. In their hearts, Wallace concluded, they resembled the folks at home. As he would later tell Douglas Kiker of NBC, the outpouring of support made him realize that "they all hate black people, all of them.... They're all afraid, all of them.... That's it! They're all southern! The whole United States is southern!"[52]

As 1964 opened, Wallace began a frenetic speaking tour, testing his popularity around the country. He cleaned up his language, removed the racial jokes, and paid more attention to anticommunism and government intrusion into the private affairs of individuals. But at the heart of Wallace's message remained the question of race. Describing himself as a segregationist and not a racist, Wallace explained to a Wisconsin audience that although hating someone because of his or her skin color was evil, racial separation proved "best for both peoples." Moreover, Wallace argued, the real issue was states' rights: "If Wisconsin believes in integration, that is Wisconsin's business, and not mine." But the nation must grant Alabama "the right to choose the path it will follow."[53]

With his nomination already assured, Johnson had elected not to campaign in the 1964 Democratic presidential primaries. Wallace moved into the breach, optimistic that the reception he had received on his speaking tour would lead to a strong showing at the polls. Indeed, he stole the show. In a total of sixteen primaries, Wallace's name was on the ballot in nine states and he received 11 percent of the total vote, a more than respectable showing. Though Wallace's numbers were modest in New Jersey, Illinois, Pennsylvania, and Nebraska and infinitesimal in Oregon and Massachusetts, they were surprisingly strong in Wisconsin (34 percent), Indiana (30 percent), and Maryland (43 percent).[54] In just two years, he had become a national phenomenon and a hero to white supremacists, who had been kept down for decades. His showing was a troubling sign that the end was near for the unnatural, frequently troubled electoral coalition of blacks, northern working-class whites, and conservative southerners that had chosen Democratic presidents for twenty-four of the previous thirty-two years.

With Wallace as the trailblazer for a new political alignment, a number of Republican candidates watched the Alabama governor's primary campaign carefully to discover just how far they could go in appealing to racial discontent. In Texas, George Bush, a political novice seeking the Senate seat of the liberal Democrat Ralph Yarborough, adopted many of Wallace's tactics. As chairman of the Harris County Republican Party, Bush had been a racial moderate, but as a candidate he suddenly moved to the right, emphatically opposing the civil rights bill, which was just then moving through the Senate on its way to passage. Stumping across the state, Bush became a Wallace soundalike, accusing Yarborough of "trampling on the Constitution" and warning that workers would be displaced by African Americans if the civil rights bill became law. The measure benefited only the 14 percent of Texans who were black, Bush said, but he promised to look out for "the other 86 percent."[55]

A relative newcomer to Texas, the Connecticut-reared Bush may well have felt compelled to support what he perceived as local values. Barry Goldwater, on the other hand, one of only five Republicans in the Senate who would vote against the civil rights bill, followed the lead of his legal advisers, William Rehnquist and Robert Bork, arguing that the bill represented a "threat to the . . . essence of our basic system" because it gave power to the federal government that "fifty sovereign states had reserved for themselves."[56] The leader of the reactionary wing of the Republican Party, Goldwater had spelled out his views in his 1960 book *The Conscience of a Conservative*, which attacked the liberal welfare state, denounced school desegregation, and called for a reining in of the Supreme Court's power to interpret the Constitution.

Campaigning for the Republican presidential nomination, Goldwater kept a close eye on Wallace's success in the Democratic primaries, noting in a news conference that the Alabaman's support was coming from a white backlash, made up of people who didn't want "their . . . rights tampered with," people who believed that "they should have the right to say who lives near them."[57] To win the nomination, Goldwater opined, he had to "go hunting where the ducks are." African Americans and most of the East Coast dismissed his rugged conservatism, but among whites in the South, the West, and the Midwest Goldwater found an enthusiastic following that championed his nomination at the Republican convention. Though he got barely 15 percent of the eastern seaboard votes, Goldwater became the party's presidential nominee by sweeping 271 of 278 votes cast by southerners.[58]

In the November elections, both Bush and Goldwater were soundly defeated. The white backlash had not yet become a commanding voice in American politics. As the presidential adviser Richard Goodwin later wrote, the only question in the national election was not Johnson's "victory or defeat but the size of the inevitable triumph."[59] Johnson overwhelmed his opponent, winning in nearly 90 percent of the country's 435 congressional districts. Goldwater carried only six states—five in the South and his home state of Arizona. Democrats also gained seats in the House and Senate, so Johnson could look forward not only to liberal majorities in both chambers but to declining opposition from congressional southerners. In his 1965 State of the Union address, the victorious president listed among his top priorities legislation to eliminate "every remaining obstacle to the right to vote."

A few weeks earlier, Martin Luther King Jr. had launched a major effort to register voters in Alabama. King had chosen Selma in Dallas County—where only about 2 percent of the 15,000 blacks eligible to vote were registered—as the focal point of his campaign, and just as in Birmingham he began a series

of marches, this time aimed at the registrar of voters. Once again, local officials responded with violent police action, and by the end of January more
than 2,600 blacks were in jail, many of them women and children. Writing
in the *New York Times* on February 1, King explained why he and his followers had chosen to be arrested. "Have you ever been required to answer
100 questions on government, some abstruse even to a political science spe-
cialist, merely to vote? Have you ever stood in line with over a hundred others and after waiting an entire day seen less than ten given the qualifying
test? THIS IS SELMA ALABAMA. THERE ARE MORE NEGROES IN JAIL WITH ME
THAN THERE ARE ON THE VOTING ROLLS. . . . We are in jail simply because
we cannot tolerate these conditions for ourselves and our nation." King also
contacted the president, who responded publicly the next day, expressing his
concern over "the loss of any American's right to vote" and vowing "to see
that right . . . secured for all our citizens."[60]

King's campaign in Selma reached a climax on Bloody Sunday, March 7.
Attempting to begin a peaceful march to Montgomery, the state capital, six
hundred demonstrators led by Hosea Williams of SCLC and John Lewis of
SNCC were stopped at the Edmund Pettus Bridge on the way out of Selma
and attacked by state troopers and sheriff's deputies mounted on horseback.
The scene enraged people across America, who saw on television defenseless
women and children trampled by horses and beaten by baton-wielding officers. It also galvanized support for the voting rights legislation that the president presented to the nation a little over a week later. Addressing a televised
joint session of Congress, Johnson compared Selma to Lexington, Concord,
and Appomattox, calling on Americans once again "to right wrong, to do justice, [and] to serve man." In the next forty-eight hours, he continued, he
would send Congress legislation that would end "restrictions . . . used to
deny Negroes the right to vote" by establishing a federally imposed "simple
uniform standard" for registration. The bill also would empower the federal
government to send its own representatives "to register Negroes wherever
state officials refuse" to do the job. "Their cause must be our cause, too," the
president concluded. "It is not just Negroes, but it is all of us, who must overcome the crippling legacy of bigotry and injustice. And we shall overcome."[61]

Johnson was true to his word, and oversaw the swift passage of a measure he privately called the "goddamndest, toughest voting rights bill" the
attorney general could devise. Individual suits brought on a case-by-case
basis were an "impossible system of law enforcement," and a broad legislative

solution was necessary to ensure black voting rights. The day after the bill reached the Senate, it was quickly passed on to the Judiciary Committee, chaired by James Eastland of Mississippi. Southerners realized that anything more than a perfunctory filibuster was impossible, and a little over a week later the bill was returned to the floor of the Senate. "The self-styled 'liberals' are in such a majority now . . . that our small band of southern constitutionalists can muster only about twenty votes," Richard Russell of Georgia, who had been Johnson's mentor in his early days in the House, lamented. The measure passed on May 26, and two weeks later it was approved by the House, 328 to 74. Asked about the president, Russell would say only that their opinions were "so completely at variance that we do not discuss what I regard as his extreme position on this issue."[62]

The effects of the 1964 Civil Rights Act and the 1965 Voting Rights Act were immediate and dramatic. Ramsey Clark, a member of the Justice Department who would go on to become attorney general, later recalled that in relation to public facilities, compliance came "almost overnight, as if by magic" throughout the South. It happened so quickly, he observed, that "it certainly surprised and relieved many of us." Results from the Voting Rights Act were equally remarkable. Almost a quarter of a million blacks registered in the first five months after its passage, and by the summer of 1966 registration in the states where federal registrars were sent had swelled from less than 27 percent of the eligible black population to 55 percent.[63]

Johnson's presidency was at its high point. The successful passage and implementation of legislation that seemed to him "one of the most monumental laws in the entire history of American freedom" was a triumph of personal and political power. And what greater affirmation could he receive than the enthusiastic approval of Martin Luther King Jr.? "I am convinced," King wrote Johnson, "that you will go down in history as the president who issued the second and final Emancipation Proclamation."[64]

CHAPTER 11

THE NEW FEDERALISM AND ITS LEGACY

If there is any legacy I want to leave the nation, it is that I continued to move our country in the direction of colorblindness [and] further away from . . . racial quotas.

—RONALD REAGAN, MARCH 1986

Although Lyndon Johnson had begun his elected term with nearly unprecedented popular support, he chose not to seek reelection four years later, and in 1969 he walked away from the presidency bitter and bewildered by his failure to lead the nation. Much of his difficulty had come from the war in Vietnam, which Johnson had inherited and which opened deep fissures in American society. The uproar over the war could be quieted—and eventually was—by the American withdrawal from Southeast Asia. The division over race ran deeper. Racial friction represented a permanent part of American society, and the backlash that George Wallace had exploited in the 1964 Democratic primaries rapidly expanded as whites reacted to the combination of increasingly militant tactics by civil rights activists and federal programs that continued to favor blacks. As early as 1958, the Klan boasted of a membership of forty thousand, and in a CBS special a year later, the grand wizard of Georgia, Eldon Lee Edwards, explained that the group's express purpose was "maintaining segregated schools at any and all cost. . . . If the Supreme Court can't maintain our Southern way of life then we *are* going to do something about it."[1]

The new Klan fought integration with all the old methods—assassinations, church bombings, jail sentences, beatings, and intimidation. The murders of Medgar Evers in 1963 and of James Chaney, Michael Schwerner, and Andrew Goodman during Mississippi Freedom Summer of 1964, and the assassination of Martin Luther King Jr. in 1968—to name but a few victims of white violence—not only enraged black leaders but also precipitated prolonged and deadly riots in several northern cities where living and working conditions for poor blacks had deteriorated badly. Harlem in 1964 and Watts in 1965 initiated a series of inner-city rebellions that traumatized the nation's major urban centers in the middle and late 1960s. Not only among the rioters but within the black leadership, radical changes were taking place. In 1957 Martin Luther King and a group of prominent African American ministers had formed SCLC to coordinate civil rights activities among already existing national organizations like the NAACP and CORE and activist groups with ties to local churches. SNCC was founded three years later by black college students in the South, and it, too, quickly affiliated itself with SCLC. From the beginning, however, there were significant differences in the organizations which created tensions among them. The NAACP represented the old guard of the civil rights movement and was run by individuals like Roy Wilkins and Thurgood Marshall, who focused their attention on lawsuits and lobbying efforts in Washington as the most effective ways to achieve social change. Both CORE and SNCC were committed to working directly in black communities and employed aggressive, confrontational actions to bring about reform at the local level.

Nevertheless, the organizations managed to work together because there were two fundamental principles they had in common. All were interracial, willing to accept at least some whites whom they regarded as sincere allies in the struggle for racial justice. And just as Dr. King had, they made a firm commitment to nonviolence. Thurgood Marshall had argued before the Supreme Court in *Brown v. Board of Education*, and he and the other NAACP leaders believed they could work successfully within the institutional framework of American society. The students who founded CORE in 1942 had been influenced by Gandhi, and CORE members became invaluable organizers of nonviolent sits-ins and the Freedom Rides, which were patterned after the "journey of reconciliation" that one of CORE's leaders, Bayard Rustin, had made through the upper South in 1947, attempting to integrate interstate travel facilities. Rustin had been arrested in Chapel Hill, North Carolina, and put to work on a chain gang, along with two of his companions.

SNCC workers were a younger group, but their leaders—figures like Julian Bond, Bob Moses, and John Lewis—were wise beyond their years and had abjured violence in both their personal and their political lives.

James Baldwin warned in his 1963 book *The Fire Next Time* that whites soon would face a bloody black rebellion unless they "dare[d] everything" and "end[ed] the racial nightmare" consuming America. Rather than moving toward reconciliation, however, whites had embarked on their own orgy of violence, setting off the reaction of rioting and looting that swept through the nation's cities beginning in the mid-1960s. White violence also led to the destruction of the civil rights coalition that Martin Luther King Jr. had built. When John F. Kennedy was assassinated, Malcolm X, the national spokesman for Elijah Muhammad's Black Muslims, shocked whites by referring to the president's death as "chickens coming home to roost." The all-out, murderous assaults on activists like Evers and the young civil rights workers killed in Mississippi constituted the final blow for many blacks, convincing them that white-hating black nationalists like the Muslims understood America better than anyone else. Militant, apocalyptic leaders who favored black separatism and espoused violence as a necessary means of self-defense took over both CORE and SNCC in 1966. Floyd McKissick replaced James Farmer, one of CORE's founders, as the organization's director, and Stokely Carmichael ousted John Lewis as the chairman of SNCC. In the same year, Huey P. Newton and Bobby Seale—mourning the assassination of Malcolm X— founded the Black Panther Party in Oakland, California.

Rather than demanding an end to segregation and protection for the right to vote, the Panthers wanted control over their own communities and swore to defend them with armed resistance if necessary. Whites had long allowed themselves to believe that race relations in the North were generally satisfactory; suddenly they heard black power leaders on television calling them "devils" and condemning them as part of the problem rather than part of the solution. Many whites who had been mildly supportive of black aspirations responded with anger of their own, dismissing the protesters as malcontents and ingrates who refused to take responsibility for their personal failures and would never be satisfied. Even Johnson lost faith: besieged by urban riots and watching his dreams of domestic harmony go up in smoke, he later told former White House aide Joseph Califano that "a few irresponsible agitators" had gone "from city to city making trouble," spoiling all the progress that he had made.[2]

Filled with bad news, 1966 represented a pivotal year for both Johnson and the civil rights movement. Not only had a group of angry young militants divided the black leadership but working-class whites who had previously supported the president were deserting him in droves. In the midterm congressional elections, the GOP made substantial gains in both houses of Congress, and California elected a conservative Republican, Ronald Reagan, as its governor. A few days earlier, *Newsweek* reported that for the first time since the beginning of the decade the majority of whites believed that Democrats were pushing civil rights too fast.[3]

The wave of urban riots continued, sweeping through Chicago in August before moving on to Newark, Detroit, and Milwaukee the following year; and in March 1968, devastated by American failures in Vietnam and his inability to restore peace at home, Johnson announced that he would not run for reelection. With liberal Democrats in disarray, it seemed clear that southerners and disaffected blue-collar workers in the West and Midwest would effectively choose the next president. Robert Kennedy was assassinated in June, ending hopes that he could restore credibility to the war-damaged Democratic Party as an outsider at odds with the policies of the Johnson administration. In his place, the Democrats chose Hubert Humphrey at their convention in Chicago, an event marred by violent clashes between antiwar demonstrators and the police. As a candidate, Humphrey appeared dead in the water before he ever got started, weighed down by the twin evils of an unpopular war he had supported as Johnson's vice president and chaos in the streets, which the Democrats seemed unable to control—not only in the nation's urban ghettos but now on the sidewalks outside their own convention.

Meanwhile, George Wallace had reappeared, this time as a serious contender for the presidency in a third-party bid. As provocative as ever, he traveled around the country, speaking before packed audiences who were eager to hear his message absolving law-abiding working-class whites of any responsibility for the ills of American society. Rioters and demonstrators were causing the nation's problems, he declared, but "the first one of 'em to pick up a brick" in Alabama would get "a bullet in the brain." The leaders of the two major parties "kowtow to these anarchists," Wallace roared, while the "sick Supreme Court" was willing to suspend prayer in the classroom and uphold the distribution of pornography.[4] On Boston Common in the summer of 1968, Wallace spoke to a crowd of 70,000—more than the Kennedys had ever drawn. At Madison Square Garden on October 24, 20,000 turned out—as many as had come to hear Franklin Roosevelt in 1936. Across the North, whites flocked to hear a leader willing to articulate their outrage at the federal government's rush to destroy the society that for them represented America at its best. In Pittsburgh, Wallace drew 15,000; in Baltimore, 16,000; in liberal San Francisco, 12,000; in Detroit, 15,000; and in Cincinnati, 16,000.[5]

Looking for a conservative candidate less extreme than Goldwater—one who could draw away at least some of the Wallace supporters without losing the party's traditional base—the Republicans returned to the past and nominated Richard Nixon. Most political commentators had pronounced Nixon finished after his loss to Kennedy and a second disastrous defeat two years later when he ran for governor of California. Never a charismatic figure, Nixon seemed a relatively weak presidential candidate, but insiders knew him as a cunning politician, willing to alter and trim his position in whatever way necessary to attract voters.[6] Nixon had studied the Goldwater campaign and decided that the senator's fondness for blunt speech had made him appear to be a racist, attractive only to what one of Nixon's advisers called "the foam-at-the-mouth segregationists." Goldwater had mistaken outspokenness for integrity, Nixon concluded; he would appeal to southerners without offending those moderates who had conservative inclinations but resisted identification with southern racists. As John Ehrlichman, one of Nixon's closest confidants, explained, Nixon needed to present his ideas so that they allowed a potential supporter to "avoid admitting to himself that he was attracted by [their] racist appeal."[7]

School desegregation was one of those tricky issues requiring Nixon to navigate between northern moderates and southern extremists. To avoid integration, school districts in the South had been using "freedom of choice" plans, allowing students to choose their own schools. Wallace promised enthusiastic support for such efforts, which put pressure on Nixon to respond. Forced to protect his southern flank, he answered with a firm endorsement of freedom of choice and an attack on forced desegregation, but he backed away from Wallace's confrontational assertion that freedom of choice was a right that no one could take away from southerners. Instead, Nixon offered a defense of segregated schools aimed at showing northerners not only that he held moderate views but that he also wanted only the best for African American children. Mixing poor, disadvantaged youngsters with more affluent whites made things harder for blacks, he declared, because "they are two to three grades behind, and all you do is destroy their ability to compete."[8]

On election day, Nixon won by the barest of margins, outpolling Humphrey 31,785,480 to 31,275,166. Wallace triumphed in five southern states and received nearly 10 million votes, which if they had gone to Nixon would have given him 57 percent of the popular vote and a smashing victory. The Republicans' "southern strategy" was sound, but they had to somehow eliminate the maverick Wallace vote to give them the new majority they hoped to lead—statistically insignificant differences in the voting in Tennessee, North Carolina, and South Carolina, coupled with a 1 percent increase in the Democratic turnout in New Jersey and Ohio, would have created a deadlock in the electoral college.[9] In the postmortems that followed the 1968 election, most pundits agreed that race sat dead center in the nation's political realignment. The time had come, the election analysts Richard Scammon and Ben Wattenberg declared, for Democrats to drop their "pro-black" stance and move to the right on social issues. For the pollster and political scientist Samuel Lubell, racial proximity was the key to understanding white anger and the Wallace phenomenon: in the North the Alabama governor's popularity had soared in places where blacks and whites were thrown together, either in neighborhoods or in schools. In *The Hidden Crisis in American Politics*, Lubell writes that touring pro-Wallace areas in the 1968 campaign was "like inspecting a stretched-out war front," with every local Wallace headquarters "another outpost marking the borders to which Negro residential movement had pushed." As Kevin Phillips, then a youthful member of the Nixon team, remarked to the writer Garry Wills, to make sense of American politics one had to understand that its underlying "secret" was *who hates whom*.[10]

Having become president without a resounding mandate, Nixon now faced the formidable task of governing. The riots of the preceding summer had prompted President Johnson to create the National Advisory Commission on Civil Disorders, headed by Governor Otto Kerner of Illinois. In plain language, the ensuing 1,500-page Kerner Report concluded that "our nation is moving toward two societies, one black, one white—separate and unequal."[11] The report claimed that more than just the segregation and poverty of the ghetto gave birth to urban riots. With astonishing candor, it blamed whites for creating the degradation of urban black life: "What white Americans have never fully understood—but what the Negro can never forget—is that white society is deeply implicated in the ghetto. White institutions created it, white institutions maintain it, and white society condones it."

That their government would condemn them rather than the rioters who burned and looted the nation's cities rankled many white Americans. Throughout the country, whites reacted to the report with anger and incredulity—though the document the commission issued was a relatively mild indictment, given that separate and unequal societies had been in place at least since *Plessy* and even the civil rights movement of the sixties had not been able to put a final stake into its heart. Nixon immediately rejected the Kerner Report's findings, complaining that it made everyone responsible for the nation's civil disorders except the "perpetrators and planners," whom he promised to deal with even if it meant meeting force with force. But when it came time to act, Nixon moved cautiously, establishing the Philadelphia Plan to combat discrimination in the construction industry and attempting to reform the welfare system based on advice given by Daniel Moynihan, at the time an urban affairs advisor to the president, who hoped to defuse racial rhetoric and, like Roosevelt, deal with blacks along with needy whites and other minorities in the larger context of American poverty.[12]

In August 1969, Nixon unveiled his Family Assistance Plan (FAP), which eliminated much of the welfare bureaucracy and promised to provide a minimum standard of living to poor families in return for their participation in a work program. Unlike Aid to Families with Dependent Children (AFDC), which was available only to women with fatherless children, FAP would provide funds for any family below the poverty line, even with the father living at home. Instead of rewarding illegitimacy and penalizing parents who struggled to stay together, FAP was meant to encourage stability among the poor and preserve the traditional family unit by not forcing fathers to leave so their families could receive assistance. Congress expected the program to cost several billion dollars annually and add anywhere from 10 million to 13 million people to the welfare rolls.

FAP represented an innovative solution to the welfare dilemma—one that might have reduced white resentment by diluting the percentage of blacks in the program with the addition of other minorities and poor whites. It never made much headway in Congress, however, and though Nixon blamed welfare professionals and radical groups like the National Welfare

Rights Organization for its failure, opposition to the scheme had come from every direction. Among its opponents were most of the members of his own cabinet, powerful organizations like the United States Chamber of Commerce and the National Association of Manufacturers, conservative Republicans like George Will, who complained that most Americans were not interested in poverty, and a number of liberal groups like the Urban League, which questioned the program's mandatory-work provision. The scheme also lacked significant popular support, and the president himself lost interest in it as the 1972 election approached.

In a more aggressive mode, Nixon also attempted to thwart court-ordered desegregation and busing plans for twenty-three Mississippi school districts. In May 1968, in *Green v. Board of Education*, the Supreme Court had finally outlawed "freedom of choice" plans for school admission, breaking up a logjam of school desegregation cases in lower courts. In August 1969, at the urging of Mississippi's John Stennis, the powerful chairman of the Senate Armed Services Committee, Nixon ordered the Department of Health, Education, and Welfare (HEW) to request delays for integration of the school districts, and for the first time since the *Brown* decision, attorneys from the federal government argued on the side of southern segregationists against lawyers from civil rights groups. Within HEW, staff resistance to the president's action was widespread, and ultimately only two education specialists were willing to go to court and support the delay. A few months later, the Supreme Court, under the leadership of Nixon's own appointee, Warren Burger, decided unanimously against further stalling and ordered the twenty-three districts to "begin immediately to operate as unitary systems." Though Nixon's advisers at the White House continued to counsel resistance, Robert Finch, the head of HEW, publicly stated that his department was unwilling to "tolerate any further delays in abolishing the vestiges of the dual system," and soon afterward the president issued his own statement, promising that "the administration . . . will carry out the mandate of the Court and . . . enforce the law."[13]

Harry Dent, a former aide to Strom Thurmond, had joined the Nixon team at the beginning of the 1968 presidential campaign, and by 1970 he was one of the president's chief political planners in regard to Wallace and the South. Dent urged Nixon to abandon not only the Family Assistance Plan but every other social policy that cast him as a moderate, in favor of measures that would attract southerners. Nixon needed to embrace issues that would define him more clearly as a conservative, Dent argued, but in a way that would not alienate the "nominally Democrat white middle-class vote in the swing states of California, Ohio, Illinois, Pennsylvania, and New Jersey."[14] Nixon tidied up his administration, firing key officials in HEW who had resisted the delay of school desegregation and moving Robert Finch, an old California associate and close friend, to the White House as a personal adviser. When Abe Fortas, a liberal Johnson appointee, resigned under fire from the Supreme Court in May 1969, Nixon attempted to put a conservative southerner in his place, but congressional Democrats rebuffed him twice, blocking the confirmation of both Clement Haynsworth and G. Harrold Carswell. Eventually, Congress approved Harry Blackmun, a moderate midwesterner. Many political observers viewed the rejection of Haynsworth and Carswell as defeats for the president, but these episodes won him sympathy among southern voters, who not only resented the Democrats' refusal to accept either man but lauded Nixon's courage in proposing two individuals friendly to their way of thinking.

With the 1972 election looming, Nixon rejected anything that might be construed as moderation. The president aimed to out-Wallace Wallace himself, promising to cut welfare costs, stop school busing, end efforts to integrate public housing, and eliminate hiring quotas, one of the principal tactics of affirmative action which whites found particularly offensive. The term *affirmative action* had first appeared in the 1964 Civil Rights Act as an unspelled-out remedy to be used against federal contractors who violated the law's antidiscrimination employment provisions. The following year, Johnson had issued Executive Order 11246, making the secretary of labor responsible for formulating a specific plan of implementation. Focusing initially on construction companies, unions, and civil service, the Department of Labor gradually extended its reach to a wide range of industries doing business with the federal government—banks, trucking companies, steel mills, aircraft manufacturers, and so forth—forcing them to establish specific timetables to meet government-imposed hiring goals. In 1972, affirmative action came to the nation's universities, creating an immediate uproar not only in relation to employment but in student admissions.[15] Women had been added to the list of "protected classes" that needed to be "fully utilized" in order to meet the "proportional representation" that affirmative action was intended to promote—and while most university officials, at least in the North, believed that they could survive percentage increases of blacks and other minorities based on their numbers in the general population, women were another matter. The possibility of eventual female majorities among faculty members was too much for the male-dominated university community to contemplate, and many of its members reacted by vehemently opposing the new rules. Portraying themselves as defenders of equal opportunity, they insisted that everyone should be measured on the same scale, regardless of race or gender. Never fully understanding the dispute, most whites took it as another example of blacks looking for special treatment, demanding places as university teachers and students that would have gone to white candidates had they been judged on merit alone.

Never one to underestimate an opponent, Nixon embarked on a campaign of dirty tricks to make sure that George Wallace would not spoil his bid for reelection. Two years earlier, in the 1970 race for the Alabama governorship, the Nixon camp had secretly funded Wallace's opponent, Albert Brewer, whom Wallace narrowly defeated with a last-minute, fiercely racist attack that included a newspaper advertisement depicting a small white girl in a bathing suit surrounded by seven grinning black youngsters, above a caption that read, "This Could Be Alabama Four Years from Now." Having failed to derail Wallace in their first attempt, the president and his handlers devised a more complex scheme to undermine him. Employing a "Special Services Staff" they had set up at the IRS, they began collecting incriminating financial data on Wallace and his associates. Not wanting their investigation to appear politically motivated, federal officials announced that they would not charge Wallace himself but would go after his brother, Gerald, and several of Wallace's main financial backers. At that point, Wallace joined Nixon aboard the presidential helicopter on a flight from Mobile to Birmingham, and a short time later, on January 12, 1972, the indictments against his brother and his associates were dropped. The next day, Wallace announced his candidacy for president, indicating that he would not challenge Nixon as an independent but instead would enter the Democratic primaries.[16]

Nixon had not only gotten rid of Wallace as a threat to his own campaign but had also transformed him into an immediate problem for the Democrats. In Florida, the first primary he entered, Wallace faced an array of potentially formidable presidential candidates: Humphrey, George McGovern, Birch Bayh, Shirley Chisholm, Edmund Muskie, Henry "Scoop" Jackson, Vance Hartke, and Wilbur Mills. With mainline

Democrats splitting the vote, Wallace easily outdistanced the field, winning 42 percent of the vote from angry whites bent on sending the party leadership a message. As the primaries moved on, Wallace narrowly lost in Pennsylvania and Indiana, where Humphrey had strong union support and outspent him eight to one. But by the middle of May, Wallace had received more than 3 million votes, led Humphrey by 800,000, and outstripped McGovern, the eventual Democratic nominee, by more than a million. A few days later, a lone gunman, Arthur Bremer, shot Wallace at a political rally in Maryland. Wallace survived, but his confinement to a wheelchair ended his run as a national candidate. Even so, in the days immediately following the shooting, he swept primaries in Tennessee, North Carolina, Maryland, and Michigan, where he won 51 percent of the vote to McGovern's 27 percent. Could he have become the Democratic presidential nominee, finally facing Nixon in a national contest? Certainly he would have been an unlikely choice, but with Wallace riding the crest of white resentment, anything was possible, and he had made a career of overcoming the expectations of more conventional politicians.

Whichever might have happened, the impact of the shooting of George Wallace cannot be overestimated. With Wallace out of the picture, Nixon easily won the election, with more than 47 million votes to McGovern's 29 million. In the electoral college, Nixon scored an even more stunning victory, carrying 49 states and receiving 520 votes; McGovern won only Massachusetts and the District of Columbia and a mere 17 electoral votes. Most of Wallace's followers had switched to the Republicans, finally creating the "New American Majority" the president and his advisers had consistently touted and desperately hoped for—but also saddling them with an angry, unfamiliar constituency that pushed the Republican Party further and further to the right.[17]

Nixon's triumph marked a historic change in the nation's political landscape. The extended Democratic ascendancy that had made black civil rights one of the nation's top domestic priorities was over. The 1968 election had been so close that it gave no definitive sign of the nation's political direction, but after 1972 there was no mistaking the will of the people. The time had come to rein in the Democratic liberals and restore a traditional sense of order to American society.

Whatever the Republicans hoped to do, however, Watergate and Nixon's subsequent resignation ended their immediate opportunity to begin reshaping the federal government. Gerald Ford, the vice president, took office immediately, believing that the scandalous behavior of Nixon and his associates had unnerved the nation and that his job was to restore confidence in Washington. As chief executive, Ford was an oddity, having never been elected as either vice president or president. He had been appointed to the vice presidency by Nixon when Spiro Agnew was forced to resign in October 1973 for having accepted bribes when he was governor of Maryland. Ten months later, Ford moved to the White House when Nixon left office. Ford served as chief executive for a little more than two years, under difficult conditions. Nixon had presided over a struggling economy for which a new term—"stagflation," or high unemployment coupled with high inflation—was coined, and voter disenchantment over Watergate had enabled the Democrats to gain forty-six seats in the House and four in the Senate in the 1974 congressional elections. Fiscally conservative, Ford resisted Democratic efforts to combat the economic downturn with federal spending, employing presidential vetoes on nearly sixty occasions, at about three times the annual rate of any of his predecessors. Though most people regard the veto as a negative act, the president explained at a fund-raiser in Hartford, Connecticut, in 1975 that it was "about as positive as you can get" because he had used it to saved the nation billions of dollars.[18] Ford was unwilling to spend precious government resources on affirmative action and the "imposition of massive school busing programs," which he firmly opposed.[19] He holds the distinction of being the only post–World War II president not to have issued a single executive order on civil rights. Nevertheless, in 1975 Ford made a significant—though unintentional— contribution to the future of civil rights. When the renowned liberal justice William O. Douglas retired from the Supreme Court, Ford resisted suggestions that he appoint Robert Bork, who had served under Nixon as solicitor general, in which capacity he had attempted to draft legislation to end busing as a court-ordered remedy for segregated schools. Preferring a less controversial figure, Ford instead picked John Paul Stevens, a conservative member of the Seventh Circuit Court of Appeals but one without Bork's narrow understanding of the Constitution. Willing to defend the dictates of his own thinking, Stevens has gradually moved to the left as the Court has become more conservative and today is regarded as perhaps its most independent thinker.

In 1976, voters elected Jimmy Carter, a Washington outsider who was viewed as uncorrupted by the sordid politics of the Watergate era. Six years earlier, Carter had become the governor of Georgia after a bitter campaign in which he was accused of tailoring his message based on the race of his audience. In the Democratic gubernatorial primary, he proclaimed to African Americans that state officials should guarantee everyone equal opportunity, but speaking to whites he supported the need for private segregated schools in areas where black majorities existed. Carter also made a taped radio spot to be played on stations with a primarily white audience in which he declared that he wanted no part of any "bloc" vote, slurring his speech—some said intentionally—so that many listeners understood him to say "black."[20] Winning both the primary and the general election, however, he invited the all-black choir from nearby Morris Brown University to sing "The Battle Hymn of the Republic" at his inauguration and declared that "the time for racial discrimination . . . is over. No poor white or black person should ever have to bear the additional burden of being deprived of the opportunity of an education, a job, or simple justice."[21] Carter reorganized the state government, establishing a Department of Human Resources, and struggled against recalcitrant whites to support fair housing regulations, affirmative action in state civil service, and an Atlanta voluntary busing plan. Though progress was slow, by the end of his term as governor African American appointees on state boards had risen from three to fifty-five, the number of black state employees had grown from 4,840 to 6,684, and Carter had gained the respect of the majority of Georgia's black leaders.[22]

The first obstacle to Carter's bid for the Democratic presidential nomination was George Wallace. Carter had maintained a cordial relationship with Wallace when the Alabaman was riding high in the 1960s, but by 1976 he had decided that to win the presidency he had to become Wallace without racism, building a campaign that appealed to working-class whites while at the same time wooing black voters. Carter narrowly defeated Wallace in the Florida and North Carolina primaries, where, in exit polls, more voters had personally preferred the Alabaman—but Wallace's wheelchair and general health were the overriding issues. Having ended Wallace's dreams of a comeback, Carter went on to compete as a champion of the working class in every state primary and secured the nomination when no other candidate emerged to challenge him on a consistent basis. In the general election, he barely defeated Ford, winning 297 votes in the electoral college to the incumbent's 240. Just as he had hoped, he had attracted the working-class vote that Wallace had appealed to, as well as the black vote. Carter got 58 percent of blue-collar votes and somewhere in the 90 percent range of the African American vote, which was unusually large owing to a concentrated registration drive by black leaders, including Jesse Jackson, Coretta Scott King, Barbara Jordan, and Richard Hatcher.[23] As Andrew Young, the first black member of the House of Representatives from Georgia and later the United Nations ambassador, noted when he heard that Carter had carried the crucial state of Mississippi because of a large black turnout, "The hands that picked cotton finally picked the president."[24]

Having won the election, Carter was confronted by the same governing problem that Lyndon Johnson had faced: how to satisfy both blacks and working-class whites, his two most important constituencies, whose desires often conflicted. Before the election, Carter had repeatedly been accused of "fuzziness" in his thinking, but in retrospect observers realized that he had often been deliberately ambiguous in order to give individuals on both sides of an issue something to agree with. In relation to schools, he repeatedly opposed mandatory busing to force integration, but he was also against a constitutional amendment to outlaw it. As president, however, Carter had to act rather than merely express himself, and he was constantly forced to deal with situations that could not be resolved without leaving either blacks or whites dissatisfied, and sometimes both.

The Carter administration supported the 1978 Omnibus Minority Business Act, which employed "set-asides," reserving a percentage of government business for firms owned by minorities. Black banks were encouraged by the deposit of nearly 150 million federal dollars the following year, and the Small Business Administration offered management and technical advice to black-owned businesses. When it came to hiring or school admissions, however, Carter drew a sharp distinction between "flexible affirmative action programs using goals," which he approved, and "inflexible racial quotas." In 1977, the Supreme Court addressed a suit brought by a white man named Allen Bakke, who had been refused admission to the medical school of the University of California at Davis. Arguing that he was better qualified than a number of minority students who were accepted, Bakke claimed that he had been the victim of "reverse discrimination." Filing an amicus curiae brief, the Justice Department first supported Bakke's claim that "racial classifications favorable to minority groups are presumptively unconstitutional."[25] Alerted to the Justice Department's action by black leaders, Joseph Califano, the head of HEW, argued that "classifications favorable to minorities should be judged on a lenient, rational basis." The final draft of the government's brief, which contained no direct statement opposing rigid quotas, represented a victory for HEW, but it also exposed the administration's confusion on the issue. Ultimately the court found in Bakke's favor, rejecting HEW's position, which angered both black leaders, who blamed the president, and whites, who faulted him because the administration's brief had not categorically opposed quotas.

A similar muddle ensued when HEW tried to desegregate the North Carolina higher education system. Of all the southern states, North Carolina had the most black colleges, five, which traditionally had served as centers of advancement for ambitious blacks. Among other things, the government integration plan called for the elimination of duplicate noncore curricula throughout the state system, which would force students who wanted specific courses to attend a particular school. Not only white college officials objected but blacks as well, who feared that the underlying intent was the gradual elimination of their schools altogether. The desegregation of the North Carolina colleges was never completed under the Carter administration, but it created anger and suspicion both among whites, who feared that standards would erode at all-white schools, and among blacks, who wanted to preserve institutions that historically had served them well.

Carter's most significant accomplishments in relation to civil rights were the black appointments he made within his administration and to the federal judiciary. Along with Andrew Young at the United Nations, Carter appointed Patricia Harris as secretary of housing and urban development and named Eleanor Holmes Norton chairman of the Equal Employment Opportunity Commission. In the Justice Department, Drew Days from the NAACP Legal Defense Fund was made assistant attorney general for civil rights, and Wade McCree, who had been an appeals court judge, became solicitor general. Within the federal judiciary, Carter appointed as judges more blacks, Latinos, and women than all previous presidents combined: fully 14 percent of such appointments went to blacks, about the same number to women, and 7 percent to Latinos.[26]

Carter was soundly defeated in 1980 by Ronald Reagan in an election that restored the Republicans to power by revitalizing the coalition between traditional conservatives and disgruntled working-class whites. Though Carter managed to retain the African American support that had helped put him in office in 1976, winning 85 percent of the black vote, his popularity among whites had fallen dismally. By his forty-fifth month in office, the president's approval rating had dropped to 31 percent.[27] In both international and national affairs, most whites—particularly men—perceived him as weak and indecisive. Not only his compassionate foreign policy that led to the treaty for the return of the Panama Canal and his hesitancy to use force to end the yearlong imprisonment of American hostages in Iran, but his willingness at home to compromise with blacks and other minorities—who in the eyes of most whites needed to be firmly dealt with—showed his lack of manly spirit, which compared poorly to the contrived movie-hero masculinity of Ronald Reagan.

Ronald Reagan's victory brought the intellectual leaders of the New American Majority, who had found themselves on the street after Watergate, back to Washington. An uneasy mix of political cynics and zealous Christians, they had drawn different lessons from the Nixon debacle but shared a common determination not to fail a second time. Believing either that politics represented a brutal contest in which only the fittest survived or that they had been born again after having exorcised the ghost of Watergate, they now spoke of themselves as the "Moral Majority." Carter had often introduced himself as a born-again Christian, particularly when he was campaigning, but his Christianity was filled with the recognition of human fallibility and forgiveness. The Moral Majority was made of sterner stuff. Always on the lookout for corruption and sin, they were antiabortion, anti–gun control, in favor of the death penalty, and deeply suspicious of anyone who did not share their skin color and their faith in what they took to be old-fashioned values. They saw it as their mission to cleanse American society—to wage a holy war against the immigrants and outsiders, the nonbelievers and blacks, whose rejection of the traditional American way of life had led the nation to the brink of disaster.

Reagan intended to create what he termed a *New Federalism*—a Jeffersonian style of government that would give control of most social programs back to the states. Big government, he often proclaimed, offered no solution to the nation's problems. Government *was* the problem. His administration would embrace once again the doctrine of states' rights and return power to local white majorities, allowing them a free hand to run their communities without federal interference. The people who deserved primary consideration were not the losers, "who had fallen by the wayside or who can't keep up in our competitive society," Reagan declared, but the "millions of unsung men and women who get up every morning, send the kids to school, go to work, try to keep up the payment on their house, pay exorbitant taxes . . . and as a result have to sacrifice many of their own desires and dreams and hopes."[28]

As head of the Civil Rights Division of the Justice Department, Reagan chose William Bradford Reynolds, a Yale-educated attorney with little background in civil rights law but a fierce determination to eliminate affirmative action quotas and race-based preferences in hiring. Over the years, the Department of Justice had been a mainstay in the struggle for racial equality, working in concert with activist groups to advance the civil rights agenda. The failure of suits based on individual complaints to solve problems like voter registration had led the government to undertake more expansive actions that provided group remedies, but Reynolds almost immediately reversed that practice. He made it clear that the Civil Rights Division would no longer support the use of quotas or any other type of statistical formula to give individuals who were not victims of specific incidents of discrimination preferential treatment on the basis of race, gender, nationality, or religion: "Race-conscious preferences or sex-conscious preferences are . . . divisive techniques which go well beyond the remedy that is necessary to redress in full measure those injured by a particular [set of] discriminatory practices," he informed the Subcommittee on Economic Opportunities of the House Education and Labor Committee on September 23, 1981.[29] Under the rule set by Reynolds, the Justice Department would address racial problems— which, by definition, were conflicts between opposing groups—only on an individual basis that sought a remedy for a specific complainant and would not apply to others in the same position.

The Reagan administration's effort to roll back civil rights advances by limiting federal involvement became policy across the civil rights spectrum, hampering everything from school integration to affirmative action to fair employment practices, all of which had been adjudicated previously and declared legal by federal courts. In late 1981, the Mississippian Trent Lott, then a member of the House, prevailed on the administration to end the government's refusal to grant tax-exempt status to private segregated schools in the South. Avoiding public hearings, the Justice Department, along with Bob Jones University and a group of North Carolina Christian schools, filed a federal lawsuit, *Bob Jones University v. U.S.*, to force the government to reverse itself.[30] When the *New York Times* called the suit "a racist policy" that encouraged "tax-exempt hate," Reagan claimed that federal officials had no right to refuse tax-exempt status to segregated schools. At that point, well over half the 175 lawyers in the Civil Rights Division rebelled, circulating a petition declaring that exemptions for schools unwilling to integrate was a violation of existing law. Defending the administration's participation in the suit, a spokesman for Reynolds told reporters that the dissenting lawyers were welcome to leave the division. A year later, the Supreme Court decided the case by a margin of 8 to 1, rejecting the administration's call for exemptions and asserting that the existing policy was "wholly consistent with what Congress, the executive, and the courts have repeatedly declared."

Reagan also moved to reconstitute the federal judiciary so that decisions like *Jones v. U.S.* could be reversed. In eight years in office, the president named three new Supreme Court justices, moved another from associate to chief justice, and appointed 78 appeals court judges and 290 district court judges, replacing over half the federal judiciary.[31] Intent on giving the judicial branch a long-term conservative slant, he established the Office of Legal Policy to evaluate potential jurists, not only to make certain that their conservative political views were beyond reproach but that their age and health promised a long tenure on the bench.

Reagan's first appointment to the Court, in 1981, was Sandra Day O'Connor. Though a relatively lackluster choice, O'Connor, a judge on the Arizona Court of Appeals, possessed solid conservative credentials, and Reagan knew that as the Court's first female candidate she would meet with little if any serious opposition. In 1986, in a pair of moves that gave conservatives a much higher profile on the Court, he promoted Associate Justice William Rehnquist, who had been a legal adviser to both Goldwater and Nixon, to chief justice and appointed to the bench the combative Antonin Scalia. A year later, Reagan nominated Robert Bork, whom Ford had considered and then rejected as too controversial. After a series of bitter, protracted hearings, the Senate refused to confirm Bork, and Reagan settled on Anthony Kennedy, a California law professor and appeals court judge and a much less divisive candidate. At this writing, all three Reagan appointees remain on the court and have given it a decidedly conservative cast.[32]

Though not directly related to civil rights, Reagan's tax policies laid an additional burden on African Americans. While the president spoke enthu-

siastically about tax cuts—particularly for the top 10 percent of taxpayers—
for minorities they often resulted in less net income as Social Security contributions rose, offsetting marginal tax reductions.[33] Generally, the more one
made under the Reagan tax scheme, the more one's taxes were reduced. A
1992 Congressional Budget Office study revealed that during the preceding
decade, tax policy had inverted the Robin Hood principle, taking from the
poor and giving to the rich. While the after-tax income of the top 1 percent
of the population rose by 60 percent, income for the middle class remained
essentially unchanged, and for the bottom fifth of the population it dropped
10 percent. For blacks, the figures were even more disheartening. After expe-
riencing a steady improvement in their earning power through the previous
twenty years, blacks saw the bottom fall out throughout the 1980s as the
income of African Americans in the lowest 20 percent of wage earners
declined by 18 percent. On the bottom rung of the economic ladder, blacks
found themselves poorer in comparison to whites than they had been since
the 1950s.

By the beginning of the 1990s, the search for racial equality had nearly
disappeared from the nation's domestic policy agenda. Reagan had succeeded
in leading a triumphant counterrevolution that refocused attention on white
concerns rather than the needs of minorities. Known as the Great
Communicator, he legitimized white anger and redefined the civil rights
debate, turning African Americans into villains and whites into victims.
Better than anyone, Lyndon Johnson had explained the need for a compensatory civil rights program: "You do not take a person who, for years, has
been hobbled by chains and liberate him, bring him to the starting line of a
race and then say, 'You are free to compete with all others,' and still justly
believe that you have been completely fair," he told Congress, in a frank
recognition that blacks would have to be given special consideration when it
came to jobs, schools, and housing in order to reach a point where they could
compete equally. It was not enough, Johnson noted, "just to open the gates
of opportunity." Everyone, black and white, needed to have "the ability to
walk through those gates."[34]

The underlying message, of course, was that for blacks to advance, whites
would have to make temporary sacrifices. "An understanding heart by all
Americans . . . is a large part of the answer," Johnson added. Sacrifice had a
noble sound to it, but in everyday practice people across the country were
afraid that it might mean the loss of a job or a place in school, long bus rides

for one's children, or new and frightening neighbors. Many whites felt not only resentment but a degree of shame as members of the dominant majority that had prospered at the expense of African Americans, but Reagan assured them that they had no reason to feel guilty. The guilty were the rioters who created havoc in the streets, the welfare queens who ate steak while decent families lived on canned spaghetti, the drug dealers who drove Cadillacs, and the gang members who killed innocent bystanders in drive-by shootings. Reagan found equally disturbing targets in the federal agencies and courts that continually catered to blacks with programs like affirmative action and school busing. All whites wanted was justice—but they wanted color-blind justice. Reagan agreed that African Americans ought to be treated as equals, but did that mean that they should receive special treatment? Instead of doing more for blacks, the real problem lay in the lack of fair play for whites. Why should they be made to step aside to allow African Americans to move ahead of them?

Reagan reassured whites of the rightness of their most shameful feelings, restoring a comfortable and accustomed racism to white middle- and working-class America. Racial prejudice needed to be eliminated, obviously; America still had its racial Neanderthals who loved to fly the Confederate flag, but they only incited blacks and made things worse. Reagan offered a more effective alternative: Never speak ill of blacks in public—at least, not directly—and defend yourself against charges of prejudice by taking shelter behind that old rampart, individual freedom. You could legitimately be against school busing without directly opposing integration. Parents had an important right to choose their children's schools—a right that needed to be protected from interference by the federal government. Reagan assured his followers that no one could fault them for putting self-interest ahead of justice. Rather than integration and equal rights, politicians in both parties began focusing on law-and-order issues, stricter judges, and welfare reform to meet the threat that minorities posed to American society. Ironically, the Reagan revolution had taken what blacks had wanted since the end of the Civil War—a color-blind society—and turned it against African Americans. Whites now were the seekers of equality, and blacks had become the enemies of that American virtue, wanting to raise themselves at the expense of whites.

◆   ◆   ◆

In 1989, George Bush, Reagan's vice president, succeeded him after a campaign mightily aided by the "Willie Horton" television advertisements, grim warnings that a vote for the Democratic candidate, Governor Michael Dukakis of Massachusetts, was a vote for the worst order of permissiveness: the early release of dangerous black convicts from prison. As president, Bush promised a "kinder, gentler" society, but the reality fell short of the mark for black people. His intentions were quickly made clear in his initial budget request when he reduced the Civil Rights Commission's funding by 59 percent.[35]

As early as 1974, when the Supreme Court limited multidistrict busing to move children between inner-city and suburban school districts in *Milliken v. Bradley*, the Congress had been fighting a legislative battle to stop dilution of the 1964 Civil Rights Act. Again in 1984, in *Grove City College v. Bell*, the Court had exerted its authority, ruling that the federal government could deny funds only to an individual program within a school that discriminated rather than to the entire institution. In 1988, Congress passed the Civil Rights Restoration Act and overrode Reagan's veto, restoring the government's power to withhold funds. The following year, a series of six federal Court decisions making it more difficult to prove job discrimination put Congress on the defensive again, and it responded with the 1991 Civil Rights Act, which granted victims of work-related discrimination the right to recover damages from employers, shifted the burden of proof from the employee to the employer, and expanded coverage to include not only race but disability, religion, gender, and national origin. Bush vetoed the measure twice, declaring that it would result in "more quota hiring of minorities and women" instead of achieving "a color-blind society . . . based on merit, not on race or gender."[36] Faced with a legislative override of his second veto, the president finally signed the bill into law on November 21, 1991. The White House promptly began drawing up an administrative directive calling for the abolition of all affirmative action programs, but when a draft was leaked to the press Bush disavowed responsibility for it, maintaining that it had been prepared without his knowledge by White House counsel C. Boyden Gray. The directive was never issued, but it damaged the president's reputation among blacks, who found it hard to believe that a subordinate had prepared the document without the president's approval.

Bush did appoint a number of African Americans to important positions, including Colin Powell as chairman of the Joint Chiefs of Staff and

Louis Sullivan as secretary of the Department of Health and Human Services. In at least two important cases, however, his choices embroiled him in controversy. In February 1989, he nominated William Lucas as assistant attorney general to head the Civil Rights Division of the Justice Department. During the confirmation hearings, it developed that Lucas had falsified information on his résumé, had been held in contempt by a federal district court for failing to care for inmates in his charge when he had been the sheriff of Wayne County, Michigan, and had been cited by customs officials for not having paid duty on jewelry he brought into the country. Lucas lost the support of Representative John Conyers (D-Mich.), who had nominated him, and ultimately was rejected by the Senate Judiciary Committee.

Bush's most controversial appointment came in 1991 when Thurgood Marshall resigned from the Supreme Court because of illness. Marshall had been not just a great black jurist but one of the truly remarkable legal figures of the twentieth century, having served as chief counsel to the NAACP, as a judge on the Second Circuit Court of Appeals, as Johnson's solicitor general, and as a member of the Supreme Court for nearly twenty-five years. The lead attorney in *Brown v. Board of Education*, he had also represented and won more cases before the Supreme Court than any other American lawyer, and as an appeals court judge he never had one of his ninety-eight majority decisions reversed by the Supreme Court. A year earlier, Bush had appointed the conservative but noncontroversial David Souter to replace William Brennan, but his selection of Clarence Thomas to succeed the venerable Marshall was a slap in the face to African Americans and their liberal supporters. Thomas was a Reagan appointee to the chairmanship of the Equal Employment Opportunity Commission who was against affirmative action, school busing, and racial quotas—though he had gained admission to Yale Law School on one. Opposed to the liberal principles that Thurgood Marshall had devoted his life to, Thomas appeared to have a single virtue that made him attractive to Bush: a philosophical kinship with white conservatives. Nor did the president's defense of Thomas as the most qualified person in the nation sit well with those who still took seriously the importance of African American advancement.

As a member of the Court, Thomas has voted with Justice Scalia about 85 percent of the time and written a number of opinions that reveal his hard-edged conservatism. In a 1992 case, *Hudson v. McMillan*, in which the Court majority ruled that the beating of a black inmate in Louisiana by

prison guards was cruel and unusual punishment, Thomas dissented, arguing that the beating—which left Hudson with a broken dental plate, loos-
ened teeth, and facial bruises—was deplorable but insufficient to warrant a
judgment against the guards. "A use of force that causes only insignificant
harm to a prisoner may be immoral, it may be tortious, it may be criminal,"
Thomas wrote, ". . . but it is not 'cruel and unusual punishment.'" In 1995, in
Missouri v. Jenkins, which involved a plan to increase spending to attract white
students to Kansas City's predominantly black school system, he agreed
with the Court's majority that the plan exceeded the city's existing desegregation order, but he also launched an unnecessary attack on *Brown v. Board
of Education.* "'Racial isolation' itself is not a harm; only state-enforced segregation is," Thomas maintained. ". . . [I]f separation itself is a harm, and if
integration therefore is the only way that blacks can receive a proper education, then there must be something inferior about blacks."[37]

The election of Arkansas governor Bill Clinton in 1992 produced a surge
of optimism among black leaders and their liberal supporters, simply
because it represented the end of the Reagan-Bush era and the return of a
Democratic president. Clinton, however, was not the old-style liberal
Democrat they were used to. Twelve years of Republican rule had convinced
the younger generation of Democratic politicians that the electorate had
irrevocably rejected the liberal policies that had begun with the New Deal
and that if the Democrats hoped ever to regain power they needed to
remake themselves politically. Clinton had projected himself from a small
southern state onto the national scene by becoming the chairman of the
Democratic Leadership Council (DLC), a policy group that had dropped
the Democrats' traditional identification with the working class, the poor,
and minorities and assumed a more conservative stance on issues like affirmative action, welfare, crime, and economic justice.

Having won the nomination over a field of old-fashioned liberals,
Clinton embarked on a campaign that put into practice the conclusions
reached by the DLC, seeking out middle-class whites, calling for greater
individual responsibility and initiative, and promising to "end welfare as we
know it." He expressed sympathy for white families that had been driven
from the cities to the suburbs by crime and rioting. He worked long and
hard to portray himself as a new kind of Democrat—but ultimately it made
little difference. In 1988, Dukakis had won 40 percent of the white vote;
Clinton got 39 percent, and his 43 percent of the popular vote was below

Dukakis's 46 percent. Only the existence of a third-party candidate, Ross Perot, who had taken white votes from Bush, made Clinton president.[38]

Once he had won the presidency, Clinton proved to have more of the sentiments of the traditional Democratic liberal than he had previously been willing to admit. Vowing to choose a cabinet that "looks just like America," he appointed four blacks, six women, two Hispanics, and three Jews. He also made Drew Days the solicitor general and tried to appoint an old friend, Lani Guinier, a black University of Pennsylvania law professor and former NAACP Legal Defense Fund lawyer, as assistant attorney general in charge of the Civil Rights Division of the Justice Department. Clinton had already run into trouble with his first two candidates for attorney general, Zoe Baird and Kimba Wood, both of whom had to withdraw their names after admitting that they had hired illegal immigrants. Ms. Guinier was immediately attacked as a "quota queen" by Republicans seeking to avenge the rejection of Robert Bork, and even moderate Democrats like Joseph Biden (D-Del.) took issue with her published views, which were misrepresented in the national press. At no time had she favored either the segregation of African Americans into black-majority voting districts or quotas to ensure congressional representation for blacks in Washington, as her opponents claimed. Beset by multiple problems in his Justice Department appointments, Clinton withdrew the Guinier nomination on June 5, 1993, making the White House appear—in the words of Jesse Jackson—"awfully weak and awfully incompetent."[39]

More than any previous president, Clinton relied on polling to decide administration policy. In 1993 alone, the White House spent nearly $2 million soliciting public opinion to determine what to do in relation to a variety of issues.[40] Nevertheless, in the first two years of his administration the president's health care reform plan had been rejected by Congress, he had been sharply criticized for his willingness to allow gays in the military, and he had chosen deficit reduction over a promised middle-class tax cut. With criticism coming from all directions, Clinton complained to the political analyst William Greider that he had fought more "damn battles" than any president in twenty years but had "not gotten one damn bit of credit from the knee-jerk liberal press."[41] The president's administration was at a low point, and the 1994 midterm congressional elections shattered any dreams he may have had of leading the nation back to liberalism. With an increase in the percentage of whites voting and a decline in minority votes,

Democrats lost fifty-four seats in the House and eight in the Senate, surrendering control of Congress for the first time since 1952. After the election, the columnist Mickey Kaus asked the obvious question, wondering how much better Clinton might have done if he had spent his time pushing the "tough, popular proposal[s]" that attracted whites rather than trying to satisfy the Congressional Black Caucus.[42]

Facing a Republican-dominated Congress that was beating the drum for a conservative revolution, Clinton had to deal with the defining question of welfare reform. Though the Center on Budget and Policy Priorities reported that programs to aid the poor amounted to only 23 percent of the nondefense budget but had suffered over 50 percent of the reductions in spending in the last two years, White House polls indicated that welfare reform remained a leading domestic issue for the majority of whites.[43] Following the advice of Dick Morris, a former Republican political consultant who had worked for Jesse Helms, Clinton attempted to "triangulate" between the policies of the Republican Congress and Democratic liberals to stake out his own position at the center of the debate. Ultimately, the Welfare Reform Act of 1996 represented a compromise between the Republican Congress and the president, but one over which Clinton had the lesser degree of control. In its broadest features, the bill aimed to end federal responsibility for welfare under a plan that would gradually turn it over to the separate states, eliminating the necessary protection for the poor that historically had forced Washington to administer the program. Recipients were required to work in order to receive benefits, and time limits were placed on their eligibility for aid. None of these measures were punitive, David Ellwood, Clinton's adviser on welfare reform, insisted, because their intent was to eliminate personal irresponsibility and instill American values such as "individual autonomy, the virtue of work, the primacy of the family, and the desire for community."[44] With the 1996 election approaching, the president felt he had no choice but to sign the bill, though he was troubled by its punitive character. Clinton was no more forceful when it came to protecting affirmative action. Staking out a defensive position ("mend it, don't end it") from the beginning, he conceded that the program needed reform—particularly in relation to quotas, preferences for unqualified individuals, and reverse discrimination; during the 1996 presidential debates, he boasted that he had done more to eliminate unfair affirmative action programs than any of his predecessors.

In spite of so little substantive success on civil rights, Clinton became immensely popular among African Americans. In part no doubt this was because of the expanding economy of the 1990s, which gave them jobs. Though their share in the fruits of prosperity remained small, life was better than it had been for at least a dozen years. In the midst of a Republican revolution, they were willing to overlook Clinton's inability to get things done—since, like them, he was surrounded by hostile forces that made it impossible for him to deliver. Blacks also appreciated the president's affability and warmth, which never seemed artificial or forced in personal contact with him. As the Harvard psychiatrist Alvin Poussaint has explained, Clinton was "the first president to have a black man, Vernon Jordan, as his best friend and golfing buddy." He was "culturally in tune to the black community. He went to black churches. He sang black hymns." Even his mishandling of the abortive Lani Guinier nomination could be forgiven. It was a "screwup," but black people "interpreted [it] not as a racial thing but that he couldn't handle the political flack he was going to get if he went ahead with her confirmation hearings."[45] Blacks could forgive Clinton's failures because their position in American society had made it easy for them to understand powerlessness. It was the story of many of their lives.

As the new century begins, it is clear that most Americans no longer view civil rights and the struggle for black equality as pressing issues. Though neither the Civil War nor two attempts at national reconstruction succeeded in establishing a just society, where the two races could live as one, many on both sides of the color line now seem resigned to an uneasy peace—at least for the time being. For whites, this resignation often finds expression in the assertion that prejudice has been overcome and that white people are not responsible for the problems of blacks. Among blacks, the resignation is more complex. Most members of the blossoming black middle class, confident of their ability to compete in the mainstream, insist that they want nothing more than equal economic opportunities and have no interest in mixing with white people socially. Many less fortunate blacks, unable to escape poverty, are mired in cynicism and despair. With poor educational and economic opportunities, they bear the brunt of discriminatory practices not only by private individuals and businesses but by public agencies that frequently view them not as citizens in need but as enemies on the attack. American society often seems to them a vast con-

spiracy aimed at depriving them of their self-respect and a chance for a
decent life.

To many readers, this may seem too harsh a judgment, and they may
fairly point to undeniable areas of progress for African Americans since the
1960s. As athletes and entertainers, a growing number have become mainstream idols, admired by millions both black and white. Without a doubt,
wanting to be "like Mike" is sincere, unqualified adoration, just as loving
Lucy was for earlier generations. Particularly in youth culture, negative racial
connotations have generally disappeared, as whites treat blacks as exemplars
in music, style, and speech, hoping to capture for themselves some share of
the African American mystique. These are the best of times for black athletes and entertainers. Not only are they enjoying remarkable economic
rewards but their transcendent popularity is a rare instance of successful cultural integration. The obvious appeal of individuals like Michael Jordan,
Halle Berry, Tiger Woods, and Oprah has swept away racial barriers; a vast
number of whites look up to African Americans as they never have before.
And these stars have become symbols of success for other blacks, suggesting
to them that a greater range of possibilities exists than they previously
believed.

Nevertheless, as revered as African American idols of pop culture have
become, the limits imposed by their celebrity make it unlikely that they will
ever be more than a footnote to the political and economic struggle for black
equality. Though their fame creates an illusion of freedom, in fact they are
closely controlled by the owners and advertisers of media corporations, who
pay them handsomely as long as they embrace values that appeal to a broad,
multicultural audience. One need only consider the acting career of the foot-
ball great Jim Brown to understand the high price that blacks pay once they
are regarded as politically unreliable. After a promising start in movies,
Brown was banished from Hollywood when it became clear that he was a
"bad" black man—a militant who not only offended whites by his forthright
speech but refused to be silenced.

The drive for African American equality has never had the support of
the majority of white Americans; instead, racial progress has come in brief
historical bursts, when a committed, militant minority—abolitionists,
Radical Republicans, civil rights activists—stirred the nation, pressuring it
to change. Though today there is considerable talk about an emerging
majority made up of separate minorities, the chances of its coalescing seem

relatively small. Neither Latinos nor Asian Americans, who have come to the United States seeking to share in the nation's prosperity, are keen to identify themselves with black problems; they aspire instead to join whites in a reconstituted majority. Like so many earlier groups, they have already entered the assimilation phase which—as the political commentator Michael Lind has put it—will gradually convert them into members of "a white-Asian-Hispanic melting-pot majority—a hard-to-differentiate group of beige Americans—offset by a minority of blacks who have been left [behind] once again."[46]

Of all the diverse minority groups that have arrived in the United States, it is the blacks who have had a uniquely heartrending experience. Slaves rather than immigrants, nothing separates them more from other, latter-day arrivals than the insuperable psychological burden they carried when they first set foot on American soil. For every immigrant, legal or illegal, the United States has been a beacon of hope, offering freedom and the opportunity for a better life; for Africans, exactly the opposite was the case. Coming ashore in chains, they were devoid of hope, deprived of autonomy, with nothing to look forward to but a life as chattel. Though hundreds of years have passed—years in which they became independent citizens, at least in name—they are still denied a full measure of the optimism that is the white American's birthright.

Most of them face substantial obstacles at every level of society. Among the thousand largest corporations in the country, only three had black CEOs in 1999, and only two had more than one African American on its board of directors as late as 2001.[47] At the managerial level of major companies, things are scarcely better. Though the number of black MBAs grew rapidly throughout the 1990s, the Bureau of Labor Statistics reported in 1999 that among the nation's 19 million managerial workers, only 7.2 percent were black—an increase of a mere 1.5 percent from ten years earlier.[48] The refusal by white businesses to accept well-qualified African Americans is a source of bitter frustration for those blacks who have conscientiously pursued middle-class goals.

Even more destructive are the social disadvantages that extend to blacks at every economic level. In relation to health, African Americans are unlikely to have adequate insurance; consequently, more of them die from cancer, heart disease, and diabetes than do whites. They also frequently go without appropriate medications and seldom undergo sophisticated procedures like bypass surgery, kidney transplants, or dialysis. Lacking appropriate care, African American babies die at more than twice the rate of white infants. Black children are labeled as retarded three time more often than white children, identified with emotional problems nearly twice as often, and diagnosed at a higher rate with specific learning disabilities.[49]

African Americans are also at a disadvantage in terms of education. At every level, from kindergarten to college, the majority of blacks and whites attend classes primarily with members of their own race; and just as they have always been, black institutions are underfunded in comparison with white schools. In reading, the average black seventeen-year-old performs only as well as the average thirteen-year-old white; in mathematics, the black student is even further behind. Among adults, only 15 percent of African Americans hold bachelor degrees, compared with 28 percent of whites; and in sixteen southern states plus Ohio and Pennsylvania, blacks are underrepresented at every level of higher education, from freshman to postgraduate or professional student.[50]

Blacks receive even poorer treatment in the criminal justice system. In the 1990s, the incarceration rate for African American males increased ten times faster than it did for whites; by the end of the decade, nearly one-third of all black men between the ages of twenty and twenty-nine were under some kind of correctional control—imprisonment, probation, or parole— compared with one in five whites. African Americans were four to five times more likely to be arrested for weapons offenses, and though blacks and whites use drugs at essentially the same rate, nearly two-thirds of those convicted of drug offenses were African American. Blacks also were given harsher punishment, receiving long sentences for possession of crack cocaine, while whites with a similar quantity of the powder form normally were incarcerated for less than a year.[51]

Health, education, and the criminal justice system are obvious areas in which African Americans have never received the same treatment as whites, but similar disparities exist in nearly every aspect of American life. In 2000, the United States Report to the United Nations Committee on the Elimination of Racial Discrimination offered a comprehensive list of current abuses. Blacks continued to suffer from the inadequate enforcement of existing laws; discrimination in employment, labor relations, housing, public accommodations, and the criminal justice system; and a lack of access to business capital, credit markets, educational opportunities, technology, and high-tech skills. In conclusion, the report noted, current government policies and the social practices of white America reflected a legacy of segregation, ignorance, stereotyping, and discrimination.[52]

Though whites want to believe that America's racial problems are solved, blacks know better, because they continue to live with the unresolved burden of the nation's past. Before Harriet Martineau met James Madison in the 1830s, she visited Baltimore, the initial southern stop on her American tour, and caught her first glimpse of slavery. Much to her surprise, she discovered that the city's white medical students, preparing to treat members of their own race, used only black cadavers to learn dissection. Whites did not like the idea of being cut up, she was told, and the "coloured people cannot resist." How strange, she reflected, that not only the "physical structure" but "the exquisite nervous system, [the seat] of moral as well as physical pleasures and pains" were assumed to be the same in the two races and yet the students maintained "contempt for these brethren in their countenances, hatred in their hearts, and insult on their tongues."[53] In this early encounter with American racism, Martineau grasped its contradictory nature. Like Baltimore's medical students, whites could not truthfully deny that African Americans were their equal as human beings—a proposition that skeptics like Thomas Jefferson proved again and again in their taste for black women. What antebellum American whites refused to do, however, was to surrender power and give up the use of blacks for their own advantage. In this sense, white attitudes today remain essentially the same. White Americans continue to believe that American society is theirs alone, and that control over blacks remains crucial to keeping it that way. Though the three great periods of racial upheaval—the Civil War, Reconstruction, and the civil rights era of the 1960s—each forced a degree of change, whites have adjusted in order to maintain a subtler, more sophisticated form of the same oppression that has been in place for over 350 years: a grinding onslaught of racial humiliation that lets African Americans know that they are less valuable and less worthy than the dominant majority and that works to suppress any hope that they can ever live on a par with their white superiors.

In one form or another, racial confrontation seems likely to continue as long as whites are concerned primarily with their own interests and ignore the promise of equality that the Constitution makes to all the nation's citizens. At present, the struggle between the races remains relatively subdued as African Americans attempt to mount a credible campaign for the payment of reparations—either by the federal government or by private corporations. Most whites seem unwilling to consider the idea, having already decided the case on the basis of the same prejudices that have held African Americans down historically. In a recent op-ed piece, the George Washington University law professor Jonathan Turley dismissed reparations as nothing more than a "scam" put forward by opportunists like Louis Farrakhan and Jesse Jackson, whose real interest was in lining their own pockets. Upset that reparations lawsuits ignored "fundamental legal elements," Turley declared that claims for "unjust enrichment" were meritless because the statute of limitations had run out "roughly 131 years ago."[54]

Such sentiments are no surprise to American blacks, who are accustomed to receiving too much law and not enough justice from the nation's legal system. It may well be that the courts are not the proper venue for the consideration of reparations, but critics of the idea ought to address the issue substantively rather than attempt to evade the ethical question it raises. The argument for reparations is remarkably simple: At least in theory, Americans put a high value on responsibility, and most people would agree that a corporation that creates an environmental catastrophe is obligated to clean up the mess it has made. In similar fashion, if American whites have injured American blacks over hundreds of years by refusing to allow them the equality they are entitled to as human beings and as citizens, shouldn't the nation admit its responsibility and repair the damage in whatever way it can? A frank acknowledgment of the shabby treatment African Americans have received—and in many instances still do—would be an important step in the direction of racial reconciliation. Unfortunately, it remains an admission that the majority of white citizens seem unwilling to make.

NOTES

INTRODUCTION

1. ˙ Pierre Chaunu, *L'Expansion Européene du XIIIe au XVe Siècle* (Paris: Presses Universitaires de France, 1969), xxii.
2. James Madison, *Notes of Debates in the Federal Convention of 1787* (New York: W. W. Norton, 1987), 224.
3. James M. Washington, ed., *A Testament of Hope: The Essential Writings and Speeches of Martin Luther King Jr.* (New York: Harper San Francisco, 1991), 314.

CHAPTER 1: "TWENTY NEGARS"

1. Philip S. Foner, *History of Black Americans*, vol. 1: *From Africa to the Emergence of the Cotton Kingdom* (Westport, Conn.: Greenwood Press, 1975), 194.
2. Gerald Montgomery West, *The Status of the Negro in Virginia During the Colonial Period* (New York: William R. Jenkins, 1889), 2.
3. Robert McColley, preface to *Slavery and Jeffersonian Virginia*, 2nd ed. (Urbana: University of Illinois Press, 1973), ix–x. Slaves may have reached the North American continent earlier than 1619. See Karen Ordahl Kupperman, "The Founding Years of Virginia—and the United States," *The Virginia Magazine of History and Biography*, vol. 4, no. 1 (winter 1996); William Thorndale, "The Virginia Census of 1619," *Magazine of Virginia Genealogy*, vol. 33 (1995), 155–70; and Betty Wood, *The Origins of American Slavery: Freedom and Bondage in the English Colonies* (New York: Hill & Wang, 1997). All of the above information comes from David Brion Davis, "A Big Business," *New York Review of Books*, June 11, 1998, 50, n. 1.
4. Winthrop D. Jordan, *White over Black: American Attitudes Toward the Negro, 1550–1812* (Chapel Hill: University of North Carolina Press, 1968), 61–62. See also 62, n. 38.

5. Edmund S. Morgan, *American Slavery, American Freedom: The Ordeal of Colonial Virginia* (New York: W. W. Norton, 1975), 223.

6. Jordan, 73–74.

7. Jordan, 75.

8. Jordan, 75–76.

9. McColley, xi. Morgan (298) suggests that by 1645 Virginia "could scarcely have had" more than five hundred slaves. For an appreciation of the difficulty in making population estimates for the colonies, see Morgan, 395–432.

10. Morgan, 298–99.

11. Philip S. Foner, vol. 1, 188.

12. Morgan, 299.

13. Morgan, 301.

14. Jordan, 67–69.

15. Jordan, 70.

16. Jordan, 84.

17. James Curtis Ballagh, *A History of Slavery in Virginia* (Baltimore, Md.: Johns Hopkins University Press, 1902), 34. See also Philip S. Foner, vol. 1, 191, 200.

18. West, 25.

19. Philip S. Foner, vol. 1, 192–93.

20. Jordan, 97.

21. Jordan, 261.

22. Jordan, 111.

23. Ballagh, 85.

24. Louis B. Wright and Marion Tinling, eds., *The Secret Diary of William Byrd of Westover* (Richmond, Va.: The Dietz Press, 1941), 113. See also Pierre Marambaud, *William Byrd of Westover, 1674–1744* (Charlottesville: University Press of Virginia, 1971), 178–79.

25. Frank J. Klingberg, ed., *The Carolina Chronicle of Dr. Francis Le Jau, 1706–1717* (Berkeley: University of California Press, 1956), 55, 130.

26. Jordan, 78–79.

27. Jordan, 168.

28. Jordan, 139.

29. Jordan, 140.

CHAPTER 2: ATTITUDES HARDEN IN THE PROMISED LAND

1. Alexis de Tocqueville, *Democracy in America*, ed. Phillips Bradley (New York: Knopf, 1989), vol. 1, 380–81.

2. Samuel Sewall, *The Selling of Joseph, a Memorial*, ed. Sidney Kaplan (Gehenna: University of Massachusetts Press, 1969), 7–17.

3. Kenneth Silverman, *The Life and Times of Cotton Mather* (New York: Harper & Row, 1984), 263–65.

4. Winthrop D. Jordan, *White over Black: American Attitudes Toward the Negro, 1550–1812*

(Chapel Hill: University of North Carolina Press, 1968), 187.

5. John C. Van Horne, "Collective Benevolence and the Common Good in Franklin's Philanthropy," in *Reappraising Benjamin Franklin: A Bicentennial Perspective*, ed. J. A. Leo Lemay (Newark: University of Delaware Press, 1993), 426–27.

6. Claude-Anne Lopez and Eugenia W. Herbert, *The Private Franklin: The Man and His Family* (New York: W. W. Norton, 1975), 291.

7. Lopez and Herbert, 293.

8. Benjamin Franklin, "Observations Concerning the Increase of Mankind," in *A Benjamin Franklin Reader*, ed. Nathan G. Goodman (New York: Thomas Y. Crowell, 1945), 331.

9. Franklin, 333.

10. Franklin, 335–36. Franklin was so intent on preserving the racial purity of America that even the arrival of German immigrants threatened to turn Pennsylvania into a "Colony of Aliens." The "lovely White and Red" was a conventional description of the English complexion. See Jordan, 8.

11. Van Horne, 433–36.

12. Lopez and Herbert, 300.

13. Lopez and Herbert, 300.

14. Lopez and Herbert, 290.

15. Lopez and Herbert, 301.

16. Van Horne, 437.

17. Thomas Jefferson, *Notes on the State of Virginia* (London: John Stockdale, 1787). Reprinted in Jefferson, *Writings*, with notes by Merrill D. Peterson (New York: Library of America, 1984), 123–325. For all their importance, Jefferson's comments on blacks are surprisingly brief, appearing primarily in Query XIV, 264–70, in population figures (Query VIII), 212–14, and in the section on manner (Query XVIII), 288–89.

18. Jordan, 17–18.

19. Jordan, 513–14.

20. Jordan, 514–15.

21. Jordan, 515–16.

22. Jordan, 300–301, 517–21.

23. Jordan, 521–25.

24. Jordan, 519.

25. Jordan, 519–20.

26. Jordan, 519.

27. Tocqueville, vol. 1, 374.

28. Sacvan Bercovich, *The Puritan Origins of the American Self* (New Haven, Conn.: Yale University Press, 1975), 50, 99.

29. Bercovich, 62, 99.

30. Bercovich, 102, 107.

31. Bercovich, 156.

32. Bercovich, 158.

33. John Adams, "A Dissertation on the Canon and Feudal Law," *Papers of John Adams*, vol. 1, eds. Robert J. Taylor, Mary-Jo Kline, and Gregg L. Lint (Cambridge, Mass.: Belknap Press, 1977), 112–13. In the same year the "Dissertation" appeared (1765), writing in the *Boston Gazette* under the pseudonym Humphry Ploughjogger, Adams revealed his contempt for blacks while at the same time he asserted the colonists' right to be free. "We won't be their Negroes," he wrote. Providence had never intended the colonists "for Negroes . . . and therefore never intended us for slaves. . . . I say we are handsome as old English folks, and so should be free." See T. H. Breen, "Ideology and Nationalism on the Eve of the American Revolution: Revisions *Once More* in Need of Revising," *The Journal of American History*, vol. 84, no. 1 (June 1997), 29. We are indebted for this information to David Brion Davis, "A Big Business," *New York Review of Books*, June 11, 1998, 50, n. 3.

34. Adams, *Papers*, 115.

35. Adams, *Papers*, 111.

36. See Reginald Horsman, *Race and Manifest Destiny: The Origins of American Racial Anglo-Saxonism* (Cambridge, Mass.: Harvard University Press, 1981), 3–4.

37. Horsman, 12. Jefferson regarded Tacitus as "the first writer in the world without a single exception." See Horsman, 19.

38. A second primary source also contributed to the Anglo-Saxon myth in a way that ultimately fit neatly into America's image of its adopted forebears. In the *Ecclesiastical History of the English People*, the Venerable Bede, a Benedictine monk who became the first great English historian, recounts the story of Pope Gregory, who at the end of the sixth century came upon a group of young boys for sale in the Roman marketplace and was struck by their "fair complexion, . . . pleasing countenances, and very beautiful hair." Gregory inquired where they came from and was told that they were from the island of Britain and "that they were called Angles." With "such fair countenances . . . and grace of outward form," the Pope responded, it was "meet that such should be co-heirs with the Angels in heaven." See A. M. Sellar, ed., *Bede's Ecclesiastical History of England* (London: G. Bell & Sons, 1912), 82.

39. Jefferson, *Writings*, 103–22.

40. Jefferson, *Writings*, 105–106.

41. Jefferson, *Writings*, 118–19.

42. Jefferson, *Writings*, 119.

43. Horsman, 19.

44. Horsman, 22.

45. John Adams, "Letter to H. Niles," February 13, 1818, *The Works of John Adams, 2nd President of the United States*, 10 vols., ed. Charles Francis Adams (Boston: Little, Brown, 1856), vol. 10, 282–83.

46. John Jay, "Federalist II," *The Federalist Papers*, 2 vols. (New York: George Macy Companies, 1945), vol. 1, 7–8.

47. George Washington, "Letter to William Livingston," June 12, 1783, *The World of the Founding Fathers*, ed. Saul K. Padover (New York: Thomas Yoseloff, 1960), 545.

48. Jay, 7.
49. Washington, 546.

CHAPTER 3: THE DARK SIDE OF THE CONSTITUTION

1. James Madison, *Notes of Debates in the Federal Convention of 1787* (New York: W. W. Norton, 1987). After Madison died, his wife, Dolley, was in desperate financial shape and hoped to sell her husband's documents to the government for publication. Congress balked at her asking price of $100,000, offering $30,000 instead, which Mrs. Madison ultimately accepted. A group led by John Calhoun tried unsuccessfully to block the arrangement, at least in part because Madison had been president of the Colonization Society when he died and they feared that part of the money would go to the society.

2. Paul Finkelman, *Slavery and the Founders: Race and Liberty in the Age of Jefferson* (Armonk, N.Y.: M. E. Sharpe, 1966), 1–2.

3. Finkelman, *Slavery and the Founders*, 3.

4. *Secret Proceedings and Debates of the Convention Assembled at Philadelphia, in the Year 1787, . . . Including "The Genuine Information" Laid Before the Legislature of Maryland, by Luther Martin* (Washington, D.C.: G. Templeman, 1836), 63.

5. Madison, *Notes*, 502.

6. Only Georgia did not send representatives.

7. Roger H. Brown, *Redeeming the Republic: Federalists, Taxation, and the Origins of the Constitution* (Baltimore, Md.: Johns Hopkins University Press, 1993), 18–19.

8. John Sheffield, *Observations on the Commerce of the American States* (London: J. Debrett, 1783), 110–11.

9. Alexander Hamilton, "The Continentalist," no. 6 (July 4, 1782), *The Papers of Alexander Hamilton*, eds. Harold C. Syrett and Jacob E. Cook (New York: Columbia University Press, 1962), vol. 3, 106.

14. Brown, 192.

15. Madison, *Notes*, 118.

16. Madison, *Notes*, 211.

17. Madison, *Notes*, 224–25.

18. Donald L. Robinson, *Slavery in the Structure of American Politics, 1765–1820* (New York: Harcourt Brace Jovanovich, 1971), 144–49.

19. Robinson, 148.

20. Robinson, 148.

21. Robinson, 154–57.

22. Robinson, 158.

23. Robinson, 180, Table III.

24. Madison, *Notes*, 103, 259.

25. Madison, *Notes*, 268. See also Robinson, 185.

26. Madison, *Notes*, 244.

27. Madison, *Notes*, 281.

28.   Madison, *Notes*, 275.

29.   James Madison, "Federalist LIV," *The Federalist Papers* (New York: George Macy Companies, 1945), vol. 2, 365–70.

30.   Madison, *Notes*, 273.

31.   Madison, *Notes*, 286.

32.   John Chester Miller, *The Wolf by the Ears: Thomas Jefferson and Slavery* (New York: The Free Press, 1977), 222.

33.   Madison, *Notes*, 271–72.

34.   Madison, *Notes*, 282.

35.   Miller, 27–29.

36.   Madison, *Notes*, 288.

37.   Staughton Lynd, *Class Conflict, Slavery, and the U.S. Constitution, Ten Essays* (Indianapolis, Ind.: Bobbs-Merrill, 1968), 189.

38.   Max Ferrand, ed., *The Records of the Federal Convention of 1787* (New Haven, Conn.: Yale University Press, 1937), vol. 2, 453–54.

39.   Madison, *Notes*, 362–63.

40.   Madison, *Notes*, 409–10.

41.   Robinson, 383–84.

42.   Madison, *Notes*, 505.

43.   Madison, *Notes*, 503–504.

44.   Madison, *Notes*, 505, 507.

45.   Madison, *Notes*, 507–10.

46.   Madison, *Notes*, 530.

47.   Madison, *Notes*, 104. See also 78, 195, 213.

48.   Madison, *Notes*, 255–56.

49.   Madison, *Notes*, 304–305.

50.   Jonathan Elliott, ed., *The Debates in the Several State Conventions on the Adoption of the Federal Constitution.* 4 vols. (Philadelphia: J. B. Lippincott, 1901) vol. 2, 115. The question of whether the northern states would become "partakers" of southern sins was frequently asked in the ratifying conventions. See Elliott, vol. 2, 203, for similar questioning by Joshua Atherton of New Hampshire.

51.   Madison, *Notes*, 653–54.

52.   Madison, *Notes*, 411–12.

CHAPTER 4: THE FOUNDING FATHERS AT HOME

1.   Fritz Hirschfeld, *George Washington and Slavery: A Documentary Portrayal* (Columbia: University of Missouri Press, 1997), 177–78.

2.   Herbert J. Storing, ed., *The Complete Anti-Federalist*, 7 vols. (Chicago: University of Chicago Press, 1981); see vol. 4, 224, and vol. 6, 51, 60–61.

3.   The Articles of Confederation had needed a unanimous vote for ratification. Article VII of the Constitution stated that nine states would be "sufficient for the

Establishment of this Constitution." On June 21, 1788, New Hampshire became the ninth state to ratify.

4. Hirschfeld, 34.

5. Hirschfeld, 36.

6. Hirschfeld, 67–68.

7. Benjamin Quarles, *The Negro in the American Revolution* (Chapel Hill: University of North Carolina Press, 1996), 15–18.

8. Quarles, 19.

9. Philip S. Foner, *History of Black Americans*, vol. 1, *From Africa to the Emergence of the Cotton Kingdom* (Westport, Conn.: Greenwood Press, 1975), p. 317. See also Hirschfeld, 143–44.

10. Philip S. Foner, vol. 1, 47.

11. Virginia, the Carolinas, and Georgia continued to balk at putting weapons in the hands of blacks. Virginians eventually allowed free blacks to enlist in the army as laborers and the army inevitably accepted runaways (from the Deep South) who falsified their status; but even after 1778, when the British shifted the focus of their military operations below the Mason-Dixon line, whites in the Deep South stubbornly refused to allow slaves to bear arms. Instead, they utilized slaves to build fortifications and move supplies; in the case of slaves who had been confiscated from loyalist owners, they reversed the northern practice of granting freedom in exchange for military service and offered them as enlistment bonuses to white recruits. Slaves were "an acceptable form of currency," and could be sold to other soldiers. Madison argued that it would be better to use slaves as soldiers rather than as a means of inducing whites to enlist. Even when the British overran Charleston in 1780 and Nathaniel Greene, the commander of the Continental Army in the South, requested that slaves be enlisted to recapture the city, the South Carolina legislature refused, apparently preferring British occupation to the prospect of armed blacks. Quarles, 67, 108.

12. Hirschfeld, 186.

13. Hirschfeld, 13–14.

14. Hirschfeld, 14.

15. Hirschfeld, 187–88.

16. Hirschfeld, 189.

17. Hirschfeld, 74.

18. Hirschfeld, 209–15.

19. Hirschfeld, 211–12.

20. Hirschfeld, 213–14.

21. For a popular nineteenth-century account of Gabriel's revolt, see Thomas Wentworth Higginson, *Black Rebellion: Five Slave Revolts* (New York: Da Capo Press, 1998), 71–100. First published as five separate essays in *The Atlantic Monthly* in 1870–71, they were collected in a single volume as *Black Rebellion* in 1998.

22. See John Chester Miller, *The Wolf by the Ears: Thomas Jefferson and Slavery* (New York: The Free Press, 1977), 138–41. Also see Donald L. Robinson, *Slavery in the Structure*

of American Politics, 1765–1820 (New York: Harcourt Brace Jovanovich, 1971), 361–77.

23. John Chester Miller, 148–53.

24. John Chester Miller, 154–55.

25. John Chester Miller, 159.

26. For a balanced examination of the Jefferson-Hemings relationship written prior to publication of the DNA evidence, see Annette Gordon-Reed, *Thomas Jefferson and Sally Hemings: An American Controversy* (Charlottesville: University of Virginia Press, 1997). See Joseph J. Ellis, *American Sphinx: The Character of Thomas Jefferson* (New York: Vintage Books, 1998), 363–67, for the effect of the DNA evidence. "A sexual relationship between Jefferson and Hemings can never be proven absolutely, but it is now proven beyond a reasonable doubt."

27. Randall Kennedy, *Race, Crime, and the Law* (New York: Vintage Books, 1998), 34–35.

28. John Chester Miller, 163–64.

29. John Chester Miller, 167.

30. John Chester Miller, 207.

31. John Chester Miller, 165, 173–75.

32. Thomas Jefferson, "Letter to Edward Coles," August 15, 1814, *The World of the Founding Fathers*, ed. Saul K. Padover (New York: Thomas Yoseloff, 1960), 304.

33. Thomas Jefferson, *Notes on the State of Virginia* (London: John Stockdale, 1787). Reprinted in Jefferson, *Writings*, with notes by Merrill D. Peterson (New York: Library of America, 1984), 288–89.

34. John Chester Miller, 278.

35. John Chester Miller, 92.

36. John Chester Miller, 241.

37. Winthrop D. Jordan, *White over Black: American Attitudes Toward the Negro, 1550–1812* (Chapel Hill: University of North Carolina Press, 1968), 303–304.

38. James Madison, "Notes for the *National Gazette* Essays," *The Papers of James Madison*, 17 vols., ed. Robert A. Rutland et al. (Charlottesville: University Press of Virginia, 1983), vol. 14, 163.

39. Madison, *National Gazette*, 163.

40. Drew R. McCoy, *The Last of the Fathers: James Madison and the Republican Legacy* (Cambridge: Cambridge University Press, 1989), 238.

41. McCoy, 279.

42. McCoy, 245.

43. McCoy, 249.

44. McCoy, 250.

45. McCoy, 251.

46. See Kenneth S. Greenberg, ed., *The Confessions of Nat Turner and Related Documents* (Boston: Bedford Books, 1996).

47. See Thomas Roderick Dew, "Abolition of Negro Slavery," in *The Ideology of Slavery: Proslavery Thought in the Antebellum South, 1830–1860*, ed. Drew Gilpin Faust (Baton Rouge: Louisiana State University Press, 1981), 23–77. "Abolition of Negro Slavery"

was the first published version of the *Review of the Debate in the Virginia Legislature*. "Abolition" appeared in *American Quarterly Review* in September 1832, and the *Review* was printed a few months later in pamphlet form.

48. Harriet Martineau, *Retrospect of Western Travel* (New York: Charles Lohman, 1838), vol. 1, 142.
49. McCoy, 305–306.
50. Martineau, 142–43.
51. Hirschfeld, 123–28.
52. McCoy, 290–95.
53. Thomas Jefferson, "Letter," 302–304.

CHAPTER 5: FREED BLACKS

1. Winthrop D. Jordan, *White over Black: American Attitudes Toward the Negro, 1550–1812* (Chapel Hill: University of North Carolina Press, 1968), 543–45.
2. In editions of Edwards's sermon published after his death, editors dropped his suggestion that whites should surrender America to blacks and replaced it with a conventional plea for colonization.
3. Thomas Jefferson, *Notes on the State of Virginia* (London: John Stockdale, 1787). Reprinted in Jefferson, *Writings*, with notes by Merrill D. Peterson (New York: Library of America, 1984), 264.
4. Drew R. McCoy, *The Last of the Fathers: James Madison and the Republican Legacy* (Cambridge: Cambridge University Press, 1989), 283.
5. McCoy, 277–81.
6. McCoy, 285.
7. Harriet Martineau, *Retrospect of Western Travel* (New York: Charles Lohman, 1838), vol. 1, 142–43.
8. For Madison and Martineau, see McCoy, 300–307.
9. Ira Berlin, *Slaves Without Masters: The Free Negro in the Antebellum South* (New York: The New Press, 1974), 46, table 2; 48; 136, table 6.
10. Gary B. Nash, "Introduction," in *The Negro in the American Revolution*, by Benjamin Quarles (Chapel Hill: University of North Carolina Press, 1996), xxiii.
11. Benjamin Quarles, *The Negro in the American Revolution* (Chapel Hill: University of North Carolina Press, 1996), 58.
12. Fritz Hirschfeld, *George Washington and Slavery: A Documentary Portrayal* (Columbia: University of Missouri Press, 1997), 150.
13. See Arthur Zilversmit, *The First Emancipation: The Abolition of Slavery in the North* (Chicago: University of Chicago Press, 1967).
14. Philip S. Foner, *History of Black Americans*, vol. 1, *From Africa to the Emergence of the Cotton Kingdom* (Westport, Conn.: Greenwood Press, 1975), p. 352.
15. Philip S. Foner, 83–84.
16. Zilversmit, 124.

17. Zilversmit, 194–99.

18. Berlin, 187–88.

19. Berlin, 92.

20. Zilversmit, 222–23.

21. David Brion Davis, *The Problem of Slavery in the Age of Revolution, 1770–1823* (Ithaca, N.Y.: Cornell University Press, 1975), 196–97.

22. Jordan, 421.

23. Leon F. Litwack, *North of Slavery: The Negro in the Free States, 1790–1860* (Chicago: University of Chicago Press, 1961), 207.

24. Berlin, 76–78.

25. Litwack, 123–25.

26. Litwack, 126–31.

27. Berlin, 88–89.

28. Berlin, 89.

29. Berlin, 199.

30. Zilversmit, 225.

31. Martineau, 143.

32. Berlin, 92.

33. Berlin, 93.

34. Alexis de Tocqueville, *Democracy in America*, ed. Phillips Bradley (New York: Knopf, 1989), vol. 1, 359.

35. Litwack, 68.

36. Litwack, 71.

37. Litwack, 72–74.

38. Barbara Jeanne Fields, *Slavery and Freedom on the Middle Ground: Maryland During the Nineteenth Century* (New Haven, Conn.: Yale University Press, 1985), 69.

39. Litwack, 57–58.

40. Litwack, 54–59.

41. Litwack, 50–51.

42. Litwack, 53–54.

CHAPTER 6: THE RISE OF INTERREGIONAL TENSION

1. Donald L. Robinson, *Slavery in the Structure of American Politics, 1765–1820* (New York: Harcourt Brace Jovanovich, 1971), 303.

2. Robinson, 268.

3. Robinson, 265–67.

4. Joseph J. Ellis, *American Sphinx: The Character of Thomas Jefferson* (New York: Vintage Books, 1998), 247.

5. Reginald Horsman, *Race and Manifest Destiny: The Origins of American Racial Anglo-Saxonism* (Cambridge, Mass.: Harvard University Press, 1981), 86.

6. Robinson, 393.

7.   Robinson, 395; 528, n. 45.

8.   Robinson, 528, n. 45.

9.   Everett S. Brown, ed., *William Plumer's Memorandum of Proceedings in the United States Senate, 1803–1807* (New York: Macmillan, 1923), 130.

10.   Robinson, 324.

11.   Philip S. Foner, *History of Black Americans*, vol. 2, *From the Emergence of the Cotton Kingdom to the Eve of the Compromise of 1850* (Westport, Conn: Greenwood Press, 1983), 352.

12.   Robinson, 409, 411–13.

13.   Robinson, 413–14.

14.   Robinson, 419.

15.   Ellis, 316.

16.   Philip S. Foner, vol. 2, 355–57. See also Robinson, 416–17.

17.   Robinson, 417.

18.   Ellis, 323.

19.   Jefferson to John Holmes, April 22, 1820, in Paul Leicester Ford, ed., *The Writings of Thomas Jefferson*, 10 vols. (New York: G. P. Putnam's Sons, 1892–99), vol. 10, 157–58.

20.   Jefferson's desire to educate did not extend to blacks, however. In 1817, as the executor of General Thaddeus Kosciusko's estate, he refused to carry out one of the provisions of his old friend's will. Kosciusko had wanted to sell about $17,000 in securities to purchase, free, and educate young slaves; but Jefferson refused to carry through with the project, eventually using the money for other things that had nothing to do with blacks. John Chester Miller, *The Wolf by the Ears: Thomas Jefferson and Slavery* (New York: The Free Press, 1977), 256.

21.   Miller, 258.

22.   Miller, 262.

23.   Philip S. Foner, vol. 2, 369, 373.

24.   While many slaves gained their freedom through emancipation laws or the generosity of their masters, a substantial number of the approximately 234,000 free Negroes in the nation in 1822 had bought their liberty with their own means.

25.   Thomas Wentworth Higginson, *Black Rebellion: Five Slave Revolts* (New York: Da Capo Press, 1998), 101–61. See also chapter 7, note 7. In a recent article in the *William and Mary Quarterly*, Michael Johnson offers a different interpretation of the Vesey revolt. According to Johnson, Vesey was a victim of a white conspiracy rather than the instigator of an uprising, a view that apparently is supported by significant contemporary material. See Jon Weiner, "Denmark Vesey: A New Verdict," *The Nation*, March 11, 2002, 21–24.

26.   Philip S. Foner, vol. 2, 146.

27.   Leon F. Litwack, *North of Slavery: The Negro in the Free States, 1790–1860* (Chicago: University of Chicago Press, 1961), 52.

28.   Henry Mayer, *All on Fire: William Lloyd Garrison and the Abolition of Slavery* (New York: St. Martin's Press, 1998), 122.

29.   Philip S. Foner, vol. 2, 365; Mayer, 122.

30.   Benjamin Quarles, *Black Abolitionists* (New York: Oxford University Press, 1969), 8.

31.   Philip S. Foner, vol. 2, 394–98.

32.   Philip S. Foner, vol. 2, 440.

33.   Philip S. Foner, vol. 2, 399–402, 406.

34.   Mayer, 195.

35.   Leonard L. Richards, *"Gentlemen of Property and Standing": Anti-Abolition Mobs in Jacksonian America* (New York: Oxford University Press, 1970), 52.

36.   Mayer, 197–99. See also David Grimsted, *American Mobbing, 1828–1861* (New York: Oxford University Press, 1998), 19–21.

37.   Grimsted, 20–21.

38.   Grimsted, 22–23.

39.   William Lee Miller, *Arguing About Slavery: John Quincy Adams and the Great Battle in the United States Congress* (New York: Alfred A. Knopf, 1996), 117.

40.   William Lee Miller, 144–45.

41.   William Lee Miller, 261–63.

42.   Richards, 58–59.

43.   Philip S. Foner, vol. 2, 420.

44.   Philip S. Foner, vol. 2, 419–20.

45.   Philip S. Foner, vol. 2, 401.

46.   Philip S. Foner, vol. 2, 421–22.

47.   Philip S. Foner, vol. 2, 427–28. Also see Lawrence Lader, *The Bold Brahmins: New England's War Against Slavery, 1831–1863* (New York: E. P. Dutton, 1961), 76–82.

48.   Philip S. Foner, vol. 2, 540–41.

49.   The Whig Party first appeared in 1830 as the major challenger to Andrew Jackson's Democratic Party. The Whigs would be replaced as the principal opposition in 1856 by the Republicans.

50.   Philip S. Foner, vol. 2, 542.

51.   Philip S. Foner, vol. 2, 544.

52.   Florida became a state in March 1845, ten months ahead of Texas, giving the South a temporary advantage in the Senate. The following year Iowa and Wisconsin were admitted to the Union, restoring the balance between the regions.

53.   Philip S. Foner, v. 2, 546–47. Also see Richard H. Sewell, *A House Divided: Sectionalism and Civil War, 1848–1865* (Baltimore, Md.: Johns Hopkins University Press, 1988), 24–25.

54.   Philip S. Foner, vol. 2, 550.

55.   Philip S. Foner, vol. 2, 552–55.

56.   Avery O. Craven, *The Growth of Southern Nationalism, 1848–1861* (Baton Rouge: Louisiana State University Press, 1953), 57.

57.   Craven, 54–55.

58.   Sewell, 30–31. See also Craven, 55–56. Meeting Calhoun, Harriet Martineau described him as "a cast-iron man, who looks as if he had never been born and never could be extinguished." See William Lee Miller, 115.

59.   Craven, 59.

60. Craven, 78.

61. Craven, 79–80.

62. Mayer, 396.

63. Mayer, 396.

64. The Utah Territory also was established along with the New Mexico Territory.

65. Sewell, 36–37.

66. Sewell, 34; Craven, 103.

67. Mayer, 310–11.

68. Philip S. Foner, *History of Black Americans*, vol. 3, *From the Compromise of 1850 to the End of the Civil War* (Westport, Conn.: Greenwood Press, 1983), 12.

69. Philip S. Foner, vol. 3, 17–18, 22.

70. Philip S. Foner, vol. 3, 47–64. None of the individuals charged with treason were ever convicted.

71. Philip S. Foner, vol. 3, 57, 69.

72. Sewell, 43.

73. Sewell, 42–47.

74. Sewell, 44.

75. Sewell, 46–47.

76. Sewell, 45–46.

77. Sewell, 47.

78. Sewell, 48.

79. Sewell, 49.

CHAPTER 7: THE ADVENT OF THE CONFEDERACY

1. Philip S. Foner, *History of Black Americans*, vol. 3, *From the Compromise of 1850 to the End of the Civil War* (Westport, Conn.: Greenwood Press, 1983), 210.

2. Richard H. Sewell, *A House Divided: Sectionalism and Civil War, 1848–1865* (Baltimore, Md.: Johns Hopkins University Press, 1988), 51–52. Also see Lawrence Lader, *The Bold Brahmins: New England's War Against Slavery, 1831–1863* (New York: E. P. Dutton, 1961), 220–23.

3. Lader, 222.

4. Lader, 222–26.

5. Sewell, 51.

6. For substantial treatments of *Dred Scott*, see Sewell, 56–61, and Foner, vol. 3, 214–39. Also see David M. Potter, *The Impending Crisis, 1848–1861* (New York: Harper & Row, 1976), 267–96, and Paul Finkelman, *Dred Scott vs. Sandford: A Brief History with Documents* (Boston: Bedford Books, 1997).

7. Philip S. Foner, vol. 3, 215.

8. Philip S. Foner, vol. 3, 225.

9. Lader, 227–29.

10. Sewell, 62–68.

11.   Sewell, 63.

12.   Sewell, 64.

13.   Sewell, 65.

14.   Sewell, 67–68.

15.   Potter, *Impending Crisis*, 362–84. Also see Sewell, 69–72; Foner, vol. 3, 253–54; and Henry Mayer, *All on Fire: William Lloyd Garrison and the Abolition of Slavery* (New York: St. Martin's Press, 1998), 474–80, 494–98.

16.   The other members of the "Secret Six" included Thomas Wentworth Higginson, who would go on to command the first black regiment in the Union Army and write *Black Rebellions*; Samuel Gridley Howe, a philanthropist, known for his work with the blind, who had fought in Greece during that nation's war for independence; George Stearns, who had made a fortune manufacturing lead pipe and linseed oil and previously had sent rifles to the antislavery fighters in Kansas; Theodore Parker, a Unitarian minister, who was among the best-known clergymen in the United States; and Franklin B. Sanborn, a young schoolteacher, who had met Brown and introduced him to many of the other men.

17.   Sewell, 70.

18.   Avery O. Craven, *The Growth of Southern Nationalism, 1848–1861* (Baton Rouge: Louisiana State University Press, 1953), 308–309.

19.   Mayer, 505.

20.   Sewell, 74–76.

21.   Philip S. Foner, vol. 3, 233–36.

22.   Philip S. Foner, vol. 3, 276–77.

23.   Sewell, 76; Potter, *Impending Crisis*, 429–30.

24.   Philip S. Foner, vol. 3, 281.

25.   Sewell, 76.

26.   Philip S. Foner, vol. 3, 292.

27.   Philip S. Foner, vol. 3, 292–93.

28.   David M. Potter, *Lincoln and His Party in the Secession Crisis* (Baton Rouge: Louisiana State University Press, 1942), 319.

29.   Potter, *Lincoln and His Party*, 329–30.

30.   Potter, *Impending Crisis*, 567.

31.   In the first draft of his inaugural speech, Lincoln had rashly promised to use all the power at his disposal to reclaim the captured installations, but after careful consideration he apparently had second thoughts and decided to avoid a potentially serious confrontation, ultimately promising only to preserve the property and places remaining under federal control.

32.   Potter, *Impending Crisis*, 570–71.

33.   Potter, *Impending Crisis*, 579.

34.   Potter, *Impending Crisis*, 582–83. The first shell in the bombardment of Sumter was fired by the Virginia firebrand Edmund Ruffin, who by 1860 was sixty-seven years old. In his diary, when the war ended, he recorded his "unmitigated hatred to Yankee rule—to all political, social, and business connections with Yankees, and the perfidious, malignant and vile Yankee race," and then committed suicide. See Sewell, 195.

35. Sewell, 86.
36. Sewell, 86.
37. Philip S. Foner, vol. 3, 294–95.
38. Leonard L. Richards, *The Slave Power: The Free North and Southern Domination, 1780–1860* (Baton Rouge: Louisiana State University Press, 2000), 9.
39. Donald L. Robinson, *Slavery in the Structure of American Politics, 1765–1820* (New York: Harcourt Brace Jovanovich, 1971), 278–80.
40. See Richard E. Ellis, *Jacksonian Democracy, States' Rights, and the Nullification Crisis* (New York: Oxford University Press, 1987).
41. Potter, *Lincoln and His Party*, 160, n. 11.

CHAPTER 8: THE TOILS OF RECONSTRUCTION

1. Brooks D. Simpson, *The Reconstruction Presidents* (Lawrence: University Press of Kansas, 1998), 63.
2. In August 1862, Lincoln had summoned a group of black leaders to the White House, asking that they publicly support colonization. Nearly all of them refused, saying blacks had no desire to leave the United States. Frederick Douglass replied bluntly, telling Lincoln that instead he ought to "declare slavery abolished, and favor our peaceful colonization in the rebel States, or some portion of them. We would cheerfully return there, and give our most willing aid to deliver our loyal colored brethren and other Unionists from the tyranny of rebels to our government." See Philip S. Foner, *History of Black Americans*, vol. 3, *From the Compromise of 1850 to the End of the Civil War* (Westport, Conn.: Greenwood Press, 1983), 341–43.
3. Richard H. Sewell, *A House Divided: Sectionalism and Civil War, 1848–1865* (Baltimore, Md.: Johns Hopkins University Press, 1988), 168.
4. Sewell, 172.
5. Simpson, 56.
6. Stetson Kennedy, *After Appomattox: How the South Won the War* (Gainesville: University Press of Florida, 1995), 53.
7. Simpson, 67.
8. James M. McPherson, "The Ballot and Land for the Freedmen," in *Reconstruction: An Anthology of Revisionist Writing*, eds. Kenneth M. Stampp and Leon F. Litwack (Baton Rouge: Louisiana State University Press, 1969), 138.
9. Eric Foner, *Reconstruction: America's Unfinished Revolution, 1863–1877* (New York: Harper & Row, 1988), 70–71.
10. Kennedy, 48.
11. Kennedy, 49.
12. Kennedy, 53–54.
13. John Samuel Ezell, *The South Since 1865* (Norman: University of Oklahoma Press, 1998), 80.
14. Eric Foner, 273.

15.   Simpson, 91; Kennedy, 52.

16.   McPherson, 134–35.

17.   C. Vann Woodward, "The Political Legacy of Reconstruction," in *Reconstruction: An Anthology of Revisionist Writings*, ed. Kenneth M. Stampp and Leon F. Litwack (Baton Rouge: Louisiana State University Press, 1969), 518.

18.   Woodward, 517–19.

19.   Woodward, 520–21.

20.   W. E. B. Du Bois, *Black Reconstruction in America: An Essay Toward a History of the Part Which Black Folk Played in the Attempt to Reconstruct Democracy in America* (Cleveland: World, 1969), 290.

21.   Du Bois, 371.

22.   Du Bois, 372.

23.   Eric Foner, 315.

24.   Eric Foner, 340.

25.   Eric Foner, 342–43.

26.   Alexander Keyssar, *The Right to Vote: The Contested History of Democracy in the United States* (New York: Basic Books, 2000), 95.

27.   Keyssar, 99.

28.   Eric Foner, 446–47.

29.   Simpson, 144.

30.   Du Bois, 504.

31.   Simpson, 140.

32.   Simpson, 141.

33.   Kennedy, 98–99.

34.   Hinton Rowan Helper, *Nojoque: A Question for a Continent* (New York: George W. Carleton, 1867), p. 368.

35.   Eric Foner, 427–28.

36.   Eric Foner, 429.

37.   Eric Foner, 454.

38.   Kennedy, 106.

39.   Everette Swinney, *Suppressing the Ku Klux Klan: The Enforcement of the Reconstruction Amendments* (New York and London: Garland, 1987), 132–33.

40.   Eric Foner, 454.

41.   Eric Foner, 455.

42.   Eric Foner, 456.

43.   Eric Foner, 458–59.

44.   "What I desired above all was to secure a retreat for that portion of the laboring classes of our former slave States, who might find themselves under unbelievable pressure," the president told an audience gathered to celebrate his seventy-fourth birthday, on April 27, 1896. "And I believed that the mere knowledge of that fact on the part not only of the freedmen but of their former masters, would serve to prevent anything like widespread injustice." See Simpson, 145–46.

45.   Eric Foner, 495.
46.   Eric Foner, 496.
47.   Kennedy, 218.
48.   Eric Foner, 499.
49.   Eric Foner, 500–501.
50.   Eric Foner, 502.
51.   Kennedy, 220–21.
52.   Kennedy, 224.
53.   Simpson, 162.
54.   Simpson, 168.
55.   Simpson, 167.
56.   Eric Foner, 554.
57.   Simpson, 177.
58.   Simpson, 178–79.
59.   Simpson, 180.
60.   Eric Foner, 562.
61.   Kennedy, 284.
62.   Simpson, 190.
63.   Eric Foner, 576–80.
64.   Eric Foner, 581.
65.   Eric Foner, 582.
66.   Kennedy, 283.
67.   Eric Foner, 602.
68.   Kennedy, 286.

CHAPTER 9: "SEPARATE BUT EQUAL"

1.   William Cohen, *At Freedom's Edge: Black Mobility and the Southern White Quest for Racial Control, 1861–1915* (Baton Rouge: Louisiana State University Press, 1991), 164.
2.   Cohen, 155.
3.   Paul Cuffe, a black sea captain from Massachusetts, was an exception who encouraged African Americans to return to Africa. In 1816, he carried thirty-eight American blacks to Sierra Leone.
4.   Cohen, 154.
5.   See Nell Painter, *Exodusters: Black Migration to Kansas after Reconstruction* (New York: Knopf, 1976).
6.   Cohen, 256.
7.   Cohen, 203.
8.   See J. Morgan Kousser, *The Shaping of Southern Politics: Suffrage Restrictions and the Establishment of the One-Party South, 1880–1910* (New Haven, Conn.: Yale University Press, 1974), 45–62.

9. Kousser, 51–52.

10. Kousser, 76.

11. James Allen et al., *Without Sanctuary, Lynching Photography in America* (Santa Fe, N.M.: Twin Palms, 2000), plates 59 and 60.

12. See Jacqueline Jones Royster, ed., *Southern Horrors and Other Writings: The Anti-Lynching Campaign of Ida B. Wells, 1892–1900* (Boston: Bedford Books, 1997).

13. Royster, 127.

14. Cohen, 236–37.

15. Cohen, 231.

16. See Brook Thomas, ed., *Plessy v. Ferguson: A Brief History with Documents* (Boston: Bedford Books, 1997).

17. C. Vann Woodward, *American Counterpoint: Slavery and Racism in the North-South Dialogue* (Boston: Little, Brown, 1971), 224.

18. Thomas, 31–34.

19. Thomas, 34–38.

20. Robert Francis Engs, *Educating the Disenfranchised and Disinherited: Samuel Chapman Armstrong and Hampton Institute, 1839–1883* (Knoxville: University of Tennessee Press, 1999), 1.

21. James D. Anderson, *The Education of Blacks in the South, 1860–1935* (Chapel Hill: University of North Carolina Press, 1988), 32.

22. Anderson, 72.

23. Anderson, 54.

24. Anderson, 107.

25. Richard Hofstadter, *Social Darwinism in American Thought*, 4th ed. (Boston: Beacon Press, 1992), 57–59.

26. Mike Hawkins, *Social Darwinism in European and American Thought, 1860–1945* (Cambridge: Cambridge University Press, 1997), 201–203.

27. John David Smith, *An Old Creed for the New South: Proslavery Ideology and Historiography, 1865–1918* (Westport, Conn.: Greenwood Press, 1985), 116–17.

28. Woodrow Wilson, *Division and Reunion, 1829–1889* (New York: Collier Books, 1961). See also David W. Blight, *Race and Reunion: The Civil War in American Memory* (Cambridge, Mass.: Harvard University Press, 2001), 383–91: at the fifty-year Gettysburg celebration, Wilson's viewpoint had become the nation's.

29. Nancy J. Weiss, "The Negro and the New Freedom, Fighting Wilsonian Segregation," *Political Science Quarterly* 84 (1969), 64.

30. Weiss, *PSQ*, 65.

31. Weiss, *PSQ*, 72.

32. Grace Elizabeth Hale, " 'For Colored' and 'For White': Segregating Consumption in the South," in *Jumpin' Jim Crow, Southern Politics from Civil War to Civil Rights*, eds. Jane Dailey, Glenda Elizabeth Gilmore, and Bryant Simon (Princeton, N.J.: Princeton University Press, 2000), 166–68.

33. Lewis H. Carlson and George A. Colburn, *In Their Place: White America Defines Her Minorities, 1850–1950* (New York: John Wiley, 1972), 99–102.

34. Carlson and Colburn, 80–81.

35. Joe William Trotter Jr., *The Great Migration in Historical Perspective: New Dimensions of Race, Class, and Gender* (Bloomington: Indiana University Press, 1991), 85.

36. Carole Marks, *Farewell—We're Good and Gone: The Great Black Migration* (Bloomington: Indiana University Press, 1989), 59.

37. Marks, 19.

38. William M. Tuttle Jr., *Race Riot: Chicago in the Red Summer of 1919* (Urbana: University of Illinois Press, 1996), 14.

39. Theodore Kornweibel Jr., *"Seeing Red": Federal Campaigns Against Black Militancy, 1919–1925* (Bloomington: Indiana University Press, 1998), 1–18.

40. Kornweibel, 57.

41. Kornweibel, 20.

42. Kornweibel, 77–78.

43. Kornweibel, 102.

44. Kornweibel, 134, 141.

45. Kornweibel, 81.

46. Alfred Brophy and Randall Kennedy, *Reconstructing the Dreamland: The Tulsa Race Riot of 1921* (New York: Oxford University Press, 2002); James S. Hirsch, *Riot and Remembrance: The Tulsa Race War and Its Legacy* (New York: Houghton Mifflin, 2002); and Tim Madigan, *Massacre, Destruction and the Tulsa Race Riot of 1921* (New York: St. Martin's, 2001).

47. See John M. Barry, *Rising Tide: The Great Mississippi Flood of 1927 and How It Changed America* (New York: Simon & Schuster, 1997).

48. Patricia Sullivan, *Days of Hope: Race and Democracy in the New Deal Era* (Chapel Hill: University of North Carolina Press, 1996), 21.

49. Sullivan, 22.

50. Roger Biles, *A New Deal for the American People* (DeKalb: Northern Illinois University Press, 1991), 174.

51. Biles, 176–80.

52. Sullivan 46–48.

53. Nancy J. Weiss, *Farewell to the Party of Lincoln* (Princeton, N.J.: Princeton University Press, 1983), 106. See also Maureen H. Beasley, Holly C. Shulman, and Henry R. Beasley, eds., *The Eleanor Roosevelt Encyclopedia* (Westport, Conn.: Greenwood Press, 2001), 29–30.

54. Sullivan, 59.

55. Sullivan, 61.

56. Sullivan, 105.

57. Sullivan, 107.

58. Sullivan, 99–100.

59. Sullivan, 120.

60. Sullivan, 123, 127.

61. Sullivan, 130–31.

62. Sullivan, 135–36, 147.

63. Sullivan, 164.

64. Sullivan, 166–67.

65. Sullivan, 137.
66. Sullivan, 211–12.

CHAPTER 10: CIVIL RIGHTS VICTORIES; CIVIL RIGHTS BACKLASH

1. Patricia Sullivan, *Days of Hope: Race and Democracy in the New Deal Era* (Chapel Hill: University of North Carolina Press, 1996), 181.
2. Donald R. McCoy and Richard T. Reutten, *Quest and Response: Minority Rights and the Truman Administration* (Lawrence: University Press of Kansas, 1973), 21–22.
3. Sullivan, 223–24.
4. Sullivan, 230–40, 243.
5. McCoy and Reutten, 73–74.
6. McCoy and Reutten, 127–28.
7. McCoy and Reutten, 129–31.
8. McCoy and Reutten, 187–88.
9. McCoy and Reutten, 159–60.
10. McCoy and Reutten, 342.
11. McCoy and Reutten, 344.
12. McCoy and Reutten, 341.
13. McCoy and Reutten, 345, 332.
14. McCoy and Reutten, 350–51.
15. McCoy and Reutten, 318.
16. McCoy and Reutten, 322.
17. Robert Fredrick Burk, *The Eisenhower Administration and Black Civil Rights* (Knoxville: University of Tennessee Press, 1984), 23.
18. Burk, 68–88.
19. Norman C. Amaker, *Civil Rights and the Reagan Administration* (Washington, D.C.: Urban Institute Press, 1988), 14.
20. Burk, 161.
21. Burk, 150.
22. Burk, 145–50.
23. Burk, 151.
24. Burk, 152.
25. A. James Riechley, *Conservatives in an Age of Change: The Nixon and Ford Administrations* (Washington, D.C.: Brookings Institution, 1981), 177.
26. Burk, 159, 167, 173.
27. Burk, 175.
28. Burk, 189.
29. Burk, 206, 219.
30. See Burk, 204–27.
31. See Steven F. Lawson, *Black Ballots: Voting Rights in the South, 1944–1969* (New York: Columbia University Press, 1976), 227–30. See also Carl M. Brauer, *John F. Kennedy*

and the Second Reconstruction (New York: Columbia University Press, 1977), 113–14.

32. Lawson, 247.
33. Burk, 264.
34. Brauer, 16.
35. Brauer, 47–50.
36. Brauer, 62–64.
37. See Brauer, 98–109. See also Mark Stern, *Calculating Visions: Kennedy, Johnson, and Civil Rights* (New Brunswick, N.J.: Rutgers University Press, 1992), 58–62.
38. See Brauer, 229–41. See also Stern, 80–81.
39. Stern, 91.
40. Stern, 115–16.
41. Stern, 119–22.
42. Stern, 161.
43. Stern, 161.
44. Stern, 165.
45. Stern, 185.
46. Edward D. Berkowitz, *America's Welfare State: From Roosevelt to Reagan* (Baltimore, Md.: Johns Hopkins University Press, 1991), 92. ADC was changed to AFDC (Aid to Families with Dependent Children) in 1962.
47. Berkowitz, 91.
48. Berkowitz, 101–102.
49. Berkowitz, 44.
50. Dan T. Carter, *From George Wallace to Newt Gingrich: Race in the Conservative Counterrevolution, 1963–1994* (Baton Rouge: Louisiana State University Press, 1996), 2.
51. Carter, 4.
52. Carter, 6.
53. Stephan Lesher, *George Wallace, American Populist* (Reading, Mass.: Addison-Wesley, 1994), 280.
54. Carter, xii.
55. Carter, xii–xiii.
56. Taylor Branch, *Pillar of Fire: America in the King Years, 1963–65* (New York: Simon & Schuster, 1998), 357, see footnote *.
57. Lesher, 295.
58. Stern, 193.
59. Stern, 210.
60. Stern, 220–21.
61. Stern, 226.
62. Stern, 222, 227–28.
63. Stern, 185, 228.
64. Stern, 228.

CHAPTER 11: THE NEW FEDERALISM AND ITS LEGACY

1. Wyn Craig Wade, *The Fiery Cross: The Ku Klux Klan in America* (New York: Oxford University Press, 1998), 305.

2. Doris Kearns, *Lyndon Johnson and the American Dream* (New York: Harper & Row, 1976), 305.

3. Mark Stern, *Calculating Visions: Kennedy, Johnson, and Civil Rights* (New Brunswick N.J.: Rutgers University Press, 1992), 229.

4. Dan T. Carter, *From George Wallace to Newt Gingrich: Race in the Conservative Counterrevolution, 1963–1994* (Baton Rouge: Louisiana State University Press, 1996), 20.

5. Carter, 19.

6. Roger Ailes, one of the leaders of the Nixon election campaign, compared him to a boy who, on Christmas morning, got a briefcase while all his friends received footballs—and was happy about it. See Carter, 27.

7. Carter, 30.

8. Carter, 33.

9. Carter, 35.

10. See Carter, 40–43. Also see Richard Scammon and Ben Wattenberg, *The Real Majority: How the Silent Center of the American Electorate Chooses Its President* (New York: Coward-McCann & Geoghegan, 1970); Samuel Lubell, *The Hidden Crisis in American Politics* (New York: W. W. Norton, 1970); and Kevin Phillips, *The Emerging Republican Majority* (New Rochelle, N.Y.: Arlington House, 1970).

11. The eleven-member National Advisory Commission on Civil Disorders chaired by Otto Kerner, the governor of Illinois, issued its report on February 29, 1968.

12. Carter, 36–39.

13. A. James Reichley, *Conservatives in an Age of Change: The Nixon and Ford Administrations* (Washington, D.C.: Brookings Institution, 1981), 182–85.

14. Carter, 44.

15. See the "Affirmative Action" entry, *Stanford Encyclopedia of Philosophy* <**www.seop.leeds.ac.uk/entries/affirmative-action/**>, 1–2.

16. Carter, 46–49.

17. See Carter, 53, n. 50. Nixon apparently was delighted with his new constituency, telling his aide, H. R. Haldeman, that southerners were "Americans to the core," who hadn't been "poisoned by the elite universities and the media" and still retained their "patriotism," "strong moral and spiritual values," and "anti-permissiveness."

18. Samuel B. Hoff, "Presidential Success in the Veto Process: The Legislative Record of Gerald R. Ford," in *Gerald R. Ford and the Politics of Post-Watergate America*, eds. Bernard J. Firestone and Alexej Ugrinsky (Westport, Conn.: Greenwood Press, 1993), vol. 1, 293–308.

19. Howard Ball, "Confronting Institutional Schizophrenia: The Effort to Depoliticize the U.S. Department of Justice, 1974–1976," in *Gerald R. Ford and the Politics of Post-Watergate America*, eds. Bernard J. Firestone and Alexej Ugrinsky (Westport, Conn.: Greenwood Press, 1993), vol. 1, 105.

20. Betty Glad, *Jimmy Carter in Search of the Great White House* (New York: W. W. Norton, 1980), 133.

21. Glad, 141.

22. Glad, 186.

23. Glad, 403.

24. John Dumbrell, *The Carter Presidency: A Reevaluation* (New York: Manchester University Press, 1993), 89.

25. Dumbrell, 93.

26. Norman C. Amaker, *Civil Rights and the Reagan Administration* (Washington, D.C.: Urban Institute Press, 1988), 27. See also Sheldon Goldman, *Picking Federal Judges: Lower Court Selections from Roosevelt Through Reagan* (New Haven, Conn.: Yale University Press, 1997), 350.

27. Dumbrell, 90–91, 50.

28. Ronnie Dugger, *On Reagan: The Man and His Presidency* (New York: McGraw-Hill, 1983), 293.

29. Amaker, 22.

30. Carter, 56–57.

31. Carter, 58–59.

32. Nicholas Laham, *The Reagan Presidency and the Politics of Race: In Pursuit of Colorblind Justice and Limited Government* (Westport, Conn.: Praeger, 1998), 66–67. Chief Justice Rehnquist has been a foe of civil rights dating back to *Brown v. Board of Education*, when he clerked for Justice Robert H. Jackson, sending him a memo urging that separate but equal should not be overturned. The Rehnquist Court has gradually turned its back on civil rights. In 1992, it withdrew judicial supervision over school integration, and its rulings on affirmative action have reversed the supportive efforts of the Court throughout the 1970s and early 1980s.

33. Carter, 62–63.

34. Message to Congress, February 15, 1967. Cited in Robert A. Caro, *The Path to Power: the Years of Lyndon Johnson* (New York: Alfred A. Knopf, 1982), 352.

35. Steven A. Shull, *American Civil Rights Policy from Truman to Clinton: The Role of Presidential Leadership* (Armonk, N.Y.: M. E. Sharpe, 1999), 109.

36. Jeremy D. Mayer, *Running on Race: Racial Politics in Presidential Campaigns, 1960–2000* (New York: Random House, 2002), 231.

37. Mayer, 261–62.

38. Kevin Merida and Michael A. Fletcher, "Supreme Discomfort," *Washington Post*, August 4, 2002, 16–17.

39. Philip A. Klinkner, "Bill Clinton and the Politics of the New Liberalism," in *Without Justice for All: The New Liberalism and Our Retreat from Racial Equality*, ed. Adolph Reed Jr. (Boulder Colo.: Westview Press, 1999), p. 19.

40. Shull, 135.; Jeffrey E. Cohen, *Presidential Responsiveness and Public Policy-making: The Public and the Policies That Presidents Choose* (Ann Arbor: University of Michigan Press, 1997), 13.

41. Klinkner, 20.

42. Klinkner, 22.

43. Klinkner, 23.

44. Mimi Abramovitz and Ann Withorn, "Playing by the Rules: Welfare Reform and the New Authoritarian State," in *Without Justice for All: The New Liberalism and Our Retreat from Racial Equality*, ed. Adolph Reed Jr. (Boulder, Colo.: Westview Press, 1999), 163.

45. DeWayne Wickham, *Bill Clinton and Black America* (New York: Ballantine Books, 2002), 123.

46. Michael Lind, "The Beige and the Black," *New York Times Magazine*, August 16, 1998, 38–39.

47. Frank McCoy, "All Boarded Up," *Africana.com Lifestyles*, 3–4.

48. "Black MBAs Convene in Chicago to Examine Critical Issues in Business," <www.nbmbaa.org/NewsFlashes/NewsFlash-09-21-00.htm>, 1.

49. *Washington Post*, National Weekly Edition, March 19–25, 2001; *New York Times*, March 20, 2002, and June 25, 2002.

50. *Los Angeles Times*, August 25, 1998.

51. *New York Times*, April 26, 2000; *Los Angeles Times*, May 22, 2000.

52. *Los Angeles Times*, September 22, 2000.

53. Harriet Martineau, *Retrospect of Western Travel* (New York: Charles Lohman, 1838), vol. 1, 107.

54. Jonathan Turley, "Reparations: A Scam Cloaked in Racial Pain," *Los Angeles Times*, September 9, 2002, sect. B, 11.

SELECTED BIBLIOGRAPHY

Anderson, Eric, and Alfred A. Moss Jr. *Northern Philanthropy and Southern Black Education, 1902–1930.* Columbia: University of Missouri Press, 1999.

Anderson, James D. *The Education of Blacks in the South, 1860–1935.* Chapel Hill: University of North Carolina Press, 1988.

Aptheker, Herbert. *One Continual Cry: David Walker's Appeal to the Colored Citizens of the World (1829–1830).* New York: Humanities Press, 1965.

Ayers, Edward L. *Southern Crossing: A History of the American South, 1877–1906.* New York: Oxford University Press, 1995.

Bailyn, Bernard, ed. *The Debate on the Constitution: Federalist and Anti-Federalist Speeches, Articles, and Letters During the Struggle over Ratification.* 2 vols. New York: Viking Press, 1993.

Baker, Ray Stannard. *Following the Color Line: American Negro Citizenship in the Progressive Era.* New York: Harper & Row, 1964.

Barone, Michael. *Our Country: The Shaping of America from Roosevelt to Reagan.* New York: Free Press, 1990.

Beck, E. M., and Stewart E. Tolnay. *A Festival of Violence: An Analysis of Lynchings, 1882–1930.* Urbana: University of Illinois Press, 1992.

Bercovich, Sacvan. *The Puritan Origins of the American Self.* New Haven, Conn.: Yale University Press, 1975.

Berkowitz, Edward D. *America's Welfare State: From Roosevelt to Reagan.* Baltimore, Md.: Johns Hopkins University Press, 1991.

Berlin, Ira. *Many Thousands Gone: The First Two Centuries of Slavery in North America.* Cambridge, Mass.: Harvard University Press, 1998.

———. *Slaves Without Masters: The Free Negro in the Antebellum South.* New York: New Press, 1974.

Berlin, Ira, Joseph P. Reidy, and Leslie S. Rowland, eds. *Freedom's Soldiers: The Black Military Experience in the Civil War.* Cambridge: Cambridge University Press, 1998.

Berman, William C. *America's Right Turn, From Nixon to Clinton.* Baltimore, Md.: Johns Hopkins University Press, 1998.

Berthoff, Rowland. *An Unsettled People: Social Order and Disorder in American History.* New York: Harper & Row, 1975.

Blassingame, John W. *The Slave Community: Plantation Life in the Antebellum South.* New York: Oxford University Press, 1979.

Blight, David W. *Race and Reunion: The Civil War in American Memory.* Cambridge, Mass.: Harvard University Press, 2001.

Boorstin, Daniel J. *The Lost World of Thomas Jefferson.* Chicago: University of Chicago Press, 1948.

Branch, Taylor. *Parting the Waters: America in the King Years, 1954–1963.* New York: Simon & Schuster, 1988.

———. *Pillar of Fire: America in the King Years, 1963–65.* New York: Simon & Schuster, 1998.

Brauer, Carl M. *John F. Kennedy and the Second Reconstruction.* New York: Columbia University Press, 1977.

Bruce, Dickson D., Jr. *The Rhetoric of Conservatism: The Virginia Convention of 1829–1830 and the Conservative Tradition of the South.* San Marino, Calif.: Huntington Library, 1982.

Brundage, W. Fitzhugh, ed. *Under the Sentence of Death: Lynching in the South.* Chapel Hill: University of North Carolina Press, 1997.

Burk, Robert Fredrick. *The Eisenhower Administration and Black Civil Rights.* Knoxville: University of Tennessee Press, 1984.

Burns, James MacGregor, ed. *To Heal and to Build: The Programs of President Lyndon B. Johnson.* New York: McGraw-Hill, 1968.

Caro, Robert A. *The Path to Power: The Years of Lyndon Johnson.* New York: Alfred A. Knopf, 1982.

Carter, Dan T. *From George Wallace to Newt Gingrich: Race in the Conservative Counterrevolution, 1963–1994.* Baton Rouge: Louisiana State University Press, 1996.

———. *The Politics of Rage: George Wallace, the Origins of the New Conservatism, and the Transformation of American Politics.* Baton Rouge: Louisiana State University Press, 1995.

Chalmers, David M. *Hooded Americanism: The History of the Ku Klux Klan.* Durham, N.C.: Duke University Press, 1987.

Cohen, William. *At Freedom's Edge: Black Mobility and the Southern White Quest for Racial Control, 1861–1915.* Baton Rouge: Louisiana State University Press, 1991.

Couto, Richard A. *Ain't Gonna Let Nobody Turn Me Round: The Pursuit of Racial Justice in the Rural South.* Philadelphia: Temple University Press, 1991.

Craven, Avery O. *The Growth of Southern Nationalism, 1848–1861.* Baton Rouge: Louisiana State University Press, 1953.

Craven, Wesley F. *The Colonies in Transition, 1660–1773.* New York: Harper & Row, 1968.

———. *The Southern Colonies in the Seventeenth Century, 1602–1689.* Baton Rouge: Louisiana State University Press, 1949.

Dailey, Jane, Glenda Elizabeth Gilmore, and Bryant Simon, eds. *Jumpin' Jim Crow: Southern Politics from Civil War to Civil Rights.* Princeton, N.J.: Princeton University Press, 2000.

Davis, David Brion. *The Problem of Slavery in the Age of Revolution, 1770–1823.* Ithaca, N.Y.: Cornell University Press, 1975.

———. *Slavery and Human Progress.* New York: Oxford University Press, 1984.

Degler, Carl N. *The Other South: Southern Dissenters in the Nineteenth Century.* San Francisco: Harper & Row, 1924.

Du Bois, W. E. B. *Black Reconstruction in America: 1860–1880.* Cleveland: World, 1969.

Dugger, Ronnie. *On Reagan: The Man and His Presidency.* New York: McGraw-Hill, 1983.

Dumbrell, John. *The Carter Presidency: A Reevaluation.* New York: Manchester University Press, 1993.

Dumond, Dwight L. *Anti-Slavery: The Crusade for Freedom in America.* New York: W. W. Norton, 1961.

Ehrlich, Walter. *They Have No Rights: Dred Scott's Struggle for Freedom.* Westport, Conn.: Greenwood Press, 1979.

Elliott, Jonathan, ed. *The Debates in the Several State Conventions on the Adoption of the Federal Constitution.* 4 vols. Philadelphia: J. B. Lippincott, 1901.

Ellis, Joseph J. *American Sphinx: The Character of Thomas Jefferson.* New York: Vintage, 1998.

Ellis, Richard E. *The Union at Risk: Jacksonian Democracy, States' Rights, and the Nullification Crisis.* New York: Oxford University Press, 1987.

Farrand, Max, ed. *The Records of the Federal Convention of 1787.* 4 vols. New Haven, Conn.: Yale University Press, 1937.

Faust, Drew Galpin, ed. *The Ideology of Slavery: Proslavery Thought in the Antebellum South, 1830–1860.* Baton Rouge: Louisiana State University Press, 1981.

Fehrenbacher, Don E., completed and edited by Ward M. McAfee. *The Slaveholding Republic: An Account of the United States Government's Relations to Slavery.* New York: Oxford University Press, 2001.

Fields, Barbara Jeanne. *Slavery and Freedom on the Middle Ground: Maryland During the Nineteenth Century.* New Haven, Conn.: Yale University Press, 1985.

Finkelman, Paul. *Dred Scott vs. Sandford: A Brief History with Documents.* Boston: Bedford Books, 1997.

———. *Slavery and the Founders: Race and Liberty in the Age of Jefferson.* Armonk, N.Y.: M. E. Sharpe, 1996.

Fogel, Robert W. *Without Consent or Contract: The Rise and Fall of American Slavery.* New York: W.W. Norton, 1989.

Foner, Eric. *Reconstruction: America's Unfinished Revolution, 1863–1877.* New York: Harper & Row, 1988.

Foner, Philip S. *History of Black Americans.* 3 vols. Westport, Conn.: Greenwood Press, 1975–83. Vol. 1, *From Africa to the Emergence of the Cotton Kingdom.* Vol. 2, *Kingdom to the Eve of the Compromise of 1850.* Vol. .3, *From the Compromise of 1850 to the End of the Civil War.*

Formisano, Ronald P. *Boston Against Busing: Race, Class, and Ethnicity in the 1960s and 1970s*. Chapel Hill: University of North Carolina Press, 1991.

Franklin, John Hope. *The Free Negro in North Carolina*. Chapel Hill: University of North Carolina Press, 1943.

———. *The Militant South, 1860–1861*. Cambridge, Mass.: Harvard University Press, 1956.

———. *Reconstruction After the Civil War*. Chicago: University of Chicago Press, 1994.

Fredrickson, George M. *The Black Image in the White Mind: The Debate on Afro-American Character and Destiny, 1817–1914*. Hanover, N.H.: Wesleyan University Press, 1987.

Genovese, Eugene D. *Roll, Jordan, Roll: The World the Slaves Made*. New York: Pantheon, 1974.

Gilreath, James, ed. *Thomas Jefferson and the Education of a Citizen*. Washington, D.C.: Library of Congress, 1999.

Glaser, James M. *Race, Campaign Politics, and the Realignment in the South*. New Haven, Conn.: Yale University Press, 1996.

Goldman, Sheldon. *Picking Federal Judges: Lower Court Selection from Roosevelt Through Reagan*. New Haven, Conn.: Yale University Press, 1997.

Gordon-Reed, Annette. *Thomas Jefferson and Sally Hemings: An American Controversy*. Charlottesville: University Press of Virginia, 1997.

Gossett, Thomas F. *Race: The History of an Idea in America*. New York: Oxford University Press, 1997.

Graham, Hugh Davis. *The Civil Rights Era: Origins and Development of National Policy*. New York: Oxford University Press, 1990.

Greenberg, Kenneth S., ed. *The Confessions of Nat Turner and Related Documents*. Boston: Bedford Books, 1996.

Grimsted, David. *American Mobbing, 1828–1861: Toward Civil War*. New York: Oxford University Press, 1998.

Hale, Grace Elizabeth. *Making Whiteness: The Culture of Segregation in the South, 1890–1940*. New York: Pantheon, 1998.

Halliday, E. M. *Understanding Thomas Jefferson*. New York: HarperCollins, 2001.

Harris, William C. *With Charity for All: Lincoln and the Restoration of the Union*. Lexington: University Press of Kentucky, 1997.

Helper, Hinton Rowan. *The Impending Crisis in the South: How to Mend It*. Edited by George M. Fredrickson. Cambridge, Mass.: Belknap Press, 1968.

Higgenbotham, A. Leon, Jr. *In the Matter of Color: Race and the American Legal Process, the Colonial Period*. New York: Oxford University Press, 1978.

———. *Shades of Freedom: Racial Politics and the Presumption of the American Legal Process*. New York: Oxford University Press, 1996.

Higginson, Thomas Wentworth. *Black Rebellions: Five Slave Revolts*. New York: Da Capo Press, 1998.

Hirschfeld, Fritz. *George Washington and Slavery: A Documentary Portrayal*. Columbia: University of Missouri Press, 1997.

Hofstadter, Richard. *Social Darwinism in American Thought, 1860–1915.* Philadelphia: University of Pennsylvania Press, 1945.

Horsman, Reginald. *Race and Manifest Destiny: The Origins of American Racial Anglo-Saxonism.* Cambridge, Mass.: Harvard University Press, 1981.

Hyman, Harold, and William M. Wiecek. *Equal Justice Under Law: Constitutional Development, 1835–1875.* New York: Harper & Row, 1982.

Jaffa, Harry V. *Crisis of the House Divided: An Interpretation of the Issues in the Lincoln-Douglas Debates.* Chicago: University of Chicago Press, 1982.

Jefferson, Thomas, and James Madison. *The Republic of Letters: The Correspondence Between Thomas Jefferson and James Madison, 1776–1826.* 3 vols. Edited by James Morton Smith. New York: W. W. Norton, 1995.

Jeffrey, Julie Roy. *The Great Silent Army of Abolitionism: Ordinary Women in the Antislavery Movement.* Chapel Hill: University of North Carolina Press, 1998.

Johannsen, Robert W. *The Frontier, the Union, and Stephen A. Douglas.* Urbana: University of Illinois Press, 1989.

Jordan, Winthrop D. *White over Black: American Attitudes Toward the Negro, 1550–1812.* Chapel Hill: University of North Carolina Press, 1968.

Kantrowitz, Stephen. *Ben Tillman and the Reconstruction of White Supremacy.* Chapel Hill: University of North Carolina Press, 2000.

Kearns, Doris. *Lyndon Johnson and the American Dream.* New York: Harper & Row, 1976.

Kennedy, Randall. *Race, Crime, and the Law.* New York: Vintage, 1998.

Kennedy, Stetson. *After Appomattox: How the South Won the War.* Gainesville: University Press of Florida, 1995.

King, Martin Luther, Jr. *The Essential Writings of Martin Luther King, Jr.* Edited by James Melvin Washington. San Francisco: Harper & Row, 1986.

Klein, Maury. *Days of Defiance: Sumter, Secession, and the Coming of the Civil War.* New York: Knopf, 1999.

Kornweibel, Theodore, Jr. *"Seeing Red": Federal Campaigns Against Black Militancy, 1919–1925.* Bloomington: Indiana University Press, 1998.

Kousser, J. Morgan. *Colorblind Injustice: Minority Voting Rights and the Undoing of the Second Reconstruction.* Chapel Hill: University of North Carolina Press, 1999.

Kozol, Jonathan. *Savage Inequalities: Children in America's Schools.* New York: HarperCollins, 1991.

Lader, Lawrence. *The Bold Brahmins: New England's War Against Slavery: 1831–1863.* New York: E. P. Dutton, 1961.

Laham, Nicholas. *The Reagan Presidency and the Politics of Race: In Pursuit of Colorblind Justice and Limited Government.* Westport, Conn.: Praeger, 1998.

Lawson, Steven F. *In Pursuit of Power: Southern Blacks and Electoral Politics, 1965–1982.* New York: Columbia University Press, 1985.

Lemann, Nicholas. *The Promised Land: The Great Black Migration and How It Changed America.* New York: Vintage, 1992.

Litwack, Leon F. *Been in the Storm So Long: The Aftermath of Slavery.* New York: Vintage, 1979.

———. *North of Slavery: The Negro in the Free States, 1790–1860.* Chicago: University of Chicago Press, 1961.

———. *Trouble in Mind: Black Southerners in the Age of Jim Crow.* New York: Knopf, 1998.

Logan, Rayford W. *The Betrayal of the Negro: From Rutherford B. Hayes to Woodrow Wilson.* New York: Da Capo Press, 1997.

Lynd, Staughton. *Class Conflict, Slavery, and the U.S. Constitution, Ten Essays.* Indianapolis: Bobbs-Merrill, 1968.

———, ed. *Reconstruction.* New York: Harper & Row, 1967.

MacLean, Nancy. *Behind the Mask of Chivalry: The Making of the Second Ku Klux Klan.* New York: Oxford University Press, 1994.

Madison, James. *Notes of Debates in the Federal Convention of 1787.* New York: W. W. Norton, 1987.

Mandle, Jay R. *Not Slave, Not Free: The African American Economic Experience Since the Civil War.* Durham, N.C.: Duke University Press, 1992.

Marks, Carole. *Farewell—We're Good and Gone: The Great Black Migration.* Bloomington: Indiana University Press, 1989.

Matthews, Richard K. *If Men Were Angels: James Madison and the Heartless Empire of Reason.* Lawrence: University Press of Kansas, 1995.

Mayer, Henry. *All on Fire: William Lloyd Garrison and the Abolition of Slavery.* New York: St. Martin's, 1998.

McColley, Robert. *Slavery and Jeffersonian Virginia.* Urbana: University of Illinois Press, 1973.

McCoy, Donald R., and Richard T. Ruetten. *Quest and Response: Minority Rights and the Truman Administration.* Lawrence: University Press of Kansas, 1973.

McCoy, Drew R. *The Last of the Fathers: James Madison and the Republican Legacy.* Cambridge: Cambridge University Press, 1989.

McCullough, David. *Truman.* New York: Simon & Schuster, 1992.

McKitrick, Eric L. *Andrew Johnson and Reconstruction.* New York: Oxford University Press, 1960.

McMillen, Neil R. *The Citizens' Council: Organized Resistance to the Second Reconstruction, 1954–1964.* Urbana: University of Illinois Press, 1991.

McPherson, James M. *The Abolitionist Legacy: From Reconstruction to the NAACP.* Princeton, N.J.: Princeton University Press, 1975.

Miller, John Chester. *The Wolf by the Ears: Thomas Jefferson and Slavery.* New York: Free Press, 1977.

Miller, William Lee. *Arguing About Slavery: John Quincy Adams and the Great Battle in the United States Congress.* New York: Knopf, 1996.

Morgan, Edmund S. *American Slavery, American Freedom: The Ordeal of Colonial Virginia.* New York: W. W. Norton, 1975.

Moseley, James G. *John Winthrop's World: History as a Story, The Story as History.* Madison: University of Wisconsin Press, 1992.

Oakes, James. *The Ruling Race: A History of American Slaveholders.* New York: W.W. Norton, 1998.

O'Brien, Gail Williams. *The Color of the Law: Race, Violence, and Justice in the Post–World War II South.* Chapel Hill: University of North Carolina Press, 1999.

Onuf, Peter S., ed. *Jeffersonian Legacies.* Charlottesville: University Press of Virginia, 1995.

Paskoff, Paul, and Daniel J. Wilson, eds. *The Cause of the South: Selections from Du Bow's Review, 1846–1867.* Baton Rouge: Louisiana State University Press, 1982.

Potter, David M. *The Impending Crisis, 1848–1861.* New York: Harper & Row, 1976.

———. *Lincoln and His Party in the Secession Crisis.* Baton Rouge: Louisiana State University Press, 1942.

———. *The South and the Sectional Conflict.* Baton Rouge: Louisiana State University Press, 1968.

Quadagno, Jill. *The Color of Welfare: How Racism Undermined the War on Poverty.* New York: Oxford University Press, 1994.

Quarles, Benjamin. *Lincoln and the Negro.* New York: Da Capo Press, 1962.

———. *The Negro in the American Revolution.* Chapel Hill: University of North Carolina Press, 1961.

Reed, Adolph, Jr., ed. *Without Justice for All: The New Liberalism and Our Retreat from Racial Equality.* Boulder, Colo.: Westview Press, 1999.

Richards, Leonard L. *"Gentlemen of Property and Standing": Anti-Abolition Mobs in Jacksonian America.* New York: Oxford University Press, 1970.

———. *The Slave Power: The Free North and Southern Domination, 1780–1860.* Baton Rouge: Louisiana State University Press, 2000.

Robinson, Donald L. *Slavery in the Structure of American Politics, 1765–1820.* New York: Harcourt Brace Jovanovich, 1971.

Royce, Edward. *The Origins of Southern Sharecropping.* Philadelphia: Temple University Press, 1993.

Royster, Jacqueline Jones, ed. *Southern Horrors and Other Writings: The Anti-Lynching Campaign of Ida B. Wells, 1892–1900.* Boston: Bedford Books, 1997.

Russell, John H. *The Free Negro in Virginia 1619–1865.* Baltimore, Md.: Johns Hopkins University Press, 1913.

Schulman, Bruce J. *From Cotton Belt to Sun Belt: Federal Policy, Economic Development, and the Transformation of the South, 1938–1980.* Durham: Duke University Press, 1994.

Sewell, Richard H. *A House Divided: Sectionalism and Civil War, 1848–1865.* Baltimore, Md.: Johns Hopkins University Press, 1988.

Simpson, Brooks D. *The Reconstruction Presidents.* Lawrence: University Press of Kansas, 1998.

Smith, John D., and Thomas H. Appleton Jr., eds. *A Mythic Land Apart: Reassessing Southerners and Their History.* Westport, Conn.: Greenwood Press, 1997.

Smith, John David. *An Old Creed for the New South: Proslavery Ideology and Historiography 1865–1918.* Westport, Conn.: Greenwood Press, 1985.

Smith, Page. *The Shaping of America*. 3 vols. New York: McGraw-Hill, 1980.

Stampp, Kenneth M. *The Peculiar Institution: Slavery and the Antebellum South*. New York: Knopf, 1965.

Stampp, Kenneth M., and Leon F. Litwack, eds. *Reconstruction: An Anthology of Revisionist Writings*. Baton Rouge: Louisiana State University Press, 1969.

Stephanson, Anders. *Manifest Destiny: American Expansion and the Empire of Right*. New York: Hill & Wang, 1995.

Stern, Mark. *Calculating Visions: Kennedy, Johnson, and Civil Rights*. New Brunswick, N.J.: Rutgers University Press, 1992.

Sullivan, Patricia. *Days of Hope: Race and Democracy in the New Deal Era*. Chapel Hill: University of North Carolina Press, 1996.

Taylor, William R. *Cavalier and Yankee: The Old South and the American National Character*. New York: Oxford University Press, 1993.

Thomas, Brook, ed. *Plessy v. Ferguson: A Brief History with Documents*. Boston: Bedford Books, 1997.

Tise, Larry E. *Proslavery: A History of the Defense of Slavery in America, 1701–1840*. Athens: University of Georgia Press, 1987.

Trotter, Joe William, Jr., ed. *The Great Migration in Historical Perspective: New Dimensions of Race, Class, and Gender*. Bloomington: Indiana University Press, 1991.

Wade, Wyn Craig. *The Fiery Cross: The Ku Klux Klan in America*. New York: Oxford University Press, 1987.

Waldrep, Christopher. *Roots of Disaster: Race and Criminal Justice in the American South, 1817–80*. Urbana: University of Illinois Press, 1998.

Weiss, Nancy J. *Farewell to the Party of Lincoln*. Princeton, N.J.: Princeton University Press, 1983.

Wilson, Douglas L., and Lucia Stanton, eds. *Jefferson Abroad*. New York: Modern Library, 1999.

Woodson, C. G. *The Education of the Negro Prior to 1861*. New York: Arno Press, 1968.

Woodward, C. Vann. *The Strange Career of Jim Crow*. New York: Oxford University Press, 1957.

Zarefsky, David. *Lincoln/Douglas and Slavery in the Crucible of Pubic Debate*. Chicago and London: University of Chicago Press, 1990.

Ziegler, Valarie H. *The Advocates of Peace in Antebellum America*. Bloomington: Indiana University Press, 1992.

Zilversmit, Arthur. *The First Emancipation: The Abolition of Slavery in the North*. Chicago: University of Chicago Press, 1967.

INDEX